♠ The
♡ Bridge Player's
◇ Comprehensive Guide
♣ to Defense

Frank Stewart

A FIRESIDE BOOK
Published by Simon & Schuster Inc.
New York London Toronto Sydney Tokyo Singapore

F

Fireside
Simon & Schuster Building
Rockefeller Center
1230 Avenue of the Americas
New York, New York 10020

First Fireside Edition, 1990
Published by arrangement with Dodd, Mead and Company

FIRESIDE and colophon are registered trademarks
of Simon & Schuster Inc.

Manufactured in the United States of America

10 9 8 7 6 5 4 3 2 1 Pbk.

Library of Congress Cataloging-in-Publication Data
Stewart, Frank, date.
   The bridge player's comprehensive guide to defense/
Frank Stewart.—1st Fireside ed.
      p.   cm.
   "A Fireside book."
   1. Contract bridge—Defensive play. I. Title.
GV1282.42.S73   1990
795.41'5—dc20   90-37419
                                                      CIP
ISBN 0-671-72460-6 Pbk.

Contents

Preface

Maybe you're an ambitious new bridge player who wants to learn all there is to know about good defensive technique; or perhaps you're an experienced player, but somehow you've let your considerable skills fall into decline. You may even be a true expert looking for one more mountain to climb. Whatever your station in the wonderful world of bridge, this book is for you.

Here are Quizzes on twenty-five of the most important areas of defensive play. Each one is introduced by example deals and an explanation of what the Quiz is all about. There are from eight to twenty problems in each Quiz. (This book contains almost four hundred problems, plus plenty of illustrative full deals and single-suit diagrams, so the reader can look forward to as many hours of instruction and enjoyment as he or she can handle. As far as I know, *The Bridge Player's Comprehensive Guide to Defense* is the most complete quiz book on defensive play ever published. In fact, it is intended as a reference book as much as to entertain and test the reader.)

In most problems, the dealer and vulnerability are specified and the bidding is given. Unless otherwise indicated (as in Quiz 25, on defense at duplicate bridge), your goal is to *beat the contract*—don't worry about overtricks or extra undertricks. The solution for each problem includes the full deal.

You may assume that your opponents are competent—that they have bid correctly, and that declarer is handling the dummy capably. Unless otherwise noted, N-S are playing standard bidding methods. All 1NT openings show 16-18 HCP, weak two-bids are in use (two clubs, therefore, is the only strong opening), jump overcalls are preemptive, and direct double raises are strong and forcing. Negative doubles make an occasional appearance. Other conventional bids are noted as they occur.

Toward the end of the book, you will find a tough Final Exam, which features still more challenging problems.

Don't feel badly if a lot of the answers elude you. While this admittedly is a book of Quizzes, and you may be looking forward to trying your skills, its real purpose is to provide instruction and improvement. As firm believers in the Socratic Method (so called because Socrates was antiquity's great teacher by question and answer), we think you will learn more if your thought processes are stimulated by questions. So whether you can provide the right answers or not, have fun and learn!

Acknowledgments

I certainly make no pretense of having devised every problem in this book independently. I did defend some of the hands; invariably, the ones I remember best are those on which I could have beaten the contract but didn't. I observed several more and constructed still others to illustrate a principle.

However, anyone who compiles a book of this kind is obliged to consult sources. To produce the best possible selection of problems, the author must pore over the works of other bridge writers. He must also search patiently for a theme that the reader will find especially clear and instructive, and that he, the author, can adapt—and perhaps embellish or improve.

Among the writers who provided inspiration in the preparation of this book are:

Albert Dormer	H.W. Kelsey
Jeremy Flint	Mike Lawrence
G.C.H. Fox	Marshall Miles
Charles H. Goren, and others	Victor Mollo
writing under the Goren byline	Terence Reese
David Greenwood	Alfred Sheinwold
Jim Jacoby	Alan Truscott
Eric Jannersten	Jan Wohlin
Edwin B. Kantar	Bobby Wolff
Edgar Kaplan	Kit Woolsey

Anyone familiar with bridge literature will recognize that this list contains the names of many of the great journalists of the game, as well as some of its finest players. I wish to recognize their skills and accomplishments, and I am happy to acknowledge my debt to each of them.

Some of the problems originate with deals published in *The Contract Bridge Bulletin* or the annual World Championship book. Both are productions of the hardworking *Bulletin* staff of the American Contract Bridge League, of which I am honored to be a part. Other problems are based on deals for which my source is *The Bridge World* magazine. *The Bridge World*, which enjoys an international reputation for excellence in the expert community, is an indispensable source for anyone attempting a book of this kind.

My thanks to Edwin B. Kantar and Harold Katz, who graciously checked portions of the manuscript for analytical error.

For convenience, players are referred to as "he" throughout this book. This is a conventional device that most bridge books adopt. There are, of course, many fine bridge players of both sexes.

This book is dedicated with pleasure to

Alfred Sheinwold

Inimitable writer whose daily illumination of bridge has entertained
and enlightened millions for decades . . . champion player . . .
bidding system innovator . . . master of many talents . . . advocate of
principle and integrity . . . good friend

The Crucial Trick: Opening Leads

If defense is the toughest part of bridge to master, as most writers maintain, then the opening lead must be the single most difficult aspect of the game. While it is possible to speculate on the best opening lead by listening carefully to the bidding and looking at one's own hand, there are woefully few times when an intelligently conceived opening lead will turn out to be a real "killer." The best anybody can aspire to is opening leads that are above average in the long run.

In considering his opening lead, a good defender always tries to imagine what declarer's plan will be. (See Quizzes 9, 10, and 13.) Often the bidding will clearly indicate what values declarer and dummy will have and how the play is likely to develop. The opening leader then launches his countermeasures while the defense enjoys the advantage of being on lead.

WEST	NORTH	EAST	SOUTH
		1 ♡	Pass
2 ♡	Pass	2 NT	Pass
3 ♡	All Pass		

South holds: ♠ J 10 9 6
♡ 8 5 3
♢ K 10 4
♣ A 9 3

Dummy will be very weak. The two-heart response shows 6-9 HCP and, since West rejected partner's try for game, he should be in the lower end of that range. Also, South can expect dummy to be distributional rather than flat, since West expressed a clear preference for the suit contract. Therefore, dummy is likely to provide declarer with some ruffing tricks and little else—and a trump lead by South is automatic.

WEST	NORTH	EAST	SOUTH
		1 NT	Pass
2 NT	Pass	3 NT	All Pass

South holds: ♠ 10 6 5 4 2
♡ J 10
♢ 6 5 3
♣ Q 7 6

Staking the defense on the spades looks against the odds, since South lacks a ready entry. However, North is marked with a few points and probably has at least four hearts, since West made no effort to find a heart fit via Stayman. At IMPs or rubber bridge, many good players would try a heart lead. Even at matchpoints, a heart lead would have considerable support.

A little originality never hurts in choosing a good opening lead. E-W are vulnerable.

WEST	NORTH	EAST	SOUTH
		1 ♠	3 ◇
3 ♡	4 ◇	Pass	Pass
4 ♠	All Pass		

South holds: ♠ 6 5 4
♡ J 8 5 3
◇ K Q 10 9 6 2
♣ —

South should lead the *two* of diamonds. If partner is awake, he should grasp the suit-preference implications of this striking lead.

Suppose South's clubs and hearts were reversed. Now he should try leading the diamond *queen*. If partner wins the ace, he will see no future in leading another diamond. Perhaps he will find the right shift.

The value of opening lead problems is suspect because there aren't always any demonstrably clear-cut answers. Even a look at the deal that inspired the problem may prove little one way or another. In most cases I have refrained from cluttering up the page with a full deal, carefully constructed to prove that my suggested answer is correct. I could, of course, just as easily construct a deal that would make my recommendation a disaster. This quiz is intended to illustrate some of the lines of reasoning that guide a good player in choosing consistently effective opening leads.

Problems

(Throughout, neither side is vulnerable.)

1.

WEST	NORTH	EAST	SOUTH
		1 ♡	Pass
2 ◇	Pass	2 ♡	Pass
4 ♡	All Pass		

South holds: ♠ K 10 3
♡ 9 6 3
◇ A 3
♣ 10 9 8 6 3

2.

WEST	NORTH	EAST	SOUTH
		1 ♠	Pass
2 ♡	Pass	2 ♠	Pass
3 ♠	Pass	4 ♠	All Pass

South holds: ♠ 5
♡ K J 9 5 3
◇ K 10 5
♣ J 10 8 3

3.

WEST	NORTH	EAST	SOUTH
		1 ♡	Pass
2 ♡	All Pass		

South holds: ♠ 10 9 5
           ♡ 7 6 5 2
           ◇ K 9 5 3
           ♣ A J

4.

WEST	NORTH	EAST	SOUTH
		1 ◇	All Pass

South holds: ♠ J 10 3
           ♡ A J 7 5 2
           ◇ 4 3
           ♣ J 7 6

5.

WEST	NORTH	EAST	SOUTH
		1 ♡	Pass
2 ♣	Pass	4 ♣	Pass
4 ♡	All Pass		

South holds: ♠ Q J 10 8 3
           ♡ 4 3
           ◇ J 3
           ♣ A 8 7 5

6.

WEST	NORTH	EAST	SOUTH
		1 ♡	Pass
1 ♠	Pass	2 ♠	Pass
2 NT	Pass	4 ♡	All Pass

South holds: ♠ A 8 6 5
           ♡ 4 3
           ◇ 10 8 3 2
           ♣ J 8 7

7.

WEST	NORTH	EAST	SOUTH
		1 ♡	Pass
1 ♠	Pass	2 ♣	All Pass

South holds: ♠ Q 10 4 3
           ♡ K J 9 3
           ◇ A 4
           ♣ 8 7 3

	WEST	NORTH	EAST	SOUTH
8.			1 ♡	Pass
	1 NT	Pass	2 ◇	Pass
	2 ♡	All Pass		

South holds: ♠ J 10 9 4
                ♡ 8 7
                ◇ J 9 7 5
                ♣ A 7 6

	WEST	NORTH	EAST	SOUTH
9.			1 ♡	Pass
	1 ♠	Pass	1 NT	Pass
	2 ♡	Pass	3 ♡	All Pass

South holds: ♠ Q 8 3
                ♡ 10 3 2
                ◇ Q 10 3
                ♣ J 9 3 2

	WEST	NORTH	EAST	SOUTH
10.			1 ♠	Pass
	1 NT	Pass	2 ♡	Pass
	3 ♡	Pass	4 ♡	All Pass

South holds: ♠ K Q 10 2
                ♡ A 5 4
                ◇ A J 8 5
                ♣ 9 2

Solutions

1. Spade three. The defense must establish tricks quickly, before declarer can draw trumps and set up dummy's diamonds. The most aggressive lead available is recommended. This is not the time to lead your ace "to look at dummy."

2. Club jack. This time your length and strength in hearts will prevent declarer from setting up dummy's suit, so a passive lead is in order.

3. Heart two. Dummy will be weakish, so there is no hurry to seek out tricks. This lead also might deprive declarer of a ruff in dummy. The lead of the club ace is against the odds, especially since the power of your jack might be wasted. Because you have four trumps, you aren't sure you want to take a ruff anyway.

4. Diamond. Partner must have good diamonds, or else he would have balanced. Perhaps your best move is to try to draw trumps.

5. Club ace, planning to continue the suit. Your partner is a heavy favorite to have a club singleton or void.

6. East's bidding suggests six hearts and three spades, while West, who suggested notrump, probably has only a four-card spade suit. Try a low spade, hoping to give partner a ruff if he has K-x (or maybe Q-x behind dummy's king) or a fast entry in trumps. Ace-underleads are rare, but here a good alternative is lacking.

7. Club three. Dummy is likely to have a stiff heart, a few clubs, and very little in high cards, so a trump lead to keep declarer from ruffing his heart losers is mandatory. Note that you have potential heart tricks to protect. I might lead a club even with Q-x-x!

8. Spade jack. This is a preference situation, as in the previous problem, but this time dummy is not likely to hit with real support. There could easily be three diamond and two hearts. With three-card heart support and a minimum response, West would have raised to two hearts at his first turn. Therefore, a trump lead is not clearly indicated.

9. Very difficult. Dummy has advertised about 9 or 10 HCP and probably three hearts. If dummy has good spades and lacks a minor-suit singleton, an attacking lead is called for; if dummy is something like

        ♠ J x x x x
        ♡ A x x
        ◇ K x x x
        ♣ x,

a trump lead might be best. Because of the dangerous-looking spade holding, my preference is for an attacking diamond three.

10. Heart ace. With such good spades, a trump lead is clear. Often it is right to lead low from A-x-x to keep communication with partner so three rounds of trumps can be played. Here, partner is unlikely ever to win a trick.

Problems

11.

	WEST	NORTH	EAST	SOUTH
			1 ♠	Pass
	1 NT	Pass	2 ◇	All Pass

South holds: ♠ 8 7 4 2
              ♡ J 8 6
              ◇ A 3
              ♣ Q J 9 2

12.

WEST	NORTH	EAST	SOUTH
			1 ♡
Pass	1 ♠	2 ◇	2 ♡
4 ◇ [1]	4 ♡	5 ◇	Dbl
All Pass			

[1]preemptive

South holds: ♠ J 4
♡ A Q J 9 3
◇ A 4 2
♣ K 10 3

13.

WEST	NORTH	EAST	SOUTH
		1 NT	Pass
4 NT	Pass	6 NT	All Pass

South holds: ♠ Q 10 7 6 3
♡ A 10 4
◇ J 10 9
♣ 9 2

14.

WEST	NORTH	EAST	SOUTH
		1 ♡	Pass
2 ♠	Pass	3 ♡	Pass
3 ♠	Pass	3 NT	Pass
4 ♡	Pass	5 ♡	Pass
6 ♡	All Pass		

South holds: ♠ A 3
♡ 7 6 4
◇ K 4 3
♣ 10 9 7 5 3

15.

WEST	NORTH	EAST	SOUTH
		1 ♡	Pass
3 ♣	Pass	3 NT	Pass
6 NT	All Pass		

South holds: ♠ K J 6 2
♡ J 9 6 4
◇ 7 6 5
♣ 9 2

16.

WEST	NORTH	EAST	SOUTH
		1 ♠	Pass
2 NT	Pass	3 ♠	Pass
4 ♠	All Pass		

South holds: ♠ Q 9 3
♡ J 10 8 3
◇ A 10 6
♣ K J 7

17.	WEST	NORTH	EAST	SOUTH
			1 ♡	Pass
	2 ♣	Pass	3 ♡	Pass
	4 ♡	All Pass		

South holds: ♠ K Q 10 7
             ♡ K 8 5 3
             ◇ 7
             ♣ A 9 5 2

18.	WEST	NORTH	EAST	SOUTH
			1 ♡	Pass
	2 ♡	Pass	3 ♡	Pass
	4 ♡	All Pass		

South holds: ♠ J 10 8 6 4
             ♡ A 6 3
             ◇ 9 7 6 4
             ♣ 3

19.	WEST	NORTH	EAST	SOUTH
	1 ♡	Pass	1 ♠	Pass
	2 ♡	Pass	2 ♠	Pass
	3 ♠	Pass	4 ♠	All Pass

South holds: ♠ A 7 6 3
             ♡ 4 2
             ◇ A J 9 5 2
             ♣ 10 4

20.	WEST	NORTH	EAST	SOUTH
			1 ♡	Pass
	2 ◇	Pass	2 ♡	Pass
	4 ♡	All Pass		

South holds: ♠ Q 2
             ♡ 10 8 3
             ◇ J 6 5 3
             ♣ J 9 5 2

Solutions

11. Club queen. There is less reason to lead a trump when it's unlikely declarer will need to ruff any spades.

12. A low diamond. Ace of diamonds, 90 percent. North bid four hearts to make, and the opponents took a sacrifice. Your side should have the majority of the high-card strength, while E-W's best hope of tricks lies with their big diamond fit. Your objective, therefore, should be to prevent the enemy from scoring extra ruffing tricks.

13. Diamond ten. Partner has no high cards, so leading away from the spade queen could be costly. Nor should you bang down the heart ace and set up declarer's honors. Stay passive, and perhaps you will score two tricks in the majors. The deceptive lead of the *ten* is unlikely to cost your side anything —you can afford to deceive partner when he'll play no part in the defense. Against *3* NT, you would, of course, lead a spade.

14. Diamond three. With dummy's spades an obvious threat, declarer has the material to take twelve tricks in due time. You must try to establish a fast trick.

15. Spade two. This is not the time to go passive, with both East and West holding long suits. Compare with Problem 13.

16. Heart jack. A normal, passive lead is okay, since dummy will have a balanced hand with few discards for declarer's losers.

17. Spade king. Your hand is too strong to lead the singleton diamond— partner will never get in to give you a ruff. Plus, you have four trumps, so a forcing defense might work better than trying for ruffs.

18. Club three. This is a near-perfect hand to lead from shortness. Partner is marked with some high cards on the auction; plus, your trump ace will let you regain the lead for a second shot at a ruff if necessary.

19. Diamond ace. Low diamond, 70 percent. With four trumps, lead your longest suit, hoping to initiate a forcing game.

20. Spade queen. Your prospects look gloomy, so try a desperation shot. On a good day, partner will have the spade king and the trump ace, and there will be a defensive trump promotion.

Problems

21.

WEST	NORTH	EAST	SOUTH
		1 ♠	Pass
2 ◇	Pass	2 ♠	Pass
3 ♡	Pass	4 ♠	Pass
5 ♠	All Pass		

South holds: ♠ 7 6 4
♡ Q 8 7 5
◇ J 4
♣ A 9 5 2

22.

WEST	NORTH	EAST	SOUTH
		1 ♣	Pass
1 ♠	Pass	1 NT	Pass
3 NT	All Pass		

South holds: ♠ 7 6 4
♡ A 6 5
◇ K 4
♣ Q J 10 3 2

23.

WEST	NORTH	EAST	SOUTH
	1 ◇	1 ♠	Pass
2 ◇¹	Dbl	Pass	Pass
3 ♠	Pass	4 ♠	All Pass

¹good hand, spade support

South holds: ♠ 7 6 4
♡ J 10 3
◇ Q 10 5 4
♣ J 10 4

24.

WEST	NORTH	EAST	SOUTH
	1 ◇	1 ♡	Pass
2 ♡	All Pass		

South holds: ♠ 10 4
♡ 10 5 3
◇ J 9 3
♣ Q 10 5 4 2

25.

WEST	NORTH	EAST	SOUTH
1 ◇	Pass	1 ♠	Pass
2 ♡	Pass	2 NT	Pass
3 ♠	Pass	3 NT	All Pass

South holds: ♠ A Q 4
♡ 5 4
◇ K J 9 8 4
♣ J 9 3

26.

WEST	NORTH	EAST	SOUTH
3 ♡	Pass	3 NT	All Pass

South holds: ♠ K 10 6 4
♡ J 6
◇ 9 6 5 4
♣ A J 3

27.

WEST	NORTH	EAST	SOUTH
	1 ♡	1 ♠	Pass
1 NT	Pass	2 ♠	Pass
3 ♠	All Pass		

South holds: ♠ 9 6 5 3
♡ Q 9 5
◇ J 2
♣ 10 7 5 3

28.

WEST	NORTH	EAST	SOUTH
		1 ♡	Pass
1 ♠	Pass	1 NT	Pass
2 NT	All Pass		

South holds: ♠ 9 3
♡ Q 10 8 3
◇ Q 9 4 2
♣ A 9 3

29.

WEST	NORTH	EAST	SOUTH
		1 ♣	Pass
1 ♡	1 ♠	1 NT	Pass
2 ♣	All Pass		

South holds: ♠ 10 5
♡ K 10 8 5
◇ Q J 9 2
♣ 8 4 2

30.

WEST	NORTH	EAST	SOUTH
		1 ♣	Pass
1 ♡	Pass	1 NT	Pass
2 NT	Pass	3 NT	All Pass

South holds: ♠ 10 2
♡ J 10 8 5 3
◇ 10 2
♣ Q 10 4 2

Solutions

21.   Club two. The opponents have graciously drawn you a map. West said everything was under control except clubs, and East denied a club control when he passed five spades. You may even beat the five-spade contract. The full deal could be:

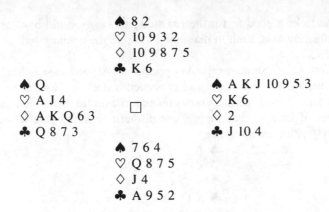

♠ 8 2
♡ 10 9 3 2
◇ 10 9 8 7 5
♣ K 6

♠ Q
♡ A J 4
◇ A K Q 6 3
♣ Q 8 7 3

♠ A K J 10 9 5 3
♡ K 6
◇ 2
♣ J 10 4

♠ 7 6 4
♡ Q 8 7 5
◇ J 4
♣ A 9 5 2

22. Club three. Despite declarer's bid, the club suit offers your best hope
to beat the contract. Leading *low* despite your sequence is best when declarer
is known to have club length. This gains when partner has a doubleton ace,
king or nine.

On other occasions, you might avoid the normal fourth-best lead from a
long, broken suit and try your lowest instead. If declarer has bid the suit,
your fourth-highest card might be too valuable to waste.

23. Diamond queen. This may be the only time you'll ever be on lead. The
lead of the queen may allow you to hold the lead and make a good shift
through dummy.

♠ 3
♡ A Q 9 2
◇ A K 9 8 2
♣ 8 7 6

♠ Q 10 8 2
♡ K 7 6
◇ J
♣ A Q 9 5 3

♠ A K J 9 5
♡ 8 5 4
◇ 7 6 3
♣ K 2

♠ 7 6 4
♡ J 10 3
◇ Q 10 5 4
♣ J 10 4

24. Spade ten. Partner has a fair hand, so try to develop a ruffing trick by
leading from shortness.

25. Diamond jack. "Surrounding plays" can be made on the opening lead.
If the diamond situation is

5 3

A Q 7 2   ☐   10 6

K J 9 8 4

you must not start your fourth-best card. Incidentally, leading the unbid suit
would be most unwise. Declarer is bound to have good clubs on this auction;

11

since he lacks a good fit for the red suits, he easily could have as many as five clubs. Put your faith in diamonds, despite the opening bid.

26. Club ace, assuming capable opposition. A good East is likely to have a heart fit, and an aggressive lead is needed if declarer is going to start with seven heart tricks. If partner shows no enthusiasm for clubs, you can switch. However, if East is a bad player, use discretion. A bad East would blithely bid 3 NT with something like:

♠ A J x
♡ x
♢ A Q x
♣ K Q 10 x x x.

27. Heart queen. A forcing defense is your best chance. With dummy marked with something in hearts and declarer likely to be short, the honor lead is most likely to accomplish something. The hearts, for instance, may lie this way:

```
              A J 8 6 3
   K 7 4 2        □        10
              Q 9 5
```

28. Spade nine. The opponents have limited values, and declarer may find it hard to assemble eight tricks without help. Neither the hearts, where you have a double stopper, nor spades, where partner should have some length, is likely to be productive. There is no reason to lead a diamond (and possibly give away a vital trick) when the contract may die of natural causes *whether or not you establish a suit.*

29. Club two. Partner has the spades under control and you have the red suits stopped up, so the only extra tricks declarer is likely to get will be with ruffs. Dummy, which removed notrump to clubs, should have some ruffing power.

30. Diamond ten. The key consideration is that partner is marked with a fair hand yet didn't overcall one spade. However, he might have considered a two-diamond overcall too dangerous even if he had a long diamond suit.

Problems

31.

WEST	NORTH	EAST	SOUTH
		1 ♣	Pass
1 ◊	Pass	3 ♣	Pass
3 ◊	Pass	3 NT	All Pass

South holds: ♠ A Q 3
♡ J 9 5 4
◊ 3 2
♣ 10 7 5 3

32.

WEST	NORTH	EAST	SOUTH
			1 ♠
2 NT[1]	Dbl	3 ♣	Pass
Pass	4 ♣	Pass	4 ♠
5 ♣	Pass	Pass	Dbl
All Pass			

[1] the "Unusual notrump," suggesting length in both minors.

South holds: ♠ K Q 9 6 5
♡ Q
◊ K 10 7 6
♣ A 6 4

33.

WEST	NORTH	EAST	SOUTH
		1 NT	Pass
2 ♣	Pass	2 ◊	All Pass (!)

South holds: ♠ K Q 9 2
♡ Q 10
◊ 8 5 2
♣ K 10 9 2

34.

WEST	NORTH	EAST	SOUTH
1 ♣	Pass	2 NT	Pass
3 NT	All Pass		

South holds: ♠ A K J 9 3
♡ 10 8 6 4 2
◊ 6 5
♣ 5

35.

WEST	NORTH	EAST	SOUTH
	1 ♣	1 ♠	Pass
3 ♠	All Pass		

South holds: ♠ 8 5 3
♡ Q J 9
◊ A J 9 3
♣ 10 4 3

36.

WEST	NORTH	EAST	SOUTH
		1 NT	Pass
2 ♣	Pass	2 ♠	Pass
3 NT	All Pass		

South holds: ♠ K J 10 9 4
♡ A 7 3
◊ K 4 3
♣ J 3

37.	WEST	NORTH	EAST	SOUTH
			1 ◇	Dbl
	All Pass			

South holds:
♠ A K 6 3
♡ Q J 9 2
◇ J
♣ K 10 6 3

38.	WEST	NORTH	EAST	SOUTH
			1 ♡	Pass
	1 ♠	Pass	1 NT	Pass
	3 NT	All Pass		

South holds:
♠ 8 6 3
♡ 7 6
◇ A K 7 5 2
♣ J 5 4

39.	WEST	NORTH	EAST	SOUTH
			1 ◇	1 ♠
	2 ♣	Pass	2 ◇	Pass
	2 ♡	Pass	2 NT	Pass
	3 NT	All Pass		

South holds:
♠ A J 10 9 4
♡ K J 3
◇ A 3 2
♣ 8 6

40.	WEST	NORTH	EAST	SOUTH
			1 NT	Pass
	2 NT	Pass	3 NT	All Pass

South holds:
♠ A J 10 9
♡ J 10 9 8
◇ 7 6 5
♣ J 3

Solutions

31. Spade ace. With both declarer and dummy holding long suits, get busy. If your hand were stronger and partner were unlikely to have an entry, the spade queen would be the best lead.

32. Club four. Club ace, 90 percent. Similar to Problem 12; however, your strong holding in West's second suit makes it even more vital to lead trumps this time. North, short in clubs, probably has general strength, while East is quite likely to be short in diamonds.

Auctions in which an opponent shows a two-suited hand (using Michaels cuebids, Landy, Astro, Brozel, and other two-suited overcalls of 1 NT, as well as the Unusual notrump) and his partner takes a preference often suggest a trump lead.

33. Diamond two. To risk a Stayman response, planning to pass any rebid, West must have a weak three-suited hand, short in clubs.

34. Heart eight. East has a spade stopper that can only be the queen, but he has only three spades, else he would have responded one spade instead of two notrump. It is best to wait for a spade lead from partner; cashing even one top spade could ruin the defense.

Where to find partner's entry? If he has a minor-suit trick to take, he probably will get in before declarer has nine tricks; but if partner owns the heart ace, you may need to lead a heart right now. Be sure to lead the *eight*, not the four. If you lead fourth best, partner may plug away at hearts instead of shifting.

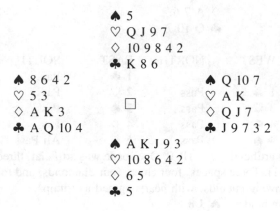

♠ 5
♥ Q J 9 7
♦ 10 9 8 4 2
♣ K 8 6

♠ 8 6 4 2   ♠ Q 10 7
♥ 5 3   ♥ A K
♦ A K 3   ♦ Q J 7
♣ A Q 10 4   ♣ J 9 7 3 2

♠ A K J 9 3
♥ 10 8 6 4 2
♦ 6 5
♣ 5

35. Spade three. With general strength, lead a trump. Compare to Problem 29.

36. Spade king. If you lead a spade, the king has to be the right card, gaining if dummy turns up with the singleton queen.

37. Diamond jack. We could have presented this problem without even showing a hand for South. A trump is the correct lead when partner converts a low-level takeout double—he is supposed to have a solid trump holding. Your strategy should be to *draw trumps*, preventing declarer from making his small trumps.

What if South had no diamonds? Well, a good partner would *find* one.

38. Diamond five. Against a suit contract you would lead a high honor, of course. But at notrump you are willing to sacrifice an early trick to establish your long cards and (hopefully) leave a diamond in partner's hand to lead back to you.

39. Spade ace. There is no point in leading the spade jack to preserve communication—partner will never get in. And dummy might well have a singleton spade honor.

40. Heart jack. There is too much chance of losing a trick with a spade lead to justify it with only a four-card suit.

Problems

41.

	WEST	NORTH	EAST	SOUTH
			Pass	Pass
	1 ♡	Pass	1 NT	Pass
	Pass	Dbl	All Pass	

South holds: ♠ Q 10 7 5 2
♡ J 3
♢ A 7 6
♣ Q 10 7

42.

	WEST	NORTH	EAST	SOUTH
			1 ♣	Pass
	1 ♠	Pass	2 ♡	Pass
	3 ♡	Pass	3 ♠	Pass
	4 ♣	Pass	4 ♢	Pass
	4 ♠	Pass	6 ♡	All Pass

One club was artificial, 17 + HCP. One spade was artificial, three controls (ace = 2, king = 1). Three spades, four clubs, four diamonds, and four spades were control-showing cuebids, with hearts agreed as trumps.

South holds: ♠ J 8
♡ Q 8 4
♢ A Q 8 2
♣ J 9 4 3

43.

	WEST	NORTH	EAST	SOUTH
				1 NT
	Pass	2 ♣	Pass	2 ♢
	Pass	Pass	2 ♡	All Pass

South holds: ♠ A J 3
♡ K 7 6
♢ A 10 4
♣ A 7 6 5

44.

WEST	NORTH	EAST	SOUTH
		3 NT[1]	All Pass

[1]"Gambling," with a long, running minor and at most one outside stopper.

South holds: ♠ A 7 5
♡ Q 6
◇ 7 6 3
♣ K J 9 5 3

45.

WEST	NORTH	EAST	SOUTH
		Pass	Pass
1 ♠	Pass	1 NT	Pass
Pass	Dbl	All Pass	

South holds: ♠ K 7 6
♡ K Q 10 9 5 3
◇ 5 4
♣ J 2

46.

WEST	NORTH	EAST	SOUTH
Pass	Pass	1 ♡	Pass
2 ♣	Pass	3 ♡	Pass
3 NT	Pass	4 ◇	Pass
4 ♠	Pass	6 ♡	All Pass

South holds: ♠ K 10 8 3
♡ 8 6 3
◇ 10 7 6 2
♣ A 6

47.

WEST	NORTH	EAST	SOUTH
	1 ♣	Pass	Pass
1 ♡	Pass	1 NT	Pass
2 NT	Pass	3 NT	Pass
Pass	Dbl	All Pass	

South holds: ♠ 10 8 3
♡ Q 7 4
◇ 10 8 6 4 2
♣ 9 3

48.

WEST	NORTH	EAST	SOUTH
		1 ◇	1 ♠
2 ◇	Pass	2 NT	Pass
3 NT	Dbl	All Pass	

South holds: ♠ K J 9 7 5
♡ Q 10 6 5
◇ A 5
♣ J 2

49.	WEST	NORTH	EAST	SOUTH
			1 ◇	Pass
	1 ♠	Pass	2 ◇	Pass
	3 ◇	Pass	3 NT	Pass
	Pass	Dbl	All Pass	

South holds: ♠ J 5
              ♡ Q 10 8 5 2
              ◇ J 9 3
              ♣ 8 7 2

50.	WEST	NORTH	EAST	SOUTH
			1 NT	Pass
	3 NT	Dbl	All Pass	

South holds: ♠ K 10 8 6 3
              ♡ 9
              ◇ J 9 6 5
              ♣ 8 6 5

Solutions

41. Heart jack. Partner has a good hand with heart length and strength.

42. When the hand actually came up, the winner was a club or spade. In the 1971 U.S. Team Trials, South laid down the diamond ace, perhaps expecting dummy to have the club ace and spade king. But the full deal was:

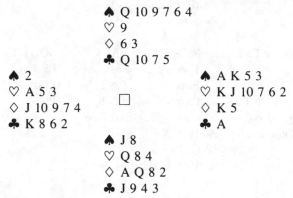

♠ Q 10 9 7 6 4
♡ 9
◇ 6 3
♣ Q 10 7 5

♠ 2   ♠ A K 5 3
♡ A 5 3   ♡ K J 10 7 6 2
◇ J 10 9 7 4   ◇ K 5
♣ K 8 6 2   ♣ A

♠ J 8
♡ Q 8 4
◇ A Q 8 2
♣ J 9 4 3

Declarer, Jim Jacoby, was impressed enough with South's decision to snatch the diamond ace that he proceeded to take a first-round trump finesse through South! The play continued: heart to the ace, club to the ace, spade ace, spade ruff, club king (pitching a spade), club ruff, heart king, and claim. The moral: Cashing out when you visualize the setting trick can backfire.

43. Club ace, intending to lead another club. Partner planned to pass any response to his Stayman inquiry, so he has a weak hand with length in diamonds, spades, and hearts.

44. The standard lead against this bidding is the spade ace. East should have seven solid diamonds, so your best chance to beat 3 NT is to run one of the black suits. You will switch to clubs or hearts if partner discourages a spade continuation.

45. Heart king. A popular conventional lead from K-Q-10-9-x-x is the *queen*, asking partner to drop the jack if he has it. This method should be shelved against gambling-style bidding, though (à la Problem 44). If you lead the queen and the situation is:

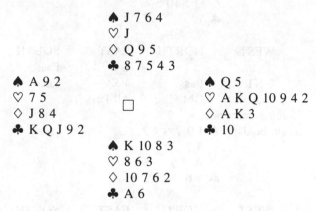

```
                    8 7
      K Q 10 9 5 3    □        A 6 2
                    J 4
```

partner will be put on a guess. If he decides your holding is Q-J-10-x-x, he may win the ace and shift!

46. Spade king. Your hand is too strong for partner to have the diamond king-queen. Instead, try to kill dummy's entry to the club suit. The full deal could be:

```
              ♠ J 7 6 4
              ♡ J
              ◇ Q 9 5
              ♣ 8 7 5 4 3
  ♠ A 9 2                      ♠ Q 5
  ♡ 7 5                        ♡ A K Q 10 9 4 2
  ◇ J 8 4          □           ◇ A K 3
  ♣ K Q J 9 2                  ♣ 10
              ♠ K 10 8 3
              ♡ 8 6 3
              ◇ 10 7 6 2
              ♣ A 6
```

47. Club nine. Partner's double conventionally demands the lead of his suit.

48. Spade seven. Partner's double asks you to lead your own suit. He has help in your suit and wants to make sure you lead it.

49. Spade jack. Partner's double conventionally requests the lead of dummy's first-bid suit.

50. Heart nine. After this unrevealing bidding, partner's double conventionally requires you to make an *unusual* lead. Usually this will be your shortest suit (unless, perhaps, you have an honor there).

Problems

51.

WEST	NORTH	EAST	SOUTH
1 ♣	Pass	1 ♡	Pass
2 ♣	Pass	2 ◇	Pass
2 ♡	Pass	2 NT	Pass
3 NT	Dbl	All Pass	

South holds: ♠ K 10 7 6 3
                ♡ 10 8 5 3
                ◇ A 4
                ♣ 9 2

52.

WEST	NORTH	EAST	SOUTH
		1 ◇	1 ♡
2 ♣	Pass	2 NT	Pass
3 NT	Dbl	All Pass	

South holds: ♠ 10 3
                ♡ K Q 10 6 4
                ◇ Q J 10 5 4
                ♣ 7

53.

WEST	NORTH	EAST	SOUTH
		1 ♡	Pass
2 NT[1]	Pass	4 ♡	Pass
Pass	Dbl	All Pass	

[1]forcing heart raise

South holds: ♠ J 9 7 6 4 2
                ♡ 8 7
                ◇ A 7 5
                ♣ 7 6

54.

WEST	NORTH	EAST	SOUTH
1 ◇	1 ♠	2 ♡	Pass
4 ♡	Pass	5 ♣	Pass
6 ♡	Dbl	All Pass	

South holds: ♠ 9 7 5 3
                ♡ 8
                ◇ Q 9 7 5 2
                ♣ J 7 3

55.

WEST	NORTH	EAST	SOUTH
		1 ♠	Pass
2 ♣	Pass	2 ◇	Pass
3 ◇	Pass	4 ◇	Pass
5 ◇	All Pass		

South holds: ♠ Q 6 4
                ♡ A Q 9 3
                ◇ 10 6 4
                ♣ 9 7 3

56.

	WEST	NORTH	EAST	SOUTH
			1 NT	Pass
	3 NT	All Pass		

South holds: ♠ J 8 7
♡ Q 10 6 2
◇ Q 10 6 2
♣ A 2

57.

	WEST	NORTH	EAST	SOUTH
			1 ♠	Pass
	3 ♠	Pass	4 NT	Pass
	5 ♡	Pass	5 NT	Pass
	6 ♣	Pass	6 ♠	All Pass

South holds: ♠ Q 8 4
♡ J 9 7 5 3
◇ Q 6 5
♣ 10 3

58.

	WEST	NORTH	EAST	SOUTH
			1 ♣	Pass
	1 ♠	Pass	2 ◇	Pass
	2 ♠	Pass	2 NT	Pass
	3 NT	All Pass		

South holds: ♠ K 9 6
♡ Q 4 2
◇ Q 5 3
♣ J 9 4 2

59.

	WEST	NORTH	EAST	SOUTH
	1 ♣	Pass	1 ♠	Pass
	2 ♡	Pass	2 NT	Pass
	3 NT	All Pass		

South holds: ♠ Q 10 7 5
♡ 10 9
◇ K 10 3
♣ J 9 4 2

60.

	WEST	NORTH	EAST	SOUTH
	1 ♣	Pass	1 NT	Pass
	2 NT	Pass	3 NT	All Pass

South holds: ♠ A Q 10 6 2
♡ 8 7
◇ K 8 5 3
♣ 9 4

51. Expert opinion varies, but I'd vote for the normal lead of the spade six. Contrast with Problem 49. There, West could have had four small spades. Here, West has rebid the clubs, so he is marked with length (and strength, since rebidding a bad five-card suit is anathema to good players). North doubtless has a good holding in clubs, and this leads him to believe that the contract will fail—but his double doesn't demand a specific lead.

52. Another controversial situation. Does partner's double suggest a heart lead, a club lead, or no lead in particular? When this very problem was put to *The Bridge World*'s panel of experts, it split like Caesar's Gaul into three parts. The vote for the club seven barely exceeded the total for various hearts, while almost as many panelists opted for a spade or the diamond queen.

My view is that since the meaning of partner's double is ambiguous, he could hardly double unless he could stand a heart lead. True, he failed to raise hearts, but he could have A-x.

53. Spade jack. Partner's out-of-the-blue double after the opponents have had a strong auction must request an unusual lead—he should be able to ruff spades. You lead the jack as a suit-preference signal, requesting a diamond return.

54. Diamond five. Partner's "Lightner" double of this voluntarily bid slam bars you from leading his suit. Normally, the lead of dummy's first-bid suit is suggested, since this is a lead you would seldom consider without partner's double.

55. Heart ace. A trump lead is out when both dummy and declarer have bid side suits; your heart tricks might disappear unless you take them immediately. The opponents avoided 3 NT, so perhaps partner has the heart king.

56. Heart two. Prefer the major suit to the minor, since West failed to investigate a major-suit contract.

57. Diamond five. You are entitled to draw a negative inference from partner's failure to double either of West's responses to Blackwood.

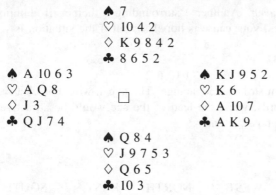

```
              ♠ 7
              ♡ 10 4 2
              ◇ K 9 8 4 2
              ♣ 8 6 5 2
♠ A 10 6 3                    ♠ K J 9 5 2
♡ A Q 8                       ♡ K 6
◇ J 3            □            ◇ A 10 7
♣ Q J 7 4                     ♣ A K 9
              ♠ Q 8 4
              ♡ J 9 7 5 3
              ◇ Q 6 5
              ♣ 10 3
```

Such clues also are available when partner fails to double a control-showing cuebid or a bid of the fourth suit, which is often made with a fragment or single stopper.

58. A spade. This problem is from *Instructions for the Defense* by Jeremy Flint and David Greenwood. In theory East should have a mild spade fit or else good trick prospects without the spades. In practice, many players bid this way with a spade singleton and not much extra high-card strength. On the actual deal, the lead of the spade king was effective even though East had his bid.

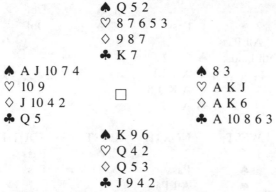

```
              ♠ Q 5 2
              ♡ 8 7 6 5 3
              ◇ 9 8 7
              ♣ K 7
♠ A J 10 7 4                  ♠ 8 3
♡ 10 9                        ♡ A K J
◇ J 10 4 2       □            ◇ A K 6
♣ Q 5                         ♣ A 10 8 6 3
              ♠ K 9 6
              ♡ Q 4 2
              ◇ Q 5 3
              ♣ J 9 4 2
```

Declarer ducked the first trick and was surprised to lose to North's spade queen at trick two. Things went from bad to worse when the heart jack was headed by the queen at trick three, and a demoralized declarer eventually finished four down!

59. Spade five, though a heart could be right. Avoid, however, a diamond lead—dummy has at least a couple, and declarer could have a concealed five-card suit. (Compare with Problem 25.)

60. Spade *queen*. Another "surrounding" theme. If dummy hits with K-J-x of spades, your cause is hopeless; but if the situation is

```
              8 7
    K 9 4      □       J 5 3
              A Q 10 6 2
```

the queen might strike an advantage. The queen would be clearly right if you had no side cards, while the lead of the ace would be attractive if you had more than one possible entry.

Problems

61.

WEST	NORTH	EAST	SOUTH
		1 NT[1]	Pass
2 ♣	Pass	2 ◊	Pass
2 ♠	Pass	3 NT	All Pass

[1]18- 20 HCP

South holds: ♠ —
♡ K 7 5 3
◊ 8 7 5
♣ J 10 8 7 5 4

62.

WEST	NORTH	EAST	SOUTH
		1 ♠	Dbl
2 ♠	Pass	4 ♠	Dbl
All Pass			

South holds: ♠ 8 3 2
♡ A J 10
◊ A K J 8
♣ A J 2

63.

WEST	NORTH	EAST	SOUTH
1 ♡	2 ◊	2 ♠	Pass
3 ♠	Pass	3 NT	Pass
4 ♠	All Pass		

South holds: ♠ 9 6 3
♡ K 7 3
◊ 10 5 3
♣ K 10 4 2

64.

WEST	NORTH	EAST	SOUTH
1 NT	Pass	2 ♠	All Pass

South holds: ♠ Q 7 4
♡ A Q J 3
◊ 9 6 3
♣ A 10 4

65.	WEST	NORTH	EAST	SOUTH
			1 ♡	Pass
	2 ◇	Pass	3 ♣	Pass
	3 ♠	Dbl	4 ♣	Pass
	5 ♡	Pass	6 ♡	All Pass

South holds: ♠ Q 10 6 3
♡ 7 6
◇ A 10 6 5 2
♣ 8 2

Solutions

61. Partner is very likely to be short in clubs on this bidding. A club lead will do, since there is nothing better, but the lead of the seven should be preferred to the jack, which might crash something valuable in partner's hand.

On a similar deal in the 1965 Bermuda Bowl, a U.S. player led the club jack and presented declarer with a ninth trick. The club lie was:

Q

K 9 3   □   A 6 2

J 10 8 7 5 4

62. Lead a trump as fast as you can. You must protect your high cards from impending ruffs—where else does declarer figure to get his tricks?

63. Club two. Your discouraging heart and spade holdings suggest that you will need some fast tricks, and your best hope lies with the club suit. On the bidding, dummy probably will table a singleton diamond, and with declarer holding something in diamonds, a diamond lead could set up a vital pitch.

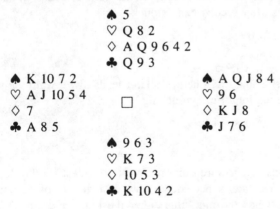

```
                    ♠ 5
                    ♡ Q 8 2
                    ◇ A Q 9 6 4 2
                    ♣ Q 9 3
  ♠ K 10 7 2                        ♠ A Q J 8 4
  ♡ A J 10 5 4          □           ♡ 9 6
  ◇ 7                               ◇ K J 8
  ♣ A 8 5                           ♣ J 7 6
                    ♠ 9 6 3
                    ♡ K 7 3
                    ◇ 10 5 3
                    ♣ K 10 4 2
```

64. Heart ace. Heart queen, 90 percent. There is nothing wrong with getting busy here when you have such a promising source of tricks. The heart king is probably in dummy, so this lead won't cost much.

65. Diamond ace. Based on a hand from H. W. Kelsey's classic book, *Killing Defense at Bridge.* East can hardly be afraid of a spade lead on this auction. Maybe his pattern is 1-5-2-5, and partner can ruff the second diamond.

Second-Hand Play

The well-known admonition to play "second hand low" is a throwback to the time of whist and auction bridge. While "second hand low" is still a fairly reliable guide for routine situations, it should be regarded as a tendency, not as a hard and fast rule.

The reason for playing low as second hand is simple: Partner is last to play, so there is less reason for second hand to do anything desperate. Second hand can *wait* and let declarer commit himself, often to his disadvantage, as third hand. If you play low as second hand, you might oblige declarer to guess what to play from third hand, force him to spend a high card to keep fourth hand from winning cheaply, avoid clashing with one of your partner's high cards on the same trick, or make declarer's job of establishing winners a little harder.

In this situation:

```
                  8 7 4
   J 9 5            □           A 10 6 3
                  K Q 2
```

declarer may be entitled to two tricks, but if East plays low the first time the suit is led from dummy, declarer must spend an entry to lead the suit again. And if declarer's holding were K-J-2, he would have to guess whether to play the king or the jack after second hand's duck.

```
                  J 6
   A Q 8 3          □            9 4
                  K 10 7 5 2
```

Needing to establish some tricks here, declarer leads low toward the jack. West can save a trick in the long run by ducking.

```
                  A J 8
   K Q 6            □            9 4 3
                  10 7 5 2
```

When declarer leads low toward dummy, West does best to play low, forcing declarer to guess. Declarer's percentage play is a finesse of dummy's eight, winning when West has the nine plus either the king or queen. West would "split his honors," as we say, only if he wanted just one fast trick.

The most spectacular example of second-hand ducking I can remember occurred in an international event when Italy's Benito Garozzo defended a spade partscore contract with A-K-x-x of hearts in front of dummy's Q-10-8-x. Garozzo refrained from leading a heart, choosing a trump lead instead. At one point, declarer led a heart toward dummy. Garozzo played low, and declarer tried dummy's eight, losing to the nine. Later on, declarer got back in and led another low heart toward dummy. Garozzo played low again (!), and this time the ten lost to the jack.

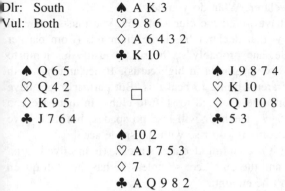

Dlr: South
Vul: Both

```
                  ♠ A K 3
                  ♡ 9 8 6
                  ◇ A 6 4 3 2
                  ♣ K 10
♠ Q 6 5                         ♠ J 9 8 7 4
♡ Q 4 2                         ♡ K 10
◇ K 9 5          □              ◇ Q J 10 8
♣ J 7 6 4                       ♣ 5 3
                  ♠ 10 2
                  ♡ A J 7 5 3
                  ◇ 7
                  ♣ A Q 9 8 2
```

On this deal from the 1983 Bermuda Bowl semifinals, two N-S pairs stopped at a heart game while the other two reached the shaky slam. Declarer won the spade lead and played a trump. If East follows with the ten, declarer inserts the jack, wins the return, and cashes the heart ace, dropping the king. Now a third round of clubs can be ruffed, and South reenters his hand with a diamond ruff to draw West's last trump.

In the Bermuda Bowl, however, *all four* Easts (Peter Weichsel and Eddie Wold of the United States, Michel Lebel of France, and Soldano De Falco of Italy) put the *king* of hearts up. Two declarers then went to the club king to lead a second heart—ten, jack, queen. West played a third trump and scored a trick with the club jack. The other two declarers immediately switched to clubs, but East overruffed dummy on the third round, and West still had to make his trump queen.

A situation players find vexing occurs when declarer leads a low card toward dummy's K-Q-x-x and you just know it's a singleton—the urge to grab your ace may be overpowering.

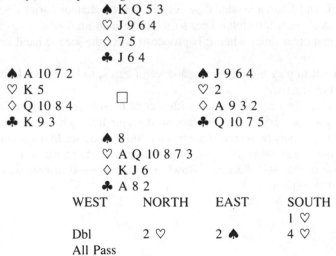

```
                  ♠ K Q 5 3
                  ♡ J 9 6 4
                  ◇ 7 5
                  ♣ J 6 4
♠ A 10 7 2                      ♠ J 9 6 4
♡ K 5                           ♡ 2
◇ Q 10 8 4       □              ◇ A 9 3 2
♣ K 9 3                         ♣ Q 10 7 5
                  ♠ 8
                  ♡ A Q 10 8 7 3
                  ◇ K J 6
                  ♣ A 8 2
```

WEST	NORTH	EAST	SOUTH
			1 ♡
Dbl	2 ♡	2 ♠	4 ♡
All Pass			

You, West, decide to lead the diamond four against the four-heart contract. Partner wins the ace and returns the two to declarer's king. Now comes the inevitable low spade from declarer. What do you do?

No doubt partner should have found the club shift, but you must deal with things as they are. You know that declarer has three diamonds (from partner return of the two), one spade, and probably six hearts (to justify his jump to game—he has at most only sixteen points in high cards). If declarer has both the club ace and queen, you aren't going to beat this. But partner might have the club queen, especially since he declined to shift to clubs. In that case you can beat it *if you duck this trick*. Declarer will lose no spades, but he'll have two club losers. Note the outcome if you rise with the spade ace.

Another way of looking at it is counting declarer's tricks. He has five hearts, a diamond, a diamond ruff, and the club ace, so unless he has the club queen as well, one spade trick won't be enough.

Positions like this are common. In general, you should *win* when you have defensive tricks ready to cash or when there is no sign of any defensive tricks except your ace. You should *duck* when the contract is in doubt, there are possible defensive tricks on the horizon and declarer will gain on the transaction if you win.

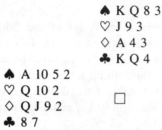

♠ K Q 8 3
♥ J 9 3
♦ A 4 3
♣ K Q 4

♠ A 10 5 2
♥ Q 10 2
♦ Q J 9 2
♣ 8 7

Dummy opened 1 NT; declarer responded three hearts and was raised to four hearts. You, West, lead the diamond queen. Dummy wins and partner plays the eight, encouraging. Declarer cashes the heart ace-king, partner showing out on the second round, and leads a spade. Rise, cash whatever diamond tricks you can, and retire. Declarer has the club ace, so the issue is in no doubt.

There are several other times when it is proper to break the second hand low tendency:

- You often want to play high from a sequence of cards, to let partner know about your holding.
- Many deceptive plays are associated with second hand high. See Quiz 23.
- Sometimes you can take a trick or prevent declarer from winning a trick too cheaply if you play high, and *it costs you nothing* to do so. In particular, many cash-out situations require you to grab a winner in second seat.

This deal arose in the 1973 Bermuda Bowl. South, believe it or not, was a many-time world champion.

Dlr: South   ♠ Q 5
Vul: N-S   ♡ A K 9 4
             ◇ J
             ♣ K 9 8 7 6 5

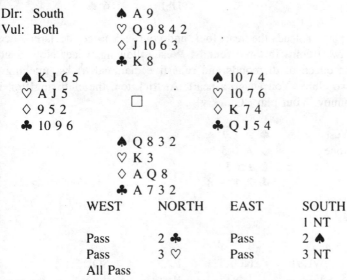

♠ 10 8 4 2		♠ A J 9 7 6 3
♡ 8 7		♡ Q 10 6 5
◇ 10 8 3 2		◇ A Q 7
♣ Q 10 3		♣ —

             ♠ K
             ♡ J 3 2
             ◇ K 9 6 5 4
             ♣ A J 4 2

WEST	NORTH	EAST	SOUTH
			1 ◇
Pass	1 ♡	1 ♠	2 ♡
2 ♠	3 ♣	4 ♠	Pass
Pass	Dbl	All Pass	

In N-S's style, the three-club bid showed at least a five-card suit and a good hand. South led a heart to the king, and North shifted to the jack of diamonds. Declarer went up with the diamond ace, cashed the ace of spades, and led the seven of diamonds away from the queen.

At this point, South had an aberration, playing low. North ruffed dummy's diamond ten and cashed the ace of hearts, but declarer took the rest, throwing two diamonds from dummy on the queen and ten of hearts.

The following deal, entitled "second hand middle," was reported by Eddie Kantar in 1978 and won a Bols Brilliancy Prize for Eddie's partner, Billy Eisenberg, who sat West.

Dlr: South   ♠ A 9
Vul: Both   ♡ Q 9 8 4 2
             ◇ J 10 6 3
             ♣ K 8

♠ K J 6 5		♠ 10 7 4
♡ A J 5		♡ 10 7 6
◇ 9 5 2		◇ K 7 4
♣ 10 9 6		♣ Q J 5 4

             ♠ Q 8 3 2
             ♡ K 3
             ◇ A Q 8
             ♣ A 7 3 2

WEST	NORTH	EAST	SOUTH
			1 NT
Pass	2 ♣	Pass	2 ♠
Pass	3 ♡	Pass	3 NT
All Pass			

Eisenberg led the ten of clubs—king, five, two. A diamond to the queen won, and declarer continued with the heart three. Here, Eisenberg put up his *jack*, and the queen won in dummy. Two more rounds of diamonds picked up the suit, and declarer exited with the heart king to West's ace. Eisenberg now led the club nine, ducked all around, and another club to declarer's ace. Declarer played to the spade ace and cashed the thirteenth diamond, but he could make no more tricks. *East* won the next heart, cashed the good club, and led a spade. Down one.

Had West followed low to the first heart, he would have been endplayed on the third round of hearts and forced to concede the ninth trick to the spade queen. (Kantar pointed out that it would do West no good to discard the heart jack on the fourth diamond—declarer could play ace and nine of spades, covering with the queen if East played the ten. The spade eight would have to score.)

Our Quiz may call upon you to avoid playing second hand low in several other situations.

Problems

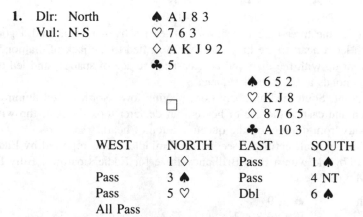

1. Dlr: North
Vul: N-S

♠ A J 8 3
♡ 7 6 3
◇ A K J 9 2
♣ 5

♠ 6 5 2
♡ K J 8
◇ 8 7 6 5
♣ A 10 3

WEST	NORTH	EAST	SOUTH
	1 ◇	Pass	1 ♠
Pass	3 ♠	Pass	4 NT
Pass	5 ♡	Dbl	6 ♠
All Pass			

West, your partner, leads the heart four, and your jack forces declarer's ace. Declarer draws trumps in three rounds, West following twice. Now South produces the queen of diamonds and runs five diamond tricks, pitching a heart and two clubs. You let go a heart. At trick ten, the club singleton is led from dummy. Your play? Quickly!

2. Dlr: West
Vul: None

♠ A J 9
♡ A 6 5
◇ J 5 3
♣ A K 9 8

♠ Q 10 4
♡ K Q J 8 2
◇ A
♣ Q 7 5 4

WEST	NORTH	EAST	SOUTH
1 ♡	1 NT	Pass	3 ◇
Pass	3 ♡	Pass	5 ◇
All Pass			

30

You, West, lead the heart king to dummy's ace. Declarer ruffs a heart and plays the diamond king. You win the ace and exit with a heart, ruffed. Declarer cashes the club ace, discards a spade on the club king, ruffs a club, returns to the diamond jack, and ruffs dummy's last club. Now a spade is led. What do you play and why?

Solutions

1. You must *duck* as smoothly as possible. Count declarer's tricks: He has four spades, five diamonds, one heart, and one ruff for a total of eleven, so he can't make it without one club trick. If he has both the club king and queen or just the king, there is nothing you can do; but if South has the club king and jack, you have a chance so long as you put him to a guess on this trick.

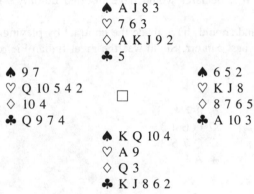

2. The deal is from the 1966 Bermuda Bowl, with the late Lew Mathe sitting West. The end position was:

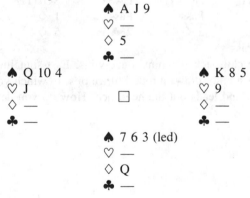

31

Mathe alertly put up the spade queen, which left declarer with no chance. The full deal:

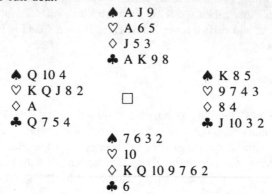

```
              ♠ A J 9
              ♡ A 6 5
              ◇ J 5 3
              ♣ A K 9 8
♠ Q 10 4                      ♠ K 8 5
♡ K Q J 8 2      □           ♡ 9 7 4 3
◇ A                          ◇ 8 4
♣ Q 7 5 4                    ♣ J 10 3 2
              ♠ 7 6 3 2
              ♡ 10
              ◇ K Q 10 9 7 6 2
              ♣ 6
```

Had Mathe played low, declarer would have inserted dummy's nine, end-playing East.

Declarer could, and should, have made the contract by playing on spades earlier, but even the best can err. South was the great Italian Pietro Forquet.

Problems

3. Dlr: West
   Vul: N-S

```
              ♠ 8 7 4
              ♡ Q 6 4 3
              ◇ Q 7 5 3
              ♣ A 9
♠ A Q 9 3
♡ K 10 8          □
◇ 8
♣ J 10 8 4 2
```

WEST	NORTH	EAST	SOUTH
Pass	Pass	Pass	1 ◇
Dbl	2 ◇	2 ♠	5 ◇
All Pass			

You, West, lead the club jack. Dummy's ace wins, East signaling with the seven. Declarer ruffs a club, draws a round of trumps, to which your partner follows with the ten, and leads out the heart ace. How do you defend?

4. Dlr: South   ♠ 6 4 2
    Vul: Both   ♡ A K Q 9 4
                     ♢ 6 5
                     ♣ 7 3 2

♠ 9 5 3
♡ J 2
♢ K J 9 4 2   □
♣ Q 10 4

WEST	NORTH	EAST	SOUTH
			1 ♣
Pass	1 ♡	Pass	2 NT
Pass	3 ♡	Pass	3 NT
All Pass			

You, West, lead the diamond four. Declarer, who has A-10-x, holds off the ace until the third round. At trick four, declarer leads a low heart toward dummy. What do you play and why?

Solutions

3. You should drop the heart king under the ace. Declarer appears to have seven diamonds, a club, and no more than two spades, so he has at least three hearts. East can be expected to hold the heart jack, else declarer would have taken a finesse in the suit. You must hope that the full deal is:

                ♠ 8 7 4
                ♡ Q 6 4 3
                ♢ Q 7 5 3
                ♣ A 9

♠ A Q 9 3   ♠ J 10 5 2
♡ K 10 8   ♡ J 9 2
♢ 8   □   ♢ 10
♣ J 10 8 4 2   ♣ K Q 7 6 3
                ♠ K 6
                ♡ A 7 5
                ♢ A K J 9 6 4 2
                ♣ 5

If you hold on to the heart king, declarer can set up dummy's fourth heart without letting your partner in to play a spade through the king. (South is marked with the spade king. He could hardly have enough to voluntarily bid an eleven-trick game, vulnerable against not, without it.)

Note that if declarer had led a low heart first, the right defense would be no less easy. You would have to play your *ten*, letting dummy's queen win, and then dump your king again if declarer led to the ace.

4. Play the heart jack. If you do not, declarer, who is likely to have two low hearts on the bidding, will insert dummy's nine, passing his heart loser to your partner, who has no more diamonds. Declarer will win any return and take three spades, four hearts, a club and a diamond. The full deal:

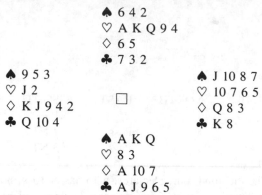

```
                   ♠ 6 4 2
                   ♡ A K Q 9 4
                   ◇ 6 5
                   ♣ 7 3 2
  ♠ 9 5 3                          ♠ J 10 8 7
  ♡ J 2                            ♡ 10 7 6 5
  ◇ K J 9 4 2     □                ◇ Q 8 3
  ♣ Q 10 4                         ♣ K 8
                   ♠ A K Q
                   ♡ 8 3
                   ◇ A 10 7
                   ♣ A J 9 6 5
```

Even if you defend correctly, partner must make a good second-hand play to defeat the contract. Declarer must win the first heart, of course, lest you cash your diamonds, and now he is limited to just three heart tricks. However, if declarer now leads a club, partner must put up his club king. If partner follows with the eight of clubs, declarer can cash his spades and exit with a club, forcing a heart lead into dummy's tenace.

Problems

5. Dlr: South
    Vul: N-S

```
                   ♠ 7
                   ♡ Q 10 8 3
                   ◇ 8 6 5 3
                   ♣ A 6 5 3
                              ♠ K 6 3
                              ♡ 7 6 5
                   □          ◇ J 10 9 7
                              ♣ Q 10 4
```

WEST	NORTH	EAST	SOUTH
			1 ♠
Pass	1 NT	Pass	2 ♡
Pass	3 ♡	Pass	4 ♡
All Pass			

West, your partner, leads ace and another heart. Declarer wins the second heart in dummy and leads a spade. How do you defend?

6. Dlr: South
Vul: E-W

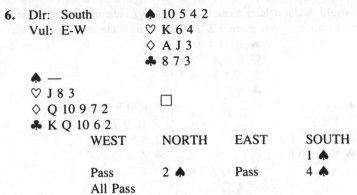

♠ 10 5 4 2
♡ K 6 4
◊ A J 3
♣ 8 7 3

♠ —
♡ J 8 3
◊ Q 10 9 7 2
♣ K Q 10 6 2

WEST	NORTH	EAST	SOUTH
			1 ♠
Pass	2 ♠	Pass	4 ♠
All Pass			

You, West, lead the king of clubs. Partner overtakes with the ace and returns a club. You cash the club ten and queen, partner pitching a low diamond. Declarer wins your heart switch with the king and leads the spade ten. Partner's king covers, and the ace wins as you show out. Do you think you can relax from here on?

Solutions

5.

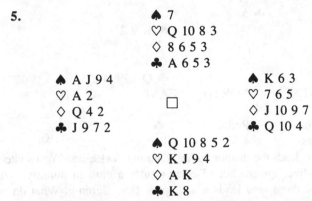

♠ 7
♡ Q 10 8 3
◊ 8 6 5 3
♣ A 6 5 3

♠ A J 9 4
♡ A 2
◊ Q 4 2
♣ J 9 7 2

♠ K 6 3
♡ 7 6 5
◊ J 10 9 7
♣ Q 10 4

♠ Q 10 8 5 2
♡ K J 9 4
◊ A K
♣ K 8

Put up the spade king, hoping it will hold so you can clear a third round of trumps. Partner's trump lead suggests a good holding in declarer's first suit, but once he continues with the second round of trumps, he is certain to have strong spades.

On this defense, declarer will lose three spades and a heart. If you play low on the spade, declarer has time to ruff two spades, concede a spade, and make his contract.

6. You can relax if declarer draws the rest of the trumps and claims. However, if he leads a diamond toward dummy, you must insert the queen. This won't cost a trick, since declarer almost surely has the diamond king and heart queen on the bidding. He is going to finesse the diamond jack anyway if he needs to. Playing second hand high may gain, however, by depriving declarer of an extra entry to dummy.

Why would declarer lead a diamond anyway? He might need to get back to dummy to finesse your partner's trump intermediates. The full deal:

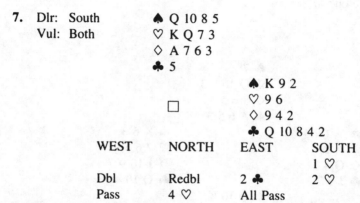

♠ 10 5 4 2
♡ K 6 4
◇ A J 3
♣ 8 7 3

♠ —
♡ J 8 3
◇ Q 10 9 7 2
♣ K Q 10 6 2

♠ K 9 8 3
♡ 10 9 7 5
◇ 8 5 4
♣ A 4

♠ A Q J 7 6
♡ A Q 2
◇ K 6
♣ J 9 5

Problems

7. Dlr: South
   Vul: Both

♠ Q 10 8 5
♡ K Q 7 3
◇ A 7 6 3
♣ 5

♠ K 9 2
♡ 9 6
◇ 9 4 2
♣ Q 10 8 4 2

WEST	NORTH	EAST	SOUTH
			1 ♡
Dbl	Redbl	2 ♣	2 ♡
Pass	4 ♡	All Pass	

West, your partner, leads the diamond king. Dummy ducks, and West switches to the club six—five, queen, ace. Declarer ruffs a club in dummy, West following with the three, and leads a low spade from dummy. What do you play and why?

8. Dlr: South
   Vul: None

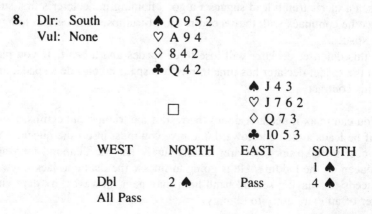

♠ Q 9 5 2
♡ A 9 4
◇ 8 4 2
♣ Q 4 2

♠ J 4 3
♡ J 7 6 2
◇ Q 7 3
♣ 10 5 3

WEST	NORTH	EAST	SOUTH
			1 ♠
Dbl	2 ♠	Pass	4 ♠
All Pass			

36

West, your partner, leads the heart king, ducked, and continues with the queen. Declarer wins the heart ace, ruffs a heart, and draws three rounds of trumps (partner discarding a diamond and a heart). Next, declarer cashes the club ace, king, and queen, as partner plays high-low. At trick ten a diamond is led from dummy. How do you defend?

Solutions

7. The full deal is:

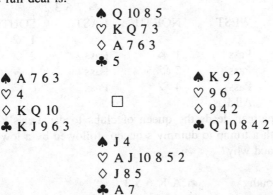

♠ Q 10 8 5
♡ K Q 7 3
◇ A 7 6 3
♣ 5

♠ A 7 6 3
♡ 4
◇ K Q 10
♣ K J 9 6 3

♠ K 9 2
♡ 9 6
◇ 9 4 2
♣ Q 10 8 4 2

♠ J 4
♡ A J 10 8 5 2
◇ J 8 5
♣ A 7

You must rise with the spade king and return a diamond. Declarer wouldn't play spades before drawing trumps if he had three spades—he might run into a ruff. Furthermore, if declarer has A-x in spades, the contract is unbeatable. (Partner's club plays mark declarer with only two clubs, and he'd be very unlikely to open the bidding on:

♠ A x
♡ J 10 x x x x
◇ J x x
♣ A x.)

8. Play the diamond queen, trying to keep declarer from passing the lead to your partner cheaply and endplaying him. You need three diamond tricks to beat this, and you won't get them unless partner's diamonds are as good as A-J-10. Be an optimist.

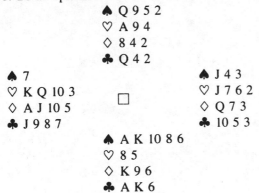

♠ Q 9 5 2
♡ A 9 4
◇ 8 4 2
♣ Q 4 2

♠ 7
♡ K Q 10 3
◇ A J 10 5
♣ J 9 8 7

♠ J 4 3
♡ J 7 6 2
◇ Q 7 3
♣ 10 5 3

♠ A K 10 8 6
♡ 8 5
◇ K 9 6
♣ A K 6

Problems

9. Dlr: South   ♠ Q J 10 5 3
    Vul: E-W   ♡ A Q 9
                    ◇ 5 4
                    ♣ 8 6 4

                            ♠ K 7 4
                     □   ♡ 4 2
                            ◇ 10 9 6 3
                            ♣ 7 5 3 2

WEST	NORTH	EAST	SOUTH
			1 ♡
Pass	1 ♠	Pass	2 ◇
Pass	3 ♡	Pass	4 ♣
Pass	4 ♡	Pass	6 ♡
All Pass			

West, your partner, leads the queen of clubs to declarer's king. Declarer continues with a trump to dummy's queen, followed by a low spade. What do you play and why?

10. Dlr: South   ♠ A K 6 5 3
    Vul: Both   ♡ J 6 3
                    ◇ A 7 4
                    ♣ J 6

                            ♠ Q 10 7
                     □   ♡ 8 7 5 4
                            ◇ Q 10 3
                            ♣ 10 7 3

WEST	NORTH	EAST	SOUTH
			1 ◇
Pass	1 ♠	Pass	1 NT
Pass	3 NT	All Pass	

West, your partner, leads the five of clubs. Declarer wins with dummy's jack and continues with a low diamond from dummy. What do you play and why?

Solutions

9.   Declarer wouldn't go to dummy to lead toward the singleton ace of spades, and if he has A-9 doubleton the contract is unlikely to fail. If declarer has the singleton nine and East plays low on the first spade, declarer will take a successful ruffing finesse against the king later and dispose of his diamond losers.

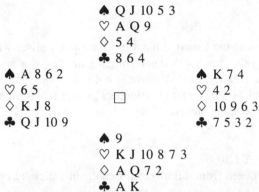

                   ♠ Q J 10 5 3
                   ♡ A Q 9
                   ◇ 5 4
                   ♣ 8 6 4

♠ A 8 6 2   ♠ K 7 4
♡ 6 5   ♡ 4 2
◇ K J 8   □   ◇ 10 9 6 3
♣ Q J 10 9   ♣ 7 5 3 2

                   ♠ 9
                   ♡ K J 10 8 7 3
                   ◇ A Q 7 2
                   ♣ A K

To beat the contract, you must go up with the spade king.

10.   You should play an honor, preferably the queen. If declarer's diamonds are K-J-x-x-(x), he is about to finesse his jack—that's one possibility you can't help. But if he has K-x-x-x-(x), he may want to duck a diamond to your partner's hand as an avoidance play. (If declarer has the club king left, he is safe as long as *you* don't gain the lead.)

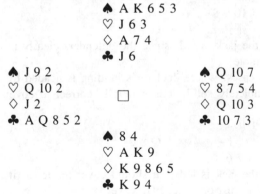

                   ♠ A K 6 5 3
                   ♡ J 6 3
                   ◇ A 7 4
                   ♣ J 6

♠ J 9 2   ♠ Q 10 7
♡ Q 10 2   ♡ 8 7 5 4
◇ J 2   □   ◇ Q 10 3
♣ A Q 8 5 2   ♣ 10 7 3

                   ♠ 8 4
                   ♡ A K 9
                   ◇ K 9 8 6 5
                   ♣ K 9 4

Note that the queen would be a mandatory play if declarer had cashed the diamond ace before leading low.

Should You Cover?

A further exception to the "second hand low" tendency arises when declarer *leads a high card*. In that case, a defender might gain by covering with a high card of his own. The idea is that if declarer is obliged to spend two of his high cards on the same trick, some of the defenders' lower-ranking cards may be promoted quickly to winning status.

Q 5

9 8 4 3   □   K 7 2

A J 10 6

If declarer leads the queen from dummy, East can gain a trick by covering with the king.

There are many lesser-known positions. For example:

10 4

Q 9 6 3   □   A 5

K J 8 7 2

If declarer leads the ten, East can gain a trick by "covering" with the ace.

In these first two instances note that declarer led an *unsupported* high card. But if this is the position:

J 10 9 8

□   Q 7 6 3

East should duck if the jack is led, since the defenders clearly have no intermediate cards to promote.

In the in-between cases, where declarer's holding is headed by a couple of honors but isn't completely solid, it is generally correct to cover the *second* honor.

J 10 4

K 9 5 3   □   Q 8 2

A 7 6

East should duck if the jack is led, but should cover the ten if it is led later. Declarer will be held to just one trick. However:

10 9 4

K 8 7 2   □   A J 3

Q 6 5

If dummy leads the ten, East, with *two* honors of his own, must cover to keep declarer from winning a trick. And:

J 10 8

K 5 4   □   Q 9

A 7 6 3 2

This time East must cover the first honor to give the defense a chance for two tricks. That's what makes bridge such a difficult game—there are exceptions to the exceptions to the rules!

The following deal was presented by Bobby Wolff in "The Aces on Bridge," his syndicated column.

Dlr: South
Vul: Both

```
                    ♠ J 8 4
                    ♡ A 7
                    ◇ K 9 8 7 6 5
                    ♣ J 2
    ♠ 6 3                         ♠ Q 10 9 5 2
    ♡ Q J 10 8 4                  ♡ 6 5 2
    ◇ Q 10 4 2        □          ◇ 3
    ♣ K 7                         ♣ A 8 6 4
                    ♠ A K 7
                    ♡ K 9 3
                    ◇ A J
                    ♣ Q 10 9 5 3
```

South plays in 3 NT, and West leads the queen of hearts. Declarer wins with the king and plays the ace and jack of diamonds. Should West cover?

Clearly, the answer is no. True, West can promote one trick for his ten by covering. But if West plays low, declarer cannot establish and cash dummy's diamonds.

The position below is somewhat enigmatic.

```
        Q J 4 3
          □        K 2
```

Should East cover the lead of the jack or queen? Not to cover will be disastrous if declarer has A-7-6-5. However, if declarer holds A-9-8-7 (which is more likely), he will look with favor on a cover—he can win and pass the nine next, bringing in the suit. But if East ducks smoothly on the first round, declarer must guess whether to continue with dummy's other honor or a low card. (West, for his part, can lead declarer astray by dropping his middle spot from 10-x-x on the first round.)

Clearly, the defenders have it easier if *dummy* is the hand leading to the trick. If *declarer* leads, his holding is concealed and some unpleasant guessing may be required. Would you cover an honor in this situation?

Dlr: South
Vul: None

```
                    ♠ A 6 3
                    ♡ 7 6 3
                    ◇ A 10 4
                    ♣ J 9 6 3
    ♠ 10 8 4
    ♡ K 10 8 4 2
    ◇ Q 5 2          □
    ♣ K 4
```

South opened 1 NT and was raised to 3 NT. Your heart lead is covered by the three, jack and queen. Now South tables the jack of diamonds.

It would be right to cover if declarer's holding was J-x or J-x-x, but if he had that, he'd be unlikely to attack diamonds at an early stage. Probably, diamonds is declarer's best suit—he might have K-J-9-8-(x). He is tempting you to cover to solve his problems. An experienced player anticipates a problem like this from the moment he sees dummy. He makes up mind to duck neither too quickly nor too slowly, and declarer will have to guess what to do.

It is usually right to withhold an honor that is safe from capture. If you have K-x-x-x of trumps in front of dummy's A-x-x, you should duck if declarer leads the queen. Barring any "smother plays" by declarer, your king will always be worth a trick.

However, it would not be so clear to duck the queen if this were a side suit. An inexperienced declarer could be trying a "Chinese finesse" by leading the unsupported queen!

The following hand, on which West must decline to cover an honor, proves that bridge is a strange game.

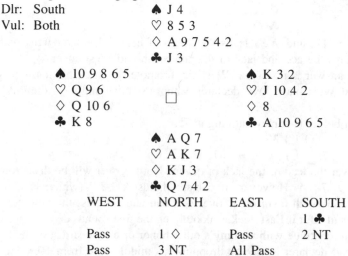

Dlr: South
Vul: Both

```
                    ♠ J 4
                    ♡ 8 5 3
                    ◇ A 9 7 5 4 2
                    ♣ J 3
    ♠ 10 9 8 6 5            ♠ K 3 2
    ♡ Q 9 6                 ♡ J 10 4 2
    ◇ Q 10 6      □         ◇ 8
    ♣ K 8                   ♣ A 10 9 6 5
                    ♠ A Q 7
                    ♡ A K 7
                    ◇ K J 3
                    ♣ Q 7 4 2
```

WEST	NORTH	EAST	SOUTH
			1 ♣
Pass	1 ◇	Pass	2 NT
Pass	3 NT	All Pass	

West's spade lead is covered by the jack, king, and ace. Declarer sees an easy make if diamonds are no worse than 3-1. He cashes the diamond king and leads the jack, planning to duck to preserve communication with dummy. But when West plays the *ten* under the jack, declarer understandably reconsiders. He plays the ace from dummy and winds up going down.

Note that if diamonds were in fact 4-0, with West holding Q-10-8-6, West again would need to refrain from covering the jack. This time declarer would take three tricks instead of five.

Problems

1. Dlr: South   ♠ K 10 8 3
   Vul: None   ♡ Q 4 3
                  ◇ 10 6 5 3
                  ♣ A K

   ♠ A 4
   ♡ J 10 9 7 5
   ◇ K Q 9   ☐
   ♣ 8 7 6

WEST	NORTH	EAST	SOUTH
			Pass
Pass	1 ◇	Pass	1 NT
All Pass			

You, West, lead the heart jack. Declarer wins the king, partner playing the two. At trick two, declarer leads the jack of spades. What do you play?

2. Dlr: South   ♠ A 10 4
   Vul: None   ♡ A 10 3
                  ◇ K 7 4
                  ♣ J 9 4 2
                            ♠ Q 8 3
                            ♡ Q 8 7 5 2
                ☐   ◇ 6 3
                            ♣ Q 10 3

WEST	NORTH	EAST	SOUTH
			1 ◇
2 ♠	3 NT	Pass	4 ♣
Pass	5 ♣	Pass	6 ♣
All Pass			

West, your partner, leads the nine of hearts, which you duck to declarer's jack. Declarer crosses to the spade ace and leads the jack of clubs. Do you cover?

Solutions

1. Win the ace. It is often right to duck in this position, giving declarer a chance to misguess if partner holds the queen, but that is a shortsighted view on this deal. If you duck, you will have to play your ace "on air" the next time declarer leads a spade toward dummy, and if partner holds Q-9-7-x-x, declarer will take two tricks when he only deserves one. The full deal:

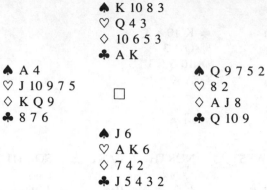

```
                    ♠ K 10 8 3
                    ♡ Q 4 3
                    ◇ 10 6 5 3
                    ♣ A K
♠ A 4                                 ♠ Q 9 7 5 2
♡ J 10 9 7 5                          ♡ 8 2
◇ K Q 9              □                ◇ A J 8
♣ 8 7 6                              ♣ Q 10 9
                    ♠ J 6
                    ♡ A K 6
                    ◇ 7 4 2
                    ♣ J 5 4 3 2
```

South could always make the contract by attacking clubs, but the line of play he chose was reasonable.

2.

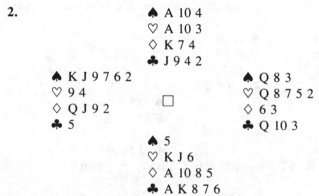

```
                    ♠ A 10 4
                    ♡ A 10 3
                    ◇ K 7 4
                    ♣ J 9 4 2
♠ K J 9 7 6 2                         ♠ Q 8 3
♡ 9 4                                 ♡ Q 8 7 5 2
◇ Q J 9 2           □                ◇ 6 3
♣ 5                                  ♣ Q 10 3
                    ♠ 5
                    ♡ K J 6
                    ◇ A 10 8 5
                    ♣ A K 8 7 6
```

This was a crucial deal from the 1963 U.S. International Team Trials. Tom Sanders was South, and the late Howard Schenken was East. When Sanders led the club jack, Schenken ducked smoothly. Tom thought this over for quite a while and finally played the ace.

One of my earlier books contained a similar-looking situation. Declarer is in six diamonds, with J-x-x-x-x of trumps in dummy across from A-K-9-x-x. He plans to play a high honor from hand, of course, but to give himself an extra chance, he should lead the diamond jack from dummy, tempting East to cover with Q-10-x.

Problems

3. Dlr: North   ♠ Q J 2
    Vul: N-S   ♡ A 9 3
                 ◇ A 9 4
                 ♣ K 6 5 3

♠ 8 6
♡ K Q 6 2   □
◇ 10 6 5 3
♣ Q J 10

WEST	NORTH	EAST	SOUTH
	1 ♣	Pass	1 ♠
Pass	1 NT	Pass	2 ♡
Pass	3 ♠	Pass	4 ♠
All Pass			

You, West, lead the queen of clubs, which holds. The club jack also wins, but declarer ruffs the third club. At trick four, declarer leads the heart jack. Do you cover?

4. Dlr: East   ♠ 10 7
    Vul: None   ♡ 7 6
                 ◇ A J 10 9 4 2
                 ♣ J 6 4

                        ♠ Q 8 6 3 2
              □   ♡ 10 4
                        ◇ K Q 6 3
                        ♣ K 2

WEST	NORTH	EAST	SOUTH
		Pass	1 ♡
Pass	1 NT	Pass	3 ♣
Pass	3 ◇	Dbl	3 ♠
Pass	4 ♣	Pass	5 ♣
All Pass			

West, your partner, leads the three of clubs, and declarer calls for dummy's jack. Do you cover?

Solutions

3. With no good intermediates in hearts, and with declarer known to have length in the suit, you certainly should duck. The full deal:

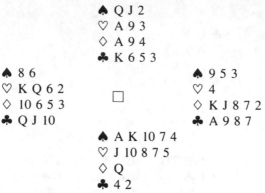

```
                    ♠ Q J 2
                    ♡ A 9 3
                    ◇ A 9 4
                    ♣ K 6 5 3
    ♠ 8 6                          ♠ 9 5 3
    ♡ K Q 6 2                      ♡ 4
    ◇ 10 6 5 3      □              ◇ K J 8 7 2
    ♣ Q J 10                       ♣ A 9 8 7
                    ♠ A K 10 7 4
                    ♡ J 10 8 7 5
                    ◇ Q
                    ♣ 4 2
```

If you cover, declarer wins the ace, draws trumps, knocks out your other heart, and claims, making four. But see what happens if you duck. Declarer must draw trumps to avoid conceding a heart ruff, and this leaves him with just one trump. You will duck again when declarer leads a second heart. He can win the nine and ace, but he lacks the entries to set up his fifth heart and will be held to nine tricks.

Incidentally, the contract would be cold if dummy had the diamond ten instead of you.

4.

```
                    ♠ 10 7
                    ♡ 7 6
                    ◇ A J 10 9 4 2
                    ♣ J 6 4
    ♠ A 9 4                          ♠ Q 8 6 3 2
    ♡ Q J 8 5                        ♡ 10 4
    ◇ 8 7 5          □               ◇ K Q 6 3
    ♣ 8 7 3                          ♣ K 2
                    ♠ K J 5
                    ♡ A K 9 3 2
                    ◇ —
                    ♣ A Q 10 9 5
```

This deal comes from the 1969 Bermuda Bowl. It was a bad year for the U.S. team, which struggled to finish third, but the United States gained here. At one table, Brazil went down in three diamonds on the N-S cards. In the replay, the U.S. pair bid as shown. On the trump lead, East unwisely *covered* the club jack with his king.

Declarer won the ace, cashed the top hearts and successfully ruffed a heart with the club four. A spade went on the diamond ace, a diamond was ruffed, and declarer ruffed another heart with the club six. Another diamond ruff put him back in hand to draw trumps and cash the good heart. He lost two spades at the finish but made his contract.

If East had refrained from covering the club jack, the result likely would have been two down. And indeed, there was nothing to gain by covering and plenty to lose.

This problem really belongs in Quiz 4.

Problems

5. Dlr: North   ♠ J 5
     Vul: N-S   ♡ A K 6 5 4
                ◇ A 6 5 4
                ♣ J 10

                           ♠ Q 9 4
                 □   ♡ Q J 10 7
                           ◇ J 7 2
                           ♣ Q 9 7

WEST	NORTH	EAST	SOUTH
	1 ♡	Pass	2 ♣
Pass	2 ◇	Pass	3 NT
All Pass			

West, your partner, leads the spade six. You cover dummy's jack, and declarer plays low. Partner overtakes your spade nine with the ten at trick two, and continues with the eight, driving out declarer's ace. Declarer goes to the heart ace and leads the jack of clubs. Do you cover?

6. Dlr: South   ♠ J 6 4
     Vul: None   ♡ A 6 4
                ◇ 7 6 5 3
                ♣ J 6 5

                           ♠ Q 7 2
                 □   ♡ 8 7 3
                           ◇ K J 9 4
                           ♣ Q 10 7

South opens 1 NT (16-18 HCP), and all pass. West, your partner, leads the heart queen, winning. The heart-ten continuation is won by dummy's king, and declarer's next play is the jack of spades. Do you cover?

Solutions

5.   ♠ J 5
                ♡ A K 6 5 4
                ◇ A 6 5 4
                ♣ J 10

♠ K 10 8 6 2   ♠ Q 9 4
♡ 9 8   □   ♡ Q J 10 7
◇ K 10 8   ◇ J 7 2
♣ 6 5 3   ♣ Q 9 7

                ♠ A 7 3
                ♡ 3 2
                ◇ Q 9 3
                ♣ A K 8 4 2

You should cover to block the club suit. If you duck, declarer will let the club jack ride and will wind up with five clubs, two hearts, a diamond, and a spade. However, if you cover, declarer is tangled up and can't reach his hand to take all his clubs. Whether he ducks your club queen or wins, returns to the club ten and tries a diamond, the contract will fail.

6.

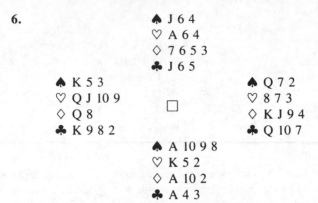

```
              ♠ J 6 4
              ♡ A 6 4
              ◇ 7 6 5 3
              ♣ J 6 5
♠ K 5 3                      ♠ Q 7 2
♡ Q J 10 9                   ♡ 8 7 3
◇ Q 8          □             ◇ K J 9 4
♣ K 9 8 2                    ♣ Q 10 7
              ♠ A 10 9 8
              ♡ K 5 2
              ◇ A 10 2
              ♣ A 4 3
```

Declarer wouldn't lead the spade jack if he had four or five spades to the ace-king-nothing. He must have either A-K-10-(x) or A-10-9-(x). In the first case you are helpless; in the second, you must be careful to duck. Note that the lead will never be in dummy again for declarer to continue with his double finesse.

Problems

7. Dlr: East
Vul: None

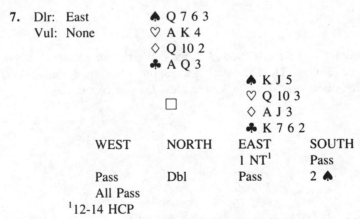

```
              ♠ Q 7 6 3
              ♡ A K 4
              ◇ Q 10 2
              ♣ A Q 3
                             ♠ K J 5
                             ♡ Q 10 3
              □              ◇ A J 3
                             ♣ K 7 6 2
```

WEST	NORTH	EAST	SOUTH
		1 NT[1]	Pass
Pass	Dbl	Pass	2 ♠
All Pass			

[1] 12-14 HCP

West, your partner, leads the ten of clubs, ducked to your king. Declarer wins your club return in dummy and leads the queen of spades. Do you cover?

8. Dlr: East   ♠ J 4
     Vul: E-W   ♡ J 5
                  ◇ 8 7 6 4
                  ♣ A J 7 5 2

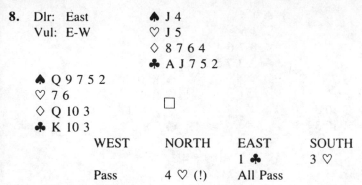

♠ Q 9 7 5 2
♡ 7 6
◇ Q 10 3
♣ K 10 3

WEST	NORTH	EAST	SOUTH
		1 ♣	3 ♡
Pass	4 ♡ (!)	All Pass	

You, West, lead the five of spades—four, ten, ace. At trick two, declarer tracks the queen of clubs. Do you cover?

Solutions

7. Declarer will have some spade length for his takeout, since North's double promised no particular spade support. Whatever declarer's holding, there is nothing to be gained by covering. You should duck in case declarer is up to some trickery.

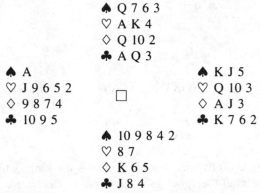

          ♠ Q 7 6 3
          ♡ A K 4
          ◇ Q 10 2
          ♣ A Q 3

♠ A   ♠ K J 5
♡ J 9 6 5 2   ♡ Q 10 3
◇ 9 8 7 4   ◇ A J 3
♣ 10 9 5   ♣ K 7 6 2

          ♠ 10 9 8 4 2
          ♡ 8 7
          ◇ K 6 5
          ♣ J 8 4

Declarer can still make the contract if you duck (by endplaying you), but there is no reason to make it a cakewalk for him.

8. Don't cover. If declarer has a seven-card heart suit for his preempt, his club queen must be singleton. If partner had two hearts and only three clubs, he would have either four or more diamonds or five spades, and the opening bid would have been different.

$\spadesuit$ J 4
$\heartsuit$ J 5
$\diamondsuit$ 8 7 6 4
$\clubsuit$ A J 7 5 2

$\spadesuit$ Q 9 7 5 2 $\spadesuit$ K 10 8 3
$\heartsuit$ 7 6 $\heartsuit$ K 2
$\diamondsuit$ Q 10 3 $\diamondsuit$ A K J
$\clubsuit$ K 10 3 $\clubsuit$ 9 8 6 4

$\spadesuit$ A 6
$\heartsuit$ A Q 10 9 8 4 3
$\diamondsuit$ 9 5 2
$\clubsuit$ Q

If you duck this trick, declarer is held to one club trick, and just nine in all. As you can see, covering allows the contract to make.

Problems

9. Dlr: South $\spadesuit$ A K 10 5
Vul: N-S $\heartsuit$ Q J 3
$\diamondsuit$ Q J 4 3
$\clubsuit$ 9 3

$\spadesuit$ Q 7 4
$\heartsuit$ K 6 5
$\diamondsuit$ 7 6
$\clubsuit$ Q J 7 5 2

WEST	NORTH	EAST	SOUTH
			1 NT[1]
Pass	2 $\clubsuit$	Pass	2 $\heartsuit$
Pass	3 NT	All Pass	

[1] 16-18 HCP

You, West, lead the five of clubs. Partner produces the king, which holds, and his return of the club four goes to declarer's ace. Declarer thinks for a few moments and leads the jack of spades. Do you cover?

10. Dlr: South $\spadesuit$ 10 5 3
Vul: N-S $\heartsuit$ A J 3
$\diamondsuit$ Q 5 3
$\clubsuit$ A J 10 4

$\spadesuit$ J 9 8 4
$\heartsuit$ 9 6
$\diamondsuit$ 6 4
$\clubsuit$ Q 9 8 7 6

WEST	NORTH	EAST	SOUTH
			1 $\spadesuit$
3 $\heartsuit$	3 NT	Pass	4 $\diamondsuit$
Pass	4 $\spadesuit$	Pass	5 $\diamondsuit$
Pass	5 $\heartsuit$	Pass	6 $\spadesuit$
All Pass			

West, your partner, leads the heart king. Declarer wins in dummy and plays the ten of spades. Do you cover?

Solutions

9.

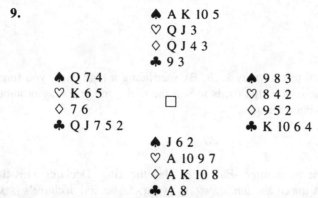

♠ A K 10 5
♥ Q J 3
♦ Q J 4 3
♣ 9 3

♠ Q 7 4   ♠ 9 8 3
♥ K 6 5   ♥ 8 4 2
♦ 7 6   ♦ 9 5 2
♣ Q J 7 5 2   ♣ K 10 6 4

♠ J 6 2
♥ A 10 9 7
♦ A K 10 8
♣ A 8

Once partner shows the club king, declarer must have all the missing high cards. That gives him two spades, a heart, four diamonds, and a club. Therefore, if you cover the spade jack, he claims. But if you duck smoothly, you might nail him. He now must guess whether to finesse in spades or hearts for his ninth trick. (If declarer runs four diamond tricks before committing himself, you will have to blank the heart king, saving enough clubs to beat the contract if you get in.)

10.

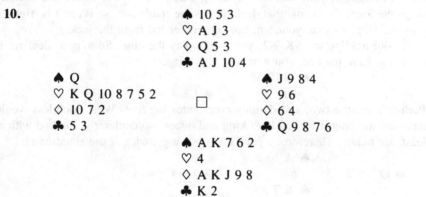

♠ 10 5 3
♥ A J 3
♦ Q 5 3
♣ A J 10 4

♠ Q   ♠ J 9 8 4
♥ K Q 10 8 7 5 2 ♥ 9 6
♦ 10 7 2   ♦ 6 4
♣ 5 3   ♣ Q 9 8 7 6

♠ A K 7 6 2
♥ 4
♦ A K J 9 8
♣ K 2

If you cover, you may never hear the end of it. Do you really think declarer would lead the ten, intending to pass it, if he held A-K-Q-x-x?

Quiz 4

Third-Hand Play

As third hand, you tend to play *high*. By sacrificing a high card, you force declarer to spend one of *his* high cards to win the trick, and you may promote some of your side's intermediates.

$$♡ 8 4 2$$

♡ Q 10 6 3   □   ♡ K 9 5

$$♡ A J 7$$

When West leads the heart three, East must play the king. Declarer wins the ace, and now West's queen and ten are worth two tricks behind declarer's jack. But if East plays a cowardly nine on partner's lead, declarer will win a thoroughly undeserved trick with the jack.

The idea of "third hand high" has many exceptions. *If there is no prospect of gain by putting up a high card in third seat, you are by no means obligated to play it.*

$$♠ Q 7 4$$

□   ♠ K 10 2

Hearts is trumps, your partner's opening lead is the spade three, and dummy plays the four. You know that declarer has the spade ace, so it can't be right to play the king. Finesse your ten, hoping partner led from the jack.

If your holding were K-9-2, you would play the nine. So long as declarer is known to have the ace, you withhold your king.

$$♠ A 10 5$$

□   ♠ J 8 4

Partner leads the two, and dummy contributes the five. West doubtless would have led the king if he had both king and queen, so declarer is marked with at least one honor. Therefore, try the eight, saving a trick if the situation is:

♠ A 10 5

♠ Q 9 6 2   □   ♠ J 8 4

♠ K 7 3

or:

♠ A 10 5

♠ K 7 6 2   □   ♠ J 8 4

♠ Q 9 3

Here is a deal from the 1974 Bermuda Bowl that shows a "third hand low" play in expert competition.

Dlr: West   ♠ K 10 7 4
Vul: E-W   ♡ K
             ◇ 8 3
             ♣ J 9 8 7 4 2

♠ Q 8 3 2		♠ J 6 5
♡ 8 3	□	♡ A 7 6 5 2
◇ J 7 6 5		◇ A 10 4
♣ Q 10 5		♣ K 3

         ♠ A 9
         ♡ Q J 10 9 4
         ◇ K Q 9 2
         ♣ A 6

WEST	NORTH	EAST	SOUTH
Garozzo	Wolff	B'donna	Hamman
Pass	Pass	1 ♡	Pass
Pass	2 ♣	Pass	3 NT
All Pass			

In one room, East's one heart opening was passed out and beaten three tricks, for + 300 to N-S.

In the replay Bob Hamman–Bobby Wolff, N-S for the United States, reached 3 NT. Benito Garozzo, West for Italy, led the spade two. When dummy played low, Giorgio Belladonna made the good play of the *five*. Declarer won his nine, but the suit was entangled.

The remainder of the play was interesting. Hamman continued with a heart to the king. Belladonna ducked this after long thought. Hamman then led to his diamond king, knocked out the heart ace, won the spade return with his ace, ran the hearts, and played ace and another club. Belladonna won the king and was forced to concede a ninth trick to dummy's spade king or declarer's diamond queen. Three IMPs to the United States.

If East had taken his heart ace at trick two (not an obvious play), the contract would have failed.

There is a special consideration if you are third to play with two or more *equal* high cards. In such a case, play the *cheapest* one. This is intended to help tell your partner what you have.

               7 6 5
  K 8 4 2   □   Q J 10
               A 9 3

West leads the two of this suit. East, with a choice of equal honors to play from, correctly puts up the *ten*. When this forces declarer's ace, West can tell that his partner has the queen and jack as well. Note that if East mistakenly plays the queen, West will have no idea where the missing honors are after declarer's ace wins.

               7
  K 9 6 4 2   □   A J 3
               Q 10 8 5

West, who is known from the bidding to have a weak hand (probably without a side entry), leads this suit against a notrump contract. If East wins the ace and returns the jack, declarer can *duck* and limit the defense to three tricks. Declarer could also duck effectively if East astutely played the *jack* at trick one, but very few players would do so—South might wind up with no tricks at all if West had A-K-9-4-2.

Sometimes a really deep finesse by third hand is worth considering.

```
              J 8
K 7 5 2        □          A 9 4
            Q 10 6 3
```

Partner leads the two against a notrump contract, and dummy plays the eight. With declarer known to have four cards in this suit, including at least one honor (partner would not lead low from K-Q-10-2), East might well play the nine. Now E-W will end with three tricks instead of two. Note, however, that East would have to grab the ace if he were defending a *suit* contract.

```
              J 5
A 9 8 4 2      □          Q 7 6
            K 10 3
```

West leads the four vs. notrump. If dummy plays low, the six from East would save a trick!

```
              9 2
A 7 4 3        □          J 8 5
            K Q 10 6
```

West leads the three against notrump, and East can save a trick by playing the eight on dummy's two.

Third hand must be alert at all times. For example, it may be necessary to unblock a suit.

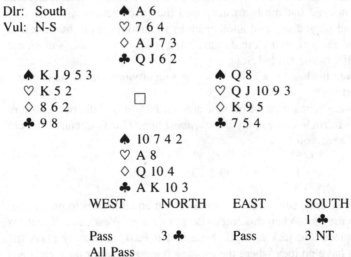

```
Dlr:  South          ♠ A 6
Vul:  N-S            ♡ 7 6 4
                     ◇ A J 7 3
                     ♣ Q J 6 2
  ♠ K J 9 5 3                        ♠ Q 8
  ♡ K 5 2                            ♡ Q J 10 9 3
  ◇ 8 6 2            □               ◇ K 9 5
  ♣ 9 8                              ♣ 7 5 4
                     ♠ 10 7 4 2
                     ♡ A 8
                     ◇ Q 10 4
                     ♣ A K 10 3
```

WEST	NORTH	EAST	SOUTH
			1 ♣
Pass	3 ♣	Pass	3 NT
All Pass			

West leads the five of spades. Declarer is afraid of a possible heart shift, and he sees a chance to block the spade suit anyway, so he rises with the ace. To defeat the contract, East must get his spade queen out of partner's way, a play that is never likely to cost.

Would you play "third hand high" as East on this deal?

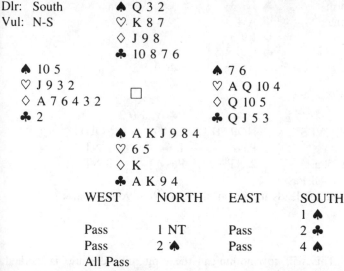

Dlr: South
Vul: N-S

♠ Q 3 2
♡ K 8 7
◇ J 9 8
♣ 10 8 7 6

♠ 10 5   ♠ 7 6
♡ J 9 3 2   ♡ A Q 10 4
◇ A 7 6 4 3 2   ◇ Q 10 5
♣ 2   ♣ Q J 5 3

♠ A K J 9 8 4
♡ 6 5
◇ K
♣ A K 9 4

WEST	NORTH	EAST	SOUTH
			1 ♠
Pass	1 NT	Pass	2 ♣
Pass	2 ♠	Pass	4 ♠
All Pass			

West chooses the doubtful lead of a club. If East puts up an honor, declarer wins, draws trumps with the ace and queen, and finesses in clubs to pick up the whole suit.

West's lead is marked by the bidding as a singleton, so East should realize that sacrificing an honor can't gain anything. Notice the difference if he plays low on the first trick. South wins cheaply in dummy, but he can't lead another club—West will ruff. Instead, declarer must draw trumps. Now, lacking a second entry to dummy, he must lose a club trick.

Problems

1. Dlr: South
   Vul: N-S

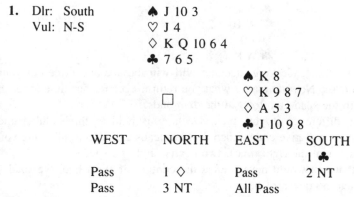

♠ J 10 3
♡ J 4
◇ K Q 10 6 4
♣ 7 6 5

♠ K 8
♡ K 9 8 7
◇ A 5 3
♣ J 10 9 8

WEST	NORTH	EAST	SOUTH
			1 ♣
Pass	1 ◇	Pass	2 NT
Pass	3 NT	All Pass	

West, your partner, leads the five of spades, and dummy contributes the jack. What do you play and why?

55

2. Dlr: North

Vul: None

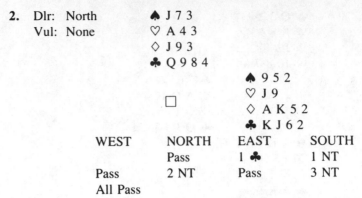

♠ J 7 3
♡ A 4 3
◇ J 9 3
♣ Q 9 8 4

♠ 9 5 2
♡ J 9
◇ A K 5 2
♣ K J 6 2

WEST	NORTH	EAST	SOUTH
	Pass	1 ♣	1 NT
Pass	2 NT	Pass	3 NT
All Pass			

West, your partner, leads the seven of clubs. Plan your defense.

Solutions

1. Play low. This will cost nothing in the long run—declarer is marked with an honor, so he always is entitled to at least one spade trick. You may gain heavily, though, if you can deny declarer a late entry to the diamond suit.

♠ J 10 3
♡ J 4
◇ K Q 10 6 4
♣ 7 6 5

♠ Q 9 6 5 2
♡ Q 6 5
◇ 8 7 2
♣ 4 3

♠ K 8
♡ K 9 8 7
◇ A 5 3
♣ J 10 9 8

♠ A 7 4
♡ A 10 3 2
◇ J 9
♣ A K Q 2

If you put up the spade king, declarer will win the ace and force out your ace of diamonds. Now no matter what you return, declarer has time to reach dummy with the spade ten to cash the diamonds.

Note the difference if you duck. Declarer is held to three clubs, one diamond (West will give count when declarer leads a diamond, allowing you to win your ace at the right time), two hearts, and two spades.

Notice that you would never defeat the contract if West had five spades to the *ace* and no queen of hearts.

2. Partner's lead marks him with two or three small clubs, so it will benefit only declarer if you play the jack.

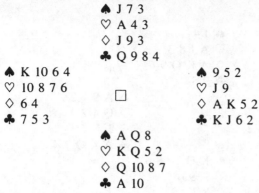

♠ J 7 3
♥ A 4 3
♦ J 9 3
♣ Q 9 8 4

♠ K 10 6 4   ♠ 9 5 2
♥ 10 8 7 6   ♥ J 9
♦ 6 4   ♦ A K 5 2
♣ 7 5 3   ♣ K J 6 2

♠ A Q 8
♥ K Q 5 2
♦ Q 10 8 7
♣ A 10

When declarer wins the club ten, he can succeed double-dummy by leading the spade queen at trick two. If South is made of flesh and blood, down one is much more likely.

Problems

3. Dlr: South   ♠ J 4
   Vul: None   ♥ A J 8 3
             ♦ A K Q 9 6
             ♣ 9 5

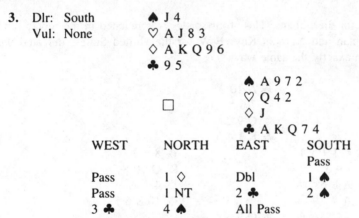

        ♠ A 9 7 2
        ♥ Q 4 2
        ♦ J
        ♣ A K Q 7 4

WEST	NORTH	EAST	SOUTH
			Pass
Pass	1 ♦	Dbl	1 ♠
Pass	1 NT	2 ♣	2 ♠
3 ♣	4 ♠	All Pass	

West, your partner, leads the jack of clubs. Plan your defense.

4. Dlr: South   ♠ A 10 3
   Vul: None   ♥ 7 6 5
             ♦ Q 9 2
             ♣ K J 4 3

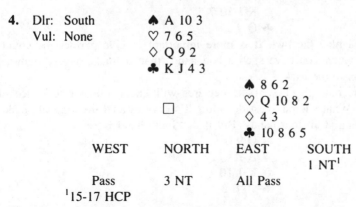

        ♠ 8 6 2
        ♥ Q 10 8 2
        ♦ 4 3
        ♣ 10 8 6 5

WEST	NORTH	EAST	SOUTH
			1 NT[1]
Pass	3 NT	All Pass	

[1] 15-17 HCP

West, your partner, leads the spade five and dummy plays low. Plan your defense.

Solutions

3.

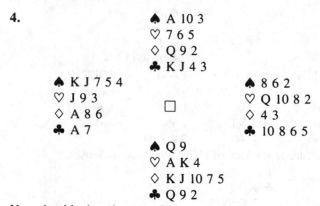

♠ J 4
♡ A J 8 3
◇ A K Q 9 6
♣ 9 5

♠ 5
♡ 10 7 5
◇ 10 7 5 4 2
♣ J 10 8 6

♠ A 9 7 2
♡ Q 4 2
◇ J
♣ A K Q 7 4

♠ K Q 10 8 6 3
♡ K 9 6
◇ 8 3
♣ 3 2

The deal is from the 1967 Bermuda Bowl final, United States vs. Italy. When the Italians were E-W, East, Walter Avarelli, overtook the club jack at trick one and shifted to the diamond jack. He won the first trump lead, underled in clubs to Giorgio Belladonna's ten, and took a diamond ruff for the setting trick.

A gain for the Italians? No—four spades was reached in the replay, and Edgar Kaplan and Norman Kay, E-W for the United States, defeated the contract in exactly the same way.

4.

♠ A 10 3
♡ 7 6 5
◇ Q 9 2
♣ K J 4 3

♠ K J 7 5 4
♡ J 9 3
◇ A 8 6
♣ A 7

♠ 8 6 2
♡ Q 10 8 2
◇ 4 3
♣ 10 8 6 5

♠ Q 9
♡ A K 4
◇ K J 10 7 5
♣ Q 9 2

You should play the *two*. It is more important to give partner the count, especially when you have such a bad hand, than to make a very nominal contribution to the trick.

After winning the first trick, declarer will knock out partner's ace of diamonds. What should West do now? It's easy to lead the king of spades when looking at all four hands. But if the South hand were

♠ Q 9 6
♡ A K Q
◇ K J 10 3
♣ 10 6 5,

West needs to lead a low club, or anything but another spade. If East plays his spade two on the opening lead, though, West has an easy time avoiding a losing play.

Problems

5. Dlr: South
Vul: N-S

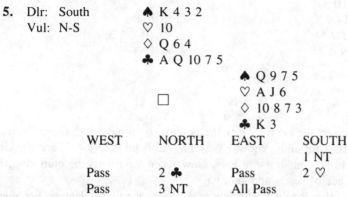

♠ K 4 3 2
♡ 10
◇ Q 6 4
♣ A Q 10 7 5

♠ Q 9 7 5
♡ A J 6
◇ 10 8 7 3
♣ K 3

WEST	NORTH	EAST	SOUTH
			1 NT
Pass	2 ♣	Pass	2 ♡
Pass	3 NT	All Pass	

West, your partner, leads the heart four. Plan your defense.

6. Dlr: South
Vul: Both

♠ K 7 4
♡ 10 6 3
◇ A J 10 6 5 4
♣ 9

♠ A J 3
♡ K Q J 9
◇ K 3
♣ J 8 6 5

WEST	NORTH	EAST	SOUTH
			1 NT
Pass	3 ◇	Pass	3 NT
All Pass			

West, your partner, leads the five of spades, and dummy plays the four. Plan your defense.

Solutions

5.

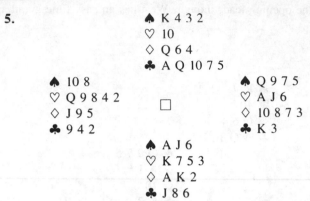

♠ K 4 3 2
♡ 10
◇ Q 6 4
♣ A Q 10 7 5

♠ 10 8
♡ Q 9 8 4 2
◇ J 9 5
♣ 9 4 2

♠ Q 9 7 5
♡ A J 6
◇ 10 8 7 3
♣ K 3

♠ A J 6
♡ K 7 5 3
◇ A K 2
♣ J 8 6

East must insert the heart jack if the defense is to have a chance. Declarer must win this—for all he knows, West has led from A-Q-8-4-2, and ducking could lead to an embarrassing loss. Now when East wins the club king, he can try the ace of hearts and another.

Note the difference if East releases the heart ace first—declarer can comfortably hold up his stopper.

The heart jack is by no means an impossible play. On the bidding, East can tell that West is much more likely to have the queen of hearts than the king.

6.

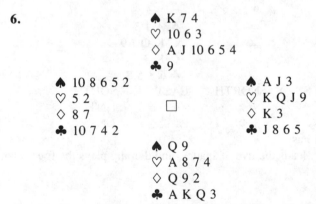

♠ K 7 4
♡ 10 6 3
◇ A J 10 6 5 4
♣ 9

♠ 10 8 6 5 2
♡ 5 2
◇ 8 7
♣ 10 7 4 2

♠ A J 3
♡ K Q J 9
◇ K 3
♣ J 8 6 5

♠ Q 9
♡ A 8 7 4
◇ Q 9 2
♣ A K Q 3

Good judgment must accompany third-hand play. Here, the textbook play of finessing the jack of spades will save a trick but lose the contract. Declarer will win the queen, lose the diamond finesse, and score up an easy overtrick.

Clearly, East can't afford to duck at trick one. He should win and shift to the heart king, setting up five fast tricks for the defense.

Problems

7. Dlr: North   ♠ A J
Vul: N-S   ♡ A Q 5
♢ Q J 10 7 6
♣ A 7 6

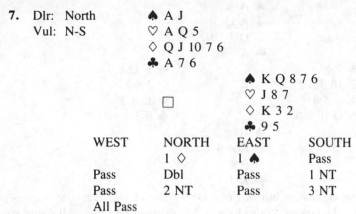

♠ K Q 8 7 6
♡ J 8 7
♢ K 3 2
♣ 9 5

WEST	NORTH	EAST	SOUTH
	1 ♢	1 ♠	Pass
Pass	Dbl	Pass	1 NT
Pass	2 NT	Pass	3 NT
All Pass			

West, your partner, leads the nine of spades, and declarer calls for dummy's jack. Plan your defense.

8. Dlr: West   ♠ 7 5 3
Vul: None   ♡ K 9 6 5 2
♢ 5
♣ K Q 5 4

♠ K Q 10
♡ 7 3
♢ A 9 6 4 2
♣ A J 9

WEST	NORTH	EAST	SOUTH
Pass	Pass	1 ♢	1 NT
Pass	2 ♢	Pass	2 ♡
Pass	4 ♡	All Pass	

West, your partner, leads the jack of diamonds. Plan your defense.

Solutions

7. South must have 10-x-x-x of spades (he could hardly bid notrump with a lesser holding), so he has the suit doubly stopped. Furthermore, if declarer has the diamond ace (and, presumably, either the club king or heart king), you aren't going to beat the contract. You must hope that partner has the diamond ace and a doubleton spade, so you can get your spades going.

The full deal:

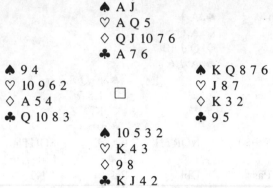

```
                    ♠ A J
                    ♡ A Q 5
                    ◇ Q J 10 7 6
                    ♣ A 7 6
  ♠ 9 4                              ♠ K Q 8 7 6
  ♡ 10 9 6 2          □              ♡ J 8 7
  ◇ A 5 4                            ◇ K 3 2
  ♣ Q 10 8 3                         ♣ 9 5
                    ♠ 10 5 3 2
                    ♡ K 4 3
                    ◇ 9 8
                    ♣ K J 4 2
```

The killing defense is not obvious even with all four hands in view—you must allow the jack of spades to win! Let declarer take one of his sure spade tricks while your partner still has a spade left to lead to you when he wins the diamond ace.

If you win the first trick, the defense is finished no matter what you return.

8.

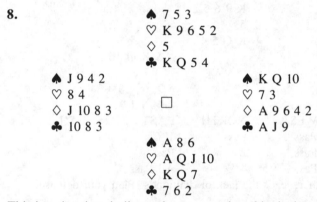

```
                    ♠ 7 5 3
                    ♡ K 9 6 5 2
                    ◇ 5
                    ♣ K Q 5 4
  ♠ J 9 4 2                          ♠ K Q 10
  ♡ 8 4                □              ♡ 7 3
  ◇ J 10 8 3                         ◇ A 9 6 4 2
  ♣ 10 8 3                           ♣ A J 9
                    ♠ A 8 6
                    ♡ A Q J 10
                    ◇ K Q 7
                    ♣ 7 6 2
```

This is a situation similar to the one mentioned in the introduction to the Quiz on second hand play. Should you take your ace, probably giving declarer two discards from dummy with the king and queen? Or should you duck and eat your diamond ace?

Here, dummy has sketchy values and several potential losers, and declarer is known to have a balanced hand, so ducking is indicated. Declarer now has four black-suit losers. If you win the diamond ace, he makes it, throwing two spades from dummy on the high diamonds.

Problems

9. Dlr: South
Vul: None

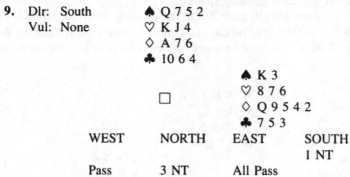

♠ Q 7 5 2
♡ K J 4
◇ A 7 6
♣ 10 6 4

□

♠ K 3
♡ 8 7 6
◇ Q 9 5 4 2
♣ 7 5 3

WEST	NORTH	EAST	SOUTH
			1 NT
Pass	3 NT	All Pass	

West, your partner, leads the jack of spades. Plan your defense.

10. Dlr: East
Vul: None

♠ A K J
♡ A 5 3
◇ 10 9 5
♣ 7 6 5 4

□

♠ 10 9 7 6
♡ K 6
◇ A K Q
♣ K Q 9 2

WEST	NORTH	EAST	SOUTH
		1 ♣ [1]	1 ♡
Pass	3 ♡ [2]	All Pass	

[1] artificial, 16+ HCP
[2] game-invitational

West, your partner, leads the ten of clubs. How do you defend?

Solutions

9.

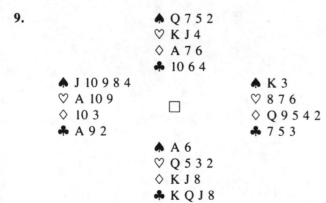

♠ Q 7 5 2
♡ K J 4
◇ A 7 6
♣ 10 6 4

♠ J 10 9 8 4
♡ A 10 9
◇ 10 3
♣ A 9 2

□

♠ K 3
♡ 8 7 6
◇ Q 9 5 4 2
♣ 7 5 3

♠ A 6
♡ Q 5 3 2
◇ K J 8
♣ K Q J 8

A routine "third hand high" situation! If declarer plays low from dummy, you must unblock the suit by going up with your king! Whether declarer wins or ducks, West will get in twice with his aces to knock out declarer's second spade stopper and cash the long spades.

If you and dummy both play low to the opening lead, declarer wins and leads a club to West's ace. He can duck on the spade return, bringing down your king. Now he has time to work on hearts to establish the other tricks he needs.

10.

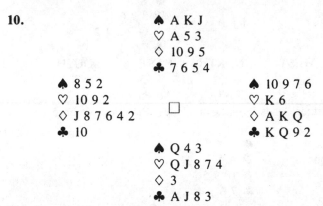

This is a deal from the 1974 Bermuda Bowl. Giorgio Belladonna was East, Benito Garozzo was West. If Belladonna had put up his club queen at trick one, the contract would have made. Declarer wins and plays ace and another heart. The best East can do is cash the club king and give partner a ruff. One diamond trick winds up the defense.

Belladonna, however, inserted his club *two* at trick one. Declarer won the jack and tried the heart ace and low one. East won the king and led the club king, West ruffing out declarer's ace. A diamond to the queen let East cash two more club tricks for down one. This contributed to a well-earned gain for Italy when the U.S. E-W pair went down in a diamond partial in the other room.

Using the Rule of Eleven

Let us look again at a situation that was touched upon in the Quiz on third-hand play:

♠ J 8 6

□   ♠ K 9 4

West leads the spade five against a four-heart contract, and dummy plays the six. It was suggested that East withhold his king and try the nine instead. But on the assumption that partner's lead is his fourth-best spade, *you can be sure that the nine will force the ace*. Think about it. Partner has three spades that outrank the five, and they must be the queen, ten, and seven since those are the only three spades higher than the five that aren't in view (besides the ace that declarer must hold).

In lieu of working out partner's holding, you may use a shortcut known as *the Rule of Eleven*.

Assuming that partner has led fourth highest, you can subtract his spot from eleven. The remainder yields the number of higher-ranking cards held by the other three hands.

Applying the Rule to the example we just saw;

J 8 6

5 led > > >   □   K 9 4

Subtract West's spot, the five, from eleven, leaving a remainder of six. So in your hand, declarer's hand and the dummy, there are six cards higher than the five. You can see five of these—the six, eight, nine, jack, and king. So declarer has only one card higher than the five, and it must be the ace.

Some people find all this a little mysterious, and textbooks usually decline to elaborate, so perhaps it would be well to explain further. Consider a suit of thirteen cards:

A K Q J 10 9 8 7 6 5 4 3 2

Now assign appropriate number values to the honors.

14 13 12 11 10 9 8 7 6 5 4 3 2

When somebody leads a fourth-best spot, three other higher cards are accounted for. In effect, "eleven" becomes the highest-ranking card remaining.

~~14~~ ~~13~~ ~~12~~ 11 10 9 8 7 6 5 4 3 2

Of these remaining cards, the ones that rank above leader's spot are held by the other three players. Therefore, their number may be obtained by simply subtracting leader's spot from eleven. That's as simple as I can make it.

The following quiz illustrates a variety of situations in which the Rule of Eleven may be helpful.

Problems

1. Dlr: South
    Vul: None

    ♠ A J 7 3
    ♡ A K Q 3
    ◇ K 5 3
    ♣ Q 4

        ♠ 10 8 2
    □ ♡ J 9 4
        ◇ A J 9 2
        ♣ K 10 5

WEST	NORTH	EAST	SOUTH
			Pass
Pass	1 ◇	Pass	1 NT
Pass	3 NT	All Pass	

West, your partner, leads the seven of diamonds and dummy plays low. Which diamond do you play?

2. Dlr: South
    Vul: Both

    ♠ J 9 7 5
    ♡ A J 7
    ◇ J 4 3 2
    ♣ 3 2

        ♠ 8
    □ ♡ K 9 5
        ◇ K 10 9 5
        ♣ 10 9 7 6 4

WEST	NORTH	EAST	SOUTH
			1 ♠
Pass	2 ♠	Pass	4 ♠
All Pass			

West, your partner, leads the heart six and dummy plays the seven. How do you defend?

Solutions

1.

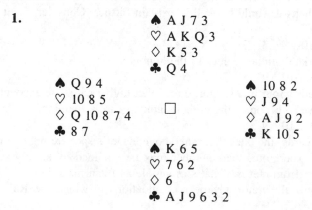

    ♠ A J 7 3
    ♡ A K Q 3
    ◇ K 5 3
    ♣ Q 4

♠ Q 9 4   ♠ 10 8 2
♡ 10 8 5   ♡ J 9 4
◇ Q 10 8 7 4 □ ◇ A J 9 2
♣ 8 7   ♣ K 10 5

    ♠ K 6 5
    ♡ 7 6 2
    ◇ 6
    ♣ A J 9 6 3 2

The Rule of Eleven reveals that declarer has no diamond that can beat the seven (eleven minus seven equals four; dummy has the king, you have the nine, jack, and ace). So you can play your two, letting partner hold the lead to come through dummy again. If you play any other diamond, the contract will make.

2. Applying the Rule of Eleven, we learn that declarer has no cards higher than the six. So the nine is good enough to win the trick. The full deal:

```
              ♠ J 9 7 5
              ♡ A J 7
              ◇ J 4 3 2
              ♣ 3 2
♠ 3 2                        ♠ 8
♡ Q 10 8 6 2      □         ♡ K 9 5
◇ Q 7 6                      ◇ K 10 9 5
♣ A Q 5                      ♣ 10 9 7 6 4
              ♠ A K Q 10 6 4
              ♡ 4 3
              ◇ A 8
              ♣ K J 8
```

Inaccurate defense would be costly this time. If East puts up his heart king, declarer will finesse the heart jack later, obtain a discard for his diamond loser, and make the contract.

Problems

3. Dlr: South
    Vul: N-S

```
♠ J 10
♡ A K
◇ Q J 9 3 2
♣ K 4 3 2
```

```
♠ Q 7 2
♡ 7 6 5 4        □
◇ K 6
♣ A 10 7 6
```

WEST	NORTH	EAST	SOUTH
			Pass
Pass	1 ◇	Pass	1 ♡
Pass	2 ♣	Pass	2 NT
Pass	3 NT	All Pass	

You, West, choose the unbid suit to lead against 3 NT. Partner produces the spade ace, and declarer follows with the four. Partner returns the six of spades to declarer's king. What do you play and why?

4. Dlr: South
Vul: None

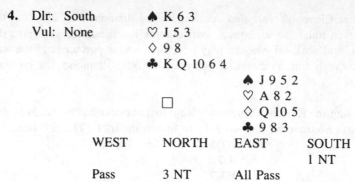

♠ K 6 3
♡ J 5 3
◇ 9 8
♣ K Q 10 6 4

♠ J 9 5 2
♡ A 8 2
◇ Q 10 5
♣ 9 8 3

WEST	NORTH	EAST	SOUTH
			1 NT
Pass	3 NT	All Pass	

West, your partner, leads the six of diamonds—eight, queen, king. Declarer continues with a club to dummy's king, winning, and leads the jack of hearts. What do you play and why?

Solutions

3. You can employ the Rule of Eleven *when your partner returns the lead of your suit*—if you know his card is his original fourth highest in the suit.

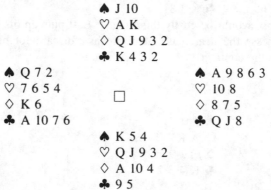

♠ J 10
♡ A K
◇ Q J 9 3 2
♣ K 4 3 2

♠ Q 7 2   ♠ A 9 8 6 3
♡ 7 6 5 4   ♡ 10 8
◇ K 6   ◇ 8 7 5
♣ A 10 7 6   ♣ Q J 8

♠ K 5 4
♡ Q J 9 3 2
◇ A 10 4
♣ 9 5

Declarer wins the second spade because he suspects that the spades are 4-4, and he fears a club switch anyway. West must be careful. If East's spade six is his original fourth-best spade (and on the bidding, it can hardly be otherwise), the Rule of Eleven applies—it indicates that declarer has no spade left that is higher than the six. So West can safely unblock his spade queen under the king. When West wins his diamond king, the defenders will be able to take all their spade tricks.

4. On the Rule of Eleven, declarer's diamond king was the only one he had higher than partner's six, so partner's suit is ready to run. Since West is a heavy favorite to have at least five diamonds (where are all the lower spots?), rise with the heart ace and fire back a diamond.

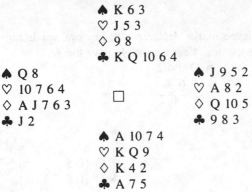

       ♠ K 6 3
       ♥ J 5 3
       ◇ 9 8
       ♣ K Q 10 6 4

♠ Q 8   ♠ J 9 5 2
♥ 10 7 6 4   ♥ A 8 2
◇ A J 7 6 3   ◇ Q 10 5
♣ J 2   ♣ 9 8 3

       ♠ A 10 7 4
       ♥ K Q 9
       ◇ K 4 2
       ♣ A 7 5

Declarer was faking a finesse when he led that jack of hearts, trying to steal his ninth trick.

Problems

5. Dlr: East   ♠ Q 9 4 2
    Vul: N-S   ♥ A 6 4
                   ◇ 9 7 6 2
                   ♣ 7 6

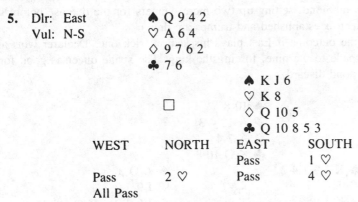

                      ♠ K J 6
                      ♥ K 8
                      ◇ Q 10 5
                      ♣ Q 10 8 5 3

WEST	NORTH	EAST	SOUTH
		Pass	1 ♥
Pass	2 ♥	Pass	4 ♥
All Pass			

West, your partner, leads the five of spades. The two is played from dummy. What do you play?

6. Dlr: South   ♠ 10 8
    Vul: None   ♥ A 10 4 3
                   ◇ A 7 4
                   ♣ K Q 10 8

                      ♠ A Q 3
                      ♥ J 9
                      ◇ J 6 3 2
                      ♣ 7 5 4 3

WEST	NORTH	EAST	SOUTH
			2 ♥
2 ♠	3 ♥	3 ♠	Pass
Pass	4 ♥	Pass	Pass
Dbl	All Pass		

West, your partner, leads the seven of spades. Plan your defense to exact the maximum penalty.

Solutions

5. The Rule of Eleven marks declarer with just one spade higher than the five, and it must be the ace. East can safely play the *six*.

♠ Q 9 4 2
♥ A 6 4
♦ 9 7 6 2
♣ 7 6

♠ 10 8 7 5   ♠ K J 6
♥ 7 3   ♥ K 8
♦ K J 4   ♦ Q 10 5
♣ J 9 4 2   ♣ Q 10 8 5 3

♠ A 3
♥ Q J 10 9 5 2
♦ A 8 3
♣ A K

Declarer will win the ace and return a spade, but East can win the jack and shift to a diamond, setting up two more winners for the defense before the spade queen is established and trumps are drawn.

Note the outcome if East plays his jack at trick one. Declarer wins and leads a spade to the nine, forcing the king. The spade queen is good for a vital diamond discard.

6.

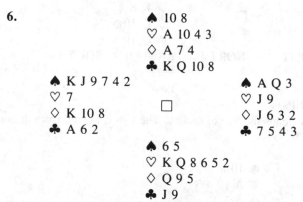

♠ 10 8
♥ A 10 4 3
♦ A 7 4
♣ K Q 10 8

♠ K J 9 7 4 2   ♠ A Q 3
♥ 7   ♥ J 9
♦ K 10 8   ♦ J 6 3 2
♣ A 6 2   ♣ 7 5 4 3

♠ 6 5
♥ K Q 8 6 5 2
♦ Q 9 5
♣ J 9

West has judged well to double four hearts instead of bidding four spades, but E-W still need to get all their tricks on defense. On the opening lead of the spade seven, East should play the *queen*, which, according to the Rule of Eleven, will win the trick. He switches to the diamond two—nine, ten, ace. Declarer draws trumps and leads a club. West takes his ace and can confidently lead another low spade to East's ace. A diamond return yields the desired two-trick set.

Of course, the defense could still beat the contract two if East played the spade ace at trick one—West could underlead his spade king later—but it's a lot easier on West's nerves if East plays the queen first.

Problems

7. Dlr: South
    Vul: E-W

           ♠ 10 5 4
           ♡ J 7 6 3
           ◇ J 6 4
           ♣ A Q 10

                    ♠ Q 8 7
                    ♡ 10 9 8
            ☐   ◇ Q 9 7
                    ♣ 8 7 6 3

WEST	NORTH	EAST	SOUTH
			1 ♣
Pass	1 ♡	Pass	2 NT
Pass	3 NT	All Pass	

West, your partner, leads the six of spades and dummy plays low. What do you play and why?

8. Dlr: North
    Vul: N-S

           ♠ 8 4
           ♡ K Q 6
           ◇ 7 6 4
           ♣ K J 10 6 5

                    ♠ K J 9
                    ♡ 9 7 4
            ☐   ◇ Q 10 9 5
                    ♣ A 7 3

WEST	NORTH	EAST	SOUTH
	Pass	Pass	1 NT
Pass	3 NT	All Pass	

West, your partner, leads the seven of spades. Your king loses to declarer's ace. The club two is led to the eight, jack, and your ace. What do you return?

Solutions

7.

           ♠ 10 5 4
           ♡ J 7 6 3
           ◇ J 6 4
           ♣ A Q 10

♠ A J 9 6 2   ♠ Q 8 7
♡ K 5 4   ♡ 10 9 8
◇ 10 8 3   ☐   ◇ Q 9 7
♣ J 4   ♣ 8 7 6 3

           ♠ K 3
           ♡ A Q 2
           ◇ A K 5 2
           ♣ K 9 5 2

West's lead of the six marks declarer with just one higher card, and this should be the ace or king—it is unlikely that declarer jumped to 2 NT with a worthless holding in spades. Therefore, East can safely insert the *seven*.

You might ask what difference it makes, since West's suit will be good in any case. But at the table East put the queen up, and South proceeded to play the hand double-dummy. He won and raced off four club tricks, disdaining the heart finesse, as West pitched a heart and a diamond. Now declarer cashed the diamond ace-king, and exited with a spade, forcing West to lead away from his heart king at the finish. 3 NT, bid and made.

It would have been a different story if East had retained the spade queen as a late entry to take partner off the endplay.

8. If you apply the Rule of Eleven, you'll see that partner's opening lead cannot be fourth best. Instead, he has made a passive lead from a worthless holding.

Do not return a spade. Shift to the ten of diamonds, where prospects are bound to be better.

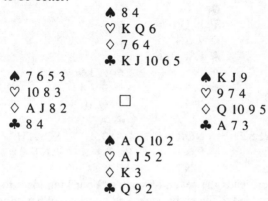

```
              ♠ 8 4
              ♡ K Q 6
              ◇ 7 6 4
              ♣ K J 10 6 5
 ♠ 7 6 5 3                   ♠ K J 9
 ♡ 10 8 3          □         ♡ 9 7 4
 ◇ A J 8 2                   ◇ Q 10 9 5
 ♣ 8 4                       ♣ A 7 3
              ♠ A Q 10 2
              ♡ A J 5 2
              ◇ K 3
              ♣ Q 9 2
```

Quiz 6

Full Circle: Fourth-Hand Play

This may seem like an odd subject for a Quiz. What problems could the defender who is *last* to play have? After all, fourth hand is well placed—he can see what everybody else has put on the trick before committing himself. In fact, there are more subtleties in defenders' play here than in any other seat.

Fourth hand has frequent opportunities for *deceptive* play. This topic is covered in depth in Quiz 23, so only one or two illustrations will be given here:

```
              A K 8 3
Q 4             □            10 9 5
              J 7 6 2
```

This suit is trumps, and declarer begins by leading low to the king. If East plays the five, declarer will have no choice but to cash the ace next, dropping West's queen. But if East follows with the nine or ten on the first lead, declarer has the losing option of returning to hand and leading the jack, trying to pin the 10-9 doubleton.

```
               10 4
8 7 2            □            K J 9 3
              A Q 6 5
```

This is a side suit. Declarer leads low to the queen and cashes the ace. If East follows with the three and nine, declarer knows he can ruff his small cards in dummy without fear of an overruff. But if East gives away no additional information by dropping the king on the second lead, declarer may have to worry about being overruffed.

```
                ♡ 6
♡ A 4 3          □            ♡ J 7
              ♡ K Q 10 9 8 5 2
```

Declarer, having opened three hearts, plays in four hearts. He wins the opening lead in dummy and plays a heart to his king. Unless there is some compelling reason to win, West should duck. If declarer has all the hearts, it hardly matters whether West wins or ducks; but if East started with J-x, West *must* duck to offer declarer an option. This is hardly the greatest play ever made—it's just routine technique that gives declarer a chance to go wrong.

```
              Q J 10 9
K 7 5           □            8 6 2
              A 4 3
```

Declarer leads the queen of this suit. West can make declarer's communications a little less fluid by allowing the first finesse to work.

Sometimes, refusing to take a winner will gain a trick by force.

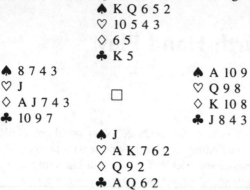

♠ K Q 6 5 2
♡ 10 5 4 3
◇ 6 5
♣ K 5

♠ 8 7 4 3
♡ J
◇ A J 7 4 3
♣ 10 9 7

♠ A 10 9
♡ Q 9 8
◇ K 10 8
♣ J 8 4 3

♠ J
♡ A K 7 6 2
◇ Q 9 2
♣ A Q 6 2

In a matchpoint duplicate game, South plays in four hearts and receives a helpful club lead, won by the king. Playing for the maximum, declarer cashes the heart ace-king and follows with two more high clubs, pitching a diamond from dummy. Now the spade jack is led, West playing the eight.

If East wins, he can do no better than cash his high trump and a diamond. Declarer easily takes four heart tricks, three clubs, one ruff in dummy, and *two* spades for ten tricks. But East knows that declarer, while he doesn't have four quick losers, is hurting for winners. So East ducks, and declarer has to come up a trick short.

(If East had one club less and one spade more, the contract still could be made. After winning the spade jack, declarer could lead his fourth club and discard dummy's last diamond. East would have no way to get in to cash his high trump, and declarer could ruff two diamonds in dummy, losing only one diamond, one heart and one club!)

On the last deal, fourth hand's refusal to take a winner costs a trick but gains one that is more important.

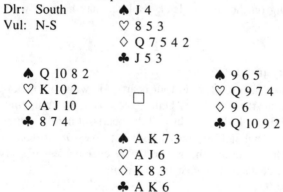

Dlr: South
Vul: N-S

♠ J 4
♡ 8 5 3
◇ Q 7 5 4 2
♣ J 5 3

♠ Q 10 8 2
♡ K 10 2
◇ A J 10
♣ 8 7 4

♠ 9 6 5
♡ Q 9 7 4
◇ 9 6
♣ Q 10 9 2

♠ A K 7 3
♡ A J 6
◇ K 8 3
♣ A K 6

South opens 2 NT, and North raises hopefully to 3 NT. West's spade lead looks poor when dummy's jack wins, but in fact declarer has just lost his late entry to dummy. Suppose he leads a low diamond to the nine and king at trick two. If West grabs this trick, preserving his second stopper, declarer will win the return, duck a diamond, and take three diamonds, three spades, two clubs, and a heart.

The difference is striking if West smoothly withholds the diamond ace. Declarer could, in theory, continue with a diamond to the king. Although the long diamonds are now dead, he can salvage an eighth trick for down one. In practice, declarer will duck the second diamond in dummy, playing East for A-9 doubleton, and now he should finish down two.

Problems

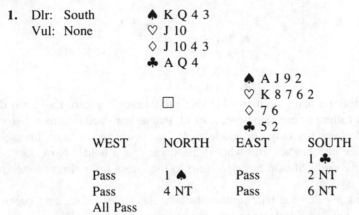

1. Dlr: South
    Vul: None

♠ K Q 4 3
♡ J 10
◇ J 10 4 3
♣ A Q 4

♠ A J 9 2
♡ K 8 7 6 2
◇ 7 6
♣ 5 2

WEST	NORTH	EAST	SOUTH
			1 ♣
Pass	1 ♠	Pass	2 NT
Pass	4 NT	Pass	6 NT
All Pass			

West, your partner, leads the diamond nine. Plan your defense.

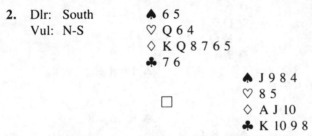

2. Dlr: South
    Vul: N-S

♠ 6 5
♡ Q 6 4
◇ K Q 8 7 6 5
♣ 7 6

♠ J 9 8 4
♡ 8 5
◇ A J 10
♣ K 10 9 8

South opened 2 NT and converted partner's three-diamond response to 3 NT. West, your partner, leads the heart jack, won by declarer's king. The diamond two is led to West's four and dummy's king. Plan your defense.

1.

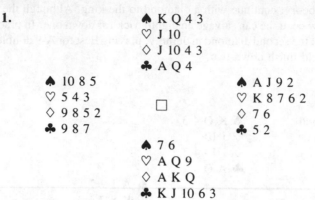

When declarer plays the inevitable spade to dummy's queen, East must duck without batting an eye. Suppose, instead, that he wins and returns a diamond. Since declarer has only one spade trick, he must take the heart finesse and will make his contract. But what if the spade queen holds? Now declarer is left in the dark. Should he try a heart to the queen or lead up to the spade king?

East knows on the bidding that declarer has the heart ace and queen, so he must not force declarer to take the heart finesse that he knows will win.

2.

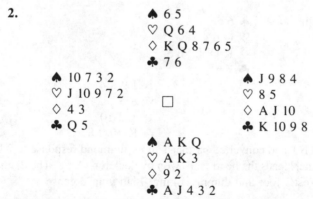

If East wins the first diamond and returns, say, a heart, declarer wins in hand, leads a diamond to the queen, concedes a diamond, and claims the rest. But note the effect if East has the elementary technique to duck the first diamond. In effect, this costs declarer an entry he needs to set up the suit, and eight tricks will be the limit.

Declarer's play, while all right at matchpoints, would be wrong at IMPs or rubber bridge. On the first round of diamonds it would be correct to play small from both hands! The contract is unbeatable on this line, assuming a 3-2 diamond break.

Suppose that the lie of the diamond suit is:

K Q 10 8 5 3

7 6   □   A J 2

9 4

Declarer astutely leads the diamond nine and plays low from the dummy. If East wins the jack, the contract will be made. An expert East would play low! Now declarer still has a chance to go down—he might continue by leading a diamond to the ten, playing West for A-J-7-6.

Problems

3. Dlr: East
    Vul: N-S

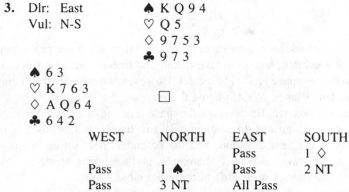

    ♠ K Q 9 4
    ♡ Q 5
    ◇ 9 7 5 3
    ♣ 9 7 3

    ♠ 6 3
    ♡ K 7 6 3
    ◇ A Q 6 4
    ♣ 6 4 2

WEST	NORTH	EAST	SOUTH
		Pass	1 ◇
Pass	1 ♠	Pass	2 NT
Pass	3 NT	All Pass	

You, West, lead a low heart. Declarer plays low from dummy and takes partner's jack with the ace. He cashes the spade ace and plays the spade eight to the queen, partner following with the five and two. Next, the diamond three is led—eight, ten. How do you defend?

4. Dlr: South
    Vul: E-W

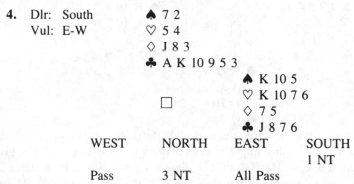

    ♠ 7 2
    ♡ 5 4
    ◇ J 8 3
    ♣ A K 10 9 5 3

    ♠ K 10 5
    ♡ K 10 7 6
    ◇ 7 5
    ♣ J 8 7 6

WEST	NORTH	EAST	SOUTH
			1 NT
Pass	3 NT	All Pass	

West, your partner, leads the spade four to the king and ace. Declarer now leads the club two and plays dummy's nine when West follows low. How do you defend?

Solutions

3.

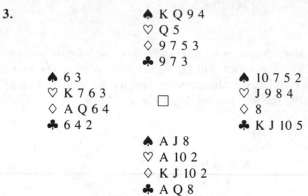

     ♠ K Q 9 4
     ♡ Q 5
     ♢ 9 7 5 3
     ♣ 9 7 3

♠ 6 3   ♠ 10 7 5 2
♡ K 7 6 3   ♡ J 9 8 4
♢ A Q 6 4   ♢ 8
♣ 6 4 2   ♣ K J 10 5

     ♠ A J 8
     ♡ A 10 2
     ♢ K J 10 2
     ♣ A Q 8

In the 1974 Spingold, eventual winner Lou Bluhm turned in a fine performance on this deal. Declarer planned to take a diamond finesse, and if it worked he could overtake the spade jack and repeat it. However, when he led the diamond three to his ten, Bluhm, West, played the *six*.

Declarer was taken in. He overtook the spade jack with the queen, expecting to make three spades tricks, three diamonds, two hearts, and a club. But East showed out on the next diamond, and the defenders now set up hearts and wound up taking two hearts, two diamonds, and a surprise spade for down one. The same contract was made at the other table.

4.

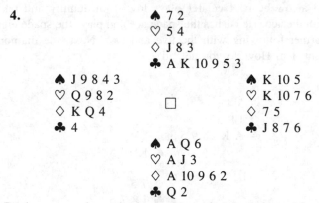

     ♠ 7 2
     ♡ 5 4
     ♢ J 8 3
     ♣ A K 10 9 5 3

♠ J 9 8 4 3   ♠ K 10 5
♡ Q 9 8 2   ♡ K 10 7 6
♢ K Q 4   ♢ 7 5
♣ 4   ♣ J 8 7 6

     ♠ A Q 6
     ♡ A J 3
     ♢ A 10 9 6 2
     ♣ Q 2

Declarer must have the bare queen of clubs left, and he is worried about a 4-1 club break. His play might cost overtricks if clubs were 3-2 but gives extra chances in case of a 4-1 split. If East wins the club jack, declarer can claim nine tricks, overtaking the club queen. If the club nine holds, declarer has two entries to dummy to double-finesse in diamonds—he hopes to win two spades, a heart, four diamonds, and three clubs, even if clubs are 4-1.

As it happens, both diamond honors are wrong, but East still must refuse to take his club jack to beat the contract.

5. Dlr: South
   Vul: N-S

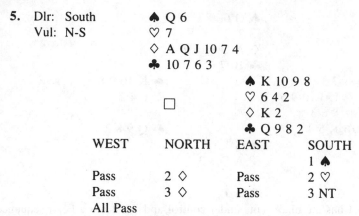

♠ Q 6
♡ 7
♢ A Q J 10 7 4
♣ 10 7 6 3

♠ K 10 9 8
♡ 6 4 2
♢ K 2
♣ Q 9 8 2

WEST	NORTH	EAST	SOUTH
			1 ♠
Pass	2 ♢	Pass	2 ♡
Pass	3 ♢	Pass	3 NT
All Pass			

West, your partner, leads the heart jack, won by declarer's queen. The diamond nine is led; your partner plays the three, and dummy the ten. Quickly! How do you defend?

6. Dlr: West
   Vul: None

♠ K 4
♡ 9 6 3
♢ A 7 5 2
♣ A K 8 4

♠ Q 10 3
♡ Q 7
♢ Q 9 3
♣ Q J 9 7 2

WEST	NORTH	EAST	SOUTH
Pass	1 ♢	Pass	1 ♠
Pass	2 ♣	Pass	2 NT
Pass	3 NT	All Pass	

West, your partner, leads the five of hearts. Declarer ducks your queen, ducks again to partner's jack when you return the suit, and wins his ace on the third round as you discard a club. Next comes a spade to the king. Plan your defense.

Solutions

5.

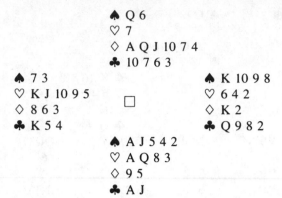

♠ Q 6
♡ 7
◇ A Q J 10 7 4
♣ 10 7 6 3

♠ 7 3
♡ K J 10 9 5
◇ 8 6 3
♣ K 5 4

♠ K 10 9 8
♡ 6 4 2
◇ K 2
♣ Q 9 8 2

♠ A J 5 4 2
♡ A Q 8 3
◇ 9 5
♣ A J

Since East has the black suits under control and West has a heart sequence, declarer cannot make the contract without dummy's diamonds. On the bidding and play, declarer will have two diamonds, so East must duck the first diamond (and without hesitation) to give the defense a chance.

6.

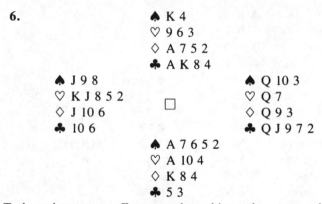

♠ K 4
♡ 9 6 3
◇ A 7 5 2
♣ A K 8 4

♠ J 9 8
♡ K J 8 5 2
◇ J 10 6
♣ 10 6

♠ Q 10 3
♡ Q 7
◇ Q 9 3
♣ Q J 9 7 2

♠ A 7 6 5 2
♡ A 10 4
◇ K 8 4
♣ 5 3

To beat the contract, East must throw his spade queen under dummy's king. If declarer's spades are as good as A-J-x-x-x, the spade queen is a doomed card anyway. But if declarer has A-x-x-x-x and East hangs on to the queen, declarer always can set up four spade tricks (and nine in all) without letting West in to cash his two good hearts. Work it out for yourself.

Problems

7. Dlr: South   ♠ J 7 6 5 2
     Vul: Both   ♡ A 7 4
               ◇ Q 5
               ♣ 7 5 3

♠ 8 3
♡ 10 8 5 2   □
◇ 10 9 7 4
♣ A 4 2

WEST	NORTH	EAST	SOUTH
			1 ♠
Pass	2 ♠	Pass	4 ♠
All Pass			

You, West, strike oil with a lead of the diamond ten—partner wins the king and ace, declarer dropping the two and jack. East shifts to a trump. Declarer wins the ace and continues a spade to the jack, East discarding a diamond. A club is led to East's nine and declarer's jack. Plan your defense.

8. Dlr: East   ♠ K 5 2
     Vul: None   ♡ 6 4
               ◇ 7 2
               ♣ K J 10 9 6 3

                   ♠ Q 10 8
        □   ♡ K J 10 8
                   ◇ 9 8
                   ♣ A 7 5 4

WEST	NORTH	EAST	SOUTH
		Pass	1 ♠
Pass	2 ♣	Pass	2 ◇
Pass	2 ♠	Pass	3 ♠
All Pass			

West, your partner, leads the spade jack. Declarer wins in hand with the ace and plays the club queen, overtaking with dummy's king. How do you defend?

Solutions

7. East's play of the club nine marks declarer with the ten, and declarer must have either the club king or queen also, else East would have split his honors. Assume that South has the king, since the contract is always down otherwise. The full deal is:

```
                    ♠ J 7 6 5 2
                    ♡ A 7 4
                    ◇ Q 5
                    ♣ 7 5 3
♠ 8 3                              ♠ 4
♡ 10 8 5 2                         ♡ Q 9 3
◇ 10 9 7 4          □             ◇ A K 8 6 3
♣ A 4 2                            ♣ Q 9 8 6
                    ♠ A K Q 10 9
                    ♡ K J 6
                    ◇ J 2
                    ♣ K J 10
```

West must *duck* the club jack, otherwise he must lead something back that will help declarer avoid a fourth loser.

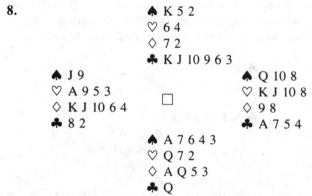

8.

```
                    ♠ K 5 2
                    ♡ 6 4
                    ◇ 7 2
                    ♣ K J 10 9 6 3
♠ J 9                              ♠ Q 10 8
♡ A 9 5 3                          ♡ K J 10 8
◇ K J 10 6 4        □             ◇ 9 8
♣ 8 2                              ♣ A 7 5 4
                    ♠ A 7 6 4 3
                    ♡ Q 7 2
                    ◇ A Q 5 3
                    ♣ Q
```

First, let's assume that East takes the club ace. On a diamond return, declarer can win, go to the trump king, pitch all three of his hearts on good clubs, and continue clubs. Whatever East does, the defense gets only two more tricks, and declarer makes four. Essentially the same thing will happen if East returns a trump. (By cashing their heart tricks, the defense can do one trick better.)

Now let us say that East *ducks* the first club, even though he knows declarer has a singleton. Declarer can do no better than continue clubs. East ducks again, and declarer pitches a heart. On the next club, East still clings to his ace and another heart is thrown. West ruffs and plays ace and a heart. Declarer ruffs but is poorly placed. He probably will go to the spade king and finesse unsuccessfully in diamonds, but no line will produce more than eight tricks.

Problems

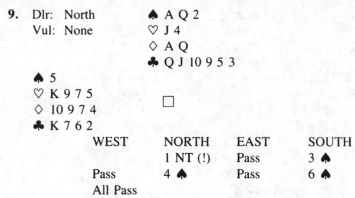

9. Dlr: North
   Vul: None

♠ A Q 2
♡ J 4
◇ A Q
♣ Q J 10 9 5 3

♠ 5
♡ K 9 7 5
◇ 10 9 7 4
♣ K 7 6 2

□

WEST	NORTH	EAST	SOUTH
	1 NT (!)	Pass	3 ♠
Pass	4 ♠	Pass	6 ♠
All Pass			

You, West, lead the ten of diamonds. Dummy wins the ace, and partner signals high. Declarer comes to the spade king, cashes the club ace, returns to the spade ace (partner completing a high-low in trumps), and leads the club queen, discarding a diamond. How do you defend?

10. Dlr: South
   Vul: N-S

♠ 7 5
♡ K J 2
◇ A 7 6 3
♣ K J 9 4

♠ K 10 6 2
♡ 7 6
◇ Q 10 5
♣ A 7 6 3

□

WEST	NORTH	EAST	SOUTH
			1 ♡
Pass	2 ♣	Pass	2 NT
Pass	3 ♡	Pass	4 ♡
All Pass			

West, your partner, leads a low trump, won by declarer's eight. Declarer considers briefly, then leads the club ten. Partner plays the eight and dummy the four. How do you defend?

Solutions

9.

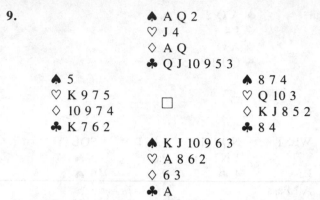

♠ A Q 2
♡ J 4
◇ A Q
♣ Q J 10 9 5 3

♠ 5
♡ K 9 7 5
◇ 10 9 7 4
♣ K 7 6 2

♠ 8 7 4
♡ Q 10 3
◇ K J 8 5 2
♣ 8 4

♠ K J 10 9 6 3
♡ A 8 6 2
◇ 6 3
♣ A

You must let the club queen hold. If you win, declarer wins any return, draws the last trump, and runs the clubs for twelve tricks. But if you duck, declarer is through. If he continues with the club jack, partner will ruff in, finishing declarer's chances of setting up clubs.

Declarer could not have made the contract by playing only one trump earlier, then taking his ruffing club finesse. East can get in with a heart and play a second trump, leaving declarer a trick short again.

10.

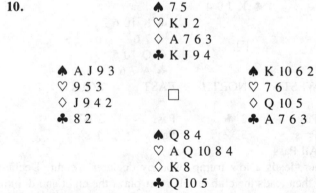

♠ 7 5
♡ K J 2
◇ A 7 6 3
♣ K J 9 4

♠ A J 9 3
♡ 9 5 3
◇ J 9 4 2
♣ 8 2

♠ K 10 6 2
♡ 7 6
◇ Q 10 5
♣ A 7 6 3

♠ Q 8 4
♡ A Q 10 8 4
◇ K 8
♣ Q 10 5

Why has declarer not drawn trumps? He must have three bad spades and can't afford to take out all of dummy's trumps until he dislodges the club ace. Assuming declarer has not rebid 2 NT with a singleton club, West's club eight indicates a doubleton. Therefore, you should duck the first club—this renders declarer helpless. If he draws no more than two trumps and then leads a second club, you win and give West a ruff. If declarer draws all the trumps, the defense has three spade tricks to take when you win the club ace.

Quiz 7

Later Leads

Generally, picking a suit to lead is the hardest part of first-hand play—once you decide on a suit, the card you lead from that suit is a matter of convention. However, very little in bridge is true a hundred percent of the time, and some imagination in choosing a lead may be called for, especially in the middle or late stages of the play.

In this Quiz, we will deal with some offbeat leads in the area of *tactics*. Leads that involve a fine point of *technique* are dealt with in Quiz 18.

Normally, you lead the top card in a sequence to prevent declarer from winning a cheap trick. However:

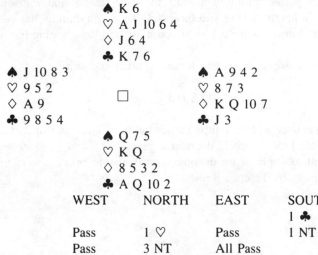

```
                 ♠ K 6
                 ♡ A J 10 6 4
                 ◇ J 6 4
                 ♣ K 7 6
  ♠ J 10 8 3                    ♠ A 9 4 2
  ♡ 9 5 2                       ♡ 8 7 3
  ◇ A 9          □              ◇ K Q 10 7
  ♣ 9 8 5 4                     ♣ J 3
                 ♠ Q 7 5
                 ♡ K Q
                 ◇ 8 5 3 2
                 ♣ A Q 10 2
```

WEST	NORTH	EAST	SOUTH
			1 ♣
Pass	1 ♡	Pass	1 NT
Pass	3 NT	All Pass	

West leads the spade jack, and dummy plays low. East can hold declarer to one spade trick by ducking here. But declarer's play is suspicious. His normal course would be to try to win the spade king; if he had Q-x-x in hand, he could preserve a tenace there. Chances are, he would like East to duck because he has nine tricks to cash if he can get in. If East works all this out, he will see that the only chance is to win and shift to the diamond *seven*.

The other side of the coin:

Dlr: North   ♠ A Q 4 3
Vul: E-W   ♡ A K 9 3 2
Matchpoints   ◇ K 4
             ♣ J 3

                     ♠ 10 7
                     ♡ J 10
         □   ◇ A 5 3
                     ♣ K Q 10 8 6 2

North opens one heart and raises South's 1 NT response to 2 NT, passed out.
West leads the spade five, won by dummy's queen. At trick two, declarer calls
for the king of diamonds, and East takes his ace.

East is afraid declarer's hand is something like:

         ♠ K 6 2
         ♡ 8 4
         ◇ Q J 10 7 2
         ♣ 9 5 4

in which case the defense must cash out. But if East leads the club king, West
may be nervous about overtaking—he will place declarer with some club length
on the bidding. Perhaps East might get the right message across by leading the
club *queen*. He could lead low, of course, but that risks finding declarer with
the club ace instead of the spade king.

Suppose you want partner in the lead badly for some reason, and your only
chance seems to be in hearts, where you have K-Q-J-x-x and dummy has A-x.
If you lead the king, dummy will duck—so you must lead low, hoping partner
owns the ten.

Next, suppose West is endplayed and forced to break this suit:

            A 10 5
  J 7 2   □   Q 8 6 3
            K 9 4

If West leads low, declarer will have little choice but to pick up the suit without
loss. If West leads the jack, he gives declarer a guess.

Here is a brilliant example of an unconventional way to break a suit, first
noted, as far as I know, by Terence Reese.

```
Dlr:  North          ♠ A 7 4
Vul:  None           ♡ J 9
                     ◇ J 10 5
                     ♣ A K J 10 3
♠ Q J 9 5                          ♠ 6 3 2
♡ Q 10 6 4          □              ♡ K 8 3
◇ K 6 3                            ◇ 8 7 4
♣ 8 5                              ♣ Q 9 6 2
                     ♠ K 10 8
                     ♡ A 7 5 2
                     ◇ A Q 9 2
                     ♣ 7 4
        WEST        NORTH       EAST        SOUTH
                    1 ♣         Pass        1 ♡
        Pass        2 ♣         Pass        3 NT
        All Pass
```

West leads the queen of spades. Declarer takes dummy's ace and loses a diamond finesse to West's king. Suppose West shifts to a low heart now—nine, king, ace. A club finesse loses to East, but the defenders can take only two heart tricks.

In an article in the December 1969 issue of *The Bridge World*, Reese noted that West could defeat the contract by shifting to the *queen* of hearts (not an obvious shot, to be sure). Declarer might duck this, wrote Reese, but he would have to win the second heart, lest East set up the fifth defensive trick with a switch back to spades. Now West would remain with the ten and six of hearts over declarer's seven.

In fact, declarer could still make the contract by catching West in a strip-squeeze, but the principle is sound. Change the deal slightly:

```
                     ♠ A 7 4
                     ♡ J 3
                     ◇ J 10 5
                     ♣ A Q J 10 3
♠ Q J 9 5                          ♠ 6 3 2
♡ Q 10 8 4          □              ♡ K 7 6
◇ K 6 3                            ◇ 8 7 4 2
♣ 8 5                              ♣ K 9 6
                     ♠ K 10 8
                     ♡ A 9 5 2
                     ◇ A Q 9
                     ♣ 7 4 2
```

Now the heart-queen shift wins for the defense. Incidentally, the lead of the queen also would suffice if declarer's heart holding were K-9-5-2.

Dlr: South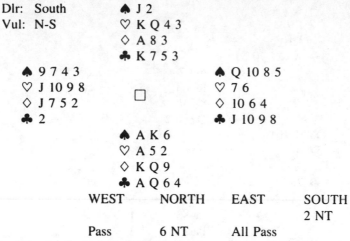
Vul: N-S

♠ J 2
♡ K Q 4 3
◇ A 8 3
♣ K 7 5 3

♠ 9 7 4 3　　　　　♠ Q 10 8 5
♡ J 10 9 8　　　　　♡ 7 6
◇ J 7 5 2　　　□　　◇ 10 6 4
♣ 2　　　　　　　　　♣ J 10 9 8

♠ A K 6
♡ A 5 2
◇ K Q 9
♣ A Q 6 4

WEST	NORTH	EAST	SOUTH
			2 NT
Pass	6 NT	All Pass	

West leads the jack of hearts. Declarer wins and tests hearts and clubs, finding that neither suit breaks favorably. After cashing three diamonds, ending in his hand, he exits with a club to East. Now East must lead the queen of spades, not a low spade, to ensure a second defensive trick.

Problems

1. Dlr: South　　♠ A 6 5
　 Vul: Both　　　♡ 10 4
　　　　　　　　　◇ K 6 2
　　　　　　　　　♣ A 10 9 6 3

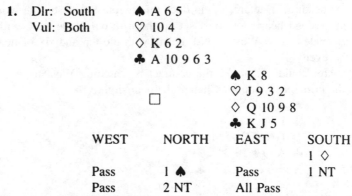

♠ K 8
♡ J 9 3 2
◇ Q 10 9 8
♣ K J 5

WEST	NORTH	EAST	SOUTH
			1 ◇
Pass	1 ♠	Pass	1 NT
Pass	2 NT	All Pass	

West, your partner, leads the four of spades. Dummy ducks, and you take your king, declarer dropping the ten. You return a spade to declarer's queen. The club queen is run to your king, and you try a shift to the diamond ten. Declarer puts in the jack, which wins. Next declarer passes the club eight, losing to your jack. What do you lead now?

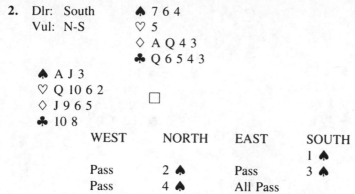

2. Dlr: South   ♠ 7 6 4
    Vul: N-S   ♡ 5
            ◇ A Q 4 3
            ♣ Q 6 5 4 3

♠ A J 3
♡ Q 10 6 2
◇ J 9 6 5
♣ 10 8

WEST	NORTH	EAST	SOUTH
			1 ♠
Pass	2 ♠	Pass	3 ♠
Pass	4 ♠	All Pass	

You, West, lead the heart two. Partner wins the ace and returns the two of trumps to declarer's king and your ace. What do you lead to trick three?

Solutions

    1. Declarer clearly has eight tricks ready to cash—two spades, three diamonds, and three clubs. Perhaps you should have shifted to hearts earlier, but you certainly must do so now. Since three fast tricks are needed, you must lead the jack, hoping that South opened on only 12 HCP, leaving West with A-Q-x of hearts.

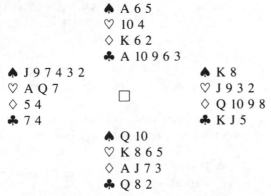

            ♠ A 6 5
            ♡ 10 4
            ◇ K 6 2
            ♣ A 10 9 6 3

♠ J 9 7 4 3 2   ♠ K 8
♡ A Q 7   ♡ J 9 3 2
◇ 5 4   ◇ Q 10 9 8
♣ 7 4   ♣ K J 5

            ♠ Q 10
            ♡ K 8 6 5
            ◇ A J 7 3
            ♣ Q 8 2

    2. Partner would not return a trump unless he had dummy's club suit locked up and unless he knew from your fourth-best lead that declarer had heart losers. You, meanwhile, can tell that declarer will take three diamond tricks at most. So your aim should be preventing ruffs. Return a low trump, which should break even at worst. In fact, the full deal is:

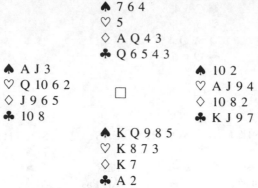

♠ 7 6 4
♡ 5
◇ A Q 4 3
♣ Q 6 5 4 3

♠ A J 3   ♠ 10 2
♡ Q 10 6 2   ♡ A J 9 4
◇ J 9 6 5   ◇ 10 8 2
♣ 10 8   ♣ K J 9 7

♠ K Q 9 8 5
♡ K 8 7 3
◇ K 7
♣ A 2

Had partner wasted his spade ten by yielding to the reflex of leading the top of a doubleton, the contract would be made. As it is, declarer is a trick short.

Problems

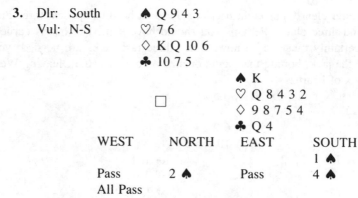

3. Dlr: South   ♠ Q 9 4 3
Vul: N-S   ♡ 7 6
◇ K Q 10 6
♣ 10 7 5

♠ K
♡ Q 8 4 3 2
◇ 9 8 7 5 4
♣ Q 4

WEST	NORTH	EAST	SOUTH
			1 ♠
Pass	2 ♠	Pass	4 ♠
All Pass			

West, your partner, leads the heart jack. Declarer wins with the king and leads a low spade to dummy's nine and your king. How do you defend?

4. Dlr: North   ♠ K 10 7 5 3
Vul: None   ♡ J 10 5
◇ 7
♣ A J 10 4

♠ 8 2
♡ K Q
◇ A 9 6 4 2
♣ 7 6 5 2

South's third-seat one spade opening is carried to four spades by North, and all pass. West, your partner, leads the diamond queen. How do you defend?

Solutions

3.

♠ Q 9 4 3
♡ 7 6
◇ K Q 10 6
♣ 10 7 5

♠ A 7 2
♡ J 10 9
◇ A 3
♣ J 9 6 3 2

♠ K
♡ Q 8 4 3 2
◇ 9 8 7 5 4
♣ Q 4

♠ J 10 8 6 5
♡ A K 5
◇ J 2
♣ A K 8

It seems clear to switch to clubs, with dummy's diamonds a threat to provide a discard or two. But if you lead the club *queen*, declarer will win and play the jack of diamonds. (A second trump would work just as well on the lie of the cards.) West wins the second diamond but cannot press the attack on clubs. Declarer will have time to knock out the other high trump, draw trumps, and take a club discard on the diamonds.

To beat the game, you must lead a low club from the Q-x. Now West can continue the suit when he gets in, establishing the defenders' club trick in time.

4. You must play partner for the heart ace. But if you lead the heart king and continue with the queen, West will play low, waiting for the third round. Grab partner's attention by leading the heart queen, then the king. A good partner will realize the significance of your unusual play, overtake, and give you a ruff.

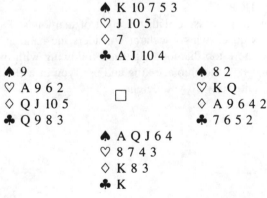

♠ K 10 7 5 3
♡ J 10 5
◇ 7
♣ A J 10 4

♠ 9
♡ A 9 6 2
◇ Q J 10 5
♣ Q 9 8 3

♠ 8 2
♡ K Q
◇ A 9 6 4 2
♣ 7 6 5 2

♠ A Q J 6 4
♡ 8 7 4 3
◇ K 8 3
♣ K

Problems

5. Dlr: South ♠ A J 6 3
Vul: E-W ♡ K 7 6
◇ 8 7 5
♣ J 5 3

♠ 9 8
♡ J 8 5 2
◇ K Q J 9 6 □
♣ 10 7

WEST	NORTH	EAST	SOUTH
			1 NT
Pass	2 ♣	Pass	2 ◇
Pass	2 NT	Pass	3 NT
All Pass			

You, West, lead a hopeful king of diamonds. Partner plays the four, and declarer the two. What do you lead at trick two?

6. Dlr: South ♠ A J 4 2
Vul: N-S ♡ 7 6 4
◇ 7 5 3
♣ J 7 2

♠ K 10 3
♡ A Q 9 3
◇ 8 6 2 □
♣ Q 10 4

WEST	NORTH	EAST	SOUTH
			2 NT[1]
Pass	3 NT	All Pass	
[1]21-22 HCP			

You, West, decide to go passive with the eight of diamonds. Partner plays low, and declarer's queen wins. Declarer considers the hand at length and finally cashes two more top diamonds, partner following with the nine and ten. South next plays off the club ace-king and puts you in with a third club, partner following suit. How do you defend?

Solutions

5.

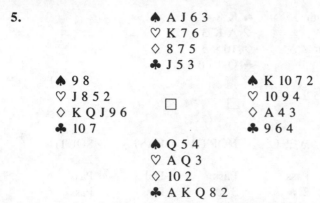

♠ A J 6 3
♡ K 7 6
◇ 8 7 5
♣ J 5 3

♠ 9 8
♡ J 8 5 2
◇ K Q J 9 6
♣ 10 7

♠ K 10 7 2
♡ 10 9 4
◇ A 4 3
♣ 9 6 4

♠ Q 5 4
♡ A Q 3
◇ 10 2
♣ A K Q 8 2

It looks as though there could be no problem here, but West managed to invent one when he carelessly continued with the diamond *queen* at trick two. East pondered this card for quite a while. It was not impossible for declarer to have

♠ Q x
♡ A Q J
◇ J 10 x x
♣ A K x x,

in which case overtaking the second diamond would give declarer an extra diamond trick and his contract. After much agonized thought, East guessed right, playing the diamond ace and returning the suit, but he had wasted a lot of valuable mental energy.

West could have saved partner all that grief by continuing with the diamond *jack* at trick two. Now East would know that it could not be wrong to overtake.

6.   Declarer must hold the heart king and spade queen to have his bid. A heart lead surely would concede the ninth trick, but you might survive with a spade, provided you lead the *king*, blocking the suit. The full deal:

♠ A J 4 2
♡ 7 6 4
◇ 7 5 3
♣ J 7 2

♠ K 10 3
♡ A Q 9 3
◇ 8 6 2
♣ Q 10 4

♠ 9 7 6 5
♡ J 10
◇ J 10 9 4
♣ 8 5 3

♠ Q 8
♡ K 8 5 2
◇ A K Q
♣ A K 9 6

After the spade king return, declarer can do no better than eight tricks. (If he wins the spade ace, dropping the queen, and continues with the jack, West must unload the ten to avoid being endplayed.)

Problems

7. Dlr: South   ♠ K 8 4
    Vul: E-W   ♡ A K 3
    Matchpoints   ◊ 10 9 3
                 ♣ Q 10 6 4

  ♠ 10 9 7 5 3
  ♡ J 9 8 5 2
  ◊ 5   □
  ♣ A 2

WEST	NORTH	EAST	SOUTH
			2 ◊
Pass	Pass	Dbl	Pass
2 ♠	3 ◊	Pass	Pass
3 ♡	Pass	Pass	4 ◊
Pass	Pass	Dbl	All Pass

Your lead of the club ace fares well—partner signals encouragement. He wins the next club with the king and gives you a ruff, South following with the jack on the third round. What do you lead to trick four?

8. Dlr: South   ♠ 5 4 2
    Vul: None   ♡ 7 6
                  ◊ Q J 10 6 4
                  ♣ A J 7

  ♠ A Q 8 6 3
  ♡ Q 4 3 2
  ◊ K 2   □
  ♣ 9 2

WEST	NORTH	EAST	SOUTH
			1 NT
Pass	3 NT	All Pass	

You, West, lead the six of spades—two, ten, jack. At trick two, declarer leads a club to the jack, winning, and continues with the queen of diamonds, passed to your king. What do you lead to trick four?

Solutions

7. Lead the nine of spades, which will force partner to take the spade ace if he has it without the queen. The full deal is:

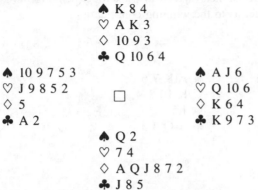

```
              ♠ K 8 4
              ♡ A K 3
              ◇ 10 9 3
              ♣ Q 10 6 4
  ♠ 10 9 7 5 3              ♠ A J 6
  ♡ J 9 8 5 2              ♡ Q 10 6
  ◇ 5          □           ◇ K 6 4
  ♣ A 2                    ♣ K 9 7 3
              ♠ Q 2
              ♡ 7 4
              ◇ A Q J 8 7 2
              ♣ J 8 5
```

Partner has heard you bid twice, vulnerable, and he won't expect you to have only 5 HCP. If you lead the spade ten or a low one at this point, you could have an accident—partner might decide to insert the spade jack, trying for +300 (especially since he can figure out that, if your spade holding were Q-10-9-x-x, your side could have scored +140 or more in spades). Declarer would win the queen and discard his other spade on the club queen, making an impossible contract.

8.

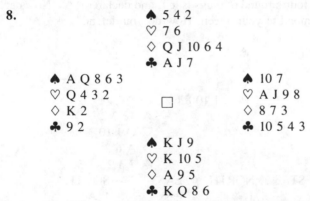

```
              ♠ 5 4 2
              ♡ 7 6
              ◇ Q J 10 6 4
              ♣ A J 7
  ♠ A Q 8 6 3              ♠ 10 7
  ♡ Q 4 3 2               ♡ A J 9 8
  ◇ K 2        □           ◇ 8 7 3
  ♣ 9 2                    ♣ 10 5 4 3
              ♠ K J 9
              ♡ K 10 5
              ◇ A 9 5
              ♣ K Q 8 6
```

At the table, West switched to a heart on winning the diamond king (good!) but to the *two* (bad!). East won the heart ace and wondered which major suit he should lead back. Looking at all four hands, a spade return is an easy winner, but from East's point of view, declarer's hand just as well could have been

```
              ♠ A K J
              ♡ Q 4 3
              ◇ A 9 5
              ♣ K 9 8 6.
```

Finally, East guessed wrong, returning a heart.

West could see nine tricks for declarer unless the defense could cash out the spades. (East's first-trick play of the spade ten marked declarer with the nine, so laying down the spade ace could not work.) He could have saved the day by leading the heart *queen* at trick four (denying the king), leaving partner in no doubt as to the winning continuation.

Problems

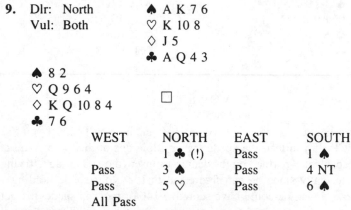

9. Dlr: North   ♠ A K 7 6
     Vul: Both   ♡ K 10 8
               ◊ J 5
               ♣ A Q 4 3

♠ 8 2
♡ Q 9 6 4
◊ K Q 10 8 4   □
♣ 7 6

WEST	NORTH	EAST	SOUTH
	1 ♣ (!)	Pass	1 ♠
Pass	3 ♠	Pass	4 NT
Pass	5 ♡	Pass	6 ♠
All Pass			

You, West, lead the diamond king to declarer's ace. Declarer draws two rounds of trumps and continues with the club king, queen, and ace. East plays the jack when a fourth round of clubs is led, and declarer ruffs. Now declarer exits with a diamond to your queen. How do you defend?

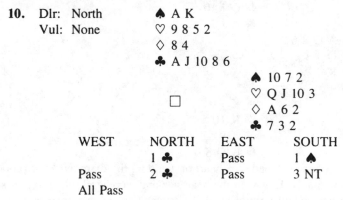

10. Dlr: North   ♠ A K
     Vul: None   ♡ 9 8 5 2
               ◊ 8 4
               ♣ A J 10 8 6

                     ♠ 10 7 2
                     ♡ Q J 10 3
            □   ◊ A 6 2
                     ♣ 7 3 2

WEST	NORTH	EAST	SOUTH
	1 ♣	Pass	1 ♠
Pass	2 ♣	Pass	3 NT
All Pass			

West, your partner, leads the queen of diamonds. How do you defend?

Solutions

9. Declarer's pattern must be 5-3-2-3 to give the defense a chance. Also, East must have the heart jack, else you are endplayed. However, even if all those wishes come true, you still must take care to lead your heart queen if you want to survive.

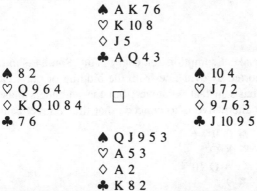

```
                    ♠ A K 7 6
                    ♡ K 10 8
                    ◇ J 5
                    ♣ A Q 4 3
    ♠ 8 2                          ♠ 10 4
    ♡ Q 9 6 4          □           ♡ J 7 2
    ◇ K Q 10 8 4                   ◇ 9 7 6 3
    ♣ 7 6                          ♣ J 10 9 5
                    ♠ Q J 9 5 3
                    ♡ A 5 3
                    ◇ A 2
                    ♣ K 8 2
```

The lead of any other card gives the contract away.

10. Win the diamond ace, and shift to the *three* of hearts. Declarer will have five club tricks, at least two spades, and one diamond. So you will have to play West for the heart ace, and with dummy holding 9-8-5-2, you can't afford to lead the queen.

```
                    ♠ A K
                    ♡ 9 8 5 2
                    ◇ 8 4
                    ♣ A J 10 8 6
    ♠ J 6 5 4                      ♠ 10 7 2
    ♡ A 7 4            □           ♡ Q J 10 3
    ◇ Q J 10 7                     ◇ A 6 2
    ♣ 9 5                          ♣ 7 3 2
                    ♠ Q 9 8 3
                    ♡ K 6
                    ◇ K 9 5 3
                    ♣ K Q 4
```

Note that if you lead your three, declarer will surely put up the king.

Expect the Worst, Assume the Best

Good defenders make assumptions on every hand. Some assumptions, called inferences, are supported by evidence from the bidding or play. Other assumptions may have no basis in fact whatever, but the defenders must make them anyway because the alternative is to concede that the contract cannot be set.

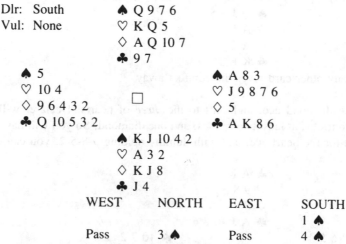

Dlr: South
Vul: None

♠ Q 9 7 6
♡ K Q 5
◇ A Q 10 7
♣ 9 7

♠ 5
♡ 10 4
◇ 9 6 4 3 2
♣ Q 10 5 3 2

♠ A 8 3
♡ J 9 8 7 6
◇ 5
♣ A K 8 6

♠ K J 10 4 2
♡ A 3 2
◇ K J 8
♣ J 4

WEST	NORTH	EAST	SOUTH
			1 ♠
Pass	3 ♠	Pass	4 ♠

West leads the three of clubs. East wins the king and shifts to the singleton diamond. Upon winning the spade ace, he returns a *low* club to partner's queen and gets a diamond ruff for down one.

Obviously, East's play risks the loss of a trick. How does he know that partner has the club queen? He doesn't, but he can tell that the defenders' cause is hopeless otherwise. So he *assumes* that the cards lie so as to allow his defense to succeed.

A part of making assumptions is to count potential defensive tricks. (This helps you avoid making too many assumptions, or assumptions that are inconsistent with the bidding or play.) Counting your tricks is easier against a game or slam contract—declarer will have most of the high cards, and your options may be severely limited.

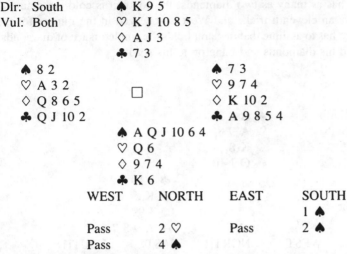

Dlr: South ♠ K 9 5
Vul: Both ♡ K J 10 8 5
  ◇ A J 3
  ♣ 7 3

♠ 8 2   ♠ 7 3
♡ A 3 2   ♡ 9 7 4
◇ Q 8 6 5   □   ◇ K 10 2
♣ Q J 10 2   ♣ A 9 8 5 4

  ♠ A Q J 10 6 4
  ♡ Q 6
  ◇ 9 7 4
  ♣ K 6

WEST	NORTH	EAST	SOUTH
			1 ♠
Pass	2 ♡	Pass	2 ♠
Pass	4 ♠		

West leads the club queen against four spades, and East wins the ace. East knows that the hand is as good as over if declarer has solid trumps and the heart ace. East must "give" West one major-suit trick, but it is too much to expect him to have two. Therefore, East must hope that partner holds the diamond queen, and it is essential to lead a diamond quickly. (An "active" defense—see Quiz 9.)

The defenders often are obliged to make other assumptions about declarer's hand.

Dlr: South ♠ 7 6
Vul: Both ♡ Q
  ◇ K J 4 3 2
  ♣ Q 10 9 5 4

♠ Q 9 4 3   ♠ 10 8 5
♡ 10 3   ♡ 8 6 2
◇ Q 9 8 7   □   ◇ 10 6 5
♣ K J 2   ♣ A 8 7 3

  ♠ A K J 2
  ♡ A K J 9 7 5 4
  ◇ A
  ♣ 6

WEST	NORTH	EAST	SOUTH
			2 ♣
Pass	3 ◇	Pass	3 ♡
Pass	4 ♣	Pass	4 ♡
Pass	5 ♡	Pass	5 ♠
Pass	6 ♡	All Pass	

West speculates with a club lead against South's six hearts. East wins the ace and shifts accurately to a trump. Declarer wins in dummy, ruffs a club, and runs all his trumps, putting West under a lot of pressure.

West can count seven trump tricks for declarer plus two side aces. It follows that if declarer has as many as two diamonds, the contract is cold—a diamond finesse will give an eleventh trick, and West is squeezed in the minors for the twelfth. So West has to assume that declarer holds the singleton ace of diamonds. He must discard his diamonds and hang on to his spades.

Problems

1. Dlr: North   ♠ A 8 3
   Vul: Both   ♡ A 9 8
   ◇ K 8
   ♣ Q J 10 5 4

   ♠ J 10 4 2
   ♡ K 5
   ◇ J 9
   ♣ A 9 8 7 6

WEST	NORTH	EAST	SOUTH
	1 ♣	Pass	1 ♡
Pass	1 NT	Pass	3 ◇
Pass	3 ♡	Pass	4 ♡
All Pass			

West, your partner, leads the two of clubs. Plan your defense.

2. Dlr: South   ♠ A Q 10 4
   Vul: E-W   ♡ 5 4
   ◇ 6 5 4
   ♣ Q 7 4 3

   ♠ J 3
   ♡ J 8 6
   ◇ A K 9 3
   ♣ A 9 6 2

WEST	NORTH	EAST	SOUTH
			1 ♡
Pass	1 ♠	Pass	3 ♡
All Pass			

North must have seen you defend before—his pass to three hearts was rather conservative. Anyway, West leads the jack of clubs. You judge to put up your ace when dummy ducks, and declarer drops the king. Plan your defense.

Solutions

1. The club ace, a club ruff, and the heart king will make up the defensive book. The setting trick must come from diamonds or spades, so you must assume that partner has either the diamond ace or the spade king. If he holds the diamond ace, your play is immaterial—you either can give partner his club ruff right now or wait until you get in with the heart king.

You therefore should assume that it's the spade king partner holds. In that case, a spade return at trick two is vital. If you return a club instead, partner will be unable to lead a spade effectively from his side, and declarer will have time to draw trumps and discard spade losers on the clubs. The full deal:

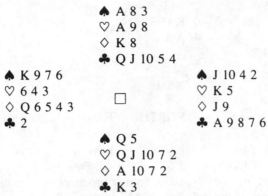

2. This will not be an easy contract to beat. There will be no spade tricks for the defense and no more in clubs. Partner can't be expected to provide two tricks in trumps, so you will have to look to diamonds for three tricks. At trick three, lead a *low* diamond, putting declarer to a guess if he has Q-10-x.

Assuming declarer misguesses, as most would, partner will win the diamond jack and return the suit for you to cash two more winners. Then the lead of the thirteenth diamond will promote the setting trick in trumps.

Problems

3. Dlr: South
Vul: N-S

♠ Q 5
♡ 10 9 8 4 3
♢ K Q 3
♣ A J 2

♠ 10 8 4 2
♡ A Q 2
♢ 10 7 4
♣ K 10 9

□

WEST	NORTH	EAST	SOUTH
			1 ♢
Pass	1 ♡	Pass	1 NT
Pass	3 NT	All Pass	

You, West, lead the two of spades. Partner produces the ace and returns the three. Declarer plays the jack from hand and dummy's queen wins the trick. Declarer now leads a heart to his jack. Plan your defense.

4. Dlr: West
Vul: N-S

♠ K Q 6 3
♡ J 3
♢ A Q 10 8
♣ K Q 4

□

♠ A 10 4
♡ 9 4
♢ 7 6 5 3 2
♣ A J 2

WEST	NORTH	EAST	SOUTH
Pass	1 NT	Pass	4 ♡
All Pass			

West, your partner, leads the two of spades against the heart game. You capture dummy's king with the ace. What do you return?

Solutions

3.

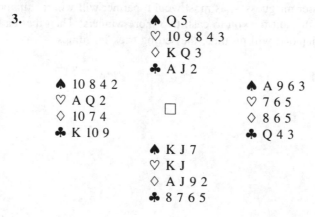

♠ Q 5
♡ 10 9 8 4 3
♢ K Q 3
♣ A J 2

♠ 10 8 4 2
♡ A Q 2
♢ 10 7 4
♣ K 10 9

♠ A 9 6 3
♡ 7 6 5
♢ 8 6 5
♣ Q 4 3

♠ K J 7
♡ K J
♢ A J 9 2
♣ 8 7 6 5

At the table, West won the heart queen and knocked out declarer's last spade stopper. Declarer gave up a further trick to the heart ace. West cashed his good spade. Declarer claimed the rest, making three.

South had to have the king of hearts for his opening bid, so at least nine offensive tricks were in view. Clearly, West should have shifted to the club ten at trick four, since a spade continuation could set up only four tricks for the defense. If declarer ducked the first club, either another club lead or a switch back to spades would establish the setting trick.

4.

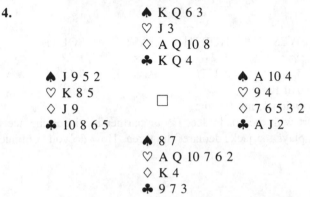

Partner must have at least one trump trick to give the defense a chance. Even so, two club tricks probably will be needed. Return a low club, playing West for the club ten and declarer for three or more clubs.

The alternative is to try a diamond, playing declarer for

♠ x x
♡ K Q 10 x x x
◇ K J x x
♣ x

However, partner would not have led a *low* spade (suggesting interest in no other suit) if he had a diamond void.

Problems

5. Dlr: East
   Vul: E-W

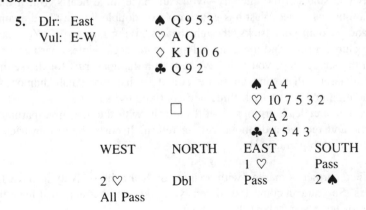

WEST	NORTH	EAST	SOUTH
		1 ♡	Pass
2 ♡	Dbl	Pass	2 ♠
All Pass			

West, your partner, leads the club king. You signal as best you can with the five, and the club six is continued to your ace. Plan your defense.

6. Dlr: North   ♠ 7 6 5 4
    Vul: None   ♡ Q 10 4
                 ◇ K Q
                 ♣ K Q 3 2

♠ A K 10 2
♡ 6 5 3
◇ A 4 3   □
♣ J 10 8

WEST	NORTH	EAST	SOUTH
	1 ♣	Pass	1 ♡
Pass	1 NT	Pass	3 ♡[1]
All Pass			

[1]invitational, not forcing

You, West, start with the spade ace. (Your partnership leads the ace from A-K-x-x.) East plays the jack, declarer the three. How do you continue?

Solutions

5.   ♠ Q 9 5 3
               ♡ A Q
               ◇ K J 10 6
               ♣ Q 9 2

♠ 7 6 2   ♠ A 4
♡ K 9 6 4   ♡ 10 7 5 3 2
◇ 8 7 5 4   □   ◇ A 2
♣ K 6   ♣ A 5 4 3

           ♠ K J 10 8
             ♡ J 8
            ◇ Q 9 3
             ♣ J 10 8 7

It seems you sold out too cheaply—you can make three hearts. But it may not be a total loss since West has gotten off to a double-dummy lead against two spades. Count your tricks, though, before giving him a ruff. You have two top clubs, a ruff, and the diamond and spade aces. Unless partner turns up with the spade king, you will have to take a diamond ruff for the setting trick. (Declarer will not misguess the suit if he has two small diamonds.) Cash the diamond ace at trick three and continue the suit.

When declarer leads trumps, you'll jump in with the ace, give partner a club ruff, and receive a diamond ruff in return. It costs the setting trick if you return a club prematurely.

6. Since partner is marked with a singleton heart, he is likely to have J-x of spades. So you can count four defensive tricks, and partner must have the club ace or heart ace to beat the contract.

At trick two, it is right to shift to a trump. There is no hurry to lead a club, since partner always will win the club ace in time for you to take your three natural spade tricks. By all means, resist the temptation to continue spades—as it happens, this would cause an embarrassing disaster.

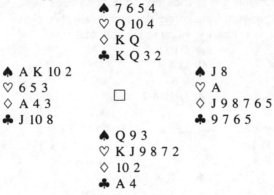

♠ 7 6 5 4
♡ Q 10 4
◇ K Q
♣ K Q 3 2

♠ A K 10 2   ♠ J 8
♡ 6 5 3   ♡ A
◇ A 4 3   ◇ J 9 8 7 6 5
♣ J 10 8   ♣ 9 7 6 5

♠ Q 9 3
♡ K J 9 8 7 2
◇ 10 2
♣ A 4

Problems

7. Dlr: East
Vul: Both

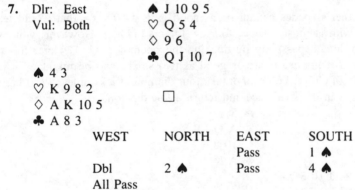

♠ J 10 9 5
♡ Q 5 4
◇ 9 6
♣ Q J 10 7

♠ 4 3
♡ K 9 8 2
◇ A K 10 5
♣ A 8 3

WEST	NORTH	EAST	SOUTH
		Pass	1 ♠
Dbl	2 ♠	Pass	4 ♠
All Pass			

You, West, lead the diamond ace—six, seven, eight. How do you continue?

8. Dlr: North
Vul: N-S

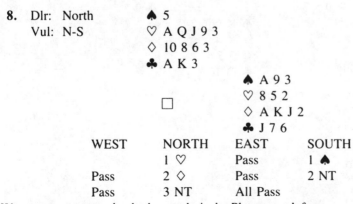

♠ 5
♡ A Q J 9 3
◇ 10 8 6 3
♣ A K 3

♠ A 9 3
♡ 8 5 2
◇ A K J 2
♣ J 7 6

WEST	NORTH	EAST	SOUTH
	1 ♡	Pass	1 ♠
Pass	2 ◇	Pass	2 NT
Pass	3 NT	All Pass	

West, your partner, leads the spade jack. Plan your defense.

Solutions

7. Partner has signaled encouragement in diamonds, and he is much more likely to have the queen than a doubleton. Lead the diamond ten (suit preference—see Quiz 15) at trick two. If East's queen wins, he will return a heart, setting up your king before declarer establishes clubs.

This defense is necessary, because the full deal is:

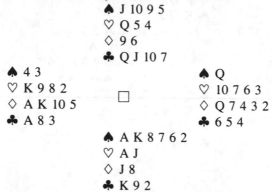

```
                  ♠ J 10 9 5
                  ♡ Q 5 4
                  ◊ 9 6
                  ♣ Q J 10 7
  ♠ 4 3                          ♠ Q
  ♡ K 9 8 2                      ♡ 10 7 6 3
  ◊ A K 10 5          □         ◊ Q 7 4 3 2
  ♣ A 8 3                       ♣ 6 5 4
                  ♠ A K 8 7 6 2
                  ♡ A J
                  ◊ J 8
                  ♣ K 9 2
```

8. Partner's spades cannot be as good as K-J-10-x-x—that would leave declarer with at most 9 HCP, too few for his bidding. However, you can't afford to defend passively by ducking the opening lead. Declarer has five heart tricks if his hearts are as good as two small, and he might well have Q-x-x-x-x of clubs. You cannot take four diamond tricks unless West has the queen, so win the spade ace and return a *low* diamond.

```
                  ♠ 5
                  ♡ A Q J 9 3
                  ◊ 10 8 6 3
                  ♣ A K 3
  ♠ J 10 8 7 4                    ♠ A 9 3
  ♡ 10 7 6                        ♡ 8 5 2
  ◊ Q 7              □           ◊ A K J 2
  ♣ 9 5 2                        ♣ J 7 6
                  ♠ K Q 6 2
                  ♡ K 4
                  ◊ 9 5 4
                  ♣ Q 10 8 4
```

Problems

9. Dlr: West   ♠ J 3
Vul: None   ♡ J 8 6 2
♦ K J 5 4 3
♣ K 6

♠ A Q 4
♡ K 4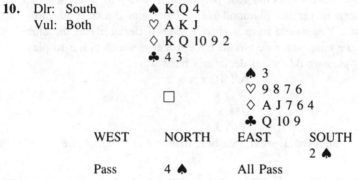
♦ A 7 2
♣ J 9 8 4 3

WEST	NORTH	EAST	SOUTH
1 ♣	Pass	1 ♠	2 ♡
2 ♠	3 ♡	All Pass	

You, West, choose a low-club lead. Partner plays the queen, and declarer's ace wins. At trick two, declarer pushes out the diamond queen. You win, East dropping the ten. What do you lead now?

10. Dlr: South   ♠ K Q 4
Vul: Both   ♡ A K J
♦ K Q 10 9 2
♣ 4 3

♠ 3
♡ 9 8 7 6
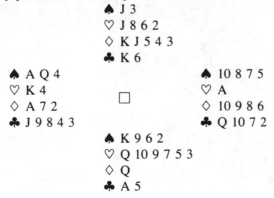   ♦ A J 7 6 4
♣ Q 10 9

WEST	NORTH	EAST	SOUTH
			2 ♠
Pass	4 ♠	All Pass	

West, your partner, leads the diamond three. Dummy's king is played. Plan your defense.

Solutions

9. A deceptively simple problem. If the defense is to take f.ve tricks, you must play partner for the trump ace. Shift to a low heart.

```
              ♠ J 3
              ♡ J 8 6 2
              ♦ K J 5 4 3
              ♣ K 6
♠ A Q 4                    ♠ 10 8 7 5
♡ K 4                      ♡ A
♦ A 7 2        □           ♦ 10 9 8 6
♣ J 9 8 4 3                ♣ Q 10 7 2
              ♠ K 9 6 2
              ♡ Q 10 9 7 5 3
              ♦ Q
              ♣ A 5
```

10. Return the ten of clubs. Almost surely, you'll need two club tricks. If declarer has the club king, you must return a club right now, since there is no further entry to your hand, and declarer eventually can get discards on the red suits.

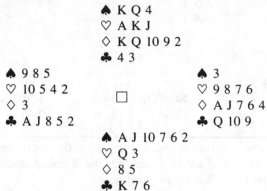

♠ K Q 4
♥ A K J
♦ K Q 10 9 2
♣ 4 3

♠ 9 8 5
♥ 10 5 4 2
♦ 3
♣ A J 8 5 2

♠ 3
♥ 9 8 7 6
♦ A J 7 6 4
♣ Q 10 9

♠ A J 10 7 6 2
♥ Q 3
♦ 8 5
♣ K 7 6

If declarer covers the club ten, partner wins and puts you back in with the club queen to get his diamond ruff. If declarer ducks, you shift back to diamonds. You would have a chance even if declarer had the club jack as well as the king, since he would have to guess which honor to play.

Your play would lose if declarer's hand were

♠ J 10 x x x x
♥ Q x
♦ x x
♣ A J x,

but this is an atypical weak two-bid, first seat and vulnerable.

Quiz 9

Get Active or Go Passive?

Most defenses against a suit contract boil down to one of two approaches. In one scenario, declarer has ample trick-taking power: lots of high cards, a good side suit in dummy, or perhaps a big trump fit combined with ruffing power. He is destined to make his contract *unless the defense can acquire the setting trick first*. In an *active* defense, therefore, the defenders are anxious to cash everything in sight, and they are willing to take chances to set up whatever tricks they need quickly.

In contrast, a passive defense is best when declarer has limited values and will have to dig hard for his tricks. In this case, the defense wants to *avoid* cashing winners, leading away from honors and breaking new suits. Getting too busy on defense can only help declarer avoid some of his potential losers— *losers that he is destined to lose in any case.*

Look at these two hands:

Dlr: South
Vul: Both

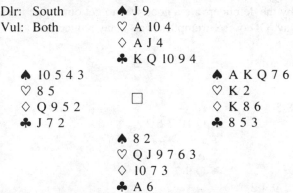

```
Dlr:  South        ♠ J 9
Vul:  Both         ♡ A 10 4
                   ◇ A J 4
                   ♣ K Q 10 9 4
♠ 10 5 4 3                      ♠ A K Q 7 6
♡ 8 5                          ♡ K 2
◇ Q 9 5 2        □             ◇ K 8 6
♣ J 7 2                        ♣ 8 5 3
                   ♠ 8 2
                   ♡ Q J 9 7 6 3
                   ◇ 10 7 3
                   ♣ A 6
```

South opened two hearts (weak), and North jumped to four hearts. West led a spade, and East cashed the queen and king. At trick three, East shifted to a diamond away from his king, and West's queen forced dummy's ace. When declarer lost the trump finesse, East was able to cash the diamond king for down one.

This was an effective *active* defense. East could see that declarer would be able to take ten tricks eventually with heart and club winners, so it was necessary to take a chance in diamonds.

Dlr: South   ♠ A K 5 4
Vul: N-S   ♡ 10 6 5
               ◊ K 7 6
               ♣ 7 5 4

♠ Q J 10 6		♠ 9 8 7 3
♡ J 4 3	□	♡ 9 8
◊ Q 10 5		◊ A 9 8 4
♣ J 9 6		♣ K 8 3

               ♠ 2
               ♡ A K Q 7 2
               ◊ J 3 2
               ♣ A Q 10 2

WEST	NORTH	EAST	SOUTH
			1 ♡
Pass	1 ♠	Pass	2 ♣
Pass	3 ♡	Pass	4 ♡
All Pass			

West leads the spade queen. Declarer takes the top spades, discarding a diamond, and plays a club to the ten and jack. Here, West must exit *safely* with a spade, which gives declarer nothing that isn't his anyhow.

The lead of either minor suit will cost a trick directly, while a trump exit gives declarer a dummy entry to take another club finesse.

Typically, trump leads by the defenders are a good way to get out of the lead without giving anything away. Of course, trump leads also may reduce declarer's trick-taking power.

Dlr: South   ♠ 8
Vul: None   ♡ K 6 5 2
               ◊ Q 8 7
               ♣ J 8 5 4 2

♠ K 5		♠ Q 10 7 6 2
♡ Q 10 8 7	□	♡ J 9
◊ 9 6 4		◊ A 3 2
♣ A K 10 6		♣ Q 9 7

               ♠ A J 9 4 3
               ♡ A 4 3
               ◊ K J 10 5
               ♣ 3

South ends in two diamonds, having opened one spade. West lays down a high club on opening lead. After seeing dummy he definitely should switch to trumps. With dummy so weak in high cards, declarer will be seeking spade ruffs.

A more spectacular example:

Dlr: East   ♠ 5
Vul: Both   ♡ J 4
           ◇ Q J 6 5 3
           ♣ 10 8 6 5 3

♠ J 9 3		♠ K 10 8 7
♡ A Q	□	♡ 7 5 2
◇ 10 9 7 2		◇ K 8 4
♣ J 9 7 2		♣ A K Q

           ♠ A Q 6 4 2
           ♡ K 10 9 8 6 3
           ◇ A
           ♣ 4

WEST	NORTH	EAST	SOUTH
		1 NT	2 ♡
2 NT	Pass	Pass	3 ♠
Pass	4 ♡	Pass	Pass
Dbl	All pass		

After West led the ten of diamonds, declarer almost made his unlikely contract. The play went: ace of diamonds, ace of spades, spade ruff, queen of diamonds covered and ruffed, spade ruff, jack of diamonds for a club discard, club ruff. With K-10-9-8 of trumps left, South was sure of two more tricks, and he conceded only 200 points despite his risky bidding.

A club lead and trump switch would make the penalty 800, but that requires a crystal ball. The technically correct lead, which results in down two, is the heart ace. West knows that his side has general strength and, since North took a heart preference, there is a danger that South will ruff some spades in dummy. On a trump lead and continuation, West loses a trump trick but gains two tricks in return.

It is strange that on some other hands, the defenders' strategy may be to *force* dummy to ruff. For example:

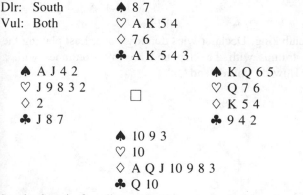

Dlr: South   ♠ 8 7
Vul: Both   ♡ A K 5 4
           ◇ 7 6
           ♣ A K 5 4 3

♠ A J 4 2		♠ K Q 6 5
♡ J 9 8 3 2	□	♡ Q 7 6
◇ 2		◇ K 5 4
♣ J 8 7		♣ 9 4 2

           ♠ 10 9 3
           ♡ 10
           ◇ A Q J 10 9 8 3
           ♣ Q 10

South plays in five diamonds after opening with a three-diamond preempt. West leads the ace of spades and continues with the two to East's queen. Declarer is marked with another spade, so clearly East should continue with a third spade, forcing dummy. Declarer can no longer pick up the diamond king.

There are, of course, plenty of other times when forcing dummy is the right defense. We'll see some of them in this Quiz and later on. Also, in Quiz 11, we will examine other defensive strategies—specifically, those that surround play in the trump suit.

Problems

1. Dlr: South
   Vul: Both

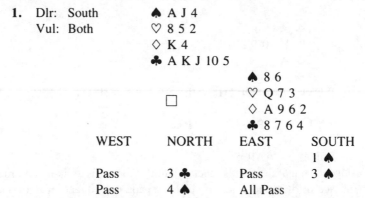

♠ A J 4
♡ 8 5 2
♢ K 4
♣ A K J 10 5

♠ 8 6
♡ Q 7 3
♢ A 9 6 2
♣ 8 7 6 4

WEST	NORTH	EAST	SOUTH
			1 ♠
Pass	3 ♣	Pass	3 ♠
Pass	4 ♠	All Pass	

West, your partner, leads the jack of diamonds. Plan your defense.

2. Dlr: South
   Vul: E-W

♠ A 10 8 5
♡ 10 5 3
♢ J 8 4
♣ A 5 3

♠ J 3
♡ Q 8 4
♢ A 9 5 2
♣ K Q 10 8

WEST	NORTH	EAST	SOUTH
			1 ♠
Pass	2 ♠	All Pass	

You, West, lead the club king. Declarer wins dummy's ace, East playing the two. Declarer draws trumps with the king and ace and continues with a diamond to his king. How do you defend?

112

Solutions

1. The situation is desperate. Declarer has only one loser in diamonds and none at all in the black suits, so the heart suit must be very kind to the defense. Furthermore, you must grab what heart tricks you can right now, before declarer draws trumps and throws his heart losers on the clubs.

West will not have the ace and king, not having led a heart, but he could have A-J-10. You must assume that is the case. Whether declarer plays the diamond king from dummy or not, win the diamond ace and lead the heart queen.

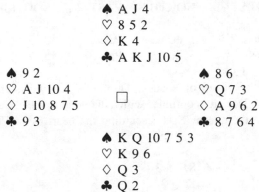

    ♠ A J 4
    ♡ 8 5 2
    ◇ K 4
    ♣ A K J 10 5

♠ 9 2   ♠ 8 6
♡ A J 10 4   ♡ Q 7 3
◇ J 10 8 7 5   ◇ A 9 6 2
♣ 9 3   ♣ 8 7 6 4

    ♠ K Q 10 7 5 3
    ♡ K 9 6
    ◇ Q 3
    ♣ Q 2

2. Dummy is flat and weak, so win the diamond ace and *return a diamond*, defending as passively as possible. The full deal:

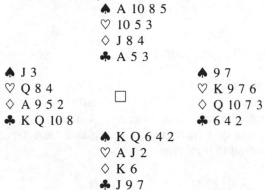

    ♠ A 10 8 5
    ♡ 10 5 3
    ◇ J 8 4
    ♣ A 5 3

♠ J 3   ♠ 9 7
♡ Q 8 4   ♡ K 9 7 6
◇ A 9 5 2   ◇ Q 10 7 3
♣ K Q 10 8   ♣ 6 4 2

    ♠ K Q 6 4 2
    ♡ A J 2
    ◇ K 6
    ♣ J 9 7

East will win the diamond ten and return a club for you to take your two tricks there. Then you can exit safely with a third diamond, forcing declarer to break the heart suit. The defense will win six tricks.

To be sure, declarer did not play to best advantage. He could have made the contract in several ways—for example, by exiting with a club after drawing trumps, forcing you to lead diamonds or hearts.

Problems

3. Dlr: South   ♠ A 8 6 3
    Vul: Both   ♡ A J
                 ◇ J 9 5 2
                 ♣ 9 4 2

♠ Q J 10 4
♡ 10 4
◇ K Q 10   □
♣ K 10 7 3

WEST	NORTH	EAST	SOUTH
			1 ♡
Pass	1 ♠	Pass	2 ◇
Pass	3 ◇	Pass	5 ◇
All Pass			

You, West, lead the queen of spades. Dummy's ace wins, and declarer discards a low club. Declarer continues with a diamond to the ace and another diamond. You win the queen, East discarding the heart two. What is your next play?

4. Dlr: South   ♠ 8 7 5 3
    Vul: N-S   ♡ K Q 3
                 ◇ Q 10 3
                 ♣ 8 7 2

♠ K Q 10 6
♡ 7 6
◇ 9 8 6   □
♣ A K 10 3

WEST	NORTH	EAST	SOUTH
			1 ♡
Dbl	2 ♡	Pass	3 ◇
Pass	4 ♡	All Pass	

You, West, lead the club ace—two, four, five. At trick two, you shift to the spade king. This time East encourages with the nine, and declarer follows low. What do you lead to trick three?

Solutions

3. Declarer's pattern probably is 0-5-5-3. If declarer has good hearts, as partner's discard suggests, you can't afford to wait for the club king to be a trick. Declarer will run hearts, throw dummy's clubs away, and ruff his losing club in dummy. Shift to a low club while you still have a trump trick for an entry.

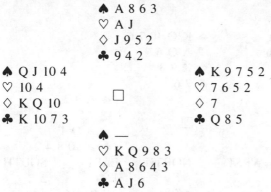

♠ A 8 6 3
♡ A J
◇ J 9 5 2
♣ 9 4 2

♠ Q J 10 4   ♠ K 9 7 5 2
♡ 10 4   ♡ 7 6 5 2
◇ K Q 10   ◇ 7
♣ K 10 7 3   ♣ Q 8 5

♠ —
♡ K Q 9 8 3
◇ A 8 6 4 3
♣ A J 6

When declarer begins to run the hearts, you can ruff in soon enough to cash the club king.

Declarer could have made the hand by starting on hearts after playing off the trump ace, but he succumbed to the lure of a possible overtrick.

4.

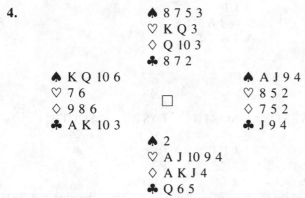

♠ 8 7 5 3
♡ K Q 3
◇ Q 10 3
♣ 8 7 2

♠ K Q 10 6   ♠ A J 9 4
♡ 7 6   ♡ 8 5 2
◇ 9 8 6   ◇ 7 5 2
♣ A K 10 3   ♣ J 9 4

♠ 2
♡ A J 10 9 4
◇ A K J 4
♣ Q 6 5

This is a deceptively difficult problem. The appearance of the dummy suggests a passive defense, and a spade continuation, forcing declarer to ruff, seems safe enough. But in fact it will help declarer to reverse the dummy. The play will go: second round of spades, ruffed; heart ace; heart to the queen; spade ruff; diamond to the ten; spade ruff; diamond to the queen; heart king, drawing the last trump; diamond to the king; diamond ace. That's ten tricks.

The *super*passive exit of a trump at trick three will ruin declarer's timing for the dummy reversal and defeat the hand.

Problems

5. Dlr: East   ♠ K Q 10 7 6
   Vul: Both   ♡ A Q 6
   ◇ K 9 3
   ♣ 7 6

	♠ A 9 2
	♡ 7 5
□	◇ A Q 4
	♣ A 10 8 4 2

WEST	NORTH	EAST	SOUTH
		1 ♣	2 ♡
Pass	4 ♡	All Pass	

West, your partner, leads the queen of clubs. When you put up the ace, declarer plays the king. How do you continue?

6. Dlr: South   ♠ 6 5
   Vul: None   ♡ J 10
   ◇ A J 6 5 4
   ♣ 7 6 5 4

♠ K Q 10 3
♡ Q 9 2
◇ 7 3 2   □
♣ K 10 8

WEST	NORTH	EAST	SOUTH
			1 ♡
Pass	1 NT	Pass	2 ♠
Pass	3 ◇	Pass	3 ♡
Pass	4 ♡	All Pass	

You, West, elect to lead the king of spades. Partner plays the nine and declarer plays small. What do you lead next?

Solutions

5.

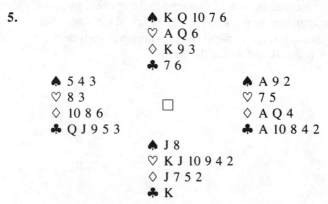

♠ K Q 10 7 6
♡ A Q 6
◇ K 9 3
♣ 7 6

♠ 5 4 3		♠ A 9 2
♡ 8 3		♡ 7 5
◇ 10 8 6	□	◇ A Q 4
♣ Q J 9 5 3		♣ A 10 8 4 2

♠ J 8
♡ K J 10 9 4 2
◇ J 7 5 2
♣ K

Dummy's spades look menacing, so you must get busy. Return a low diamond, playing declarer for at least three diamonds and West for the jack (or the ten, if declarer has J-x-x and misguesses).

6. East's signal indicates a spade honor, probably the jack. Declarer therefore has some spade losers, and he surely will want to ruff them. Dummy is weak in high cards, and the diamond suit is unlikely to run—on the bidding, declarer won't have much help in diamonds.

A trump shift is indicated, but care must be taken. The full deal:

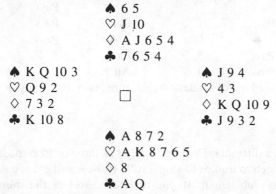

```
                    ♠ 6 5
                    ♡ J 10
                    ◇ A J 6 5 4
                    ♣ 7 6 5 4
   ♠ K Q 10 3                    ♠ J 9 4
   ♡ Q 9 2                       ♡ 4 3
   ◇ 7 3 2          □            ◇ K Q 10 9
   ♣ K 10 8                      ♣ J 9 3 2
                    ♠ A 8 7 2
                    ♡ A K 8 7 6 5
                    ◇ 8
                    ♣ A Q
```

A low trump switch still will give declarer a cakewalk—he will take six trump tricks in hand, one spade ruff, and three side aces. Try shifting to the heart *queen*, smothering two of declarer's honors at once. Now declarer gains nothing by ruffing a spade because your nine of trumps is promoted.

Double-dummy, declarer still could make the contract by declining the club finesse, stripping you of your diamonds, and throwing you in with a major suit to lead a club into his tenace.

Problems

7. Dlr: East
   Vul: Both

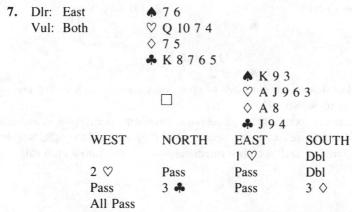

```
                    ♠ 7 6
                    ♡ Q 10 7 4
                    ◇ 7 5
                    ♣ K 8 7 6 5
                               ♠ K 9 3
                    □          ♡ A J 9 6 3
                               ◇ A 8
                               ♣ J 9 4
```

WEST	NORTH	EAST	SOUTH
		1 ♡	Dbl
2 ♡	Pass	Pass	Dbl
Pass	3 ♣	Pass	3 ◇
All Pass			

West, your partner, leads the two of hearts. Dummy plays low, and your nine holds the first trick, declarer following with the eight. Plan your defense.

8. Dlr: South   ♠ 8
     Vul: N-S   ♡ A Q 5
               ◇ A K J 6 5 4
               ♣ A Q 10

♠ K Q 10 5
♡ J 9
◇ 7 2   □
♣ K 9 8 7 6

WEST	NORTH	EAST	SOUTH
			Pass
Pass	1 ◇	Pass	Pass
1 ♠	Dbl	2 ♠	Pass
Pass	3 ◇	Pass	3 ♡
Pass	4 ♡	All Pass	

You, West, lead the king of spades—eight, nine, two. How do you continue?

Solutions

7. You are in a dilemma. Declarer surely has three or four spades, so you would like to switch to trumps to stop a ruff. However, there is a danger that declarer also has club length. If you release control of the trump suit by playing ace and another, declarer may establish clubs for all the tricks he needs.

The full deal:

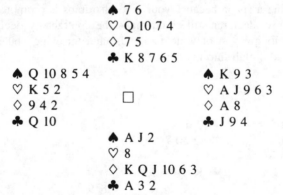

             ♠ 7 6
             ♡ Q 10 7 4
             ◇ 7 5
             ♣ K 8 7 6 5

♠ Q 10 8 5 4   ♠ K 9 3
♡ K 5 2   ♡ A J 9 6 3
◇ 9 4 2   □   ◇ A 8
♣ Q 10   ♣ J 9 4

             ♠ A J 2
             ♡ 8
             ◇ K Q J 10 6 3
             ♣ A 3 2

The winning defense is not easy to spot. East must switch to the *eight* of diamonds at trick two.

If declarer concedes a spade, East wins, cashes the diamond ace, and leads a spade. The defense can cash a spade when they win a club trick. Nor does it help declarer to duck a club immediately—he'll run into a club ruff.

8.

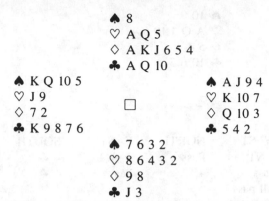

```
                    ♠ 8
                    ♡ A Q 5
                    ◊ A K J 6 5 4
                    ♣ A Q 10
♠ K Q 10 5                      ♠ A J 9 4
♡ J 9                           ♡ K 10 7
◊ 7 2            □              ◊ Q 10 3
♣ K 9 8 7 6                     ♣ 5 4 2
                    ♠ 7 6 3 2
                    ♡ 8 6 4 3 2
                    ◊ 9 8
                    ♣ J 3
```

Unless East has good hearts, declarer is bound to prevail. It won't help you to shift to trumps, though, since declarer has another source of tricks in dummy's diamonds. If you lead a heart, declarer will finesse the queen, and now the favorable lie of the minor suits will let the contract make even if East forces dummy with a spade return.

However, all is not lost. A spade continuation at trick two is more than declarer can handle.

Problems

9. Dlr: North
Vul: None

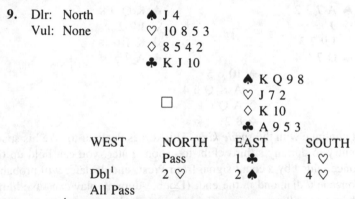

```
                    ♠ J 4
                    ♡ 10 8 5 3
                    ◊ 8 5 4 2
                    ♣ K J 10
                              ♠ K Q 9 8
                □             ♡ J 7 2
                              ◊ K 10
                              ♣ A 9 5 3
```

WEST	NORTH	EAST	SOUTH
	Pass	1 ♣	1 ♡
Dbl[1]	2 ♡	2 ♠	4 ♡
All Pass			

[1]negative, suggesting length in the unbid suits

West, your partner, leads the spade ace and continues with the two of spades to your queen. How do you continue?

10. Dlr: West ♠ 10 9
Vul: Both ♡ A Q J 10 5 4
◇ 5 4
♣ 10 6 3

♠ Q 4 3
♡ K 9 2
◇ A J 9 8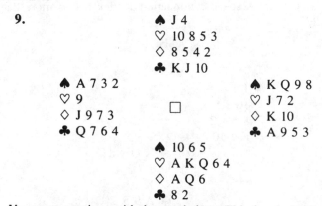
♣ A K 7

WEST	NORTH	EAST	SOUTH
1 NT	Pass	3 ♣ [1]	4 ♣
Pass	4 ♡	Pass	4 ♠
All pass			

[1]weak hand, long clubs

You, West, lead the club ace. East plays the five, and declarer follows with the queen. Plan your defense.

Solutions

9.
♠ J 4
♡ 10 8 5 3
◇ 8 5 4 2
♣ K J 10

♠ A 7 3 2   ♠ K Q 9 8
♡ 9   ♡ J 7 2
◇ J 9 7 3   ◇ K 10
♣ Q 7 6 4   ♣ A 9 5 3

♠ 10 6 5
♡ A K Q 6 4
◇ A Q 6
♣ 8 2

You must continue with the *spade king*. This forces declarer to take his spade ruff, the entry to dummy's third club, too soon. Later, you can hold up the club ace once, aided by a count signal from West, and declarer will probably have to concede a diamond in the end. (Double-dummy play can save him.)

This theme of *killing a winner or winners* declarer wants to use is so important that it has a Quiz all to itself.

10. Declarer simply could have bid four spades over three clubs, but instead he started with a cuebid. This suggests a huge spade-diamond two-suiter. If declarer has a heart in his hand, your chances look gloomy even if you kill dummy with a heart switch. The best shot for the defense looks like denying declarer a diamond ruff.

The full deal is:

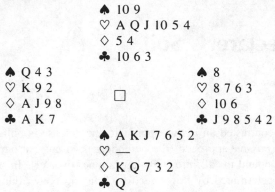

♠ 10 9
♡ A Q J 10 5 4
◇ 5 4
♣ 10 6 3

♠ Q 4 3
♡ K 9 2
◇ A J 9 8
♣ A K 7

♠ 8
♡ 8 7 6 3
◇ 10 6
♣ J 9 8 5 4 2

♠ A K J 7 6 5 2
♡ —
◇ K Q 7 3 2
♣ Q

If you lead anything but a trump at trick two, declarer is home. Say you continue with a club. Declarer ruffs and leads the diamond king to your ace. (It won't help you to duck.) A trump switch is too late now—declarer takes seven spades, a diamond, one diamond ruff, and the heart ace. If you continue clubs, South makes only six trumps in his hand, but he can ruff two diamonds in dummy.

On a trump switch at trick two, declarer can win in dummy and discard a diamond on the heart ace (but his fifth diamond is a winner anyway). When he leads a diamond to his king, you win and play the spade queen. Declarer is limited to seven spades, one diamond, and one heart.

Killing Declarer's Suit

In Quiz 9, we contrasted an *active* approach (the defense is obliged to seek fast tricks) with a *passive* approach (the defenders need only sit back and wait for tricks that are bound to fall into their laps sooner or later). In general, the right approach is determined by how much trick-taking power dummy has: if there are only a few scattered high cards, no ruffing power, and no good suit, go passive; if there are plenty of tricks, get active. (For still more on this important concept, see Quizzes 8, 13, and 20.)

One other approach must be considered. This one is based on the idea that if the defenders can deny declarer his best source of tricks, the contract is likely to fail. Here is an illustration.

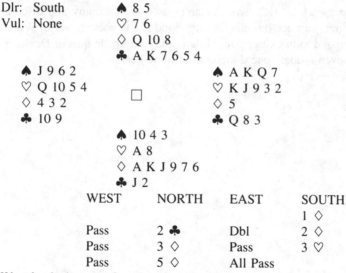

Dlr: South
Vul: None

♠ 8 5
♡ 7 6
◇ Q 10 8
♣ A K 7 6 5 4

♠ J 9 6 2
♡ Q 10 5 4
◇ 4 3 2
♣ 10 9

♠ A K Q 7
♡ K J 9 3 2
◇ 5
♣ Q 8 3

♠ 10 4 3
♡ A 8
◇ A K J 9 7 6
♣ J 2

WEST	NORTH	EAST	SOUTH
			1 ◇
Pass	2 ♣	Dbl	2 ◇
Pass	3 ◇	Pass	3 ♡
Pass	5 ◇	All Pass	

West leads the two of spades, and ninety-nine out of one hundred East defenders would take two top spades and shift to a heart. Declarer wins the ace, cashes a high trump, establishes clubs with a ruff, draws two more rounds of trumps ending in dummy, and takes a heart discard on a good club, making five.

At trick three, East should reason that declarer surely has the heart ace, so E-W have no fast heart tricks to take. The key to the defense is keeping declarer from using dummy's clubs. West's opening lead marks declarer with a third spade, so East continues with the spade ace, forcing dummy to ruff. Declarer's late entry to the club suit vanishes, and he has no way to dispose of his heart loser.

Killing declarer's suit is a very common type of defense against a notrump contract. The most spectacular example is the well-known Merrimac Coup (illustrated elsewhere). Here is another common situation, similar to one shown in Quiz 6.

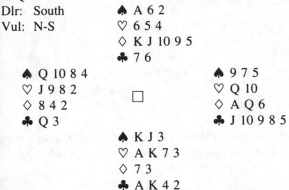

Dlr: South
Vul: N-S

♠ A 6 2
♡ 6 5 4
♢ K J 10 9 5
♣ 7 6

♠ Q 10 8 4
♡ J 9 8 2
♢ 8 4 2
♣ Q 3

♠ 9 7 5
♡ Q 10
♢ A Q 6
♣ J 10 9 8 5

♠ K J 3
♡ A K 7 3
♢ 7 3
♣ A K 4 2

South plays in 3 NT, having shown a strong, balanced hand. West leads the four of spades, which goes to declarer's jack. Declarer now plays a diamond to dummy's ten. If East wins this trick, the defense is finished: declarer wins the spade return with the king, plays his other diamond to dislodge East's ace, and takes three diamonds, three spades, and the two side ace-kings for an overtrick.

East can beat the contract by allowing dummy to win the first diamond. Declarer now has lost the timing to bring in the diamond suit, and barring an obscure throw-in, he must settle for eight tricks.

Problems

1. Dlr: North
    Vul: Both

    ♠ A K J
    ♡ A K 5 4 3
    ♢ K 4 3
    ♣ 6 2

    ♠ Q 10 4 3
    ♡ J 2
    ♢ Q 10 8 5
    ♣ K 4 3

WEST	NORTH	EAST	SOUTH
	1 ♡	Pass	1 NT
Pass	2 NT	Pass	3 NT
All Pass			

You, West, lead the three of spades. Dummy's jack wins, dampening your hopes somewhat. At trick two, declarer leads the two of clubs—five, ten. How do you defend?

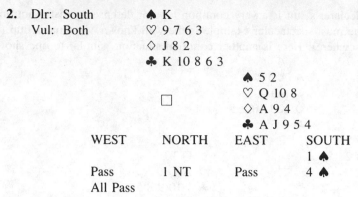

2. Dlr: South   ♠ K
     Vul: Both   ♡ 9 7 6 3
                 ◇ J 8 2
                 ♣ K 10 8 6 3

                         ♠ 5 2
               □   ♡ Q 10 8
                         ◇ A 9 4
                         ♣ A J 9 5 4

WEST	NORTH	EAST	SOUTH
			1 ♠
Pass	1 NT	Pass	4 ♠
All Pass			

West, your partner, starts the five of diamonds against South's game. You win the ace and declarer drops the queen. What is your next play?

Solutions

1.   ♠ A K J
               ♡ A K 5 4 3
               ◇ K 4 3
               ♣ 6 2

♠ Q 10 4 3   ♠ 9 6 5
♡ J 2   □   ♡ Q 10 9 7 6
◇ Q 10 8 5   ◇ 9 7 6
♣ K 4 3   ♣ A 5

               ♠ 8 7 2
               ♡ 8
               ◇ A J 2
               ♣ Q J 10 9 8 7

You should allow the club ten to hold. On the deal above, if you take the club king, declarer has time to establish clubs and will end up making two overtricks. This defense also would be necessary on other layouts—for instance, declarer could have long clubs headed by the A-Q-10 or A-J-10.

If your clubs were K-x, it still would be correct to duck the first round.

2.   ♠ K
               ♡ 9 7 6 3
               ◇ J 8 2
               ♣ K 10 8 6 3

♠ 8 4 3   ♠ 5 2
♡ K 5 4   □   ♡ Q 10 8
◇ 10 7 6 5 3   ◇ A 9 4
♣ Q 7   ♣ A J 9 5 4

               ♠ A Q J 10 9 7 6
               ♡ A J 2
               ◇ K Q
               ♣ 2

Partner has at most five diamonds, so declarer has another diamond, probably the king. Since a discard may be coming up on the jack of diamonds, shift to a trump, removing declarer's only entry to dummy. Your heart and club tricks can wait.

Playing ace and a club, trying to give partner a ruff, is a weak defense. If partner had a singleton club, he would have led it.

Problems

3. Dlr: South
Vul: N-S

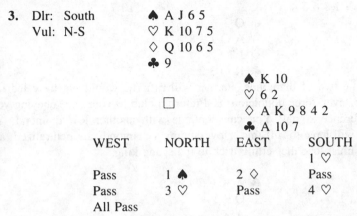

♠ A J 6 5
♥ K 10 7 5
♦ Q 10 6 5
♣ 9

♠ K 10
♥ 6 2
♦ A K 9 8 4 2
♣ A 10 7

WEST	NORTH	EAST	SOUTH
			1 ♥
Pass	1 ♠	2 ♦	Pass
Pass	3 ♥	Pass	4 ♥
All Pass			

West, your partner, leads the three of diamonds. Your king wins, and declarer drops the jack. How do you continue?

4. Dlr: South
Vul: None

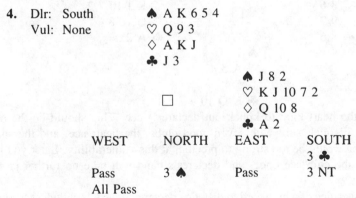

♠ A K 6 5 4
♥ Q 9 3
♦ A K J
♣ J 3

♠ J 8 2
♥ K J 10 7 2
♦ Q 10 8
♣ A 2

WEST	NORTH	EAST	SOUTH
			3 ♣
Pass	3 ♠	Pass	3 NT
All Pass			

Partner delights you by producing the heart eight on opening lead. You place your ten on dummy's nine, and declarer plays the four. What do you lead to trick two?

Solutions

3.

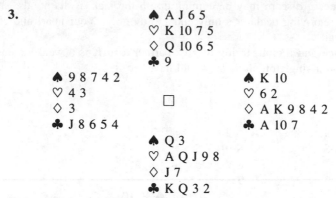

♠ A J 6 5
♡ K 10 7 5
◇ Q 10 6 5
♣ 9

♠ 9 8 7 4 2   ♠ K 10
♡ 4 3   ♡ 6 2
◇ 3   □   ◇ A K 9 8 4 2
♣ J 8 6 5 4   ♣ A 10 7

♠ Q 3
♡ A Q J 9 8
◇ J 7
♣ K Q 3 2

Return the two of diamonds. Partner will ruff (he would not have led low from the seven-three doubleton) and return a club to your ace, obeying your suit-preference signal. You can continue with another low diamond, and declarer will have to ruff this. Now dummy's diamonds are neutralized, and declarer must lose the setting trick to the spade king.

4.

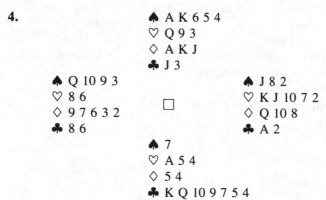

♠ A K 6 5 4
♡ Q 9 3
◇ A K J
♣ J 3

♠ Q 10 9 3   ♠ J 8 2
♡ 8 6   ♡ K J 10 7 2
◇ 9 7 6 3 2   □   ◇ Q 10 8
♣ 8 6   ♣ A 2

♠ 7
♡ A 5 4
◇ 5 4
♣ K Q 10 9 7 5 4

Return the heart king to knock out declarer's ace. This should be the only entry to his club suit; with seven good clubs, the heart ace, and the spade queen, he would be too strong to preempt at this vulnerability. Later you will hold up the club ace once, and declarer's hand will take no further part in the play.

The sacrifice of a high card to dislodge declarer's entry is called a Merrimac Coup. During the Spanish-American War, a ship of the same name was deliberately sunk by the Americans in the middle of a Cuban harbor channel. The intent was to neutralize the Spanish ships in port.

126

Problems

5. Dlr: South   ♠ A K 6 4
    Vul: Both   ♡ 6 5
                 ◇ A J 4 3 2
                 ♣ J 8

♠ J 7 2
♡ K Q 10 9 3
◇ K 10 8   ☐
♣ A 4

WEST	NORTH	EAST	SOUTH
			1 ♣
1 ♡	2 ◇	Pass	3 ♣
Pass	3 ♠	Pass	3 NT
All Pass			

You, West, lead the heart *queen*, which in your methods asks partner to drop the jack if he has it. The play to the first trick goes queen, five, two, seven. How do you continue?

6. Dlr: South   ♠ A J 6 5 4
    Vul: Both   ♡ A
                 ◇ A Q J 3 2
                 ♣ 10 5

♠ K 10 8
♡ 7 5 3
◇ 8 7   ☐
♣ K J 9 6 2

WEST	NORTH	EAST	SOUTH
			1 ♡
Pass	1 ♠	Pass	2 ♣
Pass	2 ◇	Pass	2 ♡
Pass	3 ◇	Pass	3 NT
All Pass			

You, West, lead the six of clubs. Partner's queen holds the first trick; declarer follows with the three. East returns the four of clubs to declarer's seven and your jack. What now?

Solutions

5.

        ♠ A K 6 4
        ♡ 6 5
        ◇ A J 4 3 2
        ♣ J 8

♠ J 7 2   ♠ Q 10 9 8
♡ K Q 10 9 3   □   ♡ 8 4 2
◇ K 10 8   ◇ 9 7 6
♣ A 4   ♣ 7 5 3

        ♠ 5 3
        ♡ A J 7
        ◇ Q 5
        ♣ K Q 10 9 6 2

Lead the heart ten. Declarer may be gratified with his "Bath Coup" until he realizes that the only sure entry to his club suit is gone.

As in the previous problem, you will win the second club. Then a spade shift will limit declarer to four diamonds, one heart, one club, and two spades. (If declarer cashes his second heart winner early, he sets up five defensive tricks for you.)

6. Shift to a red card. Dummy is very strong, but if declarer lacks the king of diamonds, he is sure to face entry problems. However, he may be planning to overcome them by unloading dummy's heart ace if you play a third round of clubs. The full deal:

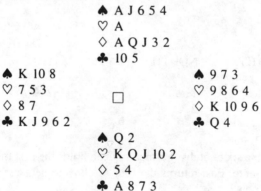

        ♠ A J 6 5 4
        ♡ A
        ◇ A Q J 3 2
        ♣ 10 5

♠ K 10 8   ♠ 9 7 3
♡ 7 5 3   □   ♡ 9 8 6 4
◇ 8 7   ◇ K 10 9 6
♣ K J 9 6 2   ♣ Q 4

        ♠ Q 2
        ♡ K Q J 10 2
        ◇ 5 4
        ♣ A 8 7 3

If you lead, say, a heart to the ace at trick three, declarer will try to reach his hand with the spade queen. When that fails, he must hope for even breaks in both spades and diamonds, which is asking a little too much.

Problems

7. Dlr: East ♠ 9 5 3
  Vul: E-W ♡ A 9 6
       ◇ Q J
       ♣ A 9 7 5 2

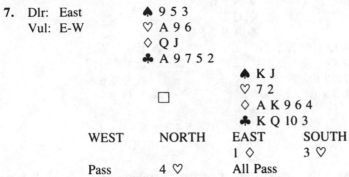

           ♠ K J
           ♡ 7 2
           ◇ A K 9 6 4
           ♣ K Q 10 3

WEST	NORTH	EAST	SOUTH
		1 ◇	3 ♡
Pass	4 ♡	All Pass	

West, your partner, leads the two of diamonds. You score the king and ace, declarer playing the five and seven. What do you do next?

8. Dlr: South ♠ J 6 4
  Vul: N-S ♡ J
       ◇ A K Q 10 7 6
       ♣ 6 5 3

♠ K Q 8 2
♡ K 5 4
◇ 9 2
♣ Q 10 8 2

WEST	NORTH	EAST	SOUTH
			1 ♡
Pass	2 ◇	Pass	3 ♣
Pass	3 ◇	Pass	3 ♡
Pass	4 ♡	All Pass	

You, West, lead the king of spades. Partner signals with the ten, and declarer drops the seven. Plan the defense.

Solutions

7. Should you shift to the spade king? Only if you have spade tricks that could disappear. Well, could they? Yes, if declarer has a singleton club— he could set up dummy's fifth club for a pitch. To do that, he would need four entries: three to ruff clubs, one to get back to his winner. The four entries are there all right—the club ace and three in trumps. So all you need to do is return a trump, and this contract is down for sure. The full deal:

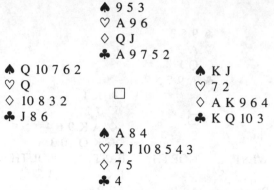

♠ 9 5 3
♥ A 9 6
♦ Q J
♣ A 9 7 5 2

♠ Q 10 7 6 2
♥ Q
♦ 10 8 3 2
♣ J 8 6

♠ K J
♥ 7 2
♦ A K 9 6 4
♣ K Q 10 3

♠ A 8 4
♥ K J 10 8 5 4 3
♦ 7 5
♣ 4

A trump shift also would work if declarer's pattern were 2-7-2-2. When you won a club trick, you could play your second trump and declarer still would be an entry short.

8.

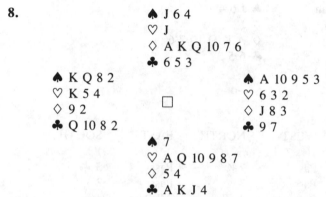

♠ J 6 4
♥ J
♦ A K Q 10 7 6
♣ 6 5 3

♠ K Q 8 2
♥ K 5 4
♦ 9 2
♣ Q 10 8 2

♠ A 10 9 5 3
♥ 6 3 2
♦ J 8 3
♣ 9 7

♠ 7
♥ A Q 10 9 8 7
♦ 5 4
♣ A K J 4

It cannot lose to shift to a diamond. When you regain the lead with the heart king, you intend to play a second diamond, cutting declarer off from dummy.

On the bidding, declarer is likely to hold six hearts and four clubs. It is perfectly true that he could have a singleton diamond and two spades, and a spade loser will go away if you shift. But this merely means that declarer will lose two clubs later instead of another spade now and one club later.

Count declarer's tricks. He has five heart tricks and at most two clubs. So even if he has a *void* in diamonds, a diamond shift cannot give away the contract, since you can ruff the third diamond.

Around the Trump Suit

There will be an extended introduction and a substantial Quiz in this section, since many interesting defensive techniques revolve around the trump suit. Our discussion will touch upon the forcing defense, trump control, ruff-and-discards, trump promotions, and the uppercut. These are all areas in which the defenders can create unexpected tricks.

Every player enjoys taking ruffing tricks with small trumps. (See Quiz 1 for more about seeking ruffs.) However, when the defenders find themselves with certain combinations of *high* trumps, ruffing still may gain.

<pre>
              7 5 3
   A J 10   □   K 6
              Q 9 8 4 2
</pre>

East ruffs something with the king, and West's trumps are worth three more tricks.

<pre>
              4 2
   A K J 8   □   Q
              10 9 7 6 5 3
</pre>

East ruffs in with the queen, and the defense takes five trump tricks instead of four.

<pre>
              Q 6 5 2
   A   □   J 10 9
              K 8 7 4 3
</pre>

If declarer leads toward the queen, E-W will take only one trick. But if West gets a ruff with the ace, East's holding is promoted.

There is a natural psychological barrier to winning trump tricks on defense. Defenders tend to regard the trump suit as declarer's inviolable domain. Many players, for example, would miss the following easy defense, which bears some relation to the positions mentioned above.

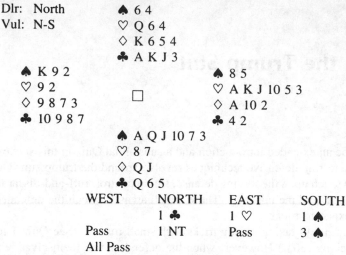

Dlr: North   ♠ 6 4
Vul: N-S   ♡ Q 6 4
           ◇ K 6 5 4
           ♣ A K J 3

♠ K 9 2   ♠ 8 5
♡ 9 2   ♡ A K J 10 5 3
◇ 9 8 7 3   ◇ A 10 2
♣ 10 9 8 7   ♣ 4 2

           ♠ A Q J 10 7 3
           ♡ 8 7
           ◇ Q J
           ♣ Q 6 5

WEST	NORTH	EAST	SOUTH
	1 ♣	1 ♡	1 ♠
Pass	1 NT	Pass	3 ♠
All Pass			

West leads a heart. On the third round, declarer ruffs with the queen, and West must *discard*. If he overruffs with the king, he gains nothing—it is as though declarer had lost a finesse to the king, which is what would happen anyway. Overruffing with a natural trump winner is seldom right.

Declarer goes to dummy with a club and plays a spade to the jack and king. Now West puts partner in with the diamond ace, and a fourth heart is led. Whether declarer ruffs low or high, West is bound to score the spade nine.

This play, called a *trump promotion*, has a first cousin, the *uppercut*.

Dlr: South   ♠ Q 7 4
Vul: None   ♡ K Q 9 6
           ◇ K Q 3
           ♣ 9 6 4

♠ J 8 3   ♠ 10
♡ A 5   ♡ J 10 8 7 4 3
◇ 10 4   ◇ 8 7 5 2
♣ A K J 8 7 2   ♣ 5 3

           ♠ A K 9 6 5 2
           ♡ 2
           ◇ A J 9 6
           ♣ Q 10

WEST	NORTH	EAST	SOUTH
			1 ♠
2 ♣	Dbl[1]	Pass	2 ♠
Pass	4 ♠	All Pass	

[1] negative

West cashes two top clubs and the heart ace. There are no more side-suit tricks for the defense, so West tries for the setting trick in trumps by leading a *low* club at trick four. East is obliged to ruff with his trump ten, and declarer, forced to spend an honor to overruff, must lose a trump trick to West.

Note that cashing the heart ace was essential. If West led a club at trick three, declarer could discard his losing heart instead of overruffing. In all the situations seen so far, the defenders *must* cash all their side-suit winners before trying to promote trump tricks; otherwise, declarer may be able to counter with a loser-on-loser play.

Timing one of these defenses correctly can be very tricky. This deal, from the 1961 European Championship, was reported by Terence Reese in *The Bridge World*.

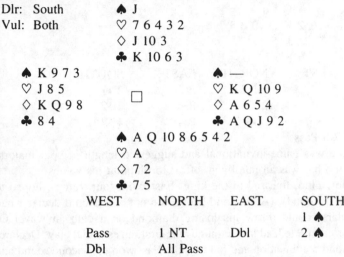

Dlr: South
Vul: Both

```
                    ♠ J
                    ♡ 7 6 4 3 2
                    ◇ J 10 3
                    ♣ K 10 6 3
♠ K 9 7 3                          ♠ —
♡ J 8 5                            ♡ K Q 10 9
◇ K Q 9 8         □                ◇ A 6 5 4
♣ 8 4                             ♣ A Q J 9 2
                    ♠ A Q 10 8 6 5 4 2
                    ♡ A
                    ◇ 7 2
                    ♣ 7 5
```

WEST	NORTH	EAST	SOUTH
			1 ♠
Pass	1 NT	Dbl	2 ♠
Dbl	All Pass		

Few players would have bid only two spades on the second round. No doubt South planned to do more later, and he must have been gratified to be doubled at the two level.

Nevertheless, E-W could have finished plus. If they cash two diamonds and two clubs, a third club from East promotes a second trump trick. The defense started well enough when West led the diamond king and shifted to a club. However, East cashed the diamond ace (a low diamond would have been better) and continued with a third diamond. Declarer played well by discarding his remaining club, and the trump promotion was gone forever: + 670 to N-S. This contributed to a hefty swing, since E-W at the other table registered + 600 in five diamonds.

In a *forcing game*, the defenders make declarer ruff so many times that he uses up all his trumps. Even if they don't establish some small trumps, the defenders may gain control of the play so they can cash winners elsewhere.

Dlr: North   ♠ A K
Vul: None   ♡ J 9 4
            ◊ Q 10 8 5
            ♣ A Q J 5

♠ 10 8 5 4 2		♠ 9 7
♡ 5		♡ A 8 7 2
◊ A 7 4 3	□	◊ K 9 6 2
♣ 9 7 3		♣ K 10 4

            ♠ Q J 6 3
            ♡ K Q 10 6 3
            ◊ J
            ♣ 8 6 2

WEST	NORTH	EAST	SOUTH
	1 NT	Pass	2 ♣
Pass	2 ◊	Pass	2 ♡
Pass	3 ♣	Pass	4 ♡
All Pass			

South's sequence was game-invitational and suggested length in both majors. North's three-club bid was an intelligent effort to pinpoint his values.

West led a low club, finessed to the king. East, with four trumps, hoped to force declarer in diamonds. (A diamond lead could not cost even if declarer had A-x, since declarer could throw his losing diamond on a club anyway.) Of course, East was careful to lead the diamond *king* first, an essential play. Declarer ruffed the diamond continuation and led trumps. East won the second round and played yet another diamond. Declarer now either had to give West the diamond ace or lose control and concede a trick to East's long trump.

In many forcing games, a defender must wait to force declarer until only one of the opposing hands has some trumps.

Dlr: South   ♠ J
Vul: N-S   ♡ J 9 4
            ◊ K Q 3 2
            ♣ J 10 8 6 2

♠ K 10 8 7 4		♠ Q 9 5 3 2
♡ A 8 2		♡ 6 5
◊ 9 5	□	◊ J 10 7 6
♣ A Q 5		♣ 7 3

            ♠ A 6
            ♡ K Q 10 7 3
            ◊ A 8 4
            ♣ K 9 4

South played in four hearts, and West led a spade. Declarer won, ruffed a spade, and led the jack of hearts. West *ducked*—had he won, he couldn't have made an effective return. However, when declarer led a second trump, West won and continued spades. Declarer ruffed in hand, drew the last trump (leaving himself with one), went to dummy with a diamond, and led the jack of clubs. West won the queen and forced out declarer's last trump with another spade lead. He later got in with the club ace and cashed a spade for down one.

Control of the trump suit can be just as important to the defenders as to declarer. For example, on many hands a defender must not release the trump ace until the proper time.

Dlr: South
Vul: Both

♠ J 5
♡ 8 5 3
♢ A 6 5 4
♣ J 7 6 5

♠ Q 10 7 4 3
♡ A 6 2
♢ K J 10
♣ Q 3

♠ 9 8
♡ 9 7
♢ Q 9 7 3
♣ K 10 9 8 4

♠ A K 6 2
♡ K Q J 10 4
♢ 8 2
♣ A 2

N-S reach an aggressive heart game. West leads a spade, won by dummy's jack. Declarer leads a heart to his king. If West wins this and plays another spade, declarer wins, draws one more trump, and safely ruffs his spade loser in dummy.

West does better to duck the first round of trumps. Declarer can't ruff his fourth spade at this point, since East can overruff; but if declarer plays a second round of trumps, West can win and lead a third round, stranding declarer with a spade loser.

Beginners are taught that giving declarer a ruff-and-discard is the unpardonable sin. Nevertheless, if declarer hasn't any losers left, a ruff-and-discard can't cost anything, and it may be an effective way of weakening declarer's trump holding. More often, it can merely be a safe way to exit.

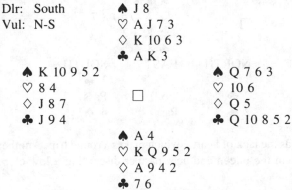

Dlr: South
Vul: N-S

♠ J 8
♡ A J 7 3
♢ K 10 6 3
♣ A K 3

♠ K 10 9 5 2
♡ 8 4
♢ J 8 7
♣ J 9 4

♠ Q 7 6 3
♡ 10 6
♢ Q 5
♣ Q 10 8 5 2

♠ A 4
♡ K Q 9 5 2
♢ A 9 4 2
♣ 7 6

In a matchpoint event, South played in the normal contract of four hearts. West led the spade ten—jack, queen, ace. Declarer drew trumps, eliminated clubs, and exited with a spade. West knew that declarer had five hearts and two clubs. If a spade continuation gave him a ruff-and-discard, then he had four diamonds, and he would only be throwing away a winner. So West led a third spade, and declarer had to lose another trick.

Problems

1. Dlr: South   ♠ K J 4
Vul: N-S   ♡ K Q 3 2
              ◊ J 6 3
              ♣ 9 5 3

♠ Q 5
♡ 8 5 4
◊ A 10 7 2   □
♣ K Q 10 4

WEST	NORTH	EAST	SOUTH
			1 NT
Pass	2 ♣	Pass	2 ♠
Pass	3 NT	Pass	4 ♡
All Pass			

You, West, lead the king of clubs—three, eight, two. The club four goes to partner's jack and declarer's ace. Declarer draws three rounds of trumps, partner discarding the five of diamonds. A spade to the jack wins, partner playing the ten. Declarer cashes the spade king and ace, East following with the seven and eight while you pitch a diamond. Declarer now exits with a club to you, East following. How do you defend?

2. Dlr: South   ♠ J 10 4
Vul: N-S   ♡ K 6 3
              ◊ Q J 10
              ♣ A J 10 3

                    ♠ K 8 7
                    ♡ A Q 10 8 7
        □   ◊ K 3 2
                    ♣ 8 7

WEST	NORTH	EAST	SOUTH
			1 ♠
Pass	2 ♣	2 ♡	Pass
Pass	2 ♠	Pass	4 ♠
All Pass			

West, your partner, leads the jack of hearts, which makes a round trip. Another heart is led, and you win the queen and ace, partner discarding a low club. How do you continue?

Solutions

1. Lead the thirteenth club. True, you are giving declarer the dreaded ruff-and-discard, but he has a losing spade to ruff, so he is going to make his two remaining trumps separately anyway. What you must avoid is breaking the diamond suit.

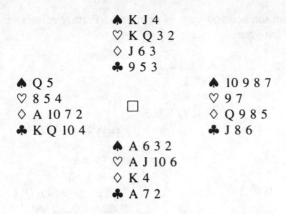

```
              ♠ K J 4
              ♡ K Q 3 2
              ◇ J 6 3
              ♣ 9 5 3
♠ Q 5                        ♠ 10 9 8 7
♡ 8 5 4           □          ♡ 9 7
◇ A 10 7 2                   ◇ Q 9 8 5
♣ K Q 10 4                   ♣ J 8 6
              ♠ A 6 3 2
              ♡ A J 10 6
              ◇ K 4
              ♣ A 7 2
```

2. Lead a fourth round of hearts. Declarer is marked with the diamond ace and a club honor on the bidding. Since he has no more side-suit losers, a ruff-and-discard won't help him.

How can it help your side? The full deal:

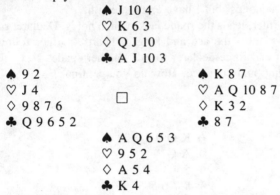

```
              ♠ J 10 4
              ♡ K 6 3
              ◇ Q J 10
              ♣ A J 10 3
♠ 9 2                        ♠ K 8 7
♡ J 4             □          ♡ A Q 10 8 7
◇ 9 8 7 6                    ◇ K 3 2
♣ Q 9 6 5 2                  ♣ 8 7
              ♠ A Q 6 5 3
              ♡ 9 5 2
              ◇ A 5 4
              ♣ K 4
```

West ruffs with the spade nine, forcing a trump honor from dummy, and your trump holding provides the setting trick.

Problems

3. Dlr: South
Vul: N-S

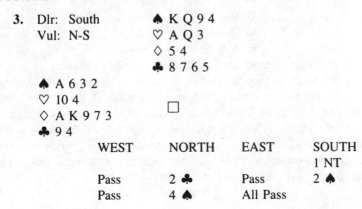

```
          ♠ K Q 9 4
          ♡ A Q 3
          ◇ 5 4
          ♣ 8 7 6 5
♠ A 6 3 2
♡ 10 4          □
◇ A K 9 7 3
♣ 9 4
```

WEST	NORTH	EAST	SOUTH
			1 NT
Pass	2 ♣	Pass	2 ♠
Pass	4 ♠	All Pass	

137

You, West, cash the ace and king of diamonds. Partner echoes, and South's queen drops. Plan your defense.

4. Dlr: North
Vul: Both

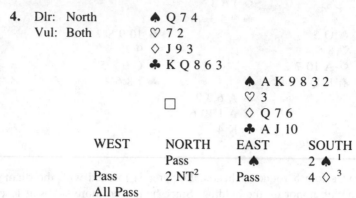

♠ Q 7 4
♡ 7 2
◊ J 9 3
♣ K Q 8 6 3

♠ A K 9 8 3 2
♡ 3
◊ Q 7 6
♣ A J 10

WEST	NORTH	EAST	SOUTH
	Pass	1 ♠	2 ♠ [1]
Pass	2 NT [2]	Pass	4 ◊ [3]
All Pass			

[1]Hearts and a minor
[2]What is your minor?
[3]Diamonds, but I have extra strength.

West, your partner, leads the spade jack, which holds. Declarer ruffs the next spade and lays down the ace and king of hearts, partner following up the line. You ruff and force declarer to ruff another spade. Next, a club is led to the two, king, and your ace. How do you continue?

Solutions

3.

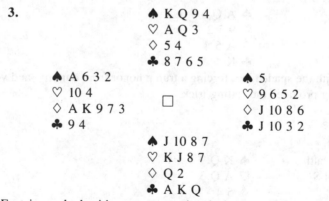

♠ K Q 9 4
♡ A Q 3
◊ 5 4
♣ 8 7 6 5

♠ A 6 3 2
♡ 10 4
◊ A K 9 7 3
♣ 9 4

♠ 5
♡ 9 6 5 2
◊ J 10 8 6
♣ J 10 3 2

♠ J 10 8 7
♡ K J 8 7
◊ Q 2
♣ A K Q

East is marked with at most another jack, so you have nothing to lose by continuing diamonds, trying to weaken declarer's trump holding. Suppose declarer takes the ruff in dummy and leads the king of spades. You must duck this, and duck again if the spade queen is led next. Now declarer is stuck: if he plays dummy's last spade, you win and force declarer to ruff a further diamond *in his hand*, losing control. As the cards lie, the best declarer can do is abandon trumps and run his side winners, conceding a trick to your small trump for down one instead of down two.

4.

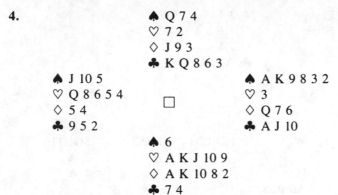

When declarer has a two-suited hand, giving him a ruff-and-discard can be an effective defense—he may want to establish his second suit by ruffing, so you make him ruff something else. Here, if you return a "safe" club or trump, declarer draws trumps in two more rounds and ruffs out West's queen of hearts, taking the rest.

Leading another spade for a ruff-and-discard cannot cost, since declarer is known to have at least ten red cards, and therefore no more fast losers. Whether he takes the ruff in his hand or in dummy, he must lose another trick either to you in trumps or to partner's heart queen.

Problems

5. Dlr: South
Vul: None

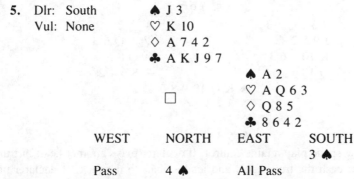

WEST	NORTH	EAST	SOUTH
			3 ♠
Pass	4 ♠	All Pass	

West, your partner, leads the two of hearts, and you capture dummy's king. How do you continue?

6. Dlr: East   ♠ J 4
Vul: None   ♡ 8 6 5 4
    ◇ J 4
    ♣ A K J 7 3

♠ A 9 8 2
♡ J 9 7 3 2
◇ A 2   □
♣ 8 4

WEST	NORTH	EAST	SOUTH
		2 ◇	2 ♠
Pass	3 ♠	Pass	4 ♠
All Pass			

You, West, lead the diamond ace—four, nine, six. How do you continue?

Solutions

5. Shift to a *low* spade. The play to the first trick tells you that declarer has three small hearts. (He wouldn't put the heart king up if he had J-x-x.) You need to stop a heart ruff, but you can't play ace of trumps and another—with all the trumps in, declarer will run the clubs, making an overtrick.

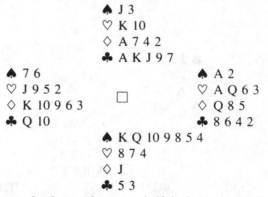

              ♠ J 3
              ♡ K 10
              ◇ A 7 4 2
              ♣ A K J 9 7
♠ 7 6   ♠ A 2
♡ J 9 5 2   ♡ A Q 6 3
◇ K 10 9 6 3   □   ◇ Q 8 5
♣ Q 10   ♣ 8 6 4 2
              ♠ K Q 10 9 8 5 4
              ♡ 8 7 4
              ◇ J
              ♣ 5 3

Your low-spade play retains control. If declarer plays another heart or trump, you win, cash the trump ace, and lead a heart to the jack. If declarer plays on clubs, West will score his small trump.

If declarer has a small singleton club and two small diamonds, a low spade switch will not defeat the contract—declarer can win in hand and play a club to the jack for ten tricks. However, the alternative diamond shift also fails. Declarer can win the ace, cash the ace and king of clubs, throwing his second diamond, ruff a club, dropping the queen, and lead a heart. Whatever the defenders do, they can take no more than two hearts and a spade.

6. Assuming that East has a reasonable weak two-bid (with more values in the diamond suit than outside it), you should shift to the nine of spades. This prevents a ruff in dummy and prepares a trump promotion while keeping control of trumps. The full deal:

♠ J 4
♡ 8 6 5 4
◇ J 4
♣ A K J 7 3

♠ A 9 8 2
♡ J 9 7 3 2
◇ A 2
♣ 8 4

♠ 3
♡ Q 10
◇ K Q 9 8 5 3
♣ 10 9 6 5

♠ K Q 10 7 6 5
♡ A K
◇ 10 7 6
♣ Q 2

If declarer wins in his hand and ruffs a diamond with the spade jack, your eight is promoted. If he wins the spade jack, you can overruff dummy on the third diamond. As the cards lie, declarer can't help himself by making an early club play.

If you lead anything but a trump at trick two, declarer can attack your communications effectively by playing a second diamond.

Problems

7. Dlr: North
Vul: N-S

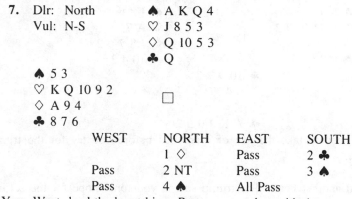

♠ A K Q 4
♡ J 8 5 3
◇ Q 10 5 3
♣ Q

♠ 5 3
♡ K Q 10 9 2
◇ A 9 4
♣ 8 7 6

WEST	NORTH	EAST	SOUTH
	1 ◇	Pass	2 ♣
Pass	2 NT	Pass	3 ♠
Pass	4 ♠	All Pass	

You, West, lead the heart king. Partner overtakes with the ace and returns a heart to your queen. What now?

8. Dlr: South   ♠ K 8
Vul: Both   ♡ J 6
♦ A K J 8 7
♣ Q J 5 3

♠ 6 3
♡ K Q 10 7 5 4 3
♦ Q 9 3   □
♣ 10

WEST	NORTH	EAST	SOUTH
			1 ♣
3 ♡	4 ♦	Pass	4 ♠
Pass	5 ♣	All Pass	

You, West, lead the king of hearts. Partner overtakes with the ace and returns a heart to your king. What do you play at trick three?

Solutions

7. Cash the ace of diamonds and play a third heart. Once East shows the heart ace, declarer needs the club ace-king and diamond king to have anything close to a hand worth a game force. Your only chance is to find partner with the spade jack.

♠ A K Q 4
♡ J 8 5 3
♦ Q 10 5 3
♣ Q

♠ 5 3   ♠ J 8 6
♡ K Q 10 9 2   ♡ A 7
♦ A 9 4   □   ♦ J 8 7 6 2
♣ 8 7 6   ♣ 10 4 3

♠ 10 9 7 2
♡ 6 4
♦ K
♣ A K J 9 5 2

Note the need to take the ace of diamonds before you try for the trump promotion.

8. Lead another heart. The trump suit is your only hope for the setting trick.

<pre>
                        ♠ K 8
                        ♡ J 6
                        ◇ A K J 8 7
                        ♣ Q J 5 3
   ♠ 6 3   ♠ 10 9 7 5 2
   ♡ K Q 10 7 5 4 3   ♡ A 9
   ◇ Q 9 3   ◇ 10 6 4 2
   ♣ 10   ♣ K 9
                        ♠ A Q J 4
                        ♡ 8 2
                        ◇ 5
                        ♣ A 8 7 6 4 2
</pre>

As it happens, today is your lucky day. If declarer ruffs low in dummy, East overruffs with the nine, forcing declarer's ace. If dummy ruffs with an honor, East will discard, of course.

Problems

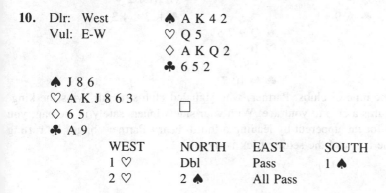

9. Dlr: North
Vul: None

<pre>
   ♠ K 10 5 2
   ♡ 7 5 3
   ◇ A K J 10
   ♣ K 3
   ♠ A 4
   ♡ 2
   ◇ 9 6 5 2
   ♣ Q 10 8 6 5 2
</pre>

WEST	NORTH	EAST	SOUTH
	1 ◇	1 ♡	1 ♠[1]
Pass	2 ♠	Pass	2 NT
Pass	4 ♠	All Pass	

[1]suggests a five-card or longer suit

You, West, lead the heart two to partner's ace. When the heart queen is returned, declarer plays the king. Plan your defense.

10. Dlr: West
Vul: E-W

<pre>
   ♠ A K 4 2
   ♡ Q 5
   ◇ A K Q 2
   ♣ 6 5 2
   ♠ J 8 6
   ♡ A K J 8 6 3
   ◇ 6 5
   ♣ A 9
</pre>

WEST	NORTH	EAST	SOUTH
1 ♡	Dbl	Pass	1 ♠
2 ♡	2 ♠	All Pass	

143

You, West, lead the heart ace—five, nine, four. You continue with the heart king, East playing the two. When the heart jack is led, dummy discards the club two, and East throws the club eight. How do you continue?

Solutions

9. Ruff with the *ace* of trumps! The 2 NT bid showed about 11 HCP, so East cannot have the club ace. The only chance of getting him in to cash the heart jack is in the trump suit. South's game try implied poorish spades, so there is a fair chance that East owns the spade queen.

♠ K 10 5 2
♡ 7 5 3
◇ A K J 10
♣ K 3

♠ A 4
♡ 2
◇ 9 6 5 2
♣ Q 10 8 6 5 2

♠ Q 8
♡ A Q J 9 8 4
◇ 7 4
♣ 9 7 4

♠ J 9 7 6 3
♡ K 10 6
◇ Q 8 3
♣ A J

If you ruff with the ace, East will gain entry to cash the setting trick before declarer can dispose of his heart loser on the diamonds. If you mistakenly ruff small and return a club, declarer wins and leads a trump to your ace. Later the spade king draws East's queen, and South chalks up his game.

10.

♠ A K 4 2
♡ Q 5
◇ A K Q 2
♣ 6 5 2

♠ J 8 6
♡ A K J 8 6 3
◇ 6 5
♣ A 9

♠ 10 3
♡ 9 2
◇ 10 9 4 3
♣ K J 8 4 3

♠ Q 9 7 5
♡ 10 7 4
◇ J 8 7
♣ Q 10 7

Lead the nine of clubs. Partner, who signaled club strength, wins the king, and returns a club to your ace. With your side winners safely in the bag, you can go for the uppercut by leading a fourth heart. Partner obliges by ruffing with the ten, and the setting trick is there.

Problems

11. Dlr: South   ♠ 7 5 3
     Vul: Both   ♡ 7 5 2
                   ◊ J 6 3
                   ♣ A Q J 8

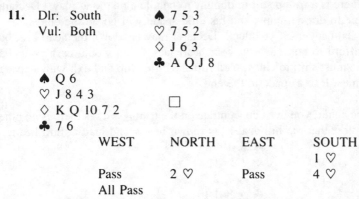

♠ Q 6
♡ J 8 4 3
◊ K Q 10 7 2
♣ 7 6

WEST	NORTH	EAST	SOUTH
			1 ♡
Pass	2 ♡	Pass	4 ♡
All Pass			

You, West, lead the king of diamonds, winning, and continue the suit. Declarer ruffs the third diamond and lays down the heart ace, felling East's queen. A club to the queen wins, and a heart is led from the table. East discards the jack of spades, and declarer inserts the heart ten. How do you defend?

12. Dlr: West   ♠ K 10 6 4
     Vul: None   ♡ 7 3
                   ◊ A K 2
                   ♣ A K J 10

♠ A
♡ K J 9 6 5 4 2
◊ J 3
♣ Q 4 3

WEST	NORTH	EAST	SOUTH
1 ♡	Dbl	Pass	1 ♠
Pass	3 ♠	Pass	4 ♠

You, West, lead the six of hearts. East wins the ace and returns a heart to declarer's queen and your king. How do you continue?

Solutions

11.

                   ♠ 7 5 3
                   ♡ 7 5 2
                   ◊ J 6 3
                   ♣ A Q J 8

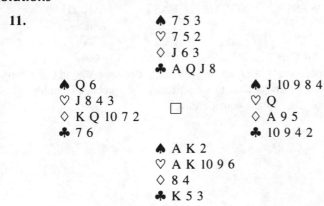

♠ Q 6   ♠ J 10 9 8 4
♡ J 8 4 3   ♡ Q
◊ K Q 10 7 2   ◊ A 9 5
♣ 7 6   ♣ 10 9 4 2

                   ♠ A K 2
                   ♡ A K 10 9 6
                   ◊ 8 4
                   ♣ K 5 3

Allow the heart ten to hold. If you win your jack, you can make ho damaging return. (There is a trump still in dummy to handle a diamond play.) Declarer will be able to draw trumps, and his little spade will go on the clubs.

Note what happens if you duck. Declarer may lay down the heart ace, but he can't afford to concede you your heart jack—you would cash your diamonds. He must shift to clubs. You ruff the third club and exit with a spade. Declarer must lose a spade in the end.

12. Once again, you must concentrate on the trump suit, as there is no other hope. Assume that the full deal is as shown below and lead a third heart.

```
              ♠ K 10 6 4
              ♡ 7 3
              ◇ A K 2
              ♣ A K J 10
  ♠ A                        ♠ J 9 2
  ♡ K J 9 6 5 4 2    □       ♡ A 8
  ◇ J 3                      ◇ 10 9 8 6 5
  ♣ Q 4 3                    ♣ 7 5 2
              ♠ Q 8 7 5 3
              ♡ Q 10
              ◇ Q 7 4
              ♣ 9 8 6
```

Partner ruffs with the nine, declarer overruffs with the queen. When you win your spade ace, you play a fourth heart, promoting partner's jack.

Problems

13. Dlr: East
    Vul: None

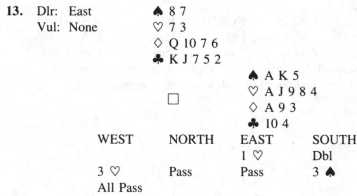

```
              ♠ 8 7
              ♡ 7 3
              ◇ Q 10 7 6
              ♣ K J 7 5 2
                        ♠ A K 5
              □         ♡ A J 9 8 4
                        ◇ A 9 3
                        ♣ 10 4
```

WEST	NORTH	EAST	SOUTH
		1 ♡	Dbl
3 ♡	Pass	Pass	3 ♠
All Pass			

West, your partner, leads a heart to your ace, declarer playing the king. Declarer ruffs your heart continuation and leads the queen of spades, West following with the three. Plan your defense.

14. Dlr: South   ♠ 6
      Vul: Both   ♡ A 7 5 3
                   ◇ K 9 6 5 3
                   ♣ 10 9 4

♠ A 8 3
♡ J 8 6   □
◇ 8 4
♣ K J 7 6 2

WEST	NORTH	EAST	SOUTH
			1 ♠
Pass	1 NT	Pass	3 ♠
All Pass			

You, West, lead the six of clubs. Partner wins the ace and returns the queen. You overtake and cash the club jack, East discarding the two of hearts. How do you continue?

Solutions

13. Duck the first spade! The full deal:

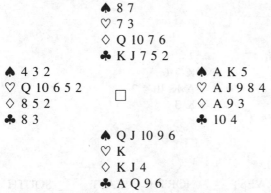

                 ♠ 8 7
                 ♡ 7 3
                 ◇ Q 10 7 6
                 ♣ K J 7 5 2

♠ 4 3 2   ♠ A K 5
♡ Q 10 6 5 2   ♡ A J 9 8 4
◇ 8 5 2   □   ◇ A 9 3
♣ 8 3   ♣ 10 4

                 ♠ Q J 10 9 6
                 ♡ K
                 ◇ K J 4
                 ♣ A Q 9 6

What can declarer do? If he continues spades, you take the ace and king and force out his last trump with a heart lead. When you win the diamond ace, you have a heart to cash.

If declarer knocks out the diamond ace at trick four, you win, cash a spade to remove dummy's remaining trump, and play a heart. At this point, you, partner, and declarer have one trump each. The best declarer can do is cash two clubs and two diamonds and lead dummy's fourth diamond, scoring his last trump *en passant* for down one.

The contract can always be made if you win the first spade.

14.

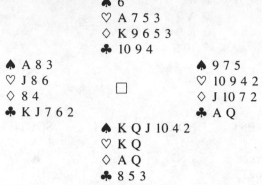

♠ 6
♡ A 7 5 3
◊ K 9 6 5 3
♣ 10 9 4

♠ A 8 3
♡ J 8 6
◊ 8 4
♣ K J 7 6 2

♠ 9 7 5
♡ 10 9 4 2
◊ J 10 7 2
♣ A Q

♠ K Q J 10 4 2
♡ K Q
◊ A Q
♣ 8 5 3

On the bidding, East must be fresh out of aces and kings. So, as usual, you turn your attention to the trump suit. A fourth round of clubs is ruffed with dummy's six. Partner overruffs with the seven, and declarer wins with the ten. When declarer leads the jack of trumps, you jump in with the ace and play another club. This time East contributes the spade nine and declarer has to overruff with the queen. Now your eight and two are good for a trick behind declarer's king. Easy, wasn't it?

Problems

15. Dlr: North
Vul: Both

♠ 7 4 2
♡ K 7 6
◊ A K 10 4 2
♣ K 3

♠ K 10 8 5 3
♡ A 3 2
◊ 8 7 5
♣ 9 5

WEST	NORTH	EAST	SOUTH
	1 ◊	Pass	1 ♡
Pass	2 ♡	Pass	4 ♡
All Pass			

Your spade lead turns out well, with partner producing the queen, ace, and another. Declarer ruffs the third spade and leads the heart queen. Plan your defense.

16. Dlr: North   ♠ K 4 2
     Vul: N-S   ♡ A
                 ◇ A Q J 10 6
                 ♣ Q 7 6 3

♠ Q 8 7 5
♡ Q J 10 8
◇ 9 2   □
♣ K J 10

WEST	NORTH	EAST	SOUTH
	1 ◇	Pass	1 ♠
Pass	2 ♣	Pass	2 ◇
Pass	2 ♠	Pass	4 ♠
All Pass			

You, West, lead the heart queen to dummy's ace, partner signaling with the nine. Declarer leads a trump from dummy—six, jack. How do you defend?

Solutions

15. Though East will have nothing more to contribute, you still have a chance if declarer had only four hearts. However, you must duck the first two rounds of trumps. If you win prematurely, declarer is safe on any return, even a spade. The full deal could be:

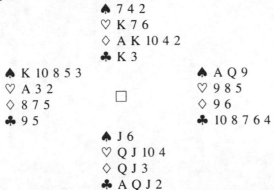

         ♠ 7 4 2
         ♡ K 7 6
         ◇ A K 10 4 2
         ♣ K 3

♠ K 10 8 5 3   ♠ A Q 9
♡ A 3 2   □   ♡ 9 8 5
◇ 8 7 5   ◇ 9 6
♣ 9 5   ♣ 10 8 7 6 4

         ♠ J 6
         ♡ Q J 10 4
         ◇ Q J 3
         ♣ A Q J 2

If you allow declarer to win the first two trumps leads, he is in a dilemma. If he leads a third trump, you win and cash two more spades. If he starts to run the minors, your partner will ruff the third diamond.

16.

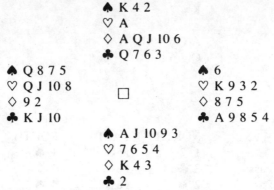

```
                    ♠ K 4 2
                    ♡ A
                    ◇ A Q J 10 6
                    ♣ Q 7 6 3
♠ Q 8 7 5                          ♠ 6
♡ Q J 10 8            □            ♡ K 9 3 2
◇ 9 2                             ◇ 8 7 5
♣ K J 10                          ♣ A 9 8 5 4
                    ♠ A J 10 9 3
                    ♡ 7 6 5 4
                    ◇ K 4 3
                    ♣ 2
```

This is a rather famous theme. West should allow the spade jack to hold! If declarer innocently continues with a spade to the king, the contract can no longer be made.

After the spade jack holds, a suspicious (or scatterbrained or inebriated) declarer could assure the contract by leading and (if West followed) passing the spade ten! This is the so-called Ann Gallagher Finesse: it is said that a charming young lady by that name once tried such a dubious "two-way finesse."

To Ruff or Not to Ruff?

Edmond Hoyle was an eighteenth-century expert on whist. Even today, his name is used to invoke learned authority over all sorts of card games. A lot of people probably think there is somebody named Hoyle alive and holding court in Las Vegas.

One of this gentleman's dicta at whist was "When in doubt, win the trick." But card-play technique has progressed in the past few hundred years, and such blanket pieces of advice no longer enjoy unquestioned acceptance.

In Quiz 11, we saw that refusing to overruff can be a necessary ingredient in a trump promotion. Here are a couple of additional positions:

```
              A 5
    J 8 3 2    □              Q
              K 10 9 7 6 4
```

This suit is trumps, and East leads a side suit in which West and declarer are void. If declarer ruffs with the ten, West must discard to wind up with two tricks.

```
              Q 4
    7 5        □              K J 9
              A 10 8 6 3 2
```

West leads a side suit in which East and dummy are void. If dummy ruffs with the queen, East must discard.

There are quite a few other situations where a defender may decline to take the short view by ruffing or overruffing. If his calculations are correct, the easy trick he is passing up will come back with interest.

Dlr: North ♠ K 5
Vul: N-S ♡ J 6 3
Matchpoints ♢ 7 6 3
     ♣ K Q 7 6 3

♠ Q J 10 8   ♠ 7 3
♡ 10 5 4   ♡ K Q 8 7
♢ K J 10 8 5 2 □ ♢ Q 9 4
♣ —   ♣ 10 9 8 4

    ♠ A 9 6 4 2
    ♡ A 9 2
    ♢ A
    ♣ A J 5 2

WEST	NORTH	EAST	SOUTH
	Pass	Pass	1 ♠
Pass	1 NT	Pass	2 ♣
Pass	3 ♣	Pass	3 ♡
Pass	3 ♠	Pass	4 ♠
All Pass			

You may not care for the bidding, but this was at matchpoints—playing in the major suit was desirable.

West led a diamond to the ace. Declarer began with three rounds of spades. West won the jack and forced declarer to ruff a diamond. Unable to play another trump, declarer began to run the clubs. However, East gave count, and West carefully waited until the fourth round of clubs to ruff in, stranding dummy's fifth club. He exited with a diamond, and declarer had to lose two heart tricks in the end for down one.

Dlr: South ♠ K Q 4
Vul: Both ♡ K 7
     ♢ A 8 6
     ♣ A 8 5 4 2

♠ 10 8 7   ♠ J 6
♡ J 9 6 4 2   ♡ A Q 10 5
♢ 9 7 3 2 □ ♢ Q J 10
♣ Q   ♣ J 10 7 6

    ♠ A 9 5 3 2
    ♡ 8 3
    ♢ K 5 4
    ♣ K 9 3

WEST	NORTH	EAST	SOUTH
			Pass
Pass	1 NT	Pass	3 ♠
Pass	4 ♠	All Pass	

On many occasions, an ill-considered ruff costs a trick immediately, and perhaps a tempo as well. On the deal above, West led a heart against four spades, and East took the ace and queen. Declarer won the diamond-queen shift in hand, cashed the club king, and played another club. West unwisely ruffed, in effect trumping his partner's winner. A diamond return knocked out the ace, but declarer drew all the trumps with the ace and king, cashed the club ace, ruffed a club, and returned to dummy with a trump to throw his diamond loser on the good club.

Ruffing in when declarer can follow with a loser usually is the wrong move. If West had patiently discarded on the second club, declarer would have had no chance to make his game.

A frequent reason for refusing to spend a trump involves *control*, another theme that was discussed in Quiz 11.

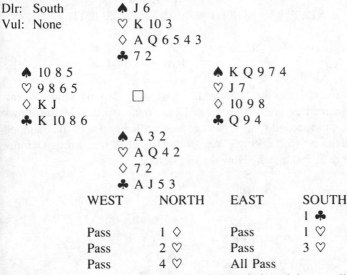

Dlr: South
Vul: None

♠ J 6
♡ K 10 3
♢ A Q 6 5 4 3
♣ 7 2

♠ 10 8 5   ♠ K Q 9 7 4
♡ 9 8 6 5   ♡ J 7
♢ K J   ♢ 10 9 8
♣ K 10 8 6   ♣ Q 9 4

♠ A 3 2
♡ A Q 4 2
♢ 7 2
♣ A J 5 3

WEST	NORTH	EAST	SOUTH
			1 ♣
Pass	1 ♢	Pass	1 ♡
Pass	2 ♡	Pass	3 ♡
Pass	4 ♡	All Pass	

Despite having only three trumps, North thought he might as well accept partner's game invitation. If diamonds came in and trumps split well, four hearts might make. If not, even three hearts probably would fail.

Declarer won the opening spade lead, took a successful diamond finesse, and continued with the diamond ace and a diamond, ruffed low. West seized the chance to overruff, and that was the end of the defense. Had West now returned a club or heart, declarer could win, draw trumps ending in dummy, and make use of the good diamonds. West actually led to the king of spades and East continued with the spade nine, hoping to force dummy. However, declarer discarded a club, allowing East to win. When East played a fourth spade, his only chance, declarer ruffed low in his hand. Whether West overruffed or discarded, declarer again could draw trumps ending in dummy and run the diamonds.

If West had discarded a club on the third round of diamonds, preserving his trump length, he would have maintained control of the hand. Against continued good defense, declarer would have been unlikely to get home.

Problems

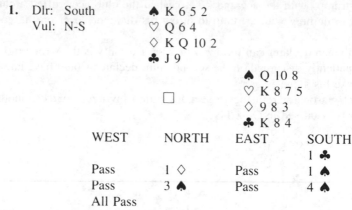

1. Dlr: South Vul: N-S

♠ K 6 5 2
♡ Q 6 4
◇ K Q 10 2
♣ J 9

♠ Q 10 8
♡ K 8 7 5
◇ 9 8 3
♣ K 8 4

WEST	NORTH	EAST	SOUTH
			1 ♣
Pass	1 ◇	Pass	1 ♠
Pass	3 ♠	Pass	4 ♠
All Pass			

West, your partner, leads the heart jack. You cover dummy's queen, and declarer's ace wins. Declarer cashes the ace and king of spades; West follows with the jack on the second round. Next come the diamond ace, the diamond jack, and a diamond to the king, West following all three times. Dummy now leads the diamond queen. How do you defend?

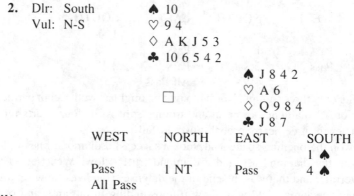

2. Dlr: South Vul: N-S

♠ 10
♡ 9 4
◇ A K J 5 3
♣ 10 6 5 4 2

♠ J 8 4 2
♡ A 6
◇ Q 9 8 4
♣ J 8 7

WEST	NORTH	EAST	SOUTH
			1 ♠
Pass	1 NT	Pass	4 ♠
All Pass			

West, your partner, leads the seven of hearts. You win and return a heart to the jack and king. When partner leads a low heart at trick three, declarer ruffs with dummy's ten of spades. How do you defend?

Solutions

1. If declarer's heart ace was a singleton, he would have maneuvered to ruff both of dummy's hearts before playing trumps. Chances are that his pattern was 4-2-3-4, and he is about to throw the losing heart on the diamond queen. You cannot prevent this, so ruffing with your high trump can't be right. If you hang on to the spade queen, you should get in to cash it (if declarer had the club ace, his opening bid would have been 1 NT), and you'd like to draw *two* of declarer's trumps for one.

154

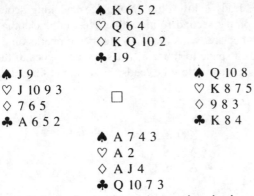

♠ K 6 5 2
♡ Q 6 4
◇ K Q 10 2
♣ J 9

♠ J 9   ♠ Q 10 8
♡ J 10 9 3   ♡ K 8 7 5
◇ 7 6 5   ◇ 9 8 3
♣ A 6 5 2   ♣ K 8 4

♠ A 7 4 3
♡ A 2
◇ A J 4
♣ Q 10 7 3

If you discard, declarer can do no better than lead a club to partner's ace. Partner forces declarer to ruff a heart. When you win the next club, you draw declarer's last trump and cash a heart for down one.

2. Discard a diamond. You will make the spade jack in any case, and if partner has something good in spades, you may gain a trick by refusing to overruff. The full deal might be:

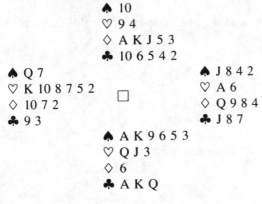

♠ 10
♡ 9 4
◇ A K J 5 3
♣ 10 6 5 4 2

♠ Q 7   ♠ J 8 4 2
♡ K 10 8 7 5 2 ♡ A 6
◇ 10 7 2   ◇ Q 9 8 4
♣ 9 3   ♣ J 8 7

♠ A K 9 6 5 3
♡ Q J 3
◇ 6
♣ A K Q

Problems

3. Dlr: East
   Vul: None

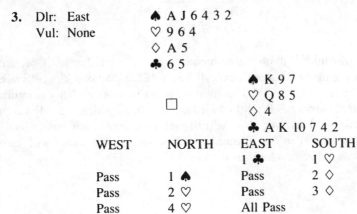

♠ A J 6 4 3 2
♡ 9 6 4
◇ A 5
♣ 6 5

♠ K 9 7
♡ Q 8 5
◇ 4
♣ A K 10 7 4 2

WEST	NORTH	EAST	SOUTH
		1 ♣	1 ♡
Pass	1 ♠	Pass	2 ◇
Pass	2 ♡	Pass	3 ◇
Pass	4 ♡	All Pass	

West, your partner, leads a low club. Your ace and king score, declarer dropping the queen on the second round while West unblocks the jack. You shift to a trump, and declarer wins the jack. He then embarks on a rather odd line of play: he leads a spade to the ace, ruffs a spade, goes to the diamond ace, and ruffs another spade. Now he leads the diamond king. Do you ruff? Why or why not?

4. Dlr: South
   Vul: N-S

   ♠ 5
   ♡ K 9 8 5
   ◇ A Q 9 8
   ♣ A 7 6 2

   ♠ A J 10 8 7 4
   ♡ J 7
   ◇ K 3
   ♣ K 9 3

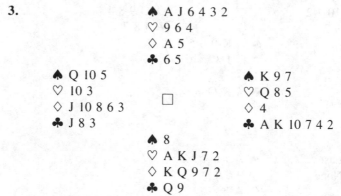

WEST	NORTH	EAST	SOUTH
			Pass
1 ♠	Dbl	Pass	2 ♡
2 ♠	3 ♡	Pass	4 ♡
All Pass			

You, West, elect to lead the ace of spades, and this drops partner's king. How do you continue?

Solutions

3.

♠ A J 6 4 3 2
♡ 9 6 4
◇ A 5
♣ 6 5

♠ Q 10 5
♡ 10 3
◇ J 10 8 6 3
♣ J 8 3

♠ K 9 7
♡ Q 8 5
◇ 4
♣ A K 10 7 4 2

♠ 8
♡ A K J 7 2
◇ K Q 9 7 2
♣ Q 9

You must discard a club on the diamond king (and discard again if declarer lays down the diamond queen next). If you ruff the diamond king, declarer will take the rest with the aid of dummy's spades no matter what you return.

Assuming partner has the J-9 or J-10 of diamonds, which is a safe bet on declarer's line of play, you can overruff when declarer finally has to lead a losing diamond and ruff it in dummy. Then your trump return will leave declarer with a diamond loser in the end.

4.

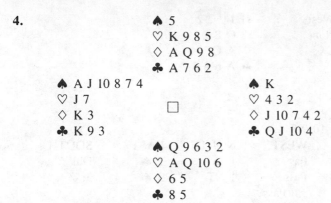

```
              ♠ 5
              ♡ K 9 8 5
              ◊ A Q 9 8
              ♣ A 7 6 2
♠ A J 10 8 7 4              ♠ K
♡ J 7                      ♡ 4 3 2
◊ K 3          □           ◊ J 10 7 4 2
♣ K 9 3                    ♣ Q J 10 4
              ♠ Q 9 6 3 2
              ♡ A Q 10 6
              ◊ 6 5
              ♣ 8 5
```

This was board 48 of the 1976 Bermuda Bowl final, United States vs. Italy. The contract and play were the same at both tables. After leading the spade ace, West continued with a low spade. Declarer *discarded* from dummy, allowing East to ruff. He won the club return, drew trumps in two rounds, and wound up with six trump tricks, a spade, a club, and two diamonds.

West's opening lead was not too inspired, but the fatal error was the spade continuation at trick two, which forced East to ruff a loser with his vital third trump. A trump shift by West would have left declarer with no way home.

Problems

5. Dlr: North
Vul: N-S

```
              ♠ Q J 9
              ♡ K 6 4
              ◊ A J 5 4 2
              ♣ K 2
                          ♠ 6 5 4 2
                          ♡ A Q 9 8
              □           ◊ K Q 10 9
                          ♣ 6
```

WEST	NORTH	EAST	SOUTH
	1 ◊	Pass	1 ♠
Pass	1 NT	Pass	3 ♣
Pass	3 ♠	Pass	4 ♠
All Pass			

West, your partner, leads the jack of hearts, winning. He continues with the heart two to your queen. Your trump shift rides to dummy's nine. Declarer cashes the club king and continues with a low club. Do you ruff? Why or why not?

6. Dlr: West   ♠ J 9 7 2
     Vul: None   ♡ Q 8
                ◇ A Q
                ♣ A 6 5 3 2

♠ 5
♡ A 6 4 2
◇ 9 5 2   □
♣ K J 10 9 8

WEST	NORTH	EAST	SOUTH
Pass	1 ♣	1 ♠	Dbl¹
Pass	1 NT	2 ♠	3 ♡
All Pass			

¹negative

You, West, lead the spade five. Partner wins the first trick with the spade ten and continues with the queen, ruffed by declarer with the heart three. Plan your defense.

Solutions

5. East must *ruff* and return a trump, a play that at worst will break even. The difference here is that East cannot overruff the dummy, and he must shift his attention to cutting down dummy's ruffing power.

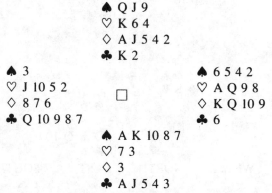

           ♠ Q J 9
           ♡ K 6 4
           ◇ A J 5 4 2
           ♣ K 2

♠ 3   ♠ 6 5 4 2
♡ J 10 5 2   ♡ A Q 9 8
◇ 8 7 6   □   ◇ K Q 10 9
♣ Q 10 9 8 7   ♣ 6

           ♠ A K 10 8 7
           ♡ 7 3
           ◇ 3
           ♣ A J 5 4 3

As the cards lie, this defense will hold declarer to five spades, two clubs, the diamond ace, and *one* ruff in dummy.

6.

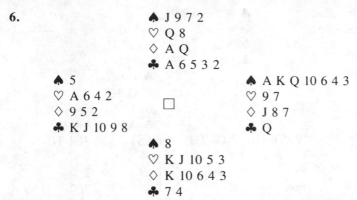

♠ J 9 7 2
♡ Q 8
◇ A Q
♣ A 6 5 3 2

♠ 5
♡ A 6 4 2
◇ 9 5 2
♣ K J 10 9 8

♠ A K Q 10 6 4 3
♡ 9 7
◇ J 8 7
♣ Q

♠ 8
♡ K J 10 5 3
◇ K 10 6 4 3
♣ 7 4

If you overruff, the contract surely will be made. The best you can do is return the club king, but declarer is in control. He can simply win dummy's ace and lead the queen of hearts. If you duck this, he cashes the ace-queen of diamonds before continuing hearts.

When declarer has a two-suited hand, the best defense usually is to force him out of control so he can't use his second suit. If you discard a club on the second spade, saving all your trumps, you can gain control if declarer tries to draw trumps. (If declarer tries some other line of play, this could turn into a very complex hand—but the defenders should manage to prevail.)

Problems

7. Dlr: South
Vul: Both

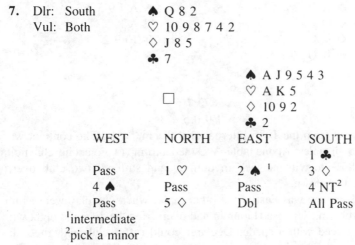

♠ Q 8 2
♡ 10 9 8 7 4 2
◇ J 8 5
♣ 7

♠ A J 9 5 4 3
♡ A K 5
◇ 10 9 2
♣ 2

WEST	NORTH	EAST	SOUTH
			1 ♣
Pass	1 ♡	2 ♠ [1]	3 ◇
4 ♠	Pass	Pass	4 NT[2]
Pass	5 ◇	Dbl	All Pass

[1]intermediate
[2]pick a minor

West, your partner, leads the spade six, and declarer ruffs your jack. He cashes the club ace and leads a low club, dummy ruffing with the eight. West has followed with the club eight and ten. How do you defend?

8. Dlr: East   ♠ A J 6 4 3 2
     Vul: None   ♡ 9 6 4
                    ◇ A 5
                    ♣ 6 5

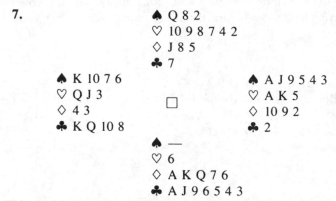

                         ♠ K 9 7
                         ♡ Q 8 5
                         ◇ 4
                         ♣ A K 10 7 4 2

WEST	NORTH	EAST	SOUTH
		1 ♣	1 ♡
Pass	1 ♠	Pass	2 ◇
Pass	2 ♡	Pass	3 ◇
Pass	4 ♡	All Pass	

If this hand looks familiar, it's the same one as Problem 3. Again you win two club tricks and shift to trumps, declarer's jack winning. This time declarer leads a diamond to the ace and a diamond back. Do you ruff? Why or why not?

Solutions

7.   ♠ Q 8 2
        ♡ 10 9 8 7 4 2
        ◇ J 8 5
        ♣ 7

♠ K 10 7 6   ♠ A J 9 5 4 3
♡ Q J 3   ♡ A K 5
◇ 4 3   ◇ 10 9 2
♣ K Q 10 8   ♣ 2

        ♠ —
        ♡ 6
        ◇ A K Q 7 6
        ♣ A J 9 6 5 4 3

This deal is from the 1985 International Team Trials. The contract was the same at both tables. At one table, West led a trump to protect his club holding. South chose to win the jack in dummy and suffered two club overruffs, finishing two down.

Bob Hamman was East at the other table, where the play went as related in our problem. Suppose Hamman had overruffed the diamond eight with the ten and forced with a spade. Declarer could ruff a club with the diamond jack, draw the remaining trumps in two rounds, concede a fourth club, and go down just one.

In practice, Hamman made the excellent play of *discarding*, applying the principle that it is wrong to help declarer keep control when he has a two-suiter. South came off dummy with a heart to Hamman's ace, and he led another spade, ruffed; South and East each had three trumps at this point. Declarer ruffed a club with the diamond jack, ruffed a heart, and ruffed a fourth club. *Now* Hamman overruffed and forced declarer out of control with

160

a further spade lead. Declarer made five trumps in hand, two ruffs in dummy and the club ace, for down three.

8. Declarer surely has some losing diamonds, else he would have simply drawn trumps and cashed out. If you ruff, you will only be ruffing one of declarer's losers with a valuable trump. The full deal:

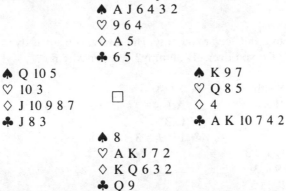

```
          ♠ A J 6 4 3 2
          ♡ 9 6 4
          ◇ A 5
          ♣ 6 5
♠ Q 10 5              ♠ K 9 7
♡ 10 3               ♡ Q 8 5
◇ J 10 9 8 7  □      ◇ 4
♣ J 8 3              ♣ A K 10 7 4 2
          ♠ 8
          ♡ A K J 7 2
          ◇ K Q 6 3 2
          ♣ Q 9
```

Note the outcome if you ruff and return, say, your last trump. Declarer now can ruff his last low diamond safely, and he also takes five trumps, three diamonds, and a spade, making the contract.

It's different if you discard a club on the second diamond. Declarer wins the king but has two little diamonds that he can't dispose of. If he tries to ruff them, you can overruff dummy twice (or return your last trump after overruffing the first time).

Problems

9. Dlr: West
Vul: None

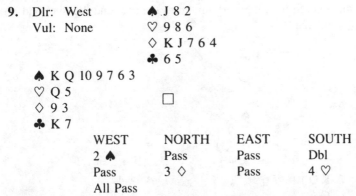

```
          ♠ J 8 2
          ♡ 9 8 6
          ◇ K J 7 6 4
          ♣ 6 5
♠ K Q 10 9 7 6 3
♡ Q 5
◇ 9 3          □
♣ K 7
```

WEST	NORTH	EAST	SOUTH
2 ♠	Pass	Pass	Dbl
Pass	3 ◇	Pass	4 ♡
All Pass			

You, West, lead the king of spades, winning. Declarer ruffs your low spade continuation and plays ace and another club to your king. You force declarer with a third spade. He ruffs with the heart ten as East pitches a diamond. Declarer cashes the diamond ace and king and ruffs a diamond with the heart ace. The position is now:

♠ —
♡ 9 8 6
◇ J 7
♣ —

♠ 10 9 7
♡ Q 5
◇ —
♣ —

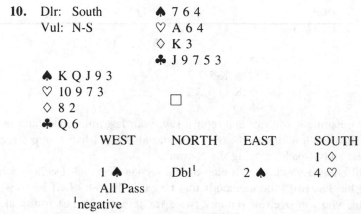

Declarer leads a club toward dummy. Hopefully, you are ready to play without a long mull. Do you overruff dummy? Why or why not?

10. Dlr: South
     Vul: N-S

♠ 7 6 4
♡ A 6 4
◇ K 3
♣ J 9 7 5 3

♠ K Q J 9 3
♡ 10 9 7 3
◇ 8 2
♣ Q 6

WEST	NORTH	EAST	SOUTH
			1 ◇
1 ♠	Dbl[1]	2 ♠	4 ♡
All Pass			

[1] negative

North's negative double with only three hearts would not be a popular choice—but it takes all kinds. You, West, lead the spade king and continue with a spade to East's ace. Declarer ruffs the third spade and cashes the heart ace and king; East follows with the jack on the second round. Declarer then plays a diamond to the king, a diamond to the ace, and the diamond queen. How do you defend?

Solutions

9.

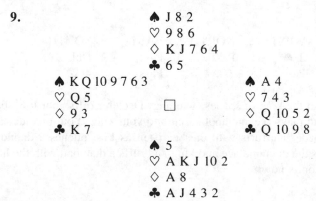

♠ J 8 2
♡ 9 8 6
◇ K J 7 6 4
♣ 6 5

♠ K Q 10 9 7 6 3
♡ Q 5
◇ 9 3
♣ K 7

♠ A 4
♡ 7 4 3
◇ Q 10 5 2
♣ Q 10 9 8

♠ 5
♡ A K J 10 2
◇ A 8
♣ A J 4 3 2

The deal was played in a crucial match at the 1974 World Mixed Team championship. West was Barbara Haberman (at that time Barbara Rappaport). Declarer was Pietro Forquet of Italy. At trick nine, with declarer having won six tricks, the position was:

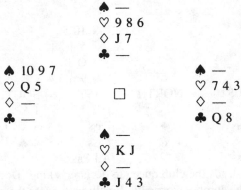

When Forquet led a club toward dummy, many Wests would have ruffed up with the queen and returned a trump. But this wouldn't be good enough—declarer would win for his seventh trick and cross-ruff for three more. Instead Haberman discarded! Forquet ruffed in dummy and saw that if East had the Q-x-x of hearts left, he needed to lead a heart to his jack. (If instead he led a diamond, East would discard his last club, overruff when declarer ruffed a club in dummy, and score a long trump.) So Forquet finessed the jack of hearts—and down he went.

10. Clearly, N-S have landed in a 4-3 fit. There is danger only if declarer has six good diamonds and the club ace. In that case, you won't beat him if you ruff the third diamond and return a club (or a spade)—declarer will be able to draw your last trump and claim with the balance of the diamonds. Instead, discard both your clubs before ruffing in. Then return a spade. The full deal:

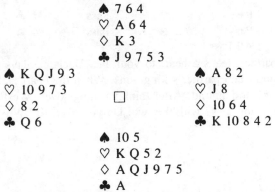

Declarer cannot ruff in hand without promoting your heart ten, so he has to ruff in dummy. However, he cannot get back to his hand to draw your last trump. If he leads a club to the ace, you ruff.

Problems

11. Dlr: South
Vul: Both

♠ K Q 7 6 3
♡ A K 10
◇ 7 6 2
♣ 8 7

□

♠ 10 5
♡ 5 4 3
◇ Q 10
♣ 9 6 5 4 3 2

WEST	NORTH	EAST	SOUTH
			1 ♡
Pass	1 ♠	Pass	3 ◇
Pass	4 ♡	Pass	4 ♠
Pass	6 ♡	All Pass	

West, your partner, leads the club queen to declarer's king. Declarer, a good player, looks over the dummy worriedly. Finally, he cashes the ace of spades, goes to the heart ace, and leads a diamond. When you follow with the ten, he consults the ceiling and eventually plays the ace. He returns to the heart king and cashes the spade king, discarding a diamond. Next, the spade queen is led. Do you ruff? Why or why not?

12. Dlr: South
Vul: N-S

♠ Q 7 4 2
♡ 7 5 3
◇ A J 5 3
♣ 6 4

□

♠ 10 9 6 5
♡ A 8 6
◇ K 8 4
♣ J 8 2

WEST	NORTH	EAST	SOUTH
			1 ♣
Pass	1 ◇	Pass	1 ♠
Pass	2 ♠	Pass	4 ♠
All Pass			

West, your partner, leads a heart to your ace. Declarer plays the queen on your heart return, and partner's king wins. When the heart jack is led next, declarer discards a diamond. After thinking things over, West produces another heart. Dummy ruffs with the two. Do you overruff? Why or why not?

Solutions

11.

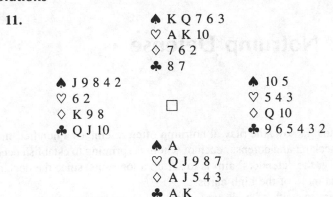

♠ K Q 7 6 3
♡ A K 10
◇ 7 6 2
♣ 8 7

♠ J 9 8 4 2
♡ 6 2
◇ K 9 8
♣ Q J 10

♠ 10 5
♡ 5 4 3
◇ Q 10
♣ 9 6 5 4 3 2

♠ A
♡ Q J 9 8 7
◇ A J 5 4 3
♣ A K

Declarer hopes for a 4-3 spade break that will let him establish the fifth spade. He sees an extra chance if you have only two spades, however. Suppose you ruff the spade queen and South overruffs. The defense now has no more trumps, while declarer has some in both his hand and dummy. He cashes his other high club and follows with a low diamond, snaring you in an endplay. You have to lead a club, and declarer gets rid of dummy's last diamond while ruffing in his hand. Then a diamond ruff sets up the suit, and South claims the rest.

To defeat South's imaginative line of play, you must refuse to ruff the spade queen.

12.   Declarer must be 4-2-2-5 for his diamond discard to make sense. But if West has the diamond queen, declarer needs the top spades and clubs to have a four-spade bid.

If you overruff dummy on the fourth heart, declarer will overruff you in turn. Then declarer will cash the high clubs, ruff a club low to establish the suit, draw trumps, and claim.

Better defense is to discard a club. Declarer will discard a club also, but now he can ruff a club neither high nor low in dummy. Unless his clubs are solid, he will have to concede the setting trick to your trumps.

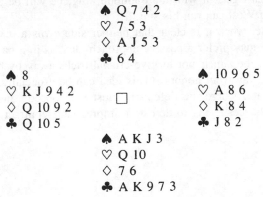

♠ Q 7 4 2
♡ 7 5 3
◇ A J 5 3
♣ 6 4

♠ 8
♡ K J 9 4 2
◇ Q 10 9 2
♣ Q 10 5

♠ 10 9 6 5
♡ A 8 6
◇ K 8 4
♣ J 8 2

♠ A K J 3
♡ Q 10
◇ 7 6
♣ A K 9 7 3

Quiz 13

Paths in Notrump Defense

As you no doubt know, the play at notrump often resembles a hundred-meter dash between declarer and defense, each of whom is sprinting to establish needed tricks. Generally, the defenders' aim is to set up a long suit, since the declaring side usually has more of the high cards.

The defenders' paucity of high cards also creates another problem—even if someone has winners established, he must get in the lead to cash them. So the defenders always have to keep *preserving communication* in mind—we'll see some examples of this. (See also Quiz 14.)

Ducking a winner to preserve an entry is a common defensive technique.

```
Dlr: South        ♠ Q 9
Vul: N-S          ♡ 7 6 4
                  ◇ A J 7 6 3
                  ♣ K 5 4

♠ A 10 7 5 2               ♠ K 6 3
♡ J 8 2          □         ♡ Q 10 9 5
◇ 8 4                      ◇ K 9 2
♣ 10 8 6                   ♣ J 9 7

                  ♠ J 8 4
                  ♡ A K 3
                  ◇ Q 10 5
                  ♣ A Q 3 2
```

West leads the five of spades against South's 3 NT. East wins the king and returns the six. When declarer plays the eight, West knows that declarer still has the jack left, for a sure stopper. He therefore allows dummy's queen to win trick two. When East gets in with the diamond king, he will be able to return his last spade, and West can run his suit.

Once in a while, when it is clear that neither side owns a ready source of tricks, the defense may prefer a passive approach. Just as in a passive defense vs. a suit contract, the aim is not to give crucial tricks away by breaking new suits and leading away from honors. (This idea can be especially important at matchpoint duplicate, where the defenders must not concede an overtrick by taking desperate chances trying to defeat an impregnable contract.)

166

Dlr: South   ♠ K 7 5 3
Vul: None   ♡ K 5 4
                 ◇ K 10 3
                 ♣ J 6 3

♠ Q 2   ♠ A 9 8 4
♡ Q 8 2   ♡ 10 7 3
◇ J 7 2   □   ◇ Q 8 6 4
♣ K 9 8 5 4   ♣ 10 2

                 ♠ J 10 6
                 ♡ A J 9 6
                 ◇ A 9 5
                 ♣ A Q 7

South opens 1 NT and is raised to 3 NT. West leads the five of clubs—jack, ten, seven. Declarer tries a heart to the jack, losing to West's queen. West can see that dummy is no powerhouse, and declarer is known to have a balanced hand also. So there is little reason for a panicky move like a switch to the queen of spades—it is best to exit safely with a heart. Let declarer attack the remaining suits.

One other possible defensive approach is neutralizing declarer's source of tricks. The subject is covered fully in Quiz 10, so only one example will be given here.

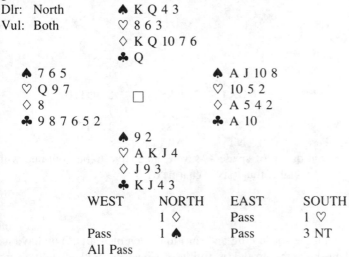

Dlr: North   ♠ K Q 4 3
Vul: Both   ♡ 8 6 3
                 ◇ K Q 10 7 6
                 ♣ Q

♠ 7 6 5   ♠ A J 10 8
♡ Q 9 7   ♡ 10 5 2
◇ 8   □   ◇ A 5 4 2
♣ 9 8 7 6 5 2   ♣ A 10

                 ♠ 9 2
                 ♡ A K J 4
                 ◇ J 9 3
                 ♣ K J 4 3

WEST	NORTH	EAST	SOUTH
	1 ◇	Pass	1 ♡
Pass	1 ♠	Pass	3 NT
All Pass			

West leads the nine of clubs to the queen and ace. If East merely returns a club, declarer wins, knocks out the ace of diamonds, and reaches dummy with a spade to cash the diamonds. He can take four diamonds, two clubs, two hearts, and a spade.

Instead, East should turn his attention to isolating the diamond suit. This can be done easily by returning the spade jack. Declarer's entry to dummy is dislodged before he is ready to use it, and the best he can do is eight tricks.

Problems

1. Dlr: South   ♠ J 3
    Vul: Both   ♡ A J 4
                         ◇ A 10 8 5 3
                         ♣ K 7 6

    ♠ K 9 7 4 2
    ♡ 10 5 3
    ◇ 7 6   □
    ♣ 9 4 2

WEST	NORTH	EAST	SOUTH
			1 ♣
Pass	1 ◇	Pass	1 NT
Pass	3 NT		

You, West, lead the four of spades. Dummy plays the jack, and partner, to your relief, covers with the queen. Declarer plays the spade six at trick one and follows with the eight when East continues with the spade ten. Plan your defense.

2. Dlr: South   ♠ 8 7
    Vul: N-S   ♡ A K J 8 6
                         ◇ J 10 9
                         ♣ Q 3 2

    ♠ Q J 10
    ♡ 5 4 3
    ◇ A Q 7 3   □
    ♣ K 10 6

WEST	NORTH	EAST	SOUTH
			1 ◇
Pass	1 ♡	Pass	1 NT
Pass	3 NT	All Pass	

You, West, try the queen of spades—seven, nine, five. You continue with the jack of spades—eight, four, six. What next?

Solutions

1. Overtake with the spade king and shift to the ten of hearts. You have no entry, so establishing the spades is fruitless. However, with that five-card diamond suit in dummy you can't afford to go passive. Perhaps partner has something good in hearts, plus an entry in diamonds.

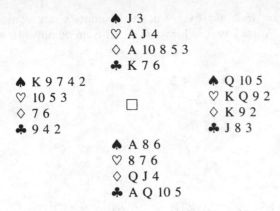

♠ J 3
♡ A J 4
◇ A 10 8 5 3
♣ K 7 6

♠ K 9 7 4 2
♡ 10 5 3
◇ 7 6
♣ 9 4 2

♠ Q 10 5
♡ K Q 9 2
◇ K 9 2
♣ J 8 3

♠ A 8 6
♡ 8 7 6
◇ Q J 4
♣ A Q 10 5

2. Declarer is certain to have at least four diamonds to the king plus the heart queen, so he has the material for nine tricks. But your partner cannot have an entry to his spades—you must look elsewhere for defensive tricks. Clubs is the only chance. You have to play East for the club jack and switch to a club at trick two.

♠ 8 7
♡ A K J 8 6
◇ J 10 9
♣ Q 3 2

♠ Q J 10
♡ 5 4 3
◇ A Q 7 3
♣ K 10 6

♠ K 9 4 3 2
♡ 7 2
◇ 6 2
♣ J 9 8 7

♠ A 6 5
♡ Q 10 9
◇ K 8 5 4
♣ A 5 4

There is one other point—if you do not lead the club *king* at trick three, you must unblock it if declarer cashes the club ace later; otherwise you could find yourself subjected to an endplay.

Problems

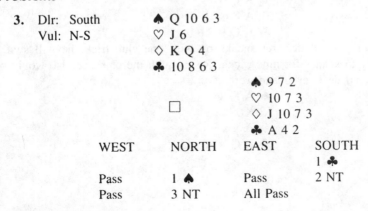

3. Dlr: South
    Vul: N-S

♠ Q 10 6 3
♡ J 6
◇ K Q 4
♣ 10 8 6 3

♠ 9 7 2
♡ 10 7 3
◇ J 10 7 3
♣ A 4 2

WEST	NORTH	EAST	SOUTH
			1 ♣
Pass	1 ♠	Pass	2 NT
Pass	3 NT	All Pass	

169

West, your partner, leads the five of hearts. Dummy's jack wins, declarer playing the four. At trick two, a low club is led from dummy. How do you defend?

4. Dlr: South   ♠ A 8 4 2
    Vul: E-W   ♡ 8 5 3
                 ◇ K 5
                 ♣ Q 10 9 5

♠ 9 6
♡ J 9 6
◇ Q 10 8 7 3   □
♣ A 8 3

WEST	NORTH	EAST	SOUTH
			1 ♣
Pass	1 ♠	Pass	2 NT
Pass	3 NT	All Pass	

You, West, lead the seven of diamonds. Declarer wins the king in dummy, partner playing the nine. Declarer continues with a club from dummy—four, king. Quickly now: Do you take this trick? If you take it, what do you lead next?

Solutions

3. Go right in with the club ace and return a heart. The idea is to spend your entry early so you can establish partner's suit while his (hoped-for) entry is preserved. The full deal:

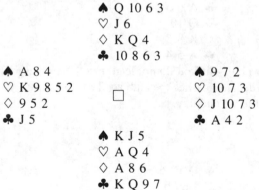

                 ♠ Q 10 6 3
                 ♡ J 6
                 ◇ K Q 4
                 ♣ 10 8 6 3

♠ A 8 4   ♠ 9 7 2
♡ K 9 8 5 2   □   ♡ 10 7 3
◇ 9 5 2   ◇ J 10 7 3
♣ J 5   ♣ A 4 2

                 ♠ K J 5
                 ♡ A Q 4
                 ◇ A 8 6
                 ♣ K Q 9 7

On this layout, if declarer sneaks by with one club trick, he will switch promptly to spades for nine tricks. Rising with the club ace also would be necessary if declarer's hand were

                 ♠ A K x
                 ♡ K x x
                 ◇ A x x
                 ♣ K Q x x

4. Let the club king hold. Of course, you won't gain a club trick if declarer also has the jack. However, you might induce him to switch suits if he thinks your partner has the club ace and you have an entry somewhere else.

Another possible benefit is illustrated by the actual deal:

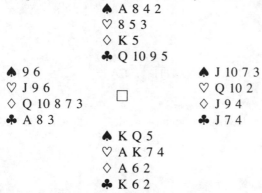

After the club king wins, declarer surely will continue with a club to the nine and jack. East returns a diamond, and your suit is set up while you still have your entry! If you win the club ace, you can establish diamonds, all right. But declarer will lose a club finesse to your partner's jack, win the return, and cash out his nine tricks.

Your *tempo* is a definite factor in a situation like this. *If you stew over your play to trick two, you might as well go ahead and win the ace.* You need to make up your mind in advance that you will cling to your entry until the time is ripe.

Problems

5. Dlr: South
Vul: None

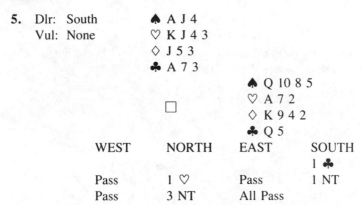

WEST	NORTH	EAST	SOUTH
			1 ♣
Pass	1 ♡	Pass	1 NT
Pass	3 NT	All Pass	

West, your partner, leads the nine of hearts. You and dummy play low, and declarer's queen wins. Declarer immediately returns the heart ten. Plan your defense.

6. Dlr: East
Vul: Both

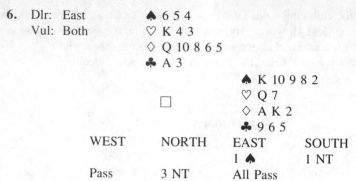

♠ 6 5 4
♡ K 4 3
◇ Q 10 8 6 5
♣ A 3

♠ K 10 9 8 2
♡ Q 7
◇ A K 2
♣ 9 6 5

WEST	NORTH	EAST	SOUTH
		1 ♠	1 NT
Pass	3 NT	All Pass	

West, your partner, leads the queen of spades. With what card do you signal at trick one?

Solutions

5. Win the second heart and return a heart. Dummy has scattered high cards, so this looks like a good time to go passive. The full deal:

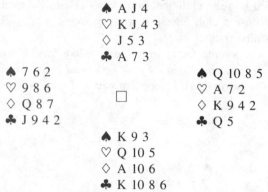

♠ A J 4
♡ K J 4 3
◇ J 5 3
♣ A 7 3

♠ 7 6 2
♡ 9 8 6
◇ Q 8 7
♣ J 9 4 2

♠ Q 10 8 5
♡ A 7 2
◇ K 9 4 2
♣ Q 5

♠ K 9 3
♡ Q 10 5
◇ A 10 6
♣ K 10 8 6

Declarer might make the contract whatever you lead back, but his chances will improve dramatically if you break a new suit for him.

6.

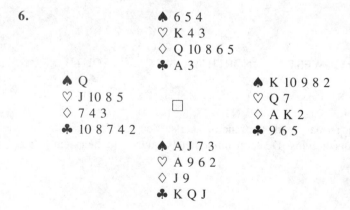

♠ 6 5 4
♡ K 4 3
◇ Q 10 8 6 5
♣ A 3

♠ Q
♡ J 10 8 5
◇ 7 4 3
♣ 10 8 7 4 2

♠ K 10 9 8 2
♡ Q 7
◇ A K 2
♣ 9 6 5

♠ A J 7 3
♡ A 9 6 2
◇ J 9
♣ K Q J

Careful. If you play the spade ten on the opening lead, declarer will duck. Partner must shift, and the defense has lost a vital tempo—declarer has time to set up diamonds. To beat the contract, *overtake* the first trick with the spade king.

Problems

7. Dlr: North
   Vul: N-S

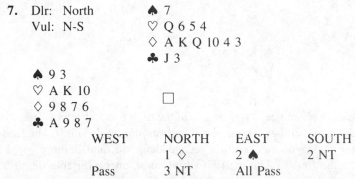

♠ 7
♡ Q 6 5 4
◇ A K Q 10 4 3
♣ J 3

♠ 9 3
♡ A K 10
◇ 9 8 7 6
♣ A 9 8 7

WEST	NORTH	EAST	SOUTH
	1 ◇	2 ♠	2 NT
Pass	3 NT	All Pass	

You, West, lead the nine of spades. Partner overtakes with the ten, and declarer wins the queen. A club to the jack wins, and declarer returns a club to his king. East has followed with the two and five. How do you defend?

8. Dlr: North
   Vul: Both

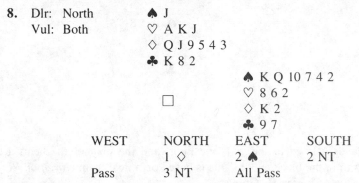

♠ J
♡ A K J
◇ Q J 9 5 4 3
♣ K 8 2

♠ K Q 10 7 4 2
♡ 8 6 2
◇ K 2
♣ 9 7

WEST	NORTH	EAST	SOUTH
	1 ◇	2 ♠	2 NT
Pass	3 NT	All Pass	

West, your partner, leads the eight of spades. Plan your defense.

Solutions

7.

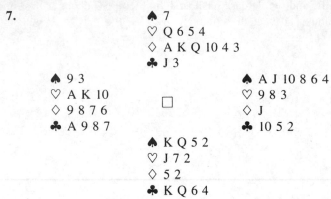

```
              ♠ 7
              ♡ Q 6 5 4
              ◇ A K Q 10 4 3
              ♣ J 3
♠ 9 3                          ♠ A J 10 8 6 4
♡ A K 10                       ♡ 9 8 3
◇ 9 8 7 6        □             ◇ J
♣ A 9 8 7                      ♣ 10 5 2
              ♠ K Q 5 2
              ♡ J 7 2
              ◇ 5 2
              ♣ K Q 6 4
```

There is virtually no choice—you must win the club ace and return a passive diamond. Declarer will have to go ahead and run dummy's suit. (If he leads a heart to the jack, you can return a second diamond, and dummy will be endplayed at the finish.) This will cost him some uncomfortable discards. The end position will be:

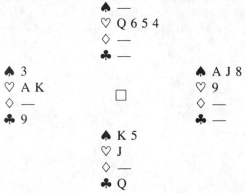

```
              ♠ —
              ♡ Q 6 5 4
              ◇ —
              ♣ —
♠ 3                            ♠ A J 8
♡ A K                          ♡ 9
◇ —              □             ◇ —
♣ 9                            ♣ —
              ♠ K 5
              ♡ J
              ◇ —
              ♣ Q
```

Declarer leads a heart to the jack and king, and the play of the heart ace squeezes him in the black suits! (This is based on a deal from *Goren on Play and Defense* by Charles H. Goren.)

8.

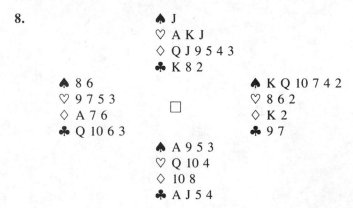

```
              ♠ J
              ♡ A K J
              ◇ Q J 9 5 4 3
              ♣ K 8 2
♠ 8 6                          ♠ K Q 10 7 4 2
♡ 9 7 5 3                      ♡ 8 6 2
◇ A 7 6          □             ◇ K 2
♣ Q 10 6 3                     ♣ 9 7
              ♠ A 9 5 3
              ♡ Q 10 4
              ◇ 10 8
              ♣ A J 5 4
```

For starters, you must assign the diamond ace to partner—there is no hope if declarer has that card.

Declarer is likely to have A-9-x-x of spades, which is good enough for a double stopper. Suppose you cover the spade jack with the queen. Declarer will *duck* this and win the spade continuation. When a diamond is led next, partner will be left without a spade to return if he wins the ace. He will have to exit in hearts or clubs, giving declarer time to establish diamonds.

Since declarer rates to have two spade stoppers anyway, East must force him to use one of them at trick one. The winning play is to let the spade jack hold! (Even if declarer's spades were A-x-x, this play might not cost the contract.)

We will see some other hands like this in Quiz 14.

Communication: Keeping Yours, Cutting Theirs

Entries are the means by which one defender or the other gains the lead. Since the defenders usually have fewer entries than declarer, they often must take special measures to keep their communications intact. This is especially true in notrump defense, where establishing and cashing long cards is frequently the goal. (See Quiz 13.)

Look at this deal:

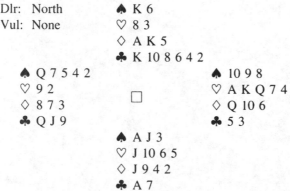

Dlr: North   ♠ K 6
Vul: None   ♡ 8 3
             ◇ A K 5
             ♣ K 10 8 6 4 2

♠ Q 7 5 4 2   ♠ 10 9 8
♡ 9 2   ☐   ♡ A K Q 7 4
◇ 8 7 3   ◇ Q 10 6
♣ Q J 9   ♣ 5 3

             ♠ A J 3
             ♡ J 10 6 5
             ◇ J 9 4 2
             ♣ A 7

North opens one club, East overcalls one heart, South jumps to 2 NT (invitational), and North goes on to 3 NT. West leads the nine of hearts.

East knows that the contract is cold unless West has a trick in clubs. Even so, declarer will prevail unless the defense can cash four heart tricks when West gets in. Clearing the heart suit will not help, since East has no fast entry on the side. Since, on the bidding, declarer is known to have one heart stopper anyway, East *ducks* the first heart, signaling with the seven.

A slightly more advanced case of keeping communication:

Dlr: North   ♠ 5 4 3
Vul: Both   ♡ A Q 2
              ◊ Q J 10 8 3
              ♣ A 3

♠ 10 2		♠ K Q 9 8 7
♡ 10 9 5 4	□	♡ J 6 3
◊ K 2		◊ A 6
♣ 10 8 7 6 5		♣ 9 4 2

           ♠ A J 6
           ♡ K 8 7
           ◊ 9 7 5 4
           ♣ K Q J

WEST	NORTH	EAST	SOUTH
	1 ◊	1 ♠	3 NT
All Pass			

When West leads the ten of spades, East must play the *nine*. If he puts up an honor, declarer *ducks* and wins the second round. The defenders are now out of touch, and declarer has time to knock out both diamond honors, making an overtrick.

However, if declarer is forced to take one of his sure spade winners at trick one, West can jump in with the diamond king when declarer leads that suit. When West returns his second spade, East's spades will be set up while he still has the diamond ace.

Of course, ruining *declarer's* communication is a technique that the defenders also must employ. Here is a simple example.

Dlr: South   ♠ 6 4
Vul: Both   ♡ 6 5 3
              ◊ A Q
              ♣ K J 10 7 6 3

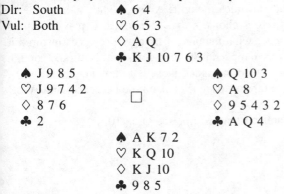

♠ J 9 8 5		♠ Q 10 3
♡ J 9 7 4 2	□	♡ A 8
◊ 8 7 6		◊ 9 5 4 3 2
♣ 2		♣ A Q 4

           ♠ A K 7 2
           ♡ K Q 10
           ◊ K J 10
           ♣ 9 8 5

South opened 1 NT and was raised to 3 NT. West led a heart to East's ace, but East knew that partner couldn't have an establishable suit plus an entry. Instead of returning a heart, East switched to diamonds, attacking declarer's entries. Declarer won in hand and finessed in clubs, but when East won the queen, another diamond play severed declarer's last link with dummy. East held up his club ace until the third round and exited with a spade—declarer had to lose two more tricks for down one.

In the 1979 Bermuda Bowl, Benito Garozzo of Italy produced a classic defense.

Dlr: South   ♠ Q J 7 3 2
Vul: Both   ♡ J 10 2
               ♢ A Q 8
               ♣ K J

♠ 8 4		♠ K 10 9 6 5
♡ Q 8 7 3	☐	♡ A 5
♢ 10 4		♢ 9 6 5
♣ A 7 6 4 2		♣ 8 5 3

               ♠ A
               ♡ K 9 6 4
               ♢ K J 7 3 2
               ♣ Q 10 9

At one table, Italy's South went down in 3 NT, adopting an inferior line of play. In the replay:

WEST	NORTH	EAST	SOUTH
Lauria	*Brachman*	*Garozzo*	*Passell*
			1 ♢
Pass	1 ♠	Pass	1 NT
Pass	2 ♣[1]	Pass	2 ♡
Pass	3 NT	All Pass	

[1] artificial force

West started the two of clubs (playing "attitude" leads). Declarer won and correctly cashed the spade ace, then went to the diamond queen and led the spade queen to East's king. What should East play now?

Even looking at all four hands, the winning defense is hardly obvious. Most Easts would return a club without much thought. A few might try the spade ten or a sneaky low heart. Garozzo's choice was a diamond—a play so full of subtlety that one is apt to ponder what manner of thought processes inspired it.

Declarer's transportation was damaged just the slightest bit. Naturally enough, he won the diamond ace and cashed the spade jack, not knowing about the 5-2 spade break. Garozzo now won three spade tricks and the heart ace, and West's club ace was the setting trick. No swing!

For more on getting declarer all tangled up, see Quiz 10.

Problems

1. Dlr: North
Vul: None

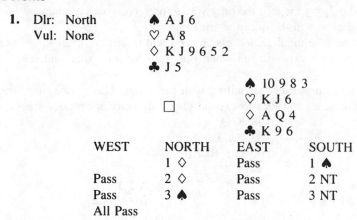

	WEST	NORTH	EAST	SOUTH
		1 ◇	Pass	1 ♠
	Pass	2 ◇	Pass	2 NT
	Pass	3 ♠	Pass	3 NT
	All Pass			

West, your partner, leads the five of hearts. Plan your defense.

2. Dlr: South
Vul: N-S

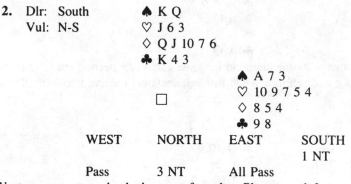

	WEST	NORTH	EAST	SOUTH
				1 NT
	Pass	3 NT	All Pass	

West, your partner, leads the two of spades. Plan your defense.

Solutions

1.

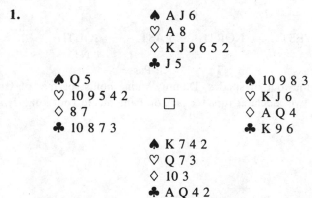

Declarer surely will play a low heart from dummy, and you need to insert the *jack*. On the bidding, West can have no more than a queen. If he has the heart queen, it doesn't matter which honor you play. But if partner's hearts are headed only by the ten, the only way to preserve your communication is to let declarer to win the queen at trick one.

When you take the diamond queen, you will return the heart king. Then maybe partner's hearts will run when you get in with the diamond ace.

2. Duck the first trick, signalling with the seven. This is one time when it would not be a good idea to expend your only entry at an early stage.

♠ K Q
♥ J 6 3
♦ Q J 10 7 6
♣ K 4 3

♠ J 9 4 2   ♠ A 7 3
♥ A 8 2   ♥ 10 9 7 5 4
♦ K 2   ♦ 8 5 4
♣ 10 7 6 5   ♣ 9 8

♠ 10 8 6 5
♥ K Q
♦ A 9 3
♣ A Q J 2

When partner wins the diamond king, he can lead a second spade. Now you take the ace and return a spade through declarer, for five tricks in all.

Problems

3. Dlr: South
Vul: Both

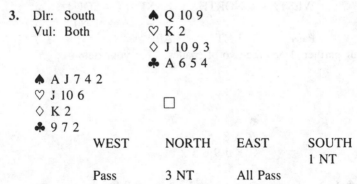

♠ Q 10 9
♥ K 2
♦ J 10 9 3
♣ A 6 5 4

♠ A J 7 4 2
♥ J 10 6
♦ K 2
♣ 9 7 2

WEST	NORTH	EAST	SOUTH
			1 NT
Pass	3 NT	All Pass	

You, West, lead the four of spades. Dummy's nine holds, partner playing the three. At trick two, declarer runs the jack of diamonds to your king. How do you continue?

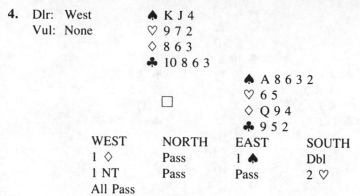

4. Dlr: West   ♠ K J 4
    Vul: None   ♡ 9 7 2
                 ◇ 8 6 3
                 ♣ 10 8 6 3

                         ♠ A 8 6 3 2
                □   ♡ 6 5
                         ◇ Q 9 4
                         ♣ 9 5 2

WEST	NORTH	EAST	SOUTH
1 ◇	Pass	1 ♠	Dbl
1 NT	Pass	Pass	2 ♡
All Pass			

West, your partner, leads the nine of spades, and declarer calls for dummy's king. How do you defend?

Solutions

3.   ♠ Q 10 9

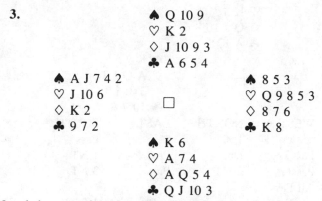

                 ♡ K 2
                 ◇ J 10 9 3
                 ♣ A 6 5 4

   ♠ A J 7 4 2   ♠ 8 5 3
   ♡ J 10 6   □   ♡ Q 9 8 5 3
   ◇ K 2   ◇ 8 7 6
   ♣ 9 7 2   ♣ K 8

               ♠ K 6
               ♡ A 7 4
               ◇ A Q 5 4
               ♣ Q J 10 3

Lead the two of spades. Even if partner has three spades and an entry, as you hope, conceding the second spade is the only way to set the contract.

A ducking play like this is easier to spot if you are declarer.

4. Play the spade eight to the first trick. Partner rebid 1 NT freely, so he can't have a singleton spade. He probably has a doubleton, plus an entry in trumps. You need to duck the first trick to keep communications for a subsequent ruff.

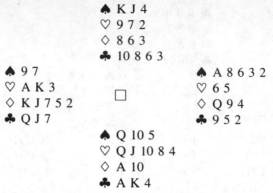

♠ K J 4
♡ 9 7 2
◇ 8 6 3
♣ 10 8 6 3

♠ 9 7   ♠ A 8 6 3 2
♡ A K 3   ♡ 6 5
◇ K J 7 5 2 ◇ Q 9 4
♣ Q J 7   ♣ 9 5 2

♠ Q 10 5
♡ Q J 10 8 4
◇ A 10
♣ A K 4

Correct defense beats the contract one trick.

Problems

5. Dlr: North   ♠ A Q 2
    Vul: N-S   ♡ K 4
                   ◇ Q J 10 8 6
                   ♣ A K 5

                          ♠ K 9 5
                          ♡ A Q J 7 5
                          ◇ 5 3
                          ♣ 10 7 6

WEST	NORTH	EAST	SOUTH
	1 ◇	1 ♡	Pass
Pass	Dbl	Pass	1 NT
Pass	2 NT	Pass	3 NT
All Pass			

West, your partner, leads the nine of hearts. Plan your defense.

6. Dlr: South   ♠ A 8 6
    Vul: Both   ♡ J 9 5 3
                   ◇ J 8 2
                   ♣ K Q 5

    ♠ K 9 5
    ♡ Q 10 6 2
    ◇ A Q 4 3
    ♣ 10 7

WEST	NORTH	EAST	SOUTH
			1 ◇
Pass	1 ♡	Pass	1 NT
Pass	2 NT	All Pass	

You, West, lead the five of spades. Dummy plays low, and East's queen wins. Declarer plays the jack on the two-of-spades return and ducks your king. Partner and declarer both follow to the third round of spades, dummy's ace winning. At trick four, declarer passes dummy's eight of diamonds to your queen, East playing the seven. What do you lead now?

Solutions

5. This deal is a relative of the second one in the introduction to this Quiz. You know declarer has one heart stopper, so you must duck the first trick completely to keep alive your chances of running the whole heart suit. The full deal is:

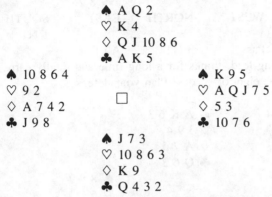

```
                    ♠ A Q 2
                    ♡ K 4
                    ◇ Q J 10 8 6
                    ♣ A K 5
  ♠ 10 8 6 4                        ♠ K 9 5
  ♡ 9 2                 □            ♡ A Q J 7 5
  ◇ A 7 4 2                         ◇ 5 3
  ♣ J 9 8                           ♣ 10 7 6
                    ♠ J 7 3
                    ♡ 10 8 6 3
                    ◇ K 9
                    ♣ Q 4 3 2
```

6. If you can find a way to get East in the lead, you should collect three spade tricks, his entry and two diamonds. But there is no time to waste—declarer is likely to have a five-card diamond suit, and he'll set up eight tricks if you defend passively.

There is no problem if partner has an ace, but he could have the heart king. In that case, you can't succeed by leading a low heart. With the nine a threat in dummy, you must lead the *queen*. The full deal:

```
                    ♠ A 8 6
                    ♡ J 9 5 3
                    ◇ J 8 2
                    ♣ K Q 5
  ♠ K 9 5                           ♠ Q 10 7 2
  ♡ Q 10 6 2            □            ♡ K 8 7
  ◇ A Q 4 3                         ◇ 7
  ♣ 10 7                            ♣ J 9 8 4 3
                    ♠ J 4 3
                    ♡ A 4
                    ◇ K 10 9 6 5
                    ♣ A 6 2
```

This is the Deschapelles Coup, the sacrifice of a high card to create an entry in partner's hand. Note what will happen if you lead a low heart.

Problems

7. Dlr: South
Vul: N-S

♠ A J
♡ J 10 7 6
◇ Q 5 4
♣ K 4 3 2

♠ K 10 9 6 4
♡ 8 5
◇ J 10 9 7
♣ 8 7

□

WEST	NORTH	EAST	SOUTH
			1 NT
Pass	3 NT	All Pass	

West, on opening lead, thinks for a long time and finally earns your favor by producing the eight of spades. Plan your defense.

8. Dlr: West
Vul: E-W

♠ A K 6 3
♡ J 9 4
◇ A 7 5
♣ Q 6 2

♠ 8 5 2
♡ 5
◇ 9 6 3 2
♣ 10 8 7 4 3

□

WEST	NORTH	EAST	SOUTH
1 ♡	Pass	Pass	1 ♠
Dbl	Redbl	2 ♣	Pass
Pass	3 ♠	All Pass	

West, your partner, leads the king, queen, and ace of hearts. Plan your defense.

Solutions

7.

♠ A J
♡ J 10 7 6
◇ Q 5 4
♣ K 4 3 2

♠ 8 5 2
♡ A Q 4 2
◇ 8 3 2
♣ Q 10 9

♠ K 10 9 6 4
♡ 8 5
◇ J 10 9 7
♣ 8 7

□

♠ Q 7 3
♡ K 9 3
◇ A K 6
♣ A J 6 5

Still another communication-saving hand. If East spends the spade king at trick one, the defense is finished. See also Problem 5.

Below are a few other positions where an unusual play by third hand is necessary to make sure communication is preserved. In each situation, the contract is notrump. East, with only one entry, places declarer with a double stopper in the suit led.

$$A\ 5\ 4$$
$$9\ 3 \qquad \square \qquad K\ J\ 10\ 8\ 2$$
$$Q\ 7\ 6$$

West leads the nine, dummy ducks, East plays the eight.

$$7\ 6$$
$$5\ 4 \qquad \square \qquad K\ Q\ J\ 9\ 8$$
$$A\ 10\ 3\ 2$$

West leads the five and East plays the eight.

$$Q\ 6$$
$$7\ 2 \qquad \square \qquad K\ J\ 9\ 5\ 4\ 3$$
$$A\ 10\ 8$$

West leads the seven and East plays the nine on dummy's six. If declarer puts up dummy's queen, East must play the nine again.

$$A\ 8\ 5\ 3$$
$$7\ 6 \qquad \square \qquad K\ Q\ 10\ 4\ 2$$
$$J\ 9$$

West leads the seven, dummy plays the three, East plays the four.

8.
$$\spadesuit\ A\ K\ 6\ 3$$
$$\heartsuit\ J\ 9\ 4$$
$$\diamondsuit\ A\ 7\ 5$$
$$\clubsuit\ Q\ 6\ 2$$

$$\spadesuit\ 9 \qquad\qquad\qquad \spadesuit\ 8\ 5\ 2$$
$$\heartsuit\ A\ K\ Q\ 7\ 6 \qquad\qquad \heartsuit\ 5$$
$$\diamondsuit\ K\ J\ 10\ 4 \quad \square \quad \diamondsuit\ 9\ 6\ 3\ 2$$
$$\clubsuit\ A\ J\ 9 \qquad\qquad\qquad \clubsuit\ 10\ 8\ 7\ 4\ 3$$

$$\spadesuit\ Q\ J\ 10\ 7\ 4$$
$$\heartsuit\ 10\ 8\ 3\ 2$$
$$\diamondsuit\ Q\ 8$$
$$\clubsuit\ K\ 5$$

This deal, which was reported by Alfred Sheinwold, is from an old U.S. Team Trial. The deal was played several times, and South usually landed in three spades. At most tables, West cashed three heart tricks and played a fourth heart. Declarer ruffed high, came to the spade queen, and led a low club. West had to let dummy's queen win. Now declarer ran his all his trumps. The end position, with West still to play to trick ten, was:

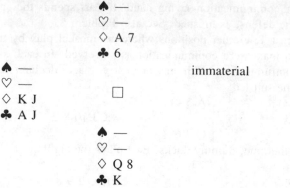

```
            ♠ —
            ♡ —
            ◇ A 7
            ♣ 6
♠ —                        immaterial
♡ —
◇ K J          ☐
♣ A J
            ♠ —
            ♡ —
            ◇ Q 8
            ♣ K
```

If West threw a diamond, declarer would score both the ace and queen. If West threw a club, declarer would exit with a club for an endplay.

At one table, many-time world champion Bob Hamman sat East, and he defeated the contract expediently. At trick three, he simply ruffed partner's heart ace with an otherwise worthless trump and returned a diamond. Five tricks for the defense were ensured.

Problems

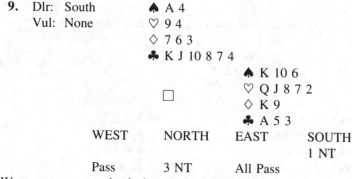

```
9.  Dlr: South      ♠ A 4
    Vul: None       ♡ 9 4
                    ◇ 7 6 3
                    ♣ K J 10 8 7 4
                            ♠ K 10 6
                            ♡ Q J 8 7 2
                ☐           ◇ K 9
                            ♣ A 5 3
        WEST    NORTH   EAST        SOUTH
                                    1 NT
        Pass    3 NT    All Pass
```

West, your partner, leads the queen of diamonds. You overtake with the king, and declarer allows it to hold. What do you lead at trick two?

10. Dlr: East   ♠ K 9 6 2
     Vul: E-W   ♡ 7 6 5
                 ◇ 10 6 3
                 ♣ A J 3

                               ♠ A Q 4
                       □   ♡ 10 8 4 2
                               ◇ J 9 2
                               ♣ Q 5 4

WEST	NORTH	EAST	SOUTH
		Pass	1 ◇
Pass	1 ♠	Pass	2 ♡
Pass	2 NT	Pass	3 ♡
Pass	4 ♣	Pass	4 NT
Pass	5 ◇	Pass	6 ◇
All Pass			

West, your partner, leads the five of spades—two, queen, jack. How do you continue?

Solutions

9. There is no urgency to return a diamond—on the bidding, partner can have no other face cards besides the diamond queen and jack. Shift gears and try to kill dummy's spade entry to the clubs. Here, though, only the lead of the spade *king* is good enough to knock the entry out in time.

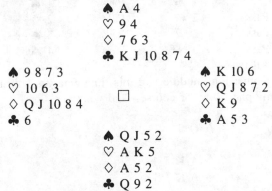

Your play gives declarer three easy spade tricks, but snatches five club tricks away. Not a bad trade. This play, sacrificing a high honor to dislodge declarer's entry, is called a Merrimac Coup. For another example, see Quiz 10.

10. The bidding (in particular, declarer's willingness to use Blackwood) mark declarer with 1-5-6-1 pattern. The setting trick will be available in hearts if partner has a singleton honor, but only if you knock declarer's entry out of dummy before he learns that a second-round finesse against you will be needed. Therefore, return a club at trick two. The full deal is:

$$
\begin{array}{c}
\spadesuit\ K\ 9\ 6\ 2 \\
\heartsuit\ 7\ 6\ 5 \\
\diamondsuit\ 10\ 6\ 3 \\
\clubsuit\ A\ J\ 3
\end{array}
$$

♠ 10 8 7 5 3		♠ A Q 4
♡ Q	□	♡ 10 8 4 2
◇ 4		◇ J 9 2
♣ K 10 8 7 6 2		♣ Q 5 4

$$
\begin{array}{c}
\spadesuit\ J \\
\heartsuit\ A\ K\ J\ 9\ 3 \\
\diamondsuit\ A\ K\ Q\ 8\ 7\ 5 \\
\clubsuit\ 9
\end{array}
$$

Problems

11. Dlr: North
    Vul: N-S

$$
\begin{array}{c}
\spadesuit\ 5 \\
\heartsuit\ J\ 7\ 5\ 3 \\
\diamondsuit\ Q\ 5 \\
\clubsuit\ A\ K\ J\ 8\ 6\ 4
\end{array}
$$

$$
□\qquad
\begin{array}{c}
\spadesuit\ A\ 3 \\
\heartsuit\ Q\ 10\ 9\ 4 \\
\diamondsuit\ A\ 7\ 4 \\
\clubsuit\ 10\ 7\ 5\ 3
\end{array}
$$

WEST	NORTH	EAST	SOUTH
	1 ♣	Pass	1 ♠
Pass	2 ♣	Pass	2 ◇
Pass	2 ♡	Pass	3 ♠
Pass	3 NT	Pass	4 ♠
All Pass			

West goes into another long huddle and this time emerges with the two of diamonds. Dummy plays low, of course. And you?

12. Dlr: South
    Vul: None

$$
\begin{array}{c}
\spadesuit\ Q\ 5 \\
\heartsuit\ J\ 3 \\
\diamondsuit\ A\ K\ 5\ 4 \\
\clubsuit\ A\ K\ J\ 8\ 4
\end{array}
$$

♠ K J 8 4 2	
♡ Q 10 7 4	□
◇ 9 2	
♣ 10 9	

WEST	NORTH	EAST	SOUTH
			1 ♡
Pass	2 ♣	Pass	2 ♡
Pass	3 ◇	Pass	3 NT
Pass	5 ♡	Pass	5 ♠
Pass	6 ♡	All Pass	

You, West, mentally flip a coin and lead the ten of clubs. Declarer wins in hand with the queen (East contributing the seven), thinks for a while, and tables the two of hearts. You put up the queen, and partner follows with the nine. How do you continue?

Solutions

11. On the bidding and opening lead, declarer is likely to have four diamonds and seven spades. He must have at least one heart, else West's opening lead would have been the heart ace. So a club void in declarer's hand is quite probable—and if he does have a club, the contract may be impossible to beat. Declarer is far more likely than West to have the diamond king, so your correct play at trick one is the *seven*, denying declarer an entry to dummy with the queen. The full deal:

```
              ♠ 5
              ♡ J 7 5 3
              ◇ Q 5
              ♣ A K J 8 6 4
♠ 9 8 6                        ♠ A 3
♡ K 6 2                        ♡ Q 10 9 4
◇ J 9 6 2          □           ◇ A 7 4
♣ Q 9 2                        ♣ 10 7 5 3
              ♠ K Q J 10 7 4 2
              ♡ A 8
              ◇ K 10 8 3
              ♣ —
```

The best play makes a two-trick difference this time. If you win the diamond ace and shift to a heart, declarer makes five. But ducking the first trick will win two diamonds, a heart, and a spade for the defense.

12.

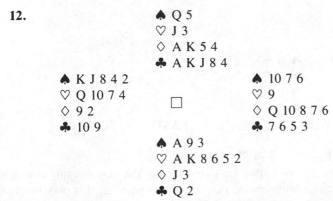

```
              ♠ Q 5
              ♡ J 3
              ◇ A K 5 4
              ♣ A K J 8 4
♠ K J 8 4 2                    ♠ 10 7 6
♡ Q 10 7 4         □           ♡ 9
◇ 9 2                          ◇ Q 10 8 7 6
♣ 10 9                         ♣ 7 6 5 3
              ♠ A 9 3
              ♡ A K 8 6 5 2
              ◇ J 3
              ♣ Q 2
```

Your best chance is to return the king of spades. Declarer will win the ace and play a heart to the jack, but then he will face the problem of getting back to his hand to draw the rest of the trumps. If his pattern is 3-6-2-2 without the queen of diamonds, he can't avoid losing the setting trick on an overruff.

Quiz 15

Talk to Partner: Defensive Signals

Most readers will be familiar with the three types of standard defensive signals. I list them here according to the priority of their use.

1. *Attitude* signals encourage or discourage the lead of a suit. A high card encourages, a low one shows apathy, discourages or, in some situations, may demand a shift. Attitude is shown when discarding or when partner is leading a suit.

2. *Count* signals tell partner how many cards you have in a suit. A high-low sequence of plays shows an even number of cards, low-high shows an odd number. With rare exceptions, this signal is used as *declarer* leads a suit.

3. *Suit-preference* signals, which arise only in special situations, are unusual in that they convey a message about a suit other than the one being played. Under the right circumstances, the play of an *unusually* high card draws attention to a high-ranking suit; an *unusually* low card shows interest in a low-ranking suit.

Suit-preference signals, though extremely useful, often are overused or abused. In fact, good judgment is needed to use *any* signal efficiently.

Dlr: East
Vul: None

```
              ♠ A J 7
              ♡ K 6 4 3
              ◇ K Q 10 7
              ♣ Q 5
♠ 9 8 4 2                      ♠ K Q 10
♡ 5                            ♡ 8 7
◇ 9 6 4 3          □          ◇ A 8
♣ A 9 6 3                      ♣ K J 10 7 4 2
              ♠ 6 5 3
              ♡ A Q J 10 9 2
              ◇ J 5 2
              ♣ 8
```

WEST	NORTH	EAST	SOUTH
		1 ♣	2 ♡
Pass	4 ♡	All Pass	

If West leads the ace of clubs, East should play the discouraging *two*. Since East obviously has a wide choice of cards to signal with, this play practically orders West to lead something else. And spades is the obvious suit to switch to.

Principle: The purpose of a signal is to *direct the defense*, not to confirm or deny certain high cards. We will see this principle applied over and over.

Dlr: South   ♠ J 9 2
Vul: N-S   ♡ J 10 3
             ◇ K Q 4
             ♣ Q 7 6 3

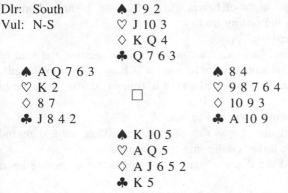

♠ A Q 7 6 3   ♠ 8 4
♡ K 2   ♡ 9 8 7 6 4
◇ 8 7   ◇ 10 9 3
♣ J 8 4 2   ♣ A 10 9

             ♠ K 10 5
             ♡ A Q 5
             ◇ A J 6 5 2
             ♣ K 5

On this deal, E-W can employ the count signal. West leads the six of spades against 3 NT. Declarer wins the jack on dummy, dropping a sneaky ten from his hand. He then passes the heart jack to West's king.

Q: How does West know not to lay down the spade ace now?

A: East should have played the spade eight at trick one, denying three cards.

(Yes, attitude signals take precedence over count. But East's attitude about spades is known when he can't beat dummy's jack, so this becomes a count situation.) Knowing declarer still has the guarded spade king, West can shift and avoid giving up the ninth trick.

A different procedure is used when giving count in the trump suit—using a high trump to signal a doubleton might be wasteful. Play high-low in trumps to show three (or five).

Here is a deal that illustrates the use of this *trump echo* as well as a common suit-preference situation.

Dlr: West   ♠ J 4
Vul: Both   ♡ K 9 4 3
            ◇ A K Q 4
            ♣ 6 5 3

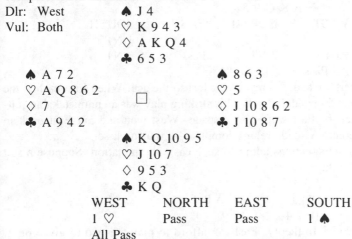

♠ A 7 2   ♠ 8 6 3
♡ A Q 8 6 2   ♡ 5
◇ 7   ◇ J 10 8 6 2
♣ A 9 4 2   ♣ J 10 8 7

           ♠ K Q 10 9 5
           ♡ J 10 7
           ◇ 9 5 3
           ♣ K Q

WEST	NORTH	EAST	SOUTH
1 ♡	Pass	Pass	1 ♠
All Pass			

N-S bid very conservatively—as it turned out, they'd have been as well off in 3 NT, even with a club lead.

West led his singleton diamond, and East dropped the jack when dummy won. East played the six on the first trump lead, and West won. He played ace and queen of hearts, East ruffing with the three. The play continued with the ten of diamonds, ruffed; the eight of hearts, ruffed by East; another diamond ruff. The ace of clubs was the setting trick.

Let's reexamine the defenders' plays:

Trick one: East's diamond jack was suit preference, suggesting the lead of the higher-ranking of the other suits (except trumps, which normally is excluded).

Trick two: East followed with his middle spot in trumps, starting an echo to show the count.

Trick three: West obediently switched to hearts.

Trick four: West's heart queen was suit preference, asking for a diamond return. East ruffed with the three, confirming three trumps.

Trick five: East returned the diamond ten, suit preference for another heart play.

Trick six: West returned the heart eight (the highest one he had left), suit preference for diamonds.

Here is suit preference used at notrump.

Dlr: South
Vul: None

```
               ♠ 8 6 5 3
               ♡ K 5
               ◇ A Q 7 4
               ♣ 8 7 4
♠ A Q 10                    ♠ 9 4 2
♡ J 9 7 6 2       ☐        ♡ A Q 8 3
◇ 8 3                      ◇ J 10 6 5
♣ 10 6 3                   ♣ J 2
               ♠ K J 7
               ♡ 10 4
               ◇ K 9 2
               ♣ A K Q 9 5
```

WEST	NORTH	EAST	SOUTH
			1 NT
Pass	2 NT	Pass	3 NT
All Pass			

West led the heart six and dummy's king lost to the ace. When East cashed the heart queen, West dropped the *jack*. This striking play was an unmistakable suit-preference signal, so East shifted to a spade. West won and put East back in with the heart eight. A spade return completed a four-trick set.

Not all signaling situations admit to such easy interpretation. Suppose a suit is distributed like this:

```
          J 9 3
K Q 6 5    ☐     A 8 2
          10 7 4
```

West leads the king. In theory, East can afford to play the two to give count, since West will know who has the ace when the king holds the trick. (With the jack in dummy, declarer would not duck if he had the ace.) But what if East wants partner to shift? This is one of many positions that require partnership discussion.

Most signaling headaches result from confusion over suit preference.

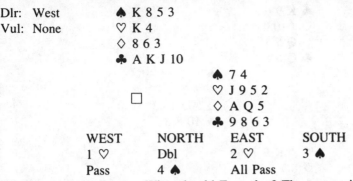

Dlr: West   ♠ K 8 5 3
Vul: None   ♡ K 4
        ◊ 8 6 3
        ♣ A K J 10

                ♠ 7 4
                ♡ J 9 5 2
        □   ◊ A Q 5
                ♣ 9 8 6 3

WEST	NORTH	EAST	SOUTH
1 ♡	Dbl	2 ♡	3 ♠
Pass	4 ♠	All Pass	

West leads the heart ace. What should East play? The answer is based on the
priorities with which the three types of signals are used. Attitude, we said,
always takes precedence. If East sticks to that principle, he will play the *two*.
When West looks at dummy, the right shift will be apparent.

Some players like suit preference so much that they would lead a *club* when
East played his lowest heart. This is contrary to our principles (not to mention
illogical, looking at the strong clubs in dummy).

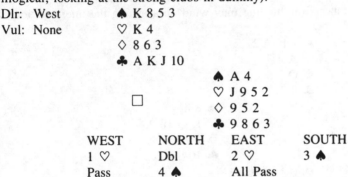

Dlr: West   ♠ K 8 5 3
Vul: None   ♡ K 4
        ◊ 8 6 3
        ♣ A K J 10

                ♠ A 4
                ♡ J 9 5 2
        □   ◊ 9 5 2
                ♣ 9 8 6 3

WEST	NORTH	EAST	SOUTH
1 ♡	Dbl	2 ♡	3 ♠
Pass	4 ♠	All Pass	

Same bidding, dummy and lead. This time, East should play the *nine*, suggesting
a heart continuation. True, dummy can win, but a passive defense could very
well be best. Therefore, there is no reason to hit the suit-preference panic
button—attitude still applies. If East can't stand the obvious switch to a diamond,
he *must not* play a low heart.

How about this hand?

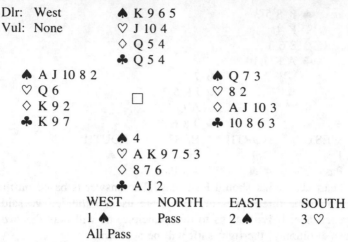

```
Dlr: West          ♠ K 9 6 5
Vul: None          ♡ J 10 4
                   ◇ Q 5 4
                   ♣ Q 5 4
   ♠ A J 10 8 2              ♠ Q 7 3
   ♡ Q 6                     ♡ 8 2
   ◇ K 9 2         □         ◇ A J 10 3
   ♣ K 9 7                   ♣ 10 8 6 3
                   ♠ 4
                   ♡ A K 9 7 5 3
                   ◇ 8 7 6
                   ♣ A J 2
```

WEST	NORTH	EAST	SOUTH
1 ♠	Pass	2 ♠	3 ♡
All Pass			

If West leads the spade ace, East should play the queen. A suit-preference signal is needed here. Declarer is about to get a discard on the spade king; but a look at dummy suggests no *obvious* switch, so attitude alone won't get the job done.

In many instances, the bidding may wind up affecting the interpretation of your signals.

```
Dlr: South         ♠ J 10 6 2
Vul: ?             ♡ A 4 3
                   ◇ Q 7 5
                   ♣ 8 7 2
   ♠ 9 3                     ♠ 8 4
   ♡ 8 7                     ♡ K Q 10 2
   ◇ A K 10 6 2    □         ◇ J 9 4 3
   ♣ K J 5 3                 ♣ 10 9 6
                   ♠ A K Q 7 5
                   ♡ J 9 6 5
                   ◇ 8
                   ♣ A Q 4
```

Suppose both sides are vulnerable, and the bidding is:

WEST	NORTH	EAST	SOUTH
			1 ♠
2 ◇	2 ♠	Pass	3 ♠
All Pass			

When West leads the diamond ace, East must play the three. Any other card might look like the beginning of a high-low with a doubleton and induce a fatal diamond continuation. There is no way East can show count here—West can only interpret his partner's play as attitude.

Should West interpret East's low-diamond play as asking for a shift to dummy's weak suit, clubs? No, dummy is flat and weak, so *no* shift is urgently needed. (Compare with the previous hand, where dummy had very strong clubs.) West should shift to a trump.

Now suppose neither side is vulnerable, and the bidding is:

WEST	NORTH	EAST	SOUTH
			1 ♠
2 ◊	2 ♠	3 ◊	3 ♠
All Pass			

This time East can play the jack or nine (count), since West cannot mistake him for a doubleton.

West may or may not find the heart shift—he is likely to exit passively with a trump again. However, say only N-S are vulnerable and the bidding is:

WEST	NORTH	EAST	SOUTH
			1 ♠
2 ◊	2 ♠	4 ◊[1]	4 ♠
All Pass			

[1]Preemptive, suggesting a sacrifice

Now East is known to have four diamonds, so his play of a high diamond can have suit-preference significance.

The problems in this Quiz include several extensions of the various signals.

Problems

1. Dlr: South   ♠ J 6 3
   Vul: E-W   ♡ 7 6 3
                 ◊ K 10 3
                 ♣ Q 8 6 3

   ♠ 4
   ♡ A K 9 4 2
   ◊ Q 7 2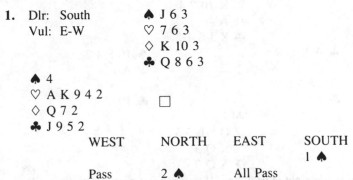
   ♣ J 9 5 2

WEST	NORTH	EAST	SOUTH
			1 ♠
Pass	2 ♠	All Pass	

You, West, lead the heart ace—three, five, eight. How do you continue?

2. Dlr: South   ♠ J 6
   Vul: None   ♡ K 10 7 4
                 ◊ A 4
                 ♣ K J 6 4 2

                          ♠ 10 8 4 2
                          ♡ A J 9
                  ☐   ◊ 10 9 6
                          ♣ 10 5 3

WEST	NORTH	EAST	SOUTH
			1 ♡
1 ♠	3 ♡	Pass	4 ♡
All Pass			

West, your partner, leads the spade ace. Plan your defense.

195

Solutions

1. Continue with the heart king. This is very unlikely to cost. True, East played his lowest heart, but when the contract is only two and no switch is attractive, a low card may be noncommittal. In fact, the full deal is:

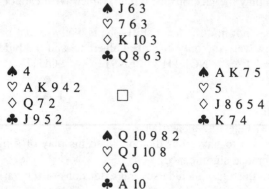

```
              ♠ J 6 3
              ♡ 7 6 3
              ◇ K 10 3
              ♣ Q 8 6 3
♠ 4                          ♠ A K 7 5
♡ A K 9 4 2       □          ♡ 5
◇ Q 7 2                      ◇ J 8 6 5 4
♣ J 9 5 2                    ♣ K 7 4
              ♠ Q 10 9 8 2
              ♡ Q J 10 8
              ◇ A 9
              ♣ A 10
```

Three rounds of hearts (West should lead the nine at trick three to discourage a club return) and careful defense thereafter will beat the contract.

2.

```
              ♠ J 6
              ♡ K 10 7 4
              ◇ A 4
              ♣ K J 6 4 2
♠ A K Q 9 5                  ♠ 10 8 4 2
♡ 2               □          ♡ A J 9
◇ J 8 7 5 2                  ◇ 10 9 6
♣ 8 7                       ♣ 10 5 3
              ♠ 7 3
              ♡ Q 8 6 5 3
              ◇ K Q 3
              ♣ A Q 9
```

Play the spade eight at trick one. If you can get partner to cash another spade, the hand is down. If you play a low spade, partner might switch to diamonds.

Problems

3. Dlr: South
Vul: N-S

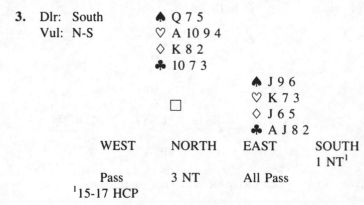

```
              ♠ Q 7 5
              ♡ A 10 9 4
              ◇ K 8 2
              ♣ 10 7 3
                            ♠ J 9 6
              □             ♡ K 7 3
                            ◇ J 6 5
                            ♣ A J 8 2
```

WEST	NORTH	EAST	SOUTH
			1 NT[1]
Pass	3 NT	All Pass	

[1]15-17 HCP

West, your partner, leads the two of spades. Declarer puts up dummy's queen, and you signal with the nine. Declarer leads a diamond to the queen, West playing the three, and leads the queen of hearts—two, four, king. What do you return?

4. Dlr: South ♠ J 5 3
   Vul: E-W   ♡ 8 4
               ◇ A Q 10 8 4
               ♣ J 4 3

                              ♠ Q 9 7 4 2
                              ♡ K J 9
                    □   ◇ K 2·
                              ♣ 9 8 7

        WEST   NORTH   EAST   SOUTH
                                        1 NT
        Pass   3 NT   All Pass

West, your partner, leads the five of hearts—four, king, two. You lead the heart jack—six, three, eight. Next, the nine of hearts—ace, queen, club three. Declarer leads the nine of diamonds and ducks it to your king. What do you return?

Solutions

3. Declarer would have played low from dummy at trick one if his spades were K-x-x, so he must have the ace. (There aren't enough HCP for partner to have both the ace and king.) Partner would give count on the diamond and heart plays, since it is safe to do so and it might be necessary. He showed an odd number of cards in each red suit, so declarer has three heart tricks and four diamonds, for nine tricks in all. You must shift to the club jack in desperation.

                    ♠ Q 7 5
                    ♡ A 10 9 4
                    ◇ K 8 2
                    ♣ 10 7 3
   ♠ K 10 4 2   ♠ J 9 6
   ♡ 8 6 2   ♡ K 7 3
   ◇ 9 7 3   □   ◇ J 6 5
   ♣ K 9 4   ♣ A J 8 2
                    ♠ A 8 3
                    ♡ Q J 5
                    ◇ A Q 10 4
                    ♣ Q 6 5

This deal is drawn from *Partnership Defense in Bridge* by Kit Woolsey, the best treatment of defensive signals available. When this book appeared in 1980, I thought it was the most important work on defensive play since Hugh Kelsey's *Killing Defense* was published in 1966.

4.

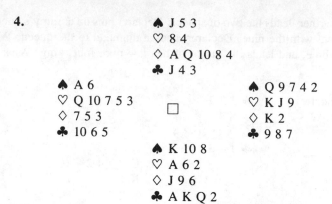

        ♠ J 5 3
        ♡ 8 4
        ◇ A Q 10 8 4
        ♣ J 4 3

♠ A 6   ♠ Q 9 7 4 2
♡ Q 10 7 5 3   ♡ K J 9
◇ 7 5 3   ◇ K 2
♣ 10 6 5   ♣ 9 8 7

        ♠ K 10 8
        ♡ A 6 2
        ◇ J 9 6
        ♣ A K Q 2

Shift to a spade. When declarer took the heart ace at trick three, all three of West's remaining hearts were good, so this is a suit-preference situation. The *queen* indicated an entry in the highest-ranking suit.

Problems

5. Dlr: West
    Vul: N-S

        ♠ Q
        ♡ A J 7 3
        ◇ Q 10 7 4
        ♣ K Q 6 5

                 ♠ K 9 5 3
                 ♡ 8
                 ◇ A 8 6 2
                 ♣ J 10 7 3

WEST	NORTH	EAST	SOUTH
2 ♠	Dbl	5 ♠	6 ♡
All Pass			

West, your partner, leads the spade ace. What do you play as East?

6. Dlr: South
    Vul: Both

        ♠ J 6 3
        ♡ Q 7 3
        ◇ K 7 3
        ♣ K J 10 4

♠ 10 9 8 7
♡ 8 5 2
◇ 10 8 5 2
♣ A 7

WEST	NORTH	EAST	SOUTH
			1 NT
Pass	3 NT	All Pass	

You, West, lead the ten of spades. Partner plays the two, and declarer wins the queen. The club three is led to the seven, jack, and two. Next comes the club four to the nine, queen, and your ace. How do you continue?

Solutions

5.

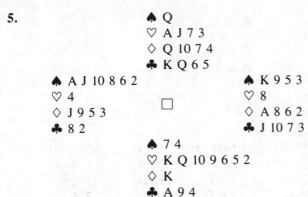

East should play the king of spades. If no diamond shift is forthcoming, and declarer squeezes East in clubs and diamonds to make the slam, all East can do is apologize for not having had a higher card with which to signal.

6. East gave count on the first round of clubs, but his second club play may be taken as suit preference. Shift to a heart.

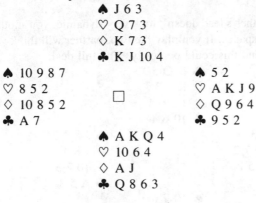

Problems

7. Dlr: West
Vul: None

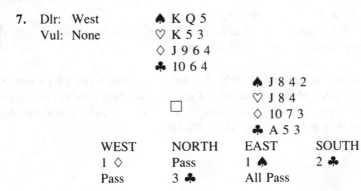

WEST	NORTH	EAST	SOUTH
1 ◇	Pass	1 ♠	2 ♣
Pass	3 ♣	All Pass	

West leads the spade ace. What do you play as East?

8. Dlr: North   ♠ K 5
      Vul: N-S   ♡ J 9 6 4
                    ◇ K 7 3
                    ♣ K 10 7 4

♠ 10 2
♡ K Q 8 3
◇ J 6   □
♣ A 8 6 5 2

WEST	NORTH	EAST	SOUTH
	Pass	Pass	1 ♠
Pass	1 NT	Pass	2 ◇
Pass	2 NT	Pass	3 ♠
Pass	4 ♠	Pass	5 ♠
Pass	6 ♠	All Pass	

You, West, lead the king of hearts—four, ten, ace. At trick two, declarer leads the three of clubs. Do you win or duck? (Quickly!)

Solutions

7. Though partner's lead doesn't look very dynamic, you should encourage with the eight of spades. If you play the two, partner will think you can stand a red-suit shift, and this could be costly. The full deal:

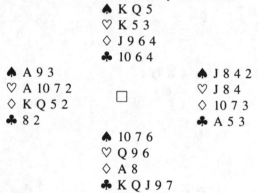

            ♠ K Q 5
            ♡ K 5 3
            ◇ J 9 6 4
            ♣ 10 6 4

♠ A 9 3   ♠ J 8 4 2
♡ A 10 7 2   ♡ J 8 4
◇ K Q 5 2   □   ◇ 10 7 3
♣ 8 2   ♣ A 5 3

            ♠ 10 7 6
            ♡ Q 9 6
            ◇ A 8
            ♣ K Q J 9 7

Declarer might manage a ninth trick in any case, but a diamond or heart shift at trick two makes it especially easy for him.

8. In a cashout situation, a defender may give count when his partner has led. Partner's ten of hearts was meant to show an even number (surely four on the bidding), so there is no heart trick for you to cash. Duck the club, hoping declarer is 6-1-4-2 and has a club guess.

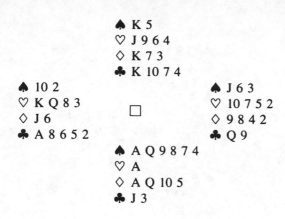

♠ K 5
♡ J 9 6 4
◇ K 7 3
♣ K 10 7 4

♠ 10 2
♡ K Q 8 3
◇ J 6
♣ A 8 6 5 2

♠ J 6 3
♡ 10 7 5 2
◇ 9 8 4 2
♣ Q 9

♠ A Q 9 8 7 4
♡ A
◇ A Q 10 5
♣ J 3

Problems

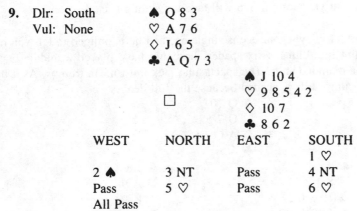

9. Dlr: South
Vul: None

♠ Q 8 3
♡ A 7 6
◇ J 6 5
♣ A Q 7 3

♠ J 10 4
♡ 9 8 5 4 2
◇ 10 7
♣ 8 6 2

WEST	NORTH	EAST	SOUTH
			1 ♡
2 ♠	3 NT	Pass	4 NT
Pass	5 ♡	Pass	6 ♡
All Pass			

West, your partner, leads the king of spades (king from ace-king vs. a slam).
What do you play as East?

10. Dlr: South
Vul: Both

♠ Q 10
♡ Q 7 5 3
◇ A Q J 5 3
♣ 6 5

♠ A
♡ 8 4 2
◇ 10 8 6 2
♣ J 10 7 4 3

WEST	NORTH	EAST	SOUTH
			1 NT
Pass	2 ♣	Pass	2 ♠
Pass	3 NT	Pass	4 ♡
All Pass			

You, West, lead the spade ace—ten, jack, four. How do you continue?

9.

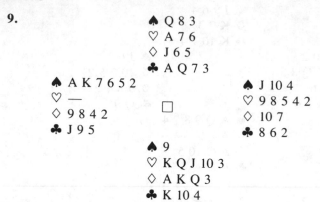

♠ Q 8 3
♡ A 7 6
◇ J 6 5
♣ A Q 7 3

♠ A K 7 6 5 2
♡ —
◇ 9 8 4 2
♣ J 9 5

♠ J 10 4
♡ 9 8 5 4 2
◇ 10 7
♣ 8 6 2

♠ 9
♡ K Q J 10 3
◇ A K Q 3
♣ K 10 4

Play the spade ten so partner will continue with his spade king. Declarer will ruff this, but your long trump will take the setting trick.

10. Partner knows your ace is singleton, and he is obliged to tell you how to put him in. With his six spades, he could have played a middle one to suggest a diamond shift. The spectacular jack must mean trumps. As it happens, a trump shift is needed because the full deal is:

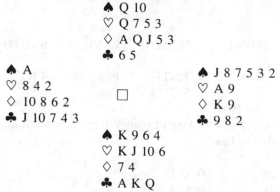

♠ Q 10
♡ Q 7 5 3
◇ A Q J 5 3
♣ 6 5

♠ A
♡ 8 4 2
◇ 10 8 6 2
♣ J 10 7 4 3

♠ J 8 7 5 3 2
♡ A 9
◇ K 9
♣ 9 8 2

♠ K 9 6 4
♡ K J 10 6
◇ 7 4
♣ A K Q

If you switch to a diamond, declarer goes up with the ace and cashes three clubs, pitching the spade queen. However he continues, the defense is helpless.

Problems

11. Dlr: South   ♠ K 6 4
      Vul: N-S   ♡ 6 5 3
                 ◇ K Q J 10 4
                 ♣ 6 4

♠ 10 9 8 5 2
♡ K 10 2
◇ A   □
♣ K 10 7 2

WEST	NORTH	EAST	SOUTH
			1 NT
Pass	3 NT	All Pass	

You, West, lead the ten of spades to the four, three, and jack. At trick two, declarer tables the three of diamonds. You take your ace, partner playing the nine. How do you continue?

12. Dlr: South   ♠ 7 6
      Vul: N-S   ♡ Q 7 3
                 ◇ J 6 3
                 ♣ Q 10 8 4 2

                 ♠ 10
      □   ♡ A J 9 5
                 ◇ Q 9 8 5
                 ♣ K J 6 5

WEST	NORTH	EAST	SOUTH
			2 ♣
Pass	2 ◇	Pass	2 ♠
Pass	2 NT	Pass	4 ♠
All Pass			

West, your partner, leads the seven of clubs—dummy ducks, and your jack forces declarer's ace. Declarer plays off the four top trumps, partner following with the five, four, three, and two while you shed your three fives. Next the nine of clubs is led. Partner follows and you take your king. What do you return?

Solutions

11. When declarer obviously will have no trouble running diamonds, it makes no sense for East to show count. The diamond nine should be suit preference, so shift to hearts.

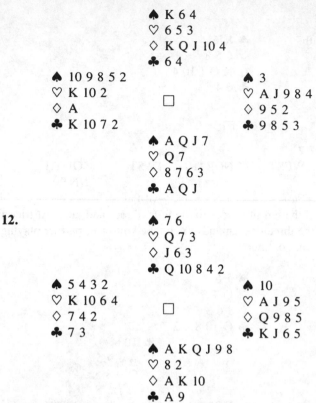

```
                    ♠ K 6 4
                    ♡ 6 5 3
                    ◇ K Q J 10 4
                    ♣ 6 4
     ♠ 10 9 8 5 2                    ♠ 3
     ♡ K 10 2                        ♡ A J 9 8 4
     ◇ A              □             ◇ 9 5 2
     ♣ K 10 7 2                      ♣ 9 8 5 3
                    ♠ A Q J 7
                    ♡ Q 7
                    ◇ 8 7 6 3
                    ♣ A Q J
```

12.
```
                    ♠ 7 6
                    ♡ Q 7 3
                    ◇ J 6 3
                    ♣ Q 10 8 4 2
     ♠ 5 4 3 2                       ♠ 10
     ♡ K 10 6 4                      ♡ A J 9 5
     ◇ 7 4 2          □             ◇ Q 9 8 5
     ♣ 7 3                           ♣ K J 6 5
                    ♠ A K Q J 9 8
                    ♡ 8 2
                    ◇ A K 10
                    ♣ A 9
```

Lead a low heart. Declarer won't have less than six spades on this bidding, so West wasn't showing count with his high-low play in trumps—he was improvising a suit-preference signal. How else could he suggest which red suit you should lead if you won a club trick?

Problems

13. Dlr: South
Vul: E-W

```
                    ♠ A 4
                    ♡ K Q 7 4
                    ◇ 7 6 3
                    ♣ J 6 5 2
     ♠ J 9 5 2
     ♡ A 5 3
     ◇ J 9 5 2        □
     ♣ 8 3
```

WEST	NORTH	EAST	SOUTH
			1 NT
Pass	2 ♣	Pass	2 ◇
Pass	3 NT	All Pass	

Declarer ducks your spade-two opening lead to East's king, and the three of spades is returned to dummy's ace. Declarer has followed with the six and ten. At trick three, a heart is led to the eight and jack, and you duck. Next comes the heart six. How do you defend?

14. Dlr: East   ♠ 6 5
    Vul: N-S   ♡ K J 9 5
                         ◇ 10 6 5
                         ♣ K 10 9 5

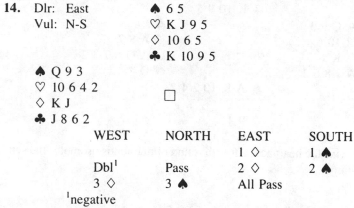

♠ Q 9 3
♡ 10 6 4 2
◇ K J
♣ J 8 6 2

WEST	NORTH	EAST	SOUTH
		1 ◇	1 ♠
Dbl[1]	Pass	2 ◇	2 ♠
3 ◇	3 ♠	All Pass	

[1]negative

You are West. Both your three-diamond bid and North's three spades were questionable, but that's all in the past. You lead the diamond king, winning, and continue with the diamond jack. East takes the ace and continues with the diamond queen. Declarer ruffs with the seven, and you overruff with the nine. How do you continue?

Solutions

13. You must duck the second heart. East's eight can't be the start of a high-low sequence with four cards. He would play the ten from 10-9-8-2.

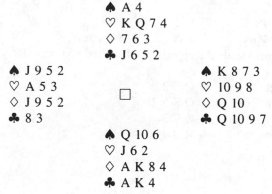

                  ♠ A 4
                  ♡ K Q 7 4
                  ◇ 7 6 3
                  ♣ J 6 5 2

♠ J 9 5 2   ♠ K 8 7 3
♡ A 5 3   ♡ 10 9 8
◇ J 9 5 2   ◇ Q 10
♣ 8 3   ♣ Q 10 9 7

                  ♠ Q 10 6
                  ♡ J 6 2
                  ◇ A K 8 4
                  ♣ A K 4

14. Lead the heart ten. East did not have suit preference available at trick three—he had to lead a high card to beat dummy. However, he had options at trick *two*. When he won the diamond ace rather than the queen, he showed a liking for hearts.

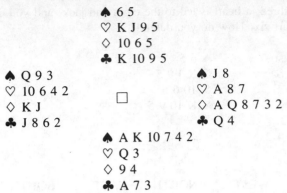

```
              ♠ 6 5
              ♡ K J 9 5
              ◇ 10 6 5
              ♣ K 10 9 5
♠ Q 9 3                    ♠ J 8
♡ 10 6 4 2        □        ♡ A 8 7
◇ K J                      ◇ A Q 8 7 3 2
♣ J 8 6 2                  ♣ Q 4
              ♠ A K 10 7 4 2
              ♡ Q 3
              ◇ 9 4
              ♣ A 7 3
```

After East wins the heart ace, a fourth round of diamonds promotes the setting trick in trumps.

Problems

15. Dlr: South   ♠ Q 9 6 4
 Vul: Both   ♡ A K J 5
          ◇ J 9
          ♣ Q 6 4

```
                          ♠ K 10 8
                          ♡ 9 3
                □         ◇ Q 8 4
                          ♣ A 10 7 5 2
```

WEST	NORTH	EAST	SOUTH
			1 ♣
Pass	1 ♡	Pass	1 ♠
Pass	4 ♠	All Pass	

West, your partner, leads the eight of clubs. Plan your defense.

16. Dlr: North   ♠ Q 8 2
 Vul: Both   ♡ Q 8 5 2
          ◇ K 7 3
          ♣ K 8 2

```
♠ A 6 4
♡ J 7 4
◇ J 10 6 5     □
♣ J 10 6
```

WEST	NORTH	EAST	SOUTH
	Pass	2 ♠	3 ♡
3 ♠	4 ♡	All Pass	

You, West, lead the spade ace—two, jack, nine. How do you continue?

Solutions

15. Win the club ace and return the ten. When partner ruffs, you don't want him to lead diamonds. If you return a lower club, partner might take it in mind to underlead the diamond ace, trying to put you in for another ruff.

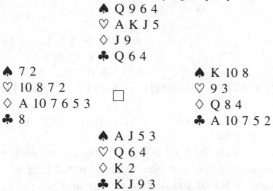

The defense can survive if partner exits with a heart, since declarer can't avoid losing the diamond ace. But a diamond underlead would be fatal. Declarer could win the king, go to dummy, finesse the trump jack, cash the ace, and run clubs, throwing dummy's last diamond.

You know that declarer has at least two diamonds. Therefore, even if West has the king of diamonds, a diamond shift cannot help the defense.

16.

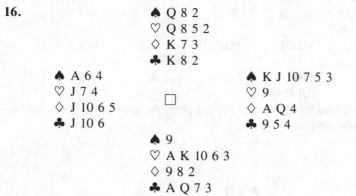

Another delicate suit-preference situation. One of the few times suit preference may be used at trick one is when the third hand has a wide choice of plays. The jack is an *unusually* high card—a *middle* spot would suggest another spade lead—so West should find the diamond shift. Note that the contract will be made on a spade continuation.

Problems

17. Dlr: East   ♠ K J 5 3
      Vul: Both   ♡ J 7 3
                  ◇ A 7 4
                  ♣ A 8 3

                                    ♠ 10
                      □   ♡ 10 8 6 4
                                      ◇ K Q 10 6
                                      ♣ 9 7 5 4

WEST	NORTH	EAST	SOUTH
		Pass	Pass
1 ♡	Dbl	2 ♡	4 ♠
All Pass			

West, your partner, leads the king of hearts (denying the ace). You play the eight to show count, and declarer wins. A spade to the king wins, and a low spade is continued. What do you discard on this trick?

18. Dlr: South   ♠ 9 5 3
      Vul: None   ♡ 10 6 4
                  ◇ K 9 4
                  ♣ A J 5 3

♠ A J 10 6 4
♡ K 3
◇ Q J 3   □
♣ 9 8 2

WEST	NORTH	EAST	SOUTH
			1 ♡
1 ♠	2 ♡	2 ♠	4 ♡
All Pass			

You, West, lead the spade ace. Partner plays the king and declarer the seven. How do you continue?

Solutions

17.

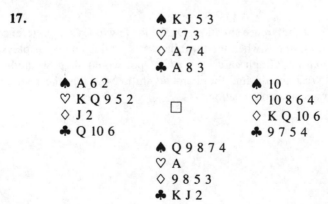

                    ♠ K J 5 3
                    ♡ J 7 3
                    ◇ A 7 4
                    ♣ A 8 3

♠ A 6 2   ♠ 10
♡ K Q 9 5 2   □   ♡ 10 8 6 4
◇ J 2   ◇ K Q 10 6
♣ Q 10 6   ♣ 9 7 5 4

                    ♠ Q 9 8 7 4
                    ♡ A
                    ◇ 9 8 5 3
                    ♣ K J 2

East's play on the opening lead was count. At trick three, he would like to suggest a diamond switch, but either a high diamond or low club pitch might cost a trick. Luckily, there is an alternative: East should discard the ten of hearts. This can be nothing else but suit preference for diamonds. If East liked clubs, he would throw his lowest heart.

18. You must continue spades. East played the spade king because it was the only encouraging card he had available. The full deal:

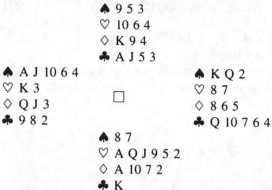

```
                    ♠ 9 5 3
                    ♡ 10 6 4
                    ◇ K 9 4
                    ♣ A J 5 3
  ♠ A J 10 6 4                    ♠ K Q 2
  ♡ K 3                           ♡ 8 7
  ◇ Q J 3          □              ◇ 8 6 5
  ♣ 9 8 2                         ♣ Q 10 7 6 4
                    ♠ 8 7
                    ♡ A Q J 9 5 2
                    ◇ A 10 7 2
                    ♣ K
```

Both the queen and two might induce West to switch to a diamond.

Problems

19. Dlr: South
Vul: N-S

```
                    ♠ Q J 7 6
                    ♡ 10 9 4
                    ◇ 7 5
                    ♣ Q J 5 4
  ♠ 9 5 2
  ♡ K 5
  ◇ A K 10 8 6 2    □
  ♣ K 10
```

WEST	NORTH	EAST	SOUTH
			1 ♡
2 ◇	2 ♡	Pass	4 ♡
All Pass			

You, West, lead the diamond ace—five, queen, three. How do you continue?

20. Dlr: East   ♠ Q
       Vul: Both   ♡ A 10 6 4
                      ◊ A Q 5 4 3
                      ♣ K Q 6

♠ J 9 6 3
♡ K 5
◊ 10 8 7   □
♣ A 10 5 2

WEST	NORTH	EAST	SOUTH
		3 ♠	Pass
4 ♠	Dbl	Pass	5 ♡
All Pass			

You, West, lead the three of spades. East wins the ace, declarer playing the ten, and returns the nine of clubs. How do you defend?

Solutions

19.   ♠ Q J 7 6
                  ♡ 10 9 4
                  ◊ 7 5
                  ♣ Q J 5 4

♠ 9 5 2   ♠ 10 8 4
♡ K 5   ♡ 8 6
◊ A K 10 8 6 2   □   ◊ Q J 4
♣ K 10   ♣ 9 8 7 6 3

           ♠ A K 3
           ♡ A Q J 7 3 2
           ◊ 9 3
           ♣ A 2

East's diamond queen promises either the jack or a singleton. The defenders may signal with the top card of sequential holdings as though they were leading to a trick. (However, it is wrong to signal with the queen from Q-x, unless the jack is in dummy.)

West therefore can underlead in diamonds, and the right card is the two. East should interpret this unusual play as suit preference for clubs—he knows West cannot have a four-card diamond suit for his two-level overcall.

20. Win the club ace and return a diamond! East's play at trick one is very significant. The spade ace cannot be a true card, since nobody would open three spades, vulnerable, on six to the ace.

```
                     ♠ Q
                     ♡ A 10 6 4
                     ◇ A Q 5 4 3
                     ♣ K Q 6
♠ J 9 6 3                              ♠ A K 8 7 5 4 2
♡ K 5                                  ♡ 7 2
◇ 10 8 7           □                   ◇ —
♣ A 10 5 2                             ♣ 9 8 4 3
                     ♠ 10
                     ♡ Q J 9 8 3
                     ◇ K J 9 6 2
                     ♣ J 7
```

There was no other way partner could hope to draw your attention to diamonds.

Quiz 16

Judicious Discards

Since the defenders have to make some discards on practically every hand, it's surprising that the literature on the subject is relatively lean. (Only Hugh Kelsey, in his excellent *More Killing Defense*, has been willing to tackle the subject in great depth.) Probably, this is because discarding can be such a big headache. Delicate reasoning often is required, and even expert partnerships can fall at a difficult hurdle. Discarding is not an easy subject to write about systematically.

Most discards fall into two broad categories. *Informative* discards give partner useful information—you can indicate a sequential holding, or show attitude, count, or suit preference. *Tactical* discards include those which unblock a suit, create an entry, or deceive declarer.

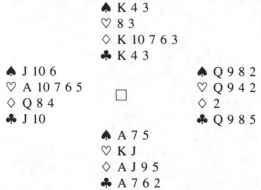

West leads the heart six against 3 NT, and declarer takes East's queen with the king. He plays a diamond to the king and a diamond back. East should discard the two of hearts, suggesting an original holding of four hearts. When West wins a diamond trick, he will know to bang down the heart ace. This is a simple informative discard.

If East's hearts were Q-9-4, he might discard the heart nine, suggesting three hearts, and West would lead a black suit, hoping partner could get in and lead a heart through. (If East started with only two hearts, he obviously would not throw away his last one.)

Many discarding problems involve simply trying to decide which winners or potential winners to keep.

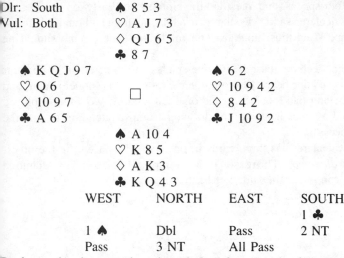

Dlr: South	♠ 8 5 3
Vul: Both	♡ A J 7 3
	◇ Q J 6 5
	♣ 8 7

♠ K Q J 9 7	♠ 6 2
♡ Q 6	♡ 10 9 4 2
◇ 10 9 7	◇ 8 4 2
♣ A 6 5	♣ J 10 9 2

	♠ A 10 4
	♡ K 8 5
	◇ A K 3
	♣ K Q 4 3

WEST	NORTH	EAST	SOUTH
			1 ♣
1 ♠	Dbl	Pass	2 NT
Pass	3 NT	All Pass	

Declarer wins the second spade and plays four rounds of diamonds. What should East's discard be? He should not throw a heart, on the principle that it is right to keep parity with dummy's length. Is it not dangerous to throw a club when declarer has bid the suit? No, declarer has nine tricks anyway if his hand is

♠ A x x
♡ x x x
◇ A K x
♣ A K Q x,

and if he holds

♠ A x x
♡ x x
◇ A K x
♣ A K x x x,

he always is down.

There is nothing worse than being subjected to a long string of declarer's winners and knowing that a wrong discard is certain to give the contract away. Luckily, many such problems can be solved by logical reasoning or by drawing inferences from the bidding or play. On the following deal, only overtricks were at stake.

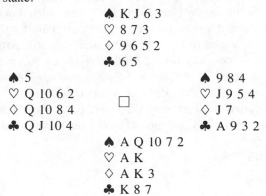

	♠ K J 6 3
	♡ 8 7 3
	◇ 9 6 5 2
	♣ 6 5

♠ 5	♠ 9 8 4
♡ Q 10 6 2	♡ J 9 5 4
◇ Q 10 8 4	◇ J 7
♣ Q J 10 4	♣ A 9 3 2

	♠ A Q 10 7 2
	♡ A K
	◇ A K 3
	♣ K 8 7

South played in four spades, and West led the club queen. East won the ace and returned a club to declarer's king. Declarer ruffed a club high and ran his trumps. On the last trump, West must unguard one of the red suits. What should he keep?

West knows that declarer started with five spades and three clubs. If declarer had four diamonds and one heart, East might have returned his singleton diamond at trick two. If declarer had four hearts and one diamond, he would have played off ace, king, and another heart before drawing trumps, intending to ruff the fourth heart if necessary.

Assuming that declarer has three cards in one red suit and two in the other, West should keep *diamonds*. The reason is very simple: If declarer has a diamond loser, only West can guard the suit. Let East protect hearts.

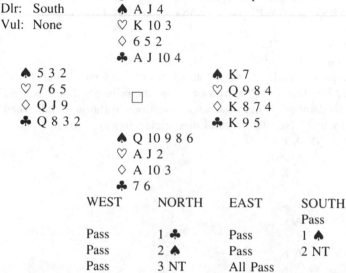

Dlr: South
Vul: None

♠ A J 4
♡ K 10 3
◇ 6 5 2
♣ A J 10 4

♠ 5 3 2
♡ 7 6 5
◇ Q J 9
♣ Q 8 3 2

♠ K 7
♡ Q 9 8 4
◇ K 8 7 4
♣ K 9 5

♠ Q 10 9 8 6
♡ A J 2
◇ A 10 3
♣ 7 6

WEST	NORTH	EAST	SOUTH
			Pass
Pass	1 ♣	Pass	1 ♠
Pass	2 ♠	Pass	2 NT
Pass	3 NT	All Pass	

West led the diamond queen. Declarer held up twice, won the third diamond and passed the spade ten to East's king. The good diamond was cashed, everybody discarding clubs. East then exited safely with his remaining spade.

The defenders should have had few problems discarding on the run of the spades. Declarer soon was known to have four spade tricks, plus two heart tricks (if East had the heart ace, he would have cashed it for the setting trick) and one each in diamonds and clubs. South couldn't have the club king, which would give him 14 HCP and an opening bid, not to mention an obvious claim for the rest. West, however, thought he needed to keep the club queen guarded. After he pitched two hearts, declarer successfully played East for the heart queen.

The defenders might have done better if West had thrown two more clubs, saving his three small hearts, while East unloaded two hearts (!) and a club.

Expert defenders are aware that declarer may draw inferences from their discards, and they sometimes try to cross him up. This fine deal arose in the 1967 Bermuda Bowl.

♠ K 8 6
♥ A 10 7
♦ A K 10 4 3
♣ J 5

♠ 9 7 5
♥ Q 9 6 3
♦ 8
♣ 10 7 6 4 3

♠ J 3
♥ K 8 5 4
♦ Q J 9 7 5
♣ Q 2

♠ A Q 10 4 2
♥ J 2
♦ 6 2
♣ A K 9 8

Pietro Forquet and Benito Garozzo of Italy, N-S, bid to six spades. West for the United States, Norman Kay, led the diamond eight, won by dummy ace. Garozzo gave the hand a typically meticulous play. He led the club jack, covered by the queen and ace, and played his other diamond toward dummy.

If West had ruffed this, declarer would only have had to guess the club position to make the slam. (Dummy would follow with a low diamond, and Garozzo would subsequently throw his heart loser on the diamond king.) However, Kay not only refused to ruff, he threw a *heart*, not his worthless fifth club, for fear of suggesting the club position to declarer.

Garozzo won dummy's diamond king and still could have made the contract with an inspired guess. In practice, he very reasonably tried a club to the nine. Kay won and alertly returned a club, dooming the slam, and the United States gained 13 IMPs. (The U.S. N-S pair stopped in game.)

Problems

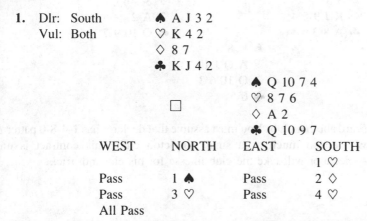

1. Dlr: South
    Vul: Both

    ♠ A J 3 2
    ♥ K 4 2
    ♦ 8 7
    ♣ K J 4 2

    ♠ Q 10 7 4
    ♥ 8 7 6
    ♦ A 2
    ♣ Q 10 9 7

WEST	NORTH	EAST	SOUTH
			1 ♥
Pass	1 ♠	Pass	2 ♦
Pass	3 ♥	Pass	4 ♥
All Pass			

West, your partner, leads the club ace and shifts to the five of diamonds. You win and return a diamond to declarer's ten and partner's jack. Next, West leads a low diamond, declarer ruffing with dummy's king. What do you discard?

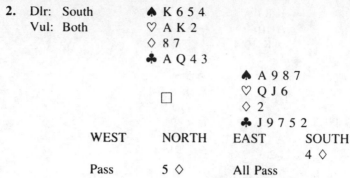

2. Dlr: South ♠ K 6 5 4
Vul: Both ♡ A K 2
◇ 8 7
♣ A Q 4 3

♠ A 9 8 7
□ ♡ Q J 6
◇ 2
♣ J 9 7 5 2

WEST	NORTH	EAST	SOUTH
			4 ◇
Pass	5 ◇	All Pass	

West, your partner, leads the spade queen, ducked in dummy. Declarer follows to the first trick but ruffs the spade-jack continuation. The diamond king goes to partner's ace, and another spade is ruffed by declarer. Next comes the diamond queen, partner's jack falling. You can spare a club on this trick. Declarer now leads another trump. Partner unhelpfully throws his last spade, and dummy pitches the heart two. What do you discard?

Solutions

1. Discard a trump! If you throw a card in either black suit, declarer might be able to establish his tenth trick there by ruffing.

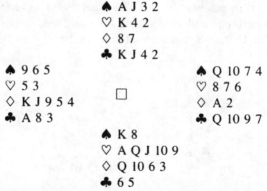

♠ A J 3 2
♡ K 4 2
◇ 8 7
♣ K J 4 2

♠ 9 6 5
♡ 5 3
◇ K J 9 5 4
♣ A 8 3

□

♠ Q 10 7 4
♡ 8 7 6
◇ A 2
♣ Q 10 9 7

♠ K 8
♡ A Q J 10 9
◇ Q 10 6 3
♣ 6 5

2. Discard another club. You must assume that declarer has 1-4-8-0 pattern. If he has even so much as a small singleton club, this contract is unbeatable—declarer will take the club finesse for his eleventh trick.

216

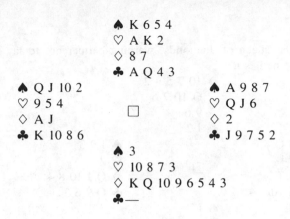

♠ K 6 5 4
♡ A K 2
◇ 8 7
♣ A Q 4 3

♠ Q J 10 2   ♠ A 9 8 7
♡ 9 5 4   ♡ Q J 6
◇ A J   ◇ 2
♣ K 10 8 6   ♣ J 9 7 5 2

♠ 3
♡ 10 8 7 3
◇ K Q 10 9 6 5 4 3
♣ —

Problems

3. Dlr: South   ♠ 10 7 5 4 2
   Vul: N-S   ♡ Q 10 7 6
                       ◇ 9 6
                       ♣ J 2

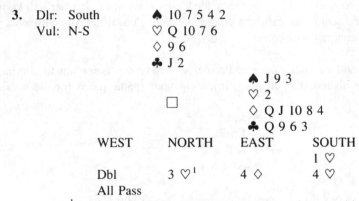

                       ♠ J 9 3
                       ♡ 2
                       ◇ Q J 10 8 4
                       ♣ Q 9 6 3

WEST	NORTH	EAST	SOUTH
			1 ♡
Dbl	3 ♡[1]	4 ◇	4 ♡
All Pass			

[1]Preemptive. With a good hand, North would start with a redouble. West, your partner, leads a trump. Declarer wins the king and leads to the trump queen. What do you discard?

4. Dlr: West   ♠ J 3
   Vul: None   ♡ J 5 3
                       ◇ K 8 5 2
                       ♣ A K 5 4

♠ Q 5
♡ K 7
◇ A Q J 10 7 3
♣ 8 7 3

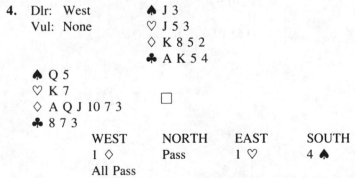

WEST	NORTH	EAST	SOUTH
1 ◇	Pass	1 ♡	4 ♠
All Pass			

You, West, lead the heart king. Partner signals high, so you continue. East cashes the heart queen and ace. What do you discard?

217

Solutions

3. Throw the queen of diamonds, warning partner not to lay down the diamond ace if he has it.

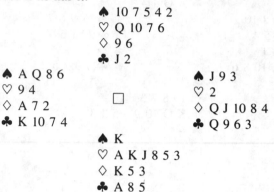

```
                    ♠ 10 7 5 4 2
                    ♡ Q 10 7 6
                    ◇ 9 6
                    ♣ J 2
    ♠ A Q 8 6                      ♠ J 9 3
    ♡ 9 4                          ♡ 2
    ◇ A 7 2           □            ◇ Q J 10 8 4
    ♣ K 10 7 4                     ♣ Q 9 6 3
                    ♠ K
                    ♡ A K J 8 5 3
                    ◇ K 5 3
                    ♣ A 8 5
```

Declarer probably will lead to the spade king at trick three. Partner will know from your discard that leading a diamond cannot gain. If he exits with a black card, the contract will be set.

4. Discard the diamond ace! Partner will have no choice but to continue with a fourth round of hearts, promoting your spade queen for the setting trick.

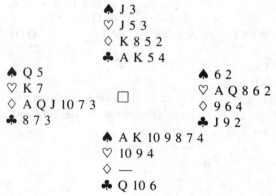

```
                    ♠ J 3
                    ♡ J 5 3
                    ◇ K 8 5 2
                    ♣ A K 5 4
    ♠ Q 5                          ♠ 6 2
    ♡ K 7                          ♡ A Q 8 6 2
    ◇ A Q J 10 7 3    □            ◇ 9 6 4
    ♣ 8 7 3                        ♣ J 9 2
                    ♠ A K 10 9 8 7 4
                    ♡ 10 9 4
                    ◇ —
                    ♣ Q 10 6
```

Problems

5. Dlr: South   ♠ 10 8 5 2
Vul: N-S   ♡ 6 5
                ◊ J 10 8 6 3
                ♣ J 5

♠ A J 3
♡ Q 10 8 7 2
◊ 2   □
♣ 9 8 7 6

WEST	NORTH	EAST	SOUTH
			2 ♣
Pass	2 ◊	Pass	2 NT
Pass	3 ♣	Pass	3 ◊
Pass	3 NT	All Pass	

South's 2 NT rebid showed a balanced 23-24 HCP; North's three clubs was Stayman. You, West, lead the seven of hearts to the five, nine, and jack. Declarer continues with the diamond ace and diamond queen. What do you discard?

6. Dlr: North   ♠ A 6
Vul: E-W   ♡ A Q 5 2
               ◊ K 3
               ♣ A 10 7 5 2

                ♠ 7 5 2
      □   ♡ K 9 8 6 3
                ◊ A Q J 10
                ♣ 3

WEST	NORTH	EAST	SOUTH
	1 ♣	Pass	1 ◊
Pass	1 ♡	Pass	1 NT
Pass	2 NT	Pass	3 NT
All Pass			

West, your partner, leads the jack of spades, and dummy's ace wins. Declarer plays a club to his king and continues with the club nine, ducking when partner's jack appears. What do you discard?

Solutions

5. Pitch the heart queen. A heart discard here says that your enthusiasm for your original suit has waned. If partner has the king of diamonds, you must dissuade him from returning a heart.

♠ 10 8 5 2
♡ 6 5
◇ J 10 8 6 3
♣ J 5

♠ A J 3
♡ Q 10 8 7 2
◇ 2
♣ 9 8 7 6

♠ Q 9 7 4
♡ 9 4 3
◇ K 9 4
♣ Q 10 3

♠ K 6
♡ A K J
◇ A Q 7 5
♣ A K 4 2

The *queen* of hearts has suit-preference implications, so perhaps partner will find the spade switch.

6.

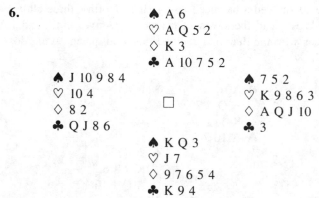

♠ A 6
♡ A Q 5 2
◇ K 3
♣ A 10 7 5 2

♠ J 10 9 8 4
♡ 10 4
◇ 8 2
♣ Q J 8 6

♠ 7 5 2
♡ K 9 8 6 3
◇ A Q J 10
♣ 3

♠ K Q 3
♡ J 7
◇ 9 7 6 5 4
♣ K 9 4

Desperate measures are called for. Declarer is marked with the spade queen, and he must have the king, too, since he went right up with dummy's ace at trick one. So he has three spade tricks, four clubs, and the heart ace for eight tricks. Even if West has the heart jack and ten shifts to a heart, declarer can strip-squeeze you in the red suits and take a ninth trick.

You must force partner to switch to a diamond right now. Pitch the heart king.

Problems

7. Dlr: West ♠ Q 10 6 3
   Vul: None ♡ 6 3
   ◊ 8 5 3
   ♣ A Q 4 2

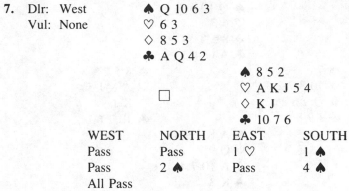

       ♠ 8 5 2
       ♡ A K J 5 4
       ◊ K J
       ♣ 10 7 6

WEST	NORTH	EAST	SOUTH
Pass	Pass	1 ♡	1 ♠
Pass	2 ♠	Pass	4 ♠
All Pass			

West, your partner, leads the two of hearts. You win the king and ace, and declarer's queen falls. At trick three, you try a shift to the king of diamonds—ace, six, three. Declarer draws three rounds of trumps, partner pitching two hearts, and continues with king, queen, and ace of clubs, discarding a diamond. After some thought, he leads dummy's fourth club. What do you discard?

8. Dlr: South ♠ A 8 6 4
   Vul: N-S ♡ 8 7
   ◊ 8 7 4
   ♣ K Q 4 3

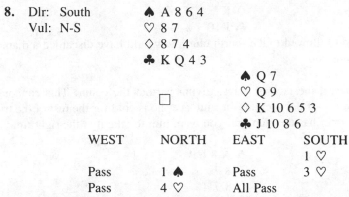

       ♠ Q 7
       ♡ Q 9
       ◊ K 10 6 5 3
       ♣ J 10 8 6

WEST	NORTH	EAST	SOUTH
			1 ♡
Pass	1 ♠	Pass	3 ♡
Pass	4 ♡	All Pass	

West, your partner, leads the five of spades, ducked to your queen. Declarer follows with the three. Your spade return goes to ten, jack, and ace. Now declarer leads a diamond to the queen, winning, and peels off three rounds of trumps, West following with the six, five, and ten. What do you discard on the third trump?

7.

        ♠ Q 10 6 3
        ♡ 6 3
        ◊ 8 5 3
        ♣ A Q 4 2

♠ 7   ♠ 8 5 2
♡ 10 8 7 2   ♡ A K J 5 4
◊ Q 9 6 2   □   ◊ K J
♣ J 9 8 5   ♣ 10 7 6

        ♠ A K J 9 4
        ♡ Q 9
        ◊ A 10 7 4
        ♣ K 3

Unload the diamond jack. Otherwise, declarer will ruff the fourth club and exit with a diamond. West cannot profitably play his queen, and when you win the jack you have to give declarer a ruff-and-discard and his contract.

Declarer could have made his game leading a diamond after playing just three rounds of clubs; but he judged that your hand was

        ♠ x x x
        ♡ A K J x x
        ◊ K
        ♣ J 10 x x.

If you had followed to the fourth club, he would have discarded a diamond, endplaying you.

8. Discard the jack of clubs, giving partner the count. This cannot cost the contract—if declarer has the club ace, he is cold for the rest of the tricks. But if partner has the club ace, you want him to take it at the right time. The full deal:

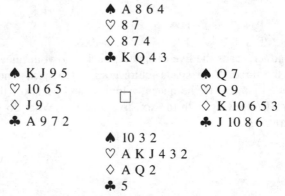

When declarer leads a club, partner will fly, cash his spade, and force declarer to ruff a spade. Declarer must lose a diamond in the end.

Problems

9. Dlr: South   ♠ A K 4 3
Vul: None   ♡ 10 4
                      ♢ 7 5 2
                      ♣ A Q 3 2

                                ♠ J 10 9 8
                 □   ♡ Q 6
                                ♢ K 3
                                ♣ J 9 8 7 6

WEST	NORTH	EAST	SOUTH
			1 ♢
Pass	1 ♠	Pass	2 ♢
Pass	3 ♣	Pass	3 NT
All Pass			

West, your partner, leads the seven of hearts—four, queen, two. You return the heart six—five, jack, ten. Partner now plays the heart nine. What do you discard?

10. Dlr: South   ♠ K Q 3 2
Vul: N-S   ♡ 9 8
                      ♢ Q J 4
                      ♣ K 7 5 2

                                ♠ J 10 9 6 5
                 □   ♡ Q J 3
                                ♢ 7
                                ♣ Q 10 9 6

WEST	NORTH	EAST	SOUTH
			1 NT[1]
Pass	2 ♣	Pass	2 ♢
Pass	3 NT	All Pass	

[1] 15-17 HCP

West, your partner, leads the six of hearts—eight, jack, king. Declarer plays a club to the king and leads the diamond queen, which wins. What do you discard when the diamond jack is led?

Solutions

9. The only thing you can do to affect the outcome is to discard the king of diamonds. This is a free shot—if declarer has six diamonds to the ace-queen-jack, your king might as well be the deuce.

                    ♠ A K 4 3
                    ♡ 10 4
                    ◇ 7 5 2
                    ♣ A Q 3 2

♠ Q 7 5 2   ♠ J 10 9 8
♡ K J 9 7 3   □   ♡ Q 6
◇ Q 9   ◇ K 3
♣ 10 5   ♣ J 9 8 7 6

                    ♠ 6
                    ♡ A 8 5 2
                    ◇ A J 10 8 6 4
                    ♣ K 4

If you hang on to the diamond king, declarer can establish diamonds without letting your partner in the lead.

10.   ♠ K Q 3 2
                        ♡ 9 8
                        ◇ Q J 4
                        ♣ K 7 5 2

♠ 8 7   ♠ J 10 9 6 5
♡ A 10 7 6 4   □   ♡ Q J 3
◇ K 8 6 3   ◇ 7
♣ J 8   ♣ Q 10 9 6

                    ♠ A 4
                    ♡ K 5 2
                    ◇ A 10 9 5 2
                    ♣ A 4 3

Throw the heart queen. The Rule of Eleven (see Quiz 5) tells you that partner's hearts are ready to run. But partner may not be so sure. From his point of view, declarer's hand just as easily could be

                    ♠ J x
                    ♡ K Q x
                    ◇ A 10 9 x x
                    ♣ A Q x,

in which case partner must lead a spade.

224

Problems

11. Dlr: South   ♠ J 4
Vul: None   ♡ 8 5
               ◇ A Q 8 6 3
               ♣ K J 6 4

♠ K 8 5 2
♡ K Q 10 7 3   □
◇ 7 2
♣ 9 3

WEST	NORTH	EAST	SOUTH
			2 NT[1]
Pass	6 NT	All Pass	

[1]21-22 HCP

You, West, lead the heart king. Declarer wins and begins running his minor-suit winners. Plan your discards.

12. Dlr: South   ♠ Q 6 3
Vul: N-S   ♡ K Q 9 4
               ◇ K 9 3 2
               ♣ 9 7

                    ♠ 8
        □   ♡ J 8 7 5 2
                    ◇ J 10 8 5
                    ♣ Q 5 4

WEST	NORTH	EAST	SOUTH
			1 NT
2 ♠	3 NT	All Pass	

West, your partner, leads the spade king, winning, and continues with the spade ace. What do you discard?

Solutions

11.   ♠ J 4
         ♡ 8 5
         ◇ A Q 8 6 3
         ♣ K J 6 4

♠ K 8 5 2   ♠ 10 9 7 3
♡ K Q 10 7 3   ♡ 9 6 2
◇ 7 2   □   ◇ 10 9 4
♣ 9 3   ♣ 8 7 5

         ♠ A Q 6
         ♡ A J 4
         ◇ K J 5
         ♣ A Q 10 2

Declarer must have every missing facecard for his 2 NT opening. You can rest assured that he will run nine minor-suit winners, coming down to:

♠ J 4
♡ 8
◊ —
♣ —

???   □   immaterial

♠ A Q
♡ J
◊ —
♣ —

At this point, declarer must guess whether to stake everything on the spade finesse or exit with a heart, endplaying West if he has come down to the heart queen and the guarded king of spades. Against unimaginative discarding by West, declarer is a favorite to read the position correctly.

West can do two things to lead declarer astray. One is to anticipate the problem and steel himself to *blank the spade king early*. Declarer is much more likely to go right if West's crucial discards are accompanied by a lot of agonized thought in the ending. The other thing West should do is *discard the heart ten*, concealing a lower spot. Declarer may think West has bared the heart queen and is ripe for the endplay.

12. Throw a club, which cannot cost a thing. As it happens, on the third round of spades partner will lead the two (suit preference), and you can pitch another club comfortably, knowing that he has the ace or king.

♠ Q 6 3
♡ K Q 9 4
◊ K 9 3 2
♣ 9 7

♠ A K 9 7 4 2   ♠ 8
♡ 6   □   ♡ J 8 7 5 2
◊ 6 4   ◊ J 10 8 5
♣ K 10 8 6   ♣ Q 5 4

♠ J 10 5
♡ A 10 3
◊ A Q 7
♣ A J 3 2

Most players would throw the heart two at the second trick because it looks like a worthless card—the "idle fifth," as it is called. In fact, East quickly threw a heart when the deal actually was played, and declarer proceeded to draw the appropriate inference and make the contract. Winning the third spade, he played a heart to the king and a heart to the *ten*. He ended with a spade, a club, three diamonds, and four hearts.

Quiz 17

Good Timing

Discussing good timing in an earlier book, I cited Hugh Kelsey's sage comment that declarer can find himself blessed with ample high cards, yet fail if he plays them in the wrong order. This admonition is even truer in defensive play, where one pair must struggle along with the worst part of the high-card strength and fewer opportunities to lead.

The following situation was mentioned in Quiz 13, but it is important enough to repeat.

```
Dlr: South        ♠ A 6 5 4
Vul: None         ♡ K 3
                  ◇ 8 5 3
                  ♣ K 8 5 2
  ♠ J 9 7 3                    ♠ Q 10 2
  ♡ Q J 10 8 6         □       ♡ 9 7 4
  ◇ A 4                        ◇ K J 6
  ♣ 9 3                        ♣ 10 7 6 4
                  ♠ K 8
                  ♡ A 5 2
                  ◇ Q 10 9 7 2
                  ♣ A Q J
```

South opens 1 NT. North tries Stayman and then puts it in 3 NT. West leads the queen of hearts. Declarer ducks the first heart, wins the second with dummy's king, and leads a low diamond. If East is well versed in the principles of notrump defense, he will put up the diamond king and return his last heart. This play can lose nothing, since declarer is about to take a successful finesse if he has the diamond ace-queen. It is vital to get the defensive timing right by preserving West's entry to the hearts.

That is a textbook situation, but other instances of defensive timing are more taxing. The next deal would be too difficult for most Wests.

Dlr: South ♠ Q J 10 4
Vul: N-S   ♡ 5 3
      ♦ Q 6 5 3
      ♣ A J 8

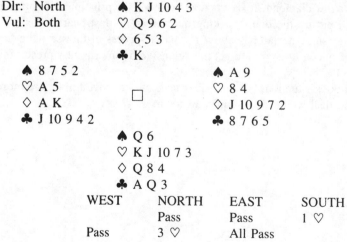

```
        ♠ Q J 10 4
        ♡ 5 3
        ♦ Q 6 5 3
        ♣ A J 8
♠ K 9 8 5              ♠ A 7 3
♡ 9 6                 ♡ K Q 10 8 4 2
♦ A 10 9 8     □      ♦ 7 2
♣ 7 4 2               ♣ 6 3
        ♠ 6 2
        ♡ A J 7
        ♦ K J 4
        ♣ K Q 10 9 5
```

WEST	NORTH	EAST	SOUTH
			1 ♣
Pass	1 ♠	2 ♡	Pass
Pass	3 ♣	Pass	3 NT
All Pass			

After N-S struggle into 3 NT, West leads the nine of hearts to the queen and ace. Declarer goes to the club jack and leads a diamond to the seven and king. West thinks that declarer is likely to have the diamond jack, too. He makes the fine play of ducking, and declarer is finished. If declarer leads another diamond, the defense can take two diamonds, two hearts, and a spade; and no other play by declarer offers any hope.

Note that if West wins the first diamond, he can do nothing to keep declarer from taking nine tricks. (Declarer, of course, mistimed *his* play—he was safe for the contract by ducking the first trick.)

Another area of defensive timing involves combining chances. Often, a defender will have two or more possible lines of play. Sometimes it won't matter in which order he tries them. On other occasions, he must take care to start with the line that will not irrevocably give away the contract if it fails.

Dlr: North ♠ K J 10 4 3
Vul: Both   ♡ Q 9 6 2
      ♦ 6 5 3
      ♣ K

```
        ♠ K J 10 4 3
        ♡ Q 9 6 2
        ♦ 6 5 3
        ♣ K
♠ 8 7 5 2             ♠ A 9
♡ A 5                ♡ 8 4
♦ A K        □       ♦ J 10 9 7 2
♣ J 10 9 4 2         ♣ 8 7 6 5
        ♠ Q 6
        ♡ K J 10 7 3
        ♦ Q 8 4
        ♣ A Q 3
```

WEST	NORTH	EAST	SOUTH
	Pass	Pass	1 ♡
Pass	3 ♡	All Pass	

West leads the king and ace of diamonds (suggesting a doubleton). In an expert game, East would follow with the jack on the second round, as a suit-preference signal for spades. But West should lead a spade regardless. Clearly, East must hold an ace to beat the contract. A spade shift can't cost if declarer has the ace; but if declarer has the *club* ace and the queen besides, a club shift will allow him to discard dummy's remaining diamond, avoiding the impending ruff.

I was West on the following deal from a recent club duplicate game.

Dlr: North
Vul: E-W
Matchpoints

♠ A Q J 6 4
♡ Q 9
◇ A 6 5
♣ Q 10 3

♠ 7 5 2
♡ A 10 7 6 3
◇ 8 3
♣ K 5 2

♠ K 10 8 3
♡ 8 5 4
◇ 9 7
♣ A J 8 4

♠ 9
♡ K J 2
◇ K Q J 10 4 2
♣ 9 7 6

WEST	NORTH	EAST	SOUTH
	1 ♠	Pass	2 ◇
Pass	2 ♠	Pass	2 NT
Pass	3 NT	All Pass	

I led a heart, won by dummy's nine. Declarer, for reasons best known to him, cashed the ace of diamonds and played a diamond to the jack before leading a second heart. Partner had high-lowed in diamonds, so I knew declarer had nine tricks to take. I grabbed the ace of hearts and shifted to a low club, and we took four tricks in the suit to put the contract down one.

Later I realized that I had misdefended. If declarer had held the jack of clubs instead of East, my defense would have given away an overtrick. I should have started by leading the *king* of clubs. If partner lacked the jack of clubs, he would signal low, and I could shift to a spade to hold declarer to just nine tricks.

On other hands, the defenders' aim is not to retain their own options but rather to keep declarer from exercising all of his. This is a deal from the 1977 Bermuda Bowl.

Dlr: North
Vul: N-S

♠ 7 2
♡ K Q J 7 4 3
◇ A 9
♣ J 6 4

♠ 8 4
♡ 10 9 5 2
◇ Q J 10 8 2
♣ 10 2

♠ 10 6 5 3
♡ A 8
◇ 5 4 3
♣ K 8 5 3

♠ A K Q J 9
♡ 6
◇ K 7 6
♣ A Q 9 7

At one table in the United States-Taiwan match, John Swanson and Paul Soloway got to six spades for the United States and went down one. The Taiwanese N-S pair in the other room also reached slam:

WEST	NORTH	EAST	SOUTH
Kantar	*Lin*	*Eisenberg*	*Tai*
	1 ♡	Pass	1 ♠
Pass	2 ♡	Pass	3 ♣
Pass	3 ♡	Pass	4 ◇
Pass	4 ♠	Pass	4 NT
Pass	5 ◇	Pass	6 ♠
All Pass			

Eddie Kantar led the queen of diamonds. Declarer won the king, drew trumps, pitching a club and a heart from dummy, and led a heart to the king and ace. Billy Eisenberg returned a diamond to dummy's ace. Hearts failed to split, but declarer continued by leading the club jack. With the lucky fall of the club ten, the slam was home. Seventeen IMPs to Taiwan.

It might have been a different story had East put it to declarer by returning the eight of clubs when he won the heart ace. South would have had to guess right then whether to stake the contract on a 3-3 heart split or finesse in clubs.

The idea of removing declarer's options can even be extended to the opening lead. Several years ago, in a team event, I held as South:

```
        ♠ 10 6 4
        ♡ 10 8 6 5 3
        ◇ 7 6 4
        ♣ K 9
```

WEST	EAST
	1 ♡
2 ♣	4 ♡
4 NT	5 ◇
6 ♡	

On opening lead, I tried the club nine, reasoning that declarer would never finesse at trick one, running the risk of a ruff, when the hearts would look solid to him. So we would take a trump trick and a surprise trick in clubs.

The story had an ironic ending. The full deal was:

```
              ♠ 9 8 7 3
              ♡ 7 2
              ◇ 10 8 3
              ♣ A 8 3 2
♠ A K 2                      ♠ Q J 5
♡ —                          ♡ A K Q J 9 4
◇ A K Q 2        □           ◇ J 9 5
♣ Q J 10 7 5 4               ♣ 6
              ♠ 10 6 4
              ♡ 10 8 6 5 3
              ◇ 7 6 4
              ♣ K 9
```

Sure enough, a club was the only lead to beat it!

Problems

1. Dlr: South   ♠ A J 4
    Vul: E-W   ♡ Q 7 4
               ◇ A 8 3
               ♣ K Q 10 3

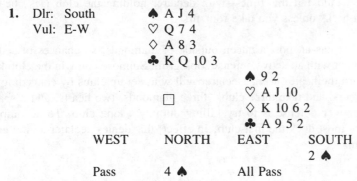

                      ♠ 9 2
                      ♡ A J 10
                      ◇ K 10 6 2
                      ♣ A 9 5 2

WEST	NORTH	EAST	SOUTH
			2 ♠
Pass	4 ♠	All Pass	

West, your partner, leads the three of hearts. Dummy plays low, and your ten wins the first trick, declarer contributing the five. How do you continue?

2. Dlr: South   ♠ J 6 5
    Vul: N-S   ♡ 7 5
               ◇ A 3 2
               ♣ A Q J 7 2

                      ♠ K 8 2
                      ♡ Q J 9 4
             □   ◇ 5 4
                      ♣ K 10 8 4

WEST	NORTH	EAST	SOUTH
			1 NT
Pass	3 NT	All Pass	

West, your partner, leads the jack of diamonds. Declarer wins the queen and leads the three of clubs to dummy's queen. Do you take the trick? Why or why not?

Solutions

1. Return the heart jack. West has at most five hearts, so you can count on two heart tricks and a club. You may need a diamond trick also, and if declarer has the diamond queen, the lead must come from partner's side.

               ♠ A J 4
               ♡ Q 7 4
               ◇ A 8 3
               ♣ K Q 10 3

♠ 8 3   ♠ 9 2
♡ K 9 6 3 2   ♡ A J 10
◇ J 9 5 4   □   ◇ K 10 6 2
♣ 7 6   ♣ A 9 5 2

               ♠ K Q 10 7 6 5
               ♡ 8 5
               ◇ Q 7
               ♣ J 8 4

Partner will know what to do when he wins the second trick. A passive defense would fail this time—with declarer holding the club jack, he can take ten tricks unless you take four first.

2. West has at most a queen outside of diamonds, so chances of setting the contract with an active defense look grim. Suppose you win the club king and return the heart queen. Declarer will win, set up clubs by conceding the fourth round and take three clubs, three diamonds, two hearts, and a spade.

A stronger defense is to try killing dummy's long club. To accomplish that, you must duck the first club. In effect, this denies declarer a vital entry to dummy.

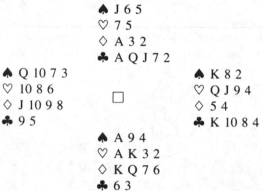

Declarer probably will come back to his hand for another club finesse, especially if East has ducked without pause. E-W should have no trouble collecting five tricks. (The contract still might be made after a very unlikely sequence of plays ending with a throw-in against East.)

Declarer could always make the contract by ducking the first round of clubs completely, but this is not a clearly indicated line. There is the threat of a damaging spade shift.

Problems

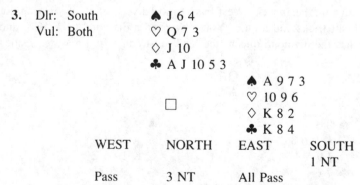

West, your partner, leads the two of spades. Declarer plays the eight under your ace. How do you continue?

4. Dlr: South   ♠ K 10 4
      Vul: Both   ♡ Q J 5 3
                   ◇ J 6 5 2
                   ♣ A 7

                             ♠ A Q 8 2
                             ♡ 9 4
                   □   ◇ 9 8 4
                             ♣ K 10 8 4

WEST	NORTH	EAST	SOUTH
			1 ♠
Pass	2 ◇	Pass	2 ♡
Pass	3 ♡	Pass	4 ♡
All Pass			

West, your partner, leads the seven of spades, and you win the queen. Plan your defense.

Solutions

3. If West has K-Q-x-x of spades, East can do no more than cash out the suit and hope to score the club king. However, declarer is likely to have a spade stopper, which means the defense will need a red-suit trick.

If declarer has his 16 HCP, West can have only one red-suit honor. If it is the heart king, the contract is ironclad. On a heart shift, declarer can *rise* with the ace, set up clubs, and take a winning diamond finesse for at least nine tricks.

Anyway, since you have something in diamonds, it seems better to play partner for the diamond queen. But timing is important. Shift to the *eight* of diamonds.

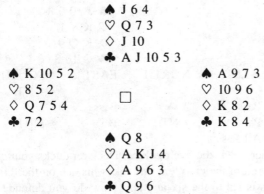

                 ♠ J 6 4
                 ♡ Q 7 3
                 ◇ J 10
                 ♣ A J 10 5 3

♠ K 10 5 2   ♠ A 9 7 3
♡ 8 5 2   □   ♡ 10 9 6
◇ Q 7 5 4   ◇ K 8 2
♣ 7 2   ♣ K 8 4

                 ♠ Q 8
                 ♡ A K J 4
                 ◇ A 9 6 3
                 ♣ Q 9 6

With West fortunately holding the diamond seven, declarer must duck, else he loses the whole diamond suit when you get in with the club king. After the diamond queen wins, West should interpret your lead of a high spot as showing no interest in a continuation and switch back to a low spade.

4.

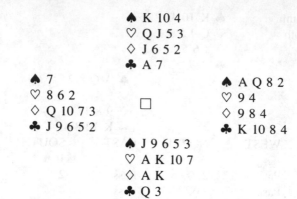

♠ K 10 4
♥ Q J 5 3
♦ J 6 5 2
♣ A 7

♠ 7
♥ 8 6 2
♦ Q 10 7 3
♣ J 9 6 5 2

♠ A Q 8 2
♥ 9 4
♦ 9 8 4
♣ K 10 8 4

♠ J 9 6 5 3
♥ A K 10 7
♦ A K
♣ Q 3

South wouldn't open one spade on J-9-x-x, so partner's lead must be a singleton. However, you will lose a valuable tempo if you cash the ace of spades before giving partner a ruff. Declarer will win the club return, draw trumps and throw dummy's club loser on a good spade.

Instead, return the spade two at trick two. Partner ruffs, and a club return ensures the contract's defeat.

Note that there is no hurry for East to lead diamonds. If West has the diamond ace or king, he is bound to make it—declarer can throw only two of dummy's diamonds on the spades.

Problems

5. Dlr: South
Vul: None

♠ Q 6
♥ J 7 6 5
♦ A J 10 7 3
♣ 7 6

♠ J 10 9 8
♥ K 8 3
♦ K Q 9
♣ Q 10 3

WEST	NORTH	EAST	SOUTH
			1 NT
Pass	2 ♣	Pass	2 ♠
Pass	2 NT	Pass	3 NT
All Pass			

West, your partner, leads the five of clubs. Declarer ducks your queen, ducks again when you return the club ten, and takes his ace on the third club. The two of diamonds is led to the six and ten. How do you defend?

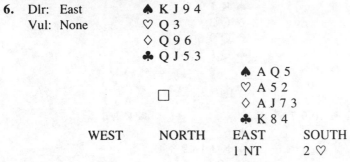

6. Dlr: East   ♠ K J 9 4
     Vul: None   ♡ Q 3
              ◊ Q 9 6
              ♣ Q J 5 3
                         ♠ A Q 5
                         ♡ A 5 2
             □   ◊ A J 7 3
                         ♣ K 8 4

WEST	NORTH	EAST	SOUTH
		1 NT	2 ♡

All Pass

West, your partner, leads an inspired king of diamonds and continues with the diamond two to your jack. How do you continue?

Solutions

5.   ♠ Q 6
            ♡ J 7 6 5
            ◊ A J 10 7 3
            ♣ 7 6

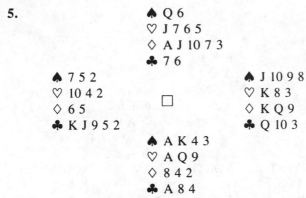

   ♠ 7 5 2   ♠ J 10 9 8
   ♡ 10 4 2   ♡ K 8 3
   ◊ 6 5   □   ◊ K Q 9
   ♣ K J 9 5 2   ♣ Q 10 3
           ♠ A K 4 3
           ♡ A Q 9
           ◊ 8 4 2
           ♣ A 8 4

Win the diamond king and return the eight of hearts, forcing declarer to choose prematurely between the heart finesse and another diamond finesse. It he goes up with the heart ace and tries a diamond to the jack, you will have to try to avoid looking smug as you cash the heart king.

     If you return the spade jack, declarer will win the queen and king, and finesse again in diamonds. When he learns that only three diamond tricks are available, he will have no choice but to take the heart finesse.

6.   Return a *low* diamond for partner to ruff. He will lead a trump, and you play ace and another. Declarer can win in dummy and finesse in clubs, but he still must lose a spade and another diamond for down one.

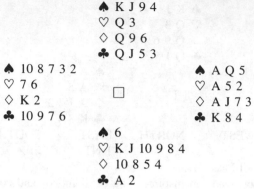

```
            ♠ K J 9 4
            ♡ Q 3
            ◇ Q 9 6
            ♣ Q J 5 3
♠ 10 8 7 3 2                    ♠ A Q 5
♡ 7 6                          ♡ A 5 2
◇ K 2              □           ◇ A J 7 3
♣ 10 9 7 6                      ♣ K 8 4
            ♠ 6
            ♡ K J 10 9 8 4
            ◇ 10 8 5 4
            ♣ A 2
```

If you cash your diamond ace at trick three, the contract will be made—depending on your next play, declarer will either score his diamond ten or ruff it in dummy for the eighth trick.

Problems

7. Dlr: South   ♠ K 5
     Vul: E-W   ♡ K 6 4
                ◇ A Q J 3
                ♣ J 7 5 3

```
                    ♠ 9 6 2
                    ♡ A 9 2
        □           ◇ 10 8 7 4
                    ♣ A 8 6
```

WEST	NORTH	EAST	SOUTH
			1 ♠
Pass	2 NT	Pass	3 ◇
Pass	4 ◇	Pass	4 ♠
All Pass			

West, your partner, leads the queen of hearts. Declarer ruffs the second heart and draws three rounds of trumps, partner following. A diamond to the jack wins, partner following low. Next, the club two is led from dummy. Do you play your ace? Why or why not?

236

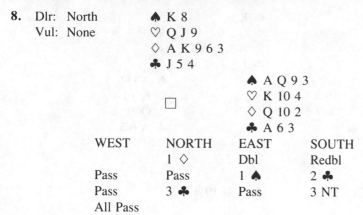

8. Dlr: North ♠ K 8
Vul: None ♡ Q J 9
♢ A K 9 6 3
♣ J 5 4

♠ A Q 9 3
□ ♡ K 10 4
♢ Q 10 2
♣ A 6 3

WEST	NORTH	EAST	SOUTH
	1 ♢	Dbl	Redbl
Pass	Pass	1 ♠	2 ♣
Pass	3 ♣	Pass	3 NT
All Pass			

West, your partner, leads the two of spades to your queen. How do you continue?

Solutions

7. You should hop up with your ace of clubs and play the heart ace, forcing out declarer's last trump. True, you take declarer off a club guess if he has K-10-x, but that danger is an illusion. Say you duck the club, and declarer's ten loses to partner's queen. Declarer ruffs a heart continuation and leads the club king to your ace. You have only minor-suit cards left, so you have to give him back the lead to finish his ten winners.

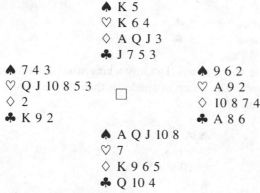

♠ K 5
♡ K 6 4
♢ A Q J 3
♣ J 7 5 3

♠ 7 4 3 ♠ 9 6 2
♡ Q J 10 8 5 3 ♡ A 9 2
♢ 2 □ ♢ 10 8 7 4
♣ K 9 2 ♣ A 8 6

♠ A Q J 10 8
♡ 7
♢ K 9 6 5
♣ Q 10 4

Correct defense will enable partner to win the club king and cash a good heart for the setting trick.

8. There are only four tricks in sight—three spades and the club ace—but you can gain a tempo by shifting to the heart king, threatening to dislodge a vital entry to declarer's hand. South must duck this or be limited to just two club tricks, and eight tricks in all (you will hold up the club ace, of course). If you can get one fast heart trick, you will shift back to spades and set up the setting trick there.

```
                        ♠ K 8
                        ♡ Q J 9
                        ◇ A K 9 6 3
                        ♣ J 5 4
    ♠ 10 7 6 2                         ♠ A Q 9 3
    ♡ 8 6 5 3                          ♡ K 10 4
    ◇ J 8 7 5            □             ◇ Q 10 2
    ♣ 7                                ♣ A 6 3
                        ♠ J 5 4
                        ♡ A 7 2
                        ◇ 4
                        ♣ K Q 10 9 8 2
```

Problems

9. Dlr: South   ♠ Q J 3
       Vul: N-S   ♡ K 4
                  ◇ 9 6 5
                  ♣ K Q J 5 4

♠ K 5
♡ Q 10 9 5
◇ A Q 10 2   □
♣ 10 8 7

WEST	NORTH	EAST	SOUTH
			1 ♠
Pass	2 ♣	Pass	2 ◇
Pass	3 ♠	Pass	4 ♠
All Pass			

You, West, lead the ten of hearts. Dummy's king wins, East playing the two and declarer the three. The queen of spades is then led and run to your king. What do you lead now?

10. Dlr: South   ♠ A 10 7 4 3
       Vul: E-W   ♡ 9 6 3
                  ◇ 10 9 6 5
                  ♣ A

♠ K J 8
♡ K 10 7 5
◇ 7   □
♣ 10 9 8 7 5

WEST	NORTH	EAST	SOUTH
			1 ♣
Pass	1 ♠	Pass	3 ♣
Pass	3 ◇	Pass	3 NT
All Pass			

You, West, lead the five of hearts, and East's jack loses to declarer's queen. Declarer goes to the club ace, East following low, and plays a spade to the two and queen. Do you win this trick? If so, what do you return?

Solutions

9. You must play East for either the club ace or the diamond king. If you lead a club and declarer turns up with the ace, you get to watch him cash eleven tricks. Keep your options open by leading the two of diamonds.

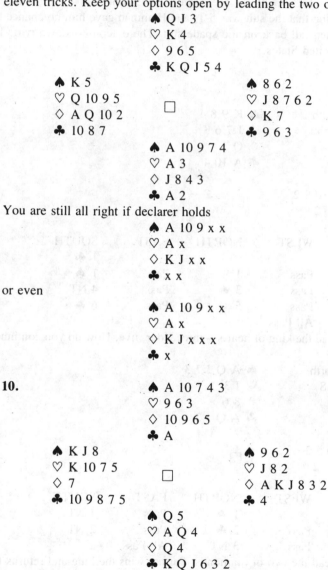

```
              ♠ Q J 3
              ♡ K 4
              ◇ 9 6 5
              ♣ K Q J 5 4
♠ K 5                        ♠ 8 6 2
♡ Q 10 9 5        □          ♡ J 8 7 6 2
◇ A Q 10 2                   ◇ K 7
♣ 10 8 7                     ♣ 9 6 3
              ♠ A 10 9 7 4
              ♡ A 3
              ◇ J 8 4 3
              ♣ A 2
```

You are still all right if declarer holds

```
              ♠ A 10 9 x x
              ♡ A x
              ◇ K J x x
              ♣ x x
```

or even

```
              ♠ A 10 9 x x
              ♡ A x
              ◇ K J x x x
              ♣ x
```

10.

```
              ♠ A 10 7 4 3
              ♡ 9 6 3
              ◇ 10 9 6 5
              ♣ A
♠ K J 8                      ♠ 9 6 2
♡ K 10 7 5        □          ♡ J 8 2
◇ 7                          ◇ A K J 8 3 2
♣ 10 9 8 7 5                 ♣ 4
              ♠ Q 5
              ♡ A Q 4
              ◇ Q 4
              ♣ K Q J 6 3 2
```

The deal is from the 1970 Bermuda Bowl. The play to the first three tricks was the same at both tables. At one table, West returned the heart king at trick four. The U.S. declarer, Bobby Wolff, won and cashed the club king. When clubs unexpectedly split 5-1, Wolff took two more rounds and then tried a spade to the ten. The spade position was as favorable as the clubs had been foul, and Wolff scored his game.

At the other table, Bob Hamman was West for the United States. After winning the spade king, Hamman alertly returned a *spade*. Of course, the Italian declarer went up with the ace, planning to run his clubs. At this stage, he had no inkling that the suit was 5-1, and Hamman gave him no chance to find out and then fall back on the spade suit. The outcome—down two, 11 IMPs to the United States.

Problems

11. Dlr: South
Vul: Both

    ♠ K 9 8 4
    ♡ J 7 6 3
    ◇ Q 3
    ♣ A 10 4

♠ 7 2
♡ K Q 10 8 2
◇ K 8 6 2
♣ 9 3

□

WEST	NORTH	EAST	SOUTH
			1 ♣
Pass	1 ♡	Pass	1 ♠
Pass	3 ♠	Pass	4 NT
Pass	5 ◇	Pass	6 ♠
All Pass			

You, West, lead the king of hearts—three, four, five. How do you continue?

12. Dlr: North
Vul: N-S

    ♠ A Q J 7 3
    ♡ J 3
    ◇ 8 6
    ♣ A Q J 2

♠ 8 5 2
♡ A 10 5 2
◇ A J 5 2
♣ 7 6

□

WEST	NORTH	EAST	SOUTH
	1 ♠	Pass	1 NT
Pass	2 ♣	Pass	2 NT
Pass	3 NT	All Pass	

You, West, lead the two of diamonds. Partner wins the king and returns the nine of diamonds to the declarer's ten and your jack. How do you continue?

11.

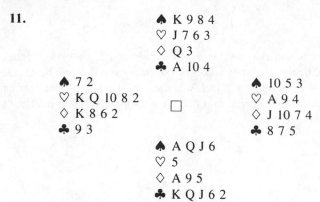

A tough problem. On this bidding, declarer surely has a singleton heart plus very good clubs and spades. A heart continuation may look safe, but declarer, playing in a 4-4 fit, may welcome the chance to score a ruff. In fact, the only move to upset declarer's timing is a *club* switch.

The contract can be made on any other return. Suppose you shift to a trump. Declarer plays dummy's nine. If partner covers, declarer can go to dummy twice in clubs for heart ruffs and overtake a spade honor to draw trumps. If East ducks, declarer remains in dummy, and can ruff two hearts and return to draw trumps without difficulty.

A heart continuation at trick two makes it even easier. Only a club shift gives declarer more problems than he can handle.

12.

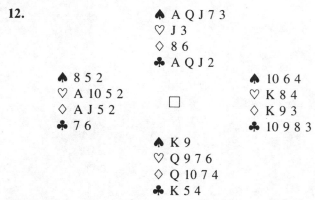

Declarer is marked with the diamond queen, and you may assume that he has the spade king, else the contract is surely unmakable. If declarer has the kings of clubs and hearts there is no defense, so you must find partner with one king. Should you try a low heart lead now or shift to clubs?

A count of tricks will give some guidance. A club lead would prove immediately fatal if declarer had that king. Not so a heart. Even if the South hand is

♠ K x
♡ K Q 9 x
♢ Q 10 x x
♣ x x x

(presumably, East would not have returned a diamond if he knew declarer had five of them), declarer cannot make the contract even if a low heart rides to his nine. You will let dummy's jack win the next heart, and declarer can take only five spades, two hearts, and one club. Nor will it help declarer to force out your diamond jack.

Card Combinations We Have Known

The proper handling of card combinations is at the heart of good declarer play, but there are many standard *defensive* card combinations as well. In fact, this is probably a more difficult area for the defenders to master. Declarer, at least, has all his resources in plain view, but playing good defense requires imagination and a developed sense of the cards.

The defenders customarily lead the highest card in a sequence to force out declarer's top cards and promote their own intermediates. Even if a defender's holding is not truly a sequence, similar results may be achieved. The position below requires West to make an honor-trapping play (often called a "surrounding" play).

```
                Q 7 3
K J 9            □              A 6 4 2
                10 8 5
```

West, deducing that his partner has the ace, leads this suit. The proper card to lead is the *jack*, which makes use of the nine as though it were the ten. Note that this play leaves declarer helpless, while no other attack by West would be sure to succeed.

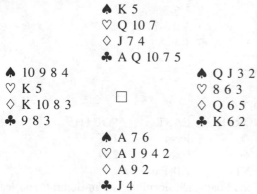

```
            ♠ K 5
            ♡ Q 10 7
            ◇ J 7 4
            ♣ A Q 10 7 5
♠ 10 9 8 4                    ♠ Q J 3 2
♡ K 5            □            ♡ 8 6 3
◇ K 10 8 3                    ◇ Q 6 5
♣ 9 8 3                      ♣ K 6 2
            ♠ A 7 6
            ♡ A J 9 4 2
            ◇ A 9 2
            ♣ J 4
```

South becomes declarer in four hearts. West leads the ten of spades. Declarer wins in dummy and finesses the ten of hearts to West's king. Looking at dummy's strong clubs, West should be anxious to shift to a diamond. But not just any diamond will do—West must table the *ten*, the card he would lead if he had a sequence headed by the ten. If West leads a low card instead and declarer plays low from dummy, the defense is ruined.

In a pinch, the defenders may have to try for a surrounding play in precarious circumstances:

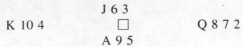

J 6 3

K 10 4   □   Q 8 7 2

A 9 5

West, who must break this suit, does best to lead the *ten*. Luckily, East comes through by holding the eight and seven as well as the queen.

Defenders who frequently try honor-trapping plays may risk becoming trapped themselves. They constantly must try to count declarer's distribution so disasters like the one below can be avoided:

10 6 4

A 7 5 2   □   K J 8 3

Q 9

East must lead this suit and proudly attempts an honor-trapping play by starting with the jack. Not a roaring success.

Another problem the defenders must contend with is blocked suits. In Quiz 4 we saw a couple of unblocking examples. Here is another:

Q 7

A 10 8 6 5 2   □   J 9

K 4 3

West leads the six of this suit against notrump. When declarer puts up dummy's queen to win the trick, East must get his jack out of the way.

A more difficult illustration of the same idea:

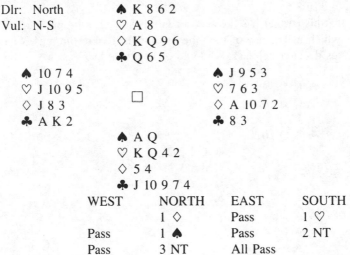

Dlr: North   ♠ K 8 6 2
Vul: N-S   ♡ A 8
                ♢ K Q 9 6
                ♣ Q 6 5

♠ 10 7 4   ♠ J 9 5 3
♡ J 10 9 5   ♡ 7 6 3
♢ J 8 3   □   ♢ A 10 7 2
♣ A K 2   ♣ 8 3

                ♠ A Q
                ♡ K Q 4 2
                ♢ 5 4
                ♣ J 10 9 7 4

WEST	NORTH	EAST	SOUTH
	1 ♢	Pass	1 ♡
Pass	1 ♠	Pass	2 NT
Pass	3 NT	All Pass	

South plays in 3 NT. He wins the heart-jack opening lead in dummy and leads a club to the jack and king. To give the defense a chance now, West must shift to the *eight* of diamonds.

244

Problems

1. Dlr: South
    Vul: N-S

♠ K 9 3 2
♡ 9
◇ A Q 7 6 4
♣ Q 5 4

                  ♠ 10 8 6 5
                □   ♡ A J 7 4
                  ◇ 9 8 5
                  ♣ K 2

WEST	NORTH	EAST	SOUTH
			1 NT
Pass	2 ♣	Pass	2 ◇
Pass	3 NT	All Pass	

West, your partner, leads the three of hearts. Plan your defense.

2. Dlr: East
    Vul: Both

♠ J 7 3
♡ J 10 9
◇ A Q 10 3
♣ A 8 4

♠ A 10 8 6
♡ A 2
◇ 2   □
♣ Q J 7 6 3 2

WEST	NORTH	EAST	SOUTH
		Pass	Pass
1 ♣	Pass	Pass	1 NT[1]
Pass	3 NT	All Pass	

[1] in the balancing seat, 12-14 HCP

You, West, lead a hopeful six of clubs. East can only contribute the five, and declarer wins the ten. At trick two, declarer leads a low heart. How do you defend?

Solutions

1. Win the heart ace and return the seven or jack of hearts. You may need to hang on to that precious heart four until the fourth round of the suit. The full deal:

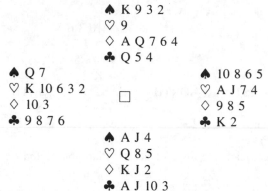

♠ K 9 3 2
♥ 9
♦ A Q 7 6 4
♣ Q 5 4

♠ Q 7   ♠ 10 8 6 5
♥ K 10 6 3 2   ♥ A J 7 4
♦ 10 3   ♦ 9 8 5
♣ 9 8 7 6   ♣ K 2

♠ A J 4
♥ Q 8 5
♦ K J 2
♣ A J 10 3

If East returns the heart four at trick two and declarer plays the eight, the suit will block and the defense can manage only four heart tricks before giving up the lead. Declarer then takes the rest.

N-S's bidding was not best, but it will cost them nothing unless East is alert.

2. It isn't often that you know *exactly* how many HCP your partner has at trick one. East probably has a red king and the queen of spades. If he had, say, the heart queen and spade king, declarer would go to dummy and lead the heart jack for a finesse.

If you beat this hand, it will be with the spade suit. Go in with the heart ace and shift to the *ten* of spades, an honor-trapping play. The full deal:

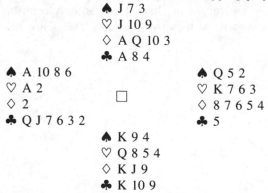

♠ J 7 3
♥ J 10 9
♦ A Q 10 3
♣ A 8 4

♠ A 10 8 6   ♠ Q 5 2
♥ A 2   ♥ K 7 6 3
♦ 2   ♦ 8 7 6 5 4
♣ Q J 7 6 3 2   ♣ 5

♠ K 9 4
♥ Q 8 5 4
♦ K J 9
♣ K 10 9

Note that *you must win the first heart*. If East wins, he cannot attack spades effectively from his side. And if you play low and East ducks as well, declarer has nine tricks (counting one he'll take in spades or a second heart).

Your opening lead didn't look too dynamic, but it was better than a low spade.

Problems

3. Dlr: South   ♠ K 5 4
    Vul: E-W   ♡ A J 8 5 3
                     ◇ 6 5
                     ♣ Q 5 4

♠ A Q 10 2
♡ 7 2
◇ K Q 10 9 3   □
♣ 8 7

WEST	NORTH	EAST	SOUTH
			1 NT
Pass	2 ♣	Pass	2 ◇
Pass	3 ♡	Pass	3 NT
All Pass			

You, West, lead the *queen* of diamonds—you and partner have adopted the popular modern treatment whereby the lead of the queen asks partner to drop the jack if he has it. However, the play to the first trick goes queen, five, two, four. What do you lead to trick two?

4. Dlr: South   ♠ 9 6 3
    Vul: Both   ♡ K J 2
                     ◇ A J 10 6 5
                     ♣ A 5

                   ♠ K Q 4
                   ♡ A 7
       □   ◇ K 9 7 2
                   ♣ 8 7 4 3

WEST	NORTH	EAST	SOUTH
			1 ♡
Pass	2 ◇	Pass	2 NT
Pass	4 ♡	All Pass	

West, your partner, leads a trump against South's heart game. You take your ace. What do you lead to trick two?

Solutions

3. Declarer is marked with the diamond ace and jack, so you must shift. Try the *queen* of spades, an honor-trapping play. Your ace-ten will remain behind declarer's hypothetical jack. The full deal might be:

♠ K 5 4
♡ A J 8 5 3
♢ 6 5
♣ Q 5 4

♠ A Q 10 2   ♠ 8 6 3
♡ 7 2   ♡ K 9 4
♢ K Q 10 9 3   ♢ 8 7 2
♣ 8 7   ♣ 10 9 6 2

♠ J 9 7
♡ Q 10 6
♢ A J 4
♣ A K J 3

If declarer ducks your queen of spades in both hands, you can lead a low spade next, maintaining a link with partner.

4. You can count one heart trick and one diamond. There aren't enough missing points for West's clubs to be as good as king-jack, so you will need two spade tricks. Against most declarers, lead the *four*, forcing a guess if South's spades are A-J-x-(x). The full deal:

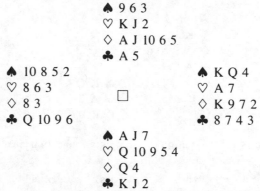

♠ 9 6 3
♡ K J 2
♢ A J 10 6 5
♣ A 5

♠ 10 8 5 2   ♠ K Q 4
♡ 8 6 3   ♡ A 7
♢ 8 3   ♢ K 9 7 2
♣ Q 10 9 6   ♣ 8 7 4 3

♠ A J 7
♡ Q 10 9 5 4
♢ Q 4
♣ K J 2

If both East and South are experts, positions like this can become a complex game of bluff and double bluff. As we have seen, an expert East invariably would lead the ten from Q-10-x or K-10-x here. So if East leads a low card instead, South might reason that East cannot have one of those holdings, and he might reject the percentage play of ducking to dummy's nine. So the next time East has K-10-x, he tries the effect of leading low, figuring that declarer might put the jack in with A-J-8. It's a real ride on a carousel.

Problems

5. Dlr: South   ♠ Q 5 2
     Vul: N-S   ♡ K Q 8 2
                    ◇ 6 5 4
                    ♣ A 5 4

♠ 7 3
♡ J 7 3
◇ Q J 10 8   □
♣ K 10 8 2

WEST	NORTH	EAST	SOUTH
			1 NT
Pass	3 NT	All Pass	

You, West, lead the queen of diamonds. Partner plays the two, and declarer's king wins. A spade is led to the queen. East produces the ace and returns the nine of diamonds to declarer's ace. Declarer cashes the king and jack of spades, East following with the eight and nine as you pitch a low club.

After some thought, declarer exits with a diamond. You win, and partner throws the club three. When you cash the fourth diamond, dummy discards a club and East lets go the club nine. What do you lead to trick eight?

6. Dlr: South   ♠ K J 2
     Vul: Both   ♡ 10 7 6 2
                    ◇ K 5 4
                    ♣ J 9 3

♠ Q 10 7 6 4
♡ A 9 3
◇ 8 7   □
♣ Q 7 2

WEST	NORTH	EAST	SOUTH
			1 ♣
Pass	1 ♡	Pass	2 ◇
Pass	3 ♣	Pass	3 NT
All Pass			

You, West, lead the six of spades. Dummy's jack wins the trick, East playing the three and declarer the five. At trick two the nine of clubs is led—eight, four, queen. What do you lead next?

Solutions

5. Lead the jack of hearts, which cannot cost. If you lead a low heart and declarer turns up with the ace-nine doubleton, a trick is lost. The full deal might be:

Declarer could have made the contract by cashing three rounds of hearts before putting you in with a diamond, but that line of play wasn't clearly indicated.

6. On the bidding, declarer probably has five clubs, four diamonds, and two cards in each major. Therefore he has nine tricks (four clubs, three spades, at least two diamonds) unless you can cash out right now. But even if the tricks are there for you, with declarer holding no better than Q-x in hearts, it may be necessary to lead your heart *nine* to avoid a blockage.

East wins the king of hearts and returns the four to your ace. Then the lead of the heart three will go through dummy's 10-7 to partner's J-8.

250

Problems

7. Dlr: North   ♠ A 6 3
      Vul: None   ♡ A 8 3
                  ◇ Q J 10 6 5
                  ♣ Q 2

                            ♠ K 5
                            ♡ Q 9 7 5
               □   ◇ A 8 3
                            ♣ 10 7 5 3

WEST	NORTH	EAST	SOUTH
	1 ◇	Pass	2 NT
Pass	3 NT	All Pass	

West, your partner, leads the jack of spades, ducked to your king. What do you play to trick two?

8. Dlr: South   ♠ 8 5 2
      Vul: None   ♡ K 9 5 3
                  ◇ A Q 10 8 4
                  ♣ A

                            ♠ Q J 9 6
                            ♡ 10 8 7 4
               □   ◇ K 5
                            ♣ K J 2

WEST	NORTH	EAST	SOUTH
			1 ♣
Pass	1 ◇	Pass	1 NT
Pass	2 ♡	Pass	2 NT
Pass	3 NT	All Pass	

West, your partner, leads the seven of clubs. Plan your defense.

Solutions

7.

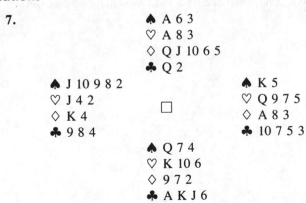

                  ♠ A 6 3
                  ♡ A 8 3
                  ◇ Q J 10 6 5
                  ♣ Q 2

♠ J 10 9 8 2   ♠ K 5
♡ J 4 2   ♡ Q 9 7 5
◇ K 4   □   ◇ A 8 3
♣ 9 8 4   ♣ 10 7 5 3

                  ♠ Q 7 4
                  ♡ K 10 6
                  ◇ 9 7 2
                  ♣ A K J 6

Some honor-trapping positions are less obvious than the ones seen so far. East knows that the spade suit holds out little hope for a set, since West cannot have two entries. East must shift to hearts, and the proper card to lead is the *nine*, entrapping dummy's eight.

Say declarer plays the ten, West covers with the jack, and dummy's ace wins. West will win the first diamond and return a heart, setting up two tricks for East while he still has the diamond ace.

No other card is sure to beat the contract. The lead of the heart five is immediately fatal if declarer plays low. If East starts with the queen and declarer guesses to win the king, neither defender can lead the suit again safely. (True, if East leads the queen, declarer might win in dummy—but the defense still will be limited to four tricks. Work out for yourself how the play will develop.)

8.

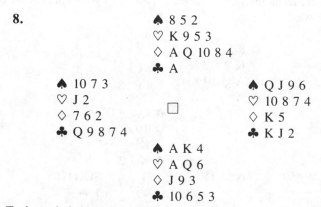

To have led the opponent's suit when the auction begged for a spade lead, West must have pretty good clubs. The Rule of Eleven (see Quiz 5) marks declarer with just one club higher than the seven. This must be the ten, since West would not lead the seven from 10-9-8-7. So you should dump your jack of clubs (or even the king) under dummy's ace.

South would have done better to bid three diamonds or two spades at his third turn—that would have led N-S to a cold five-diamond contract.

Problems

9. Dlr: South   ♠ Q 4
Vul: None   ♡ K Q J 6 3
               ◇ Q 10
               ♣ K 8 6 4

♠ J 10 9 8
♡ 10 4 2
◇ K J 7 4   □
♣ A 5

WEST	NORTH	EAST	SOUTH
			1 ◇
Pass	1 ♡	Pass	1 ♠
Pass	2 ♣	Pass	2 NT
Pass	3 NT	All Pass	

You, West, lead the jack of spades, and dummy's queen holds. At trick two, declarer plays a club to the two, queen and your ace. How do you continue?

10. Dlr: South   ♠ Q 9 6 3
Vul: Both   ♡ K 7 4
               ◇ K Q 5
               ♣ K 7 2

               ♠ 8 2
      □   ♡ 10 8 6
               ◇ A 9 6 2
               ♣ Q J 8 3

WEST	NORTH	EAST	SOUTH
			1 ♠
Pass	3 ♠	Pass	4 ♠
All Pass			

West, your partner, leads the jack of diamonds. You capture dummy's king with the ace and return the diamond two. Declarer wins in dummy, ruffs a diamond, and draws two rounds of trumps with the ace and king. Now the ace and king of clubs are cashed, and declarer exits with a club to your jack, partner following suit. How do you defend?

Solutions

  9. Declarer probably has the heart ace, else he would have started on hearts immediately instead of clubs. In that case, you can count nine tricks for him—five hearts, three spades, and a club. So you must hit diamonds despite declarer's opening bid. Partner will have to hold the diamond ace, but you still must lead the king to make sure the defensive timing is right. The full deal:

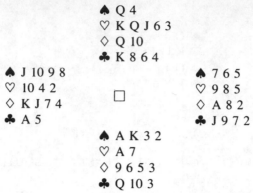

♠ Q 4
♥ K Q J 6 3
♦ Q 10
♣ K 8 6 4

♠ J 10 9 8   ♠ 7 6 5
♥ 10 4 2   □   ♥ 9 8 5
♦ K J 7 4   ♦ A 8 2
♣ A 5   ♣ J 9 7 2

♠ A K 3 2
♥ A 7
♦ 9 6 5 3
♣ Q 10 3

On the king of diamonds, East will unblock the eight. Then a diamond to the ace and a diamond back through the 9-6 to your J-7 will get the job done.

10.

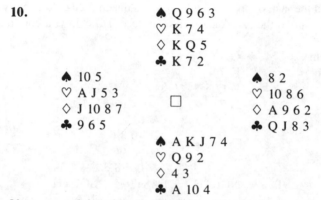

♠ Q 9 6 3
♥ K 7 4
♦ K Q 5
♣ K 7 2

♠ 10 5   ♠ 8 2
♥ A J 5 3   □   ♥ 10 8 6
♦ J 10 8 7   ♦ A 9 6 2
♣ 9 6 5   ♣ Q J 8 3

♠ A K J 7 4
♥ Q 9 2
♦ 4 3
♣ A 10 4

You are endplayed and obliged to open up hearts. As usual, be alert for "surrounding" possibilities. This time, the lead of the *eight* works. Some of these honor-trapping plays are pretty obscure, aren't they?

If you lead the ten, declarer covers with the queen—West is fixed whether he wins or ducks. If you lead low, partner has to put up the jack to force dummy's king, and declarer can lead low to the nine next to drive out the ace. Only the lead of the eight leaves declarer without recourse.

Problems

11. Dlr: South
Vul: N-S

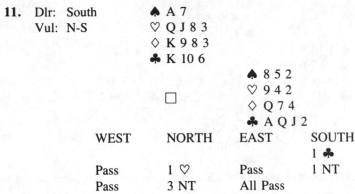

♠ A 7
♡ Q J 8 3
◇ K 9 8 3
♣ K 10 6

                    ♠ 8 5 2
                    ♡ 9 4 2
            □   ◇ Q 7 4
                    ♣ A Q J 2

WEST	NORTH	EAST	SOUTH
			1 ♣
Pass	1 ♡	Pass	1 NT
Pass	3 NT	All Pass	

West, your partner, leads the jack of spades. Declarer plays low from dummy and wins the queen in hand. At trick two, the diamond jack is run to your queen. How do you continue?

12. Dlr: South
Vul: E-W

♠ 9 5 2
♡ 10 7
◇ A 4
♣ K Q 10 9 4 3

                    ♠ K 10 8 6
                    ♡ A J 2
            □   ◇ K 9 8
                    ♣ 7 6 2

WEST	NORTH	EAST	SOUTH
			1 NT
Pass	3 NT	All Pass	

West, your partner, leads the nine of hearts. Dummy's ten covers. Plan your defense.

Solutions

11. A spade continuation is futile. If West's spades are K-J-10-x-x, declarer must have the diamond ace and the heart ace and king for nine tricks in all. You must shift, but the right answer, for some reason, is hard to spot. With dummy holding just three clubs, it is sufficient to return the club *two*. Declarer may win cheaply, but your three honors remain poised behind the king, and you are worth three tricks if partner has a red-suit entry. The full deal:

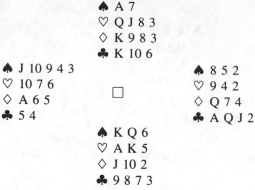

♠ A 7
♥ Q J 8 3
♦ K 9 8 3
♣ K 10 6

♠ J 10 9 4 3   ♠ 8 5 2
♥ 10 7 6   ♥ 9 4 2
♦ A 6 5   □   ♦ Q 7 4
♣ 5 4   ♣ A Q J 2

♠ K Q 6
♥ A K 5
♦ J 10 2
♣ 9 8 7 3

You give the contract away if you lead a club honor or any other suit at trick three.

12.   ♠ 9 5 2
                       ♥ 10 7
                       ♦ A 4
                       ♣ K Q 10 9 4 3

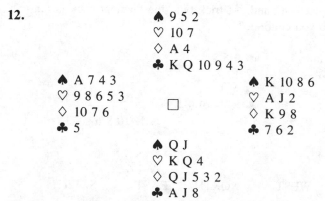

♠ A 7 4 3   ♠ K 10 8 6
♥ 9 8 6 5 3   ♥ A J 2
♦ 10 7 6   □   ♦ K 9 8
♣ 5   ♣ 7 6 2

♠ Q J
♥ K Q 4
♦ Q J 5 3 2
♣ A J 8

If you won the heart ace and shifted to the ten of spades to trap dummy's nine, sorry—I doublecrossed you. You must lead a low spade this time and collect your four spade tricks.

West has at most 4 HCP, and there is just no chance to beat the contract unless he has the spade ace. If West has, say, the spade and diamond queens, declarer has six club tricks, one diamond, two hearts, and a spade. The only alternative defense that appeals at all is a shift to the king of diamonds, trying to kill dummy if partner has the club ace. But that would leave declarer with something like

♠ A Q J
♥ K Q x x
♦ Q J x x
♣ J x,

and if he holds that hand, he can make the contract without the clubs.

Trying for an honor-trapping play is wrong here because you need *four fast spade tricks* to beat the contract.

256

One Suit at a Time

This quiz deals with an important defensive skill. Good bridge players possess something called "card sense," which gives them a natural advantage in drawing inferences. Luckily, card sense *can* be learned—so don't despair if you think you were missing when they doled it out.

Inferring the lie of an individual suit based on the play of that suit is a first step in the defenders' all-important task of reconstructing declarer's whole hand. The key to figuring these things out is to put yourself in declarer's place and consider how you would have played with various holdings. In many situations, the answer will be obvious:

$$K\ 4$$
2 led > > >   □   A Q 8 5

You are defending four spades, dummy has plenty of trumps, and this is a side suit. Partner's opening lead is two; declarer puts up the king. Who has the jack? Clearly, partner has it—otherwise declarer would have played low from dummy, hoping partner led from the queen.

It may not always be so clear what's going on. Here, for example, if declarer played low from dummy, you wouldn't be a hundred percent sure who had the jack. Expecting you to hold the ace, declarer might well play low from dummy whatever his holding was.

♠ 10
♠ K 9   □

The contract is four spades, and dummy has no entries. Declarer, who bid spades vigorously, wins the opening lead, cashes the ace of trumps, and leads the queen to your king, partner following low both times. If declarer's trumps were A-Q-J-x-x-x-x, he would start by leading low to the ten. Playing the ace first could gain nothing; even if the king fell singleton, a trick still would have to be lost to the nine. And laying down the ace first would cost a trick if either defender had K-9-x-x. So you can place declarer with an *eight*-card trump suit.

More inferences are available if you're defending a notrump contract. A simple example:

A J 9 3
Q 5 2   □

Declarer attacks this suit by leading low to the nine, losing to partner's ten. Obviously, partner has the king also—declarer's play would make little sense otherwise.

9 8 5 4
K Q J 3   □

You lead the king—four, two, six. Partner must have either the ace or the ten. If declarer held both, he could have ensured a second stopper by winning your lead.

A Q 10

7 5 3   □

Declarer leads low to the ten, losing to partner's jack. Partner is very likely to have the king, too.

K 5

2 led > > >   □   A Q 7 3

Declarer plays low from dummy, and you win the queen. If declarer's holding was x-x-x or even 10-x-x, he would have tried dummy's king immediately. You'd expect him to have J-x-x.

Reasoning out single-suit holdings will help you develop your card sense, but here we must deliver a caveat: it can be dangerous to consider a suit outside the context of the whole hand. Here are a couple of full deals on which a defender's assessment of a single suit is the key to the best defense.

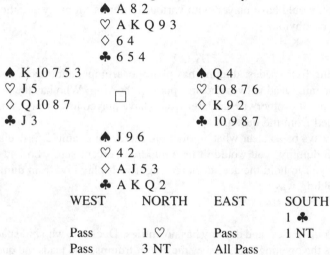

♠ A 8 2
♡ A K Q 9 3
◇ 6 4
♣ 6 5 4

♠ K 10 7 5 3   ♠ Q 4
♡ J 5   □   ♡ 10 8 7 6
◇ Q 10 8 7   ◇ K 9 2
♣ J 3   ♣ 10 9 8 7

♠ J 9 6
♡ 4 2
◇ A J 5 3
♣ A K Q 2

WEST	NORTH	EAST	SOUTH
			1 ♣
Pass	1 ♡	Pass	1 NT
Pass	3 NT	All Pass	

West leads the five of spades. If declarer were to go up with dummy's ace, hoping to block the suit, East could infer that declarer did not have K-J-x or J-10-x, and probably not K-10-x. He could safely unblock the queen.

This time, however, declarer ducks the first spade and wins the second round. Now he must develop four heart tricks without letting West in the lead, so he comes to hand with a high club and leads a heart. West can infer that declarer has only two hearts, else he would have cashed a top honor in dummy first (or he might even have played off all three top honors). So West puts up the heart jack, ruining South's plan to duck a heart safely to East.

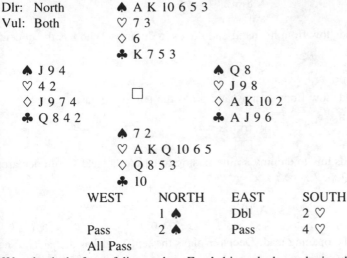

Dlr: North
Vul: Both

♠ A K 10 6 5 3
♡ 7 3
♢ 6
♣ K 7 5 3

♠ J 9 4
♡ 4 2
♢ J 9 7 4
♣ Q 8 4 2

□

♠ Q 8
♡ J 9 8
♢ A K 10 2
♣ A J 9 6

♠ 7 2
♡ A K Q 10 6 5
♢ Q 8 5 3
♣ 10

WEST	NORTH	EAST	SOUTH
	1 ♠	Dbl	2 ♡
Pass	2 ♠	Pass	4 ♡
All Pass			

West leads the four of diamonds to East's king, declarer playing the five. Declarer wins the trump shift and plays a spade to the four, ten, and queen. What should East return?

East has a good picture of declarer's hand. South has at least three diamonds and should have exactly two spades to play the suit in this manner. If he had a solid seven-card trump suit, he would have ruffed a diamond for the contract— so he must have only six hearts. Since declarer did not choose to take a diamond ruff, he must have thought it wouldn't help him take ten tricks.* He must be relying on the spades, so East must return a spade, cutting declarer's link with dummy.

Problems (A)

You are defending a *suit contract*. (To make things as simple as possible, assume that the suits below are side suits, dummy has plenty of trumps, and both declarer and dummy have ample entries.)

1.

K J 3

2 led > > >   □   Q 9 4

The two is the opening lead. Declarer plays low from dummy. Which card do you play?

2.

K J 9 3

A 6 5   □

Declarer leads low to the nine, losing to partner's ten. Who has the queen? How many cards does declarer have?

---

*The play would be interesting if declarer ruffed a diamond at trick three and led a club. To beat the contract, West would have to win and lead a spade. On any other defense, East falls victim to a three-suit squeeze. Do you see how declarer can always make the contract?

3.
                     A 8 6 2

                     ☐   K J 9

Declarer leads low from his hand and ducks in dummy. Who has the queen?

4.
                     Q 6 2

    K J 9   ☐

Declarer leads low from dummy and plays the ten. Who has the ace?

5.
                     K 10 9 4

    A 6 5   ☐

Declarer leads low to dummy's nine, losing to partner's jack. Could declarer have Q-x? Q-x-x? x-x-x? x-x?

6.
                     A 10 5

    2 led > > >   ☐   Q 9 7

The two is the opening lead. Declarer plays the ten. Who has the jack? Who has the eight?

7.
                     6 4

    Q J 7 3   ☐

Declarer leads low from dummy to his ten. Could declarer have x-x-x? K-10-x? A-10-x-x?

8.
                     Q J 10 3

    K 9 5 4   ☐

Declarer leads low toward dummy. Who has the ace?

9.
                     9

    K 7 5 2   ☐

The nine is led from dummy, partner and declarer play low. Who has the ace? Who has the queen?

10.
                     10 5 3

    K Q 9 4   ☐

You lead the king, which holds. Could declarer have the ace? The jack? The ace-jack?

11.
                     7 3

    Q 10 5   ☐

Declarer leads low from dummy to the nine. Can declarer have J-9-x-x? K-9-x-x? K-J-9-x? A-9-x-x?

12.
                     A 10 2

    K 6 5 3   ☐

Declarer leads low from dummy to the queen. Who has the jack?

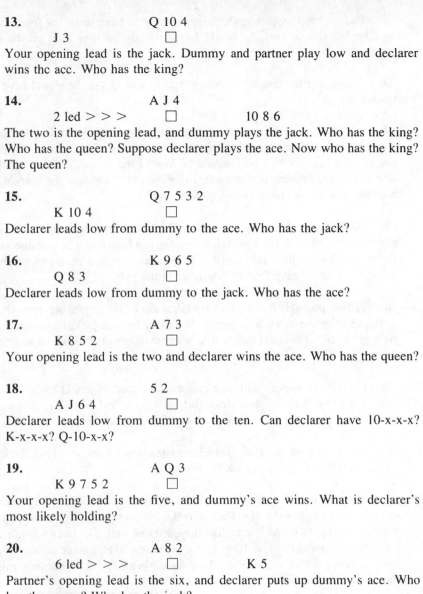

13.   Q 10 4

J 3   □

Your opening lead is the jack. Dummy and partner play low and declarer wins the ace. Who has the king?

14.   A J 4

2 led > > >   □   10 8 6

The two is the opening lead, and dummy plays the jack. Who has the king? Who has the queen? Suppose declarer plays the ace. Now who has the king? The queen?

15.   Q 7 5 3 2

K 10 4   □

Declarer leads low from dummy to the ace. Who has the jack?

16.   K 9 6 5

Q 8 3   □

Declarer leads low from dummy to the jack. Who has the ace?

17.   A 7 3

K 8 5 2   □

Your opening lead is the two and declarer wins the ace. Who has the queen?

18.   5 2

A J 6 4   □

Declarer leads low from dummy to the ten. Can declarer have 10-x-x-x? K-x-x-x? Q-10-x-x?

19.   A Q 3

K 9 7 5 2   □

Your opening lead is the five, and dummy's ace wins. What is declarer's most likely holding?

20.   A 8 2

6 led > > >   □   K 5

Partner's opening lead is the six, and declarer puts up dummy's ace. Who has the queen? Who has the jack?

Solutions (A)

(The following inferences generally are sound. However, we repeat our admonition about always considering individual suits within the context of the whole hand. When declarer is able to place the cards, or perhaps for tactical reasons, he may depart from the normal way of attacking a suit.)

1.   Play the nine, since partners seldom underlead aces against suit contracts—not at trick one, anyway.

2. Partner has the queen. Declarer is likely to have three (or four) cards —if he had one or two, he would have tried the jack or king on the first round.

3. Partner has the queen. If declarer had Q-x or Q-x-x, he would have led toward the queen.

4. Uncertain. If declarer is capable, partner may well have the ace. Declarer could have A-10 doubleton, but then he might not break the suit at all. If he had A-10-x-(x), his best play would be low to the queen; if that lost, then low to the ten. Perhaps declarer has a singleton or doubleton and is trying to establish some communication with his hand.

5. Declarer could have queen doubleton or tripleton but is more likely to have three small cards from his failure to play to a high honor before finessing. He is not likely to have two small, else he usually would have gone up with dummy's king, hoping for just one loser in the suit.

6. Partner probably has the jack (but declarer could be playing deceptively or trying to get an entry to dummy). If partner has the jack, he should have the eight also—if declarer had K-8-x, his percentage play would be low from dummy.

7. Declarer is marked with one honor, since partner would have won the trick if holding both ace and king. But if declarer had the king, he usually would have played it, trying for just one loser. He should have A-10-x-(x).

8. Partner has the ace (unless declarer somehow knows you have the king and he is trying to sneak a trick by you).

9. Partner must have the ace—even with dummy leading a singleton, it often would be right for him to duck to make declarer guess. However, partner would be unlikely to duck if he had the queen as well. Declarer's holding is probably Q-10-x-(x) or Q-J-10-x. Q-J-x-(x) is less likely, since partner might have covered with the ten from A-10-8-(x). With Q-J-8-x, declarer might have played an honor from hand.

10. Declarer might have the ace or the jack, but he can hardly have both cards—in that case, ducking would cost a trick.

11. Declarer must have either the ace or king. With K-J-9-(x), he usually would play an honor, hoping for one loser. With K-9-x-(x), he would put the king up. He should have A-9-x-(x).

12. Partner must have the jack, to judge from declarer's failure to finesse against your king.

13. Unless declarer had the singleton ace, he has both the ace and king. With A-x-(x), he would have covered your jack with the queen.

14. Declarer is marked with one honor (partner would not lead low from the king and queen). If declarer had the queen, he would duck the opening lead. When he plays the jack, he must hold the king. If declarer plays the ace, he must hold the king *and* queen for his play to make sense.

15. Partner has the jack. If declarer had it, he surely would have finessed.

16. Declarer is likely to have the ace. If his holding was J-x-(x), he would prefer to lead *toward* the king.

17. Partner should have the queen, judging from declarer's refusal to let the opening lead run to his hand. However, if some fast discards are available in dummy, declarer might proceed to win the first trick, planning to throw his queen away.

18. With the king and queen, partner normally would split his honors to ensure one trick. If declarer's holding was K-10-x-(x), he would play the king, hoping for just one loser. He should have Q-10-x-(x).

19. Declarer probably has a singleton. Again, though, he could have his reasons for going up even without a singleton. He could be planning to discard his losers in this suit, or he might need to win the first trick to gain a *tempo*.

20. Partner is likely to have the queen (since declarer did not duck the first trick), but less likely to have the jack (partner might have led the queen from queen-jack).

Problems (B)

You are defending a notrump contract. Again, assume that declarer has adequate entries in both hands.

21. J 4
3 led > > > ☐ K 9 5 2
Partner's opening lead is the three—four, king, ace. Did declarer start with A-Q-x? A-x-x? A-10-x?

22. Q 8
4 led > > > ☐ K 10 6 3
Partner's opening lead is the four, dummy plays the eight. Does declarer have A-x-x? A-J-x?

23.　　　　　　　7 4 2
　　A J 5　　　　　□

Declarer attacks this suit by leading the two to his ten. Who has queen? Who has king? Who has the nine?

24.　　　　　　　7 5 3
　　A Q 4　　　　　□

Declarer leads the three to his king. Who has the jack?

25.　　　　　　　Q 10 8 6 3
　　　　　　　　　　□　　　　K 7 5

Declarer wins the first trick in his hand, goes to dummy with another suit, and leads the three of this, a third suit. Who has the ace?

26.　　　　　　　A 3
　　Q 10 7 5 2　　　□

Your opening lead is the five; dummy's ace wins; partner and declarer play low. Who has the king? Who has the jack?

27.　　　　　　　J 9 5
　　2 led > > >　　□　　　　Q 8 4 3

Partner's opening lead is the two, dummy plays the jack. Can declarer have x-x? A-x? K-x? K-10? A-10?

28.　　　　　　　A Q 4
　　K 10 7 5 2　　　□

Your opening lead is the five; dummy's queen wins. Who has the jack?

29.　　　　　　　A 8 5 3
　　　　　　　　　　□　　　　K 6 2

Declarer leads low from dummy. Can declarer have Q-J-10-x? J-10-9-x? Q-J-9-x? Q-10-x? J-9-x-x? J-10-x-x?

30.　　　　　　　Q 10 8 3
　　A K 5 2　　　　□

Declarer leads low; you duck, and dummy's eight loses to partner's nine. Who has the jack?

31.　　　　　　　Q 3
　　J 9 5 2　　　　□

Your opening lead is the two, and dummy's queen is covered by the king and ace. Can declarer have A-10-x? A-10? A-x-x? A-x?

32.　　　　　　　K 9 8 2
　　　　　　　　　　□　　　　A Q 3

Declarer leads low from dummy. Can declarer have J-10-x? 10-x-x? J-7-x?

264

33. A J 6 2

□ K 8 5 3

Declarer leads low from dummy. Can declarer have Q-10-x? Q-x? Q-9-x?

34. K 10 4

2 led > > > □ J 8 3

Partner leads the two, dummy's ten is played, you cover with the jack, and declarer wins the ace. Who has the queen? Who has the nine?

35. A J 9 3 2

K 7 4 □

Declarer leads the two from hand and inserts dummy's nine, losing to partner's ten. Who has the queen?

36. Q J 9 5 2

□ K 3

Declarer leads the ten from hand and plays dummy's two. Who has the ace?

37. A K 9 3

Q 5 2 □

Declarer leads low from dummy to the jack. Who has the ten? How many cards does declarer have?

38. A Q 5 2

□ K 8 6 3

Declarer leads the two from dummy. Can declarer have J-10? J-10-x? J-9? J-9-x? x-x-x? x-x?

39. A 10 7

4 led > > > □ K Q 5

Partner leads the four; declarer puts up dummy's ace. Who has the jack?

40. A K 7

6 led > > > □ Q 4

Partner leads the six; declarer wins an honor in dummy. Who has the jack?

Solutions (B)

21. If declarer had either A-Q-x or A-x-x, he would have played dummy's jack to the first trick, hoping it would hold. A-10-x is his most likely holding.

22. Declarer would have put up the queen holding either A-x-x or A-J-x, hoping it would hold. You should play the king in case declarer's holding is J-x.

23. With K-Q-10-x-(x), most declarers would begin by leading low to the king or queen. (A first-round finesse of the ten would be right if entries to dummy were scarce.) Therefore, partner is likely to have one honor, and declarer might have Q-10-9-x or K-10-9-x. True, declarer is not certain to hold the nine, but he would be slightly less likely to attack the suit without it.

24. Uncertain, but partner is slightly more likely to have the jack. If declarer were attacking the suit with K-J-x-x-(x), his normal play would be low to the jack. If he was in a position where he needed just one fast trick, he might have the king-jack or only the king. In either case, however, declarers often prefer leading to the king, since a good West may try the effect of ducking with A-x-x or A-J-x.

25. Unless declarer is playing a very deep game, partner has the ace. Why would declarer go to dummy just to lead to the ace?

26. With J-x-x, declarer might have tried ducking the first trick. You might easily have led from K-Q-x-x-x. With K-J-x, he surely would have played low from dummy, making certain of three tricks. He should have either K-x-x-(x) or nothing in the suit at all.

27. A tricky situation. A good declarer, looking at A-x or K-x in hand, would play the odds and call for dummy's nine. If declarer has A-10 it doesn't matter what you do, but then declarer usually would play small from dummy without thinking about it. But with K-10 declarer would play the jack, trying to induce you to cover with the queen. (Yes, declarer could have two small cards, but it has to be against the odds—and it may be impossible on the bidding.)

28. Partner has the jack, else declarer would have played low from dummy.

29. Declarer would finesse with Q-J-10-x or Q-J-9-x, and double finesse with J-10-9-x. The other three holdings are entirely possible, and in all three cases you need to play low. (It would be equally correct to play low if your holding was K-x.)

30. Partner has the jack.

31. With A-10-x, declarer would have ducked in dummy to ensure two tricks. A-x or A-x-x is probable, A-10 possible.

32. Declarer would have come to hand to finesse if he had J-10-x-(x). With 10-x-x-(x), he might have come to hand to lead low to the eight, then low to the nine. He also has alternative plays if his holding is J-7-x-(x), but that holding is more likely than the others.

33. Declarer cannot have Q-10-x, with which he would have finessed. With Q-9-x, he might have preferred to play the ace first, then a low one. Q-x is the most probable holding.

34. It's unclear who has the queen, but we know that partner would be reluctant to lead fourth highest from a suit headed by at best the nine. Also, if declarer had A-Q-x, his play of the ten would be a little unnatural (although he could be seeking an extra entry to dummy). If partner has the queen, he must have the nine also—declarer surely would play low from dummy with A-9-x.

35. Most likely, partner has the queen. With Q-x-x, most declarers would start by leading low to the jack; with Q-x they would lead the queen, planning to finesse the nine later if the queen were covered.

36. Almost always, partner will have the ace. It might be right for you to play low, making it harder for declarer to establish the suit if he has 10-x.

37. Partner must have the ten, else declarer would have come to hand to lead the jack for a finesse. Declarer is likely to have only J-x; with J-x-x, he would have started by cashing one or both of dummy's top cards, or he might have come to hand to lead low to the nine.

38. Declarer cannot have both the jack and ten. With J-9-x, he might have cashed the ace before leading low. He might well have J-9. It would also cost declarer nothing to lead low from dummy on the first round with two or three small cards—he would plan to finesse dummy's queen later, but meanwhile he tempts you to rise with the king from K-x-(x).

39. Partner is likely to have the jack, and you should consider unblocking an honor. If declarer had J-x-(x), from his point of view he might get two tricks by ducking, setting up a later finesse.

40. According to the Rule of Eleven, declarer has just one card higher than the six. The odds are against its being the jack, but if it were, declarer might have taken his only chance to make a third trick by ducking the opening lead. If your entry situation permits it, you should consider unblocking your queen.

Problems (C)

41. Dlr: South   ♠ Q 10 5
      Vul: Both   ♡ K J 10 6 4
               ◊ A 8 5
               ♣ 10 5

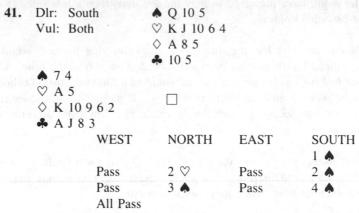

♠ 7 4
♡ A 5
◊ K 10 9 6 2   □
♣ A J 8 3

WEST	NORTH	EAST	SOUTH
			1 ♠
Pass	2 ♡	Pass	2 ♠
Pass	3 ♠	Pass	4 ♠
All Pass			

You, West, lead the ten of diamonds. Dummy's ace wins, partner playing the four and declarer the seven. Declarer draws two rounds of trumps with the ace and jack, East following low-high. Next, declarer leads the heart queen, and you take your ace. How do you continue?

42. Dlr: West   ♠ Q 7 5 2
      Vul: None   ♡ A 10 7 5
               ◊ Q 10 6
               ♣ 7 5

♠ A 10 6
♡ 9 3
◊ K 7 5 4 2   □
♣ Q J 4

WEST	NORTH	EAST	SOUTH
Pass	Pass	1 ♠	2 ♡
3 ♠	4 ♡	All Pass	

You, West, lead the ace of spades and continue with the ten. Declarer ruffs the second spade, leads a heart to the ace, and plays a club to the two, ten, and your jack. How do you continue?

43. Dlr: East   ♠ K 6
      Vul: Both   ♡ Q 5
               ◊ A Q J 10 7
               ♣ A J 4 2

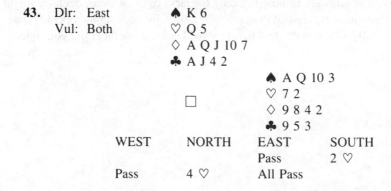

                 ♠ A Q 10 3
          □   ♡ 7 2
                 ◊ 9 8 4 2
                 ♣ 9 5 3

WEST	NORTH	EAST	SOUTH
		Pass	2 ♡
Pass	4 ♡	All Pass	

West, your partner, leads the two of spades, dummy's king losing to your ace. How do you continue?

44. Dlr: East
Vul: N-S

♠ K 8 5 3 2
♡ A 8 5 3 2
◇ 8 6
♣ K

♠ A 7
♡ 4
◇ Q J 9 5 2
♣ 9 8 7 6 3

☐

WEST	NORTH	EAST	SOUTH
		Pass	1 ♣
Pass	1 NT	Pass	2 ♡
Pass	3 ♡	Pass	3 NT
Pass	4 ♣	Pass	4 ◇
Pass	4 ♠	Pass	5 ♣
Pass	6 ♡	All Pass	

One club was strong (17+ HCP) and artificial. 1 NT conventionally showed four controls (A = 2, K = 1). The next three bids were natural, and then cuebidding led to slam.

You, West, lead the queen of diamonds. Declarer wins the king and plays the spade four to dummy's king, East following with the nine. The club king is cashed, and declarer continues with a heart to his king and the heart jack. What do you discard on this trick?

45. Dlr: South
Vul: Both

♠ A 6
♡ K 10 8 7 4
◇ K 10 9
♣ 8 7 5

☐

♠ Q 8 5 3
♡ Q 5 3
◇ A 2
♣ J 10 9 2

WEST	NORTH	EAST	SOUTH
			1 NT
Pass	2 ◇ [1]	Pass	2 ♡
Pass	3 NT[2]	Pass	4 ♡
All Pass			

[1] a "transfer" bid that conventionally asks opener to bid two hearts
[2] offers a choice of games

West, your partner, leads the jack of spades, won by declarer's king. At trick two, the heart nine is led, partner and dummy play low, and you take your queen. How do you continue?

Solutions (C)

41. Lead a low diamond. Declarer would have been obliged to duck the first trick if he had Q-x.

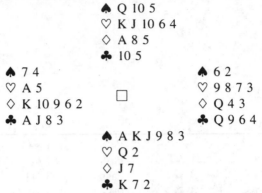

Winning the queen of diamonds, partner knows he must play you for the club ace for the fourth defensive trick. He will return a low club (promising an honor), and you will have no trouble cashing two club tricks.

42. From the club play, declarer is marked with the ace, so East must have the ace of diamonds. Shift to a low diamond, since you may need to cash out.

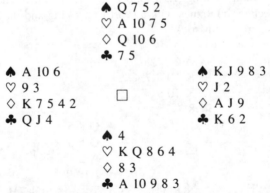

If you carelessly continue with a third spade, declarer will ruff, cash the club ace, establish clubs with a ruff, draw trumps, and discard two diamonds from dummy, making the contract.

43. Declarer has at least three small spades—with J-x-x he wouldn't have put up dummy's king. There are no tricks to be had in the minors (partner would have led a club from king-queen), so your only hope is to get all your spade tricks. Shift to a trump, hoping the full deal is:

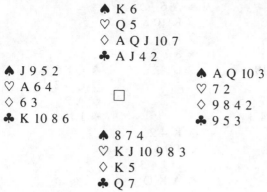

♠ K 6
♡ Q 5
◇ A Q J 10 7
♣ A J 4 2

♠ J 9 5 2   ♠ A Q 10 3
♡ A 6 4   ♡ 7 2
◇ 6 3   ◇ 9 8 4 2
♣ K 10 8 6   ♣ 9 5 3

♠ 8 7 4
♡ K J 10 9 8 3
◇ K 5
♣ Q 7

Partner will duck the first trump, retaining control, and declarer will be unable to get home.

44. Why did declarer play spades before drawing trumps? If he had a guess in the suit (with, say, Q-10-x), he would have put it off as long as possible. (In any case, if he had a guess he has guessed correctly.) It is more likely that declarer led an early spade to prepare for an endplay before you realized there was danger. The full deal:

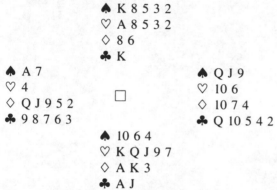

♠ K 8 5 3 2
♡ A 8 5 3 2
◇ 8 6
♣ K

♠ A 7   ♠ Q J 9
♡ 4   ♡ 10 6
◇ Q J 9 5 2   ◇ 10 7 4
♣ 9 8 7 6 3   ♣ Q 10 5 4 2

♠ 10 6 4
♡ K Q J 9 7
◇ A K 3
♣ A J

In a 1970 tournament, Victor Mitchell discarded the *ace of spades* on the second trump, defeating the contract.

Declarer could have made the slam by stripping the minors and leading a spade after playing just one trump. West could have defeated it (rather less spectacularly) by winning the first spade.

45. Declarer has at least an eight-card heart fit. If he had A-x-x, he would cash the ace and king, or at least cash the ace first. With A-J-x he certainly would cash the ace before finessing. So it seems partner must have the heart ace. In that case, there is no point in leading a club, since partner can have no points in the suit. Shift to ace and another diamond, trying for a ruff.

```
                    ♠ A 6
                    ♡ K 10 8 7 4
                    ◇ K 10 9
                    ♣ 8 7 5
♠ J 10 9 7                              ♠ Q 8 5 3
♡ A 2                  □                ♡ Q 5 3
◇ 8 7 6 5                               ◇ A 2
♣ 6 4 3                                 ♣ J 10 9 2
                    ♠ K 4 2
                    ♡ J 9 6
                    ◇ Q J 4 3
                    ♣ A K Q
```

Quiz 20

Counting and More Counting

It's a lot easier to defend well when you know what declarer has. On many hands, in fact, producing the best defense will be impossible unless you keep close track of declarer's high cards, distribution, and playing tricks.

Clues to declarer's hands are always available. He must, for example, give you a peek at his holding in the bidding. To take the simplest example, a 1 NT opening marks declarer with narrowly defined strength and pattern, so the defenders have a big head start on reconstructing his exact holding.

As the play proceeds, other bits of information surface: players will show out as suits are led, partner will signal his distribution, inferences will abound. Sometimes you'll know the whole story before the play is halfway over.

The most difficult hands are those on which you must make a crucial decision very early, before all the evidence is in. It is on such hands that you may have to try for an inferential or hypothetical count (see Quiz 21), make assumptions about the way the cards lie (see Quiz 8), or just venture your best guess.

Three different areas of counting require the defenders' attention. On the hand below, counting declarer's *high-card points* is the key to success.

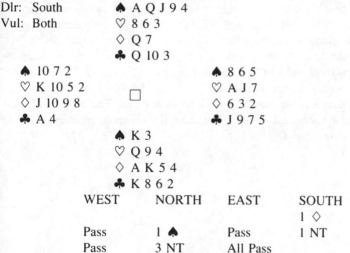

Dlr: South
Vul: Both

```
          ♠ A Q J 9 4
          ♡ 8 6 3
          ◇ Q 7
          ♣ Q 10 3
♠ 10 7 2              ♠ 8 6 5
♡ K 10 5 2           ♡ A J 7
◇ J 10 9 8           ◇ 6 3 2
♣ A 4                ♣ J 9 7 5
          ♠ K 3
          ♡ Q 9 4
          ◇ A K 5 4
          ♣ K 8 6 2
```

WEST	NORTH	EAST	SOUTH
			1 ◇
Pass	1 ♠	Pass	1 NT
Pass	3 NT	All Pass	

West leads the diamond jack. Dummy's queen wins, and declarer plays a club to the king and ace. West knows that declarer has at most 15 HCP, and he already has shown 10—the diamond ace-king and club king. Therefore, declarer's hearts cannot be as good as ace-queen, and a heart play is at the very least safe. (Really, West would expect declarer to hold the spade king—unless declarer's spades were ready to run, he would have won the first trick in hand to take a spade finesse, saving the diamond queen as a dummy entry. So declarer isn't likely to have even as much as the heart ace.)

Getting a count on declarer's *distribution* may require a knowledge of Standard bidding methods.

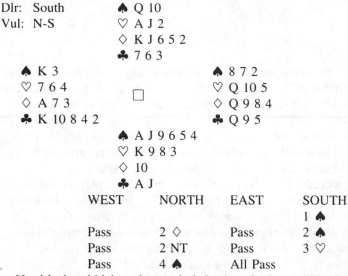

Dlr: South
Vul: N-S

♠ Q 10
♡ A J 2
◇ K J 6 5 2
♣ 7 6 3

♠ K 3
♡ 7 6 4
◇ A 7 3
♣ K 10 8 4 2

♠ 8 7 2
♡ Q 10 5
◇ Q 9 8 4
♣ Q 9 5

♠ A J 9 6 5 4
♡ K 9 8 3
◇ 10
♣ A J

WEST	NORTH	EAST	SOUTH
			1 ♠
Pass	2 ◇	Pass	2 ♠
Pass	2 NT	Pass	3 ♡
Pass	4 ♠	All Pass	

North's last bid is rather optimistic, but that's not West's problem. West leads a club to the queen and ace. At trick two, declarer tables the ten of diamonds.

In Standard, South's sequence suggests six spades, four hearts, and a minimum opening bid. Declarer is marked with the club jack from East's play of the queen, so the diamond ten must be a singleton. West therefore grabs the ace and cashes the club king. A heart switch always beats the contract now (ruining declarer's entries for a red-suit squeeze against East), but even if West never breaks the heart suit, declarer almost surely will go down.

Counting declarer's *tricks* may be most important of all. The big edge: If you know how many winners declarer has, you can tell whether to conduct an active or a passive defense. (See Quiz 9.)

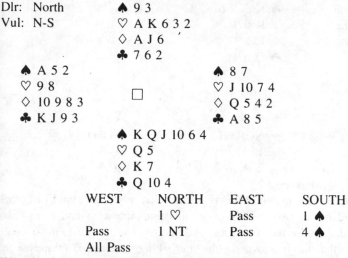

Dlr: North
Vul: N-S

North: ♠ 9 3 ♡ A K 6 3 2 ◇ A J 6 ♣ 7 6 2

West: ♠ A 5 2 ♡ 9 8 ◇ 10 9 8 3 ♣ K J 9 3

East: ♠ 8 7 ♡ J 10 7 4 ◇ Q 5 4 2 ♣ A 8 5

South: ♠ K Q J 10 6 4 ♡ Q 5 ◇ K 7 ♣ Q 10 4

WEST	NORTH	EAST	SOUTH
	1 ♡	Pass	1 ♠
Pass	1 NT	Pass	4 ♠
All Pass			

West leads the ten of diamonds against South's game. East covers dummy's jack with the queen, and declarer takes his king. He leads the spade king to West's ace.

West knows that declarer has at least six spades on the bidding, and declarer's play suggests that his suit is solid except for the ace. Declarer has two top tricks in each red suit, so ten tricks are there unless East has the club ace. On this occasion, a club switch is needed to beat the contract.

Problems

1. Dlr: South
Vul: None
Matchpoints

North: ♠ 7 6 4 ♡ J 7 ◇ Q 7 4 ♣ A K 6 5 4

West: ♠ A Q 2 ♡ K 6 4 2 ◇ J 10 9 ♣ J 7 2

WEST	NORTH	EAST	SOUTH
			1 ♡
Pass	1 NT	Pass	2 ♡
Pass	3 ♡	Pass	4 ♡
All Pass			

Playing matchpoint duplicate (where overtricks and undertricks are significant if the contract is normal), you, West, lead the jack of diamonds. When dummy hits, you see that North's first response was conservative. Declarer wins the queen in dummy and runs the heart jack to your king. How do you continue?

2. Dlr: North   ♠ K Q 7 6
Vul: None   ♡ K 6 4
Matchpoints   ◇ K J 9
    ♣ Q 6 4

♠ 8 2
♡ Q J 10 7 2
◇ A 6 5 3   □
♣ 5 3

WEST	NORTH	EAST	SOUTH
	1 ◇	Pass	1 ♠
Pass	2 ♠	Pass	4 ♠
All Pass			

You, West, lead the queen of hearts—four, nine, eight. Declarer ruffs the next heart and draws two rounds of trumps with the king and ace, East following. A diamond is led, you duck, and dummy's jack loses to the queen. Partner returns the club jack, won by declarer's king. Declarer continues with a club to the queen, a club to the ace, and the club two, ruffed in dummy as East follows. You throw two hearts.

Declarer now ruffs dummy's king of hearts and leads a diamond. Do you duck again, or do you hold declarer to his contract by grabbing your ace?

Solutions

1. Declarer has five heart tricks, three diamonds, and two clubs for his contract, so the battle is for overtricks this time. Should West lay down the spade ace or exit passively?

Declarer has shown up with 13 HCP so far—the diamond ace, diamond king, heart ace, and heart queen. He made a minimum rebid of two hearts, which is limited to 15 HCP, so East should have the spade king. If declarer's hand were

♠ K x
♡ A Q 10 x x x
◇ A K x
♣ x x,

he would have been good enough to jump to three hearts. Declarer could, however, have the queen of clubs and still be in the minimum range, so it would be dangerous not to lead spades.

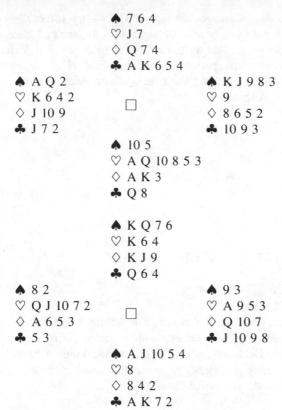

```
              ♠ 7 6 4
              ♡ J 7
              ◇ Q 7 4
              ♣ A K 6 5 4
♠ A Q 2                    ♠ K J 9 8 3
♡ K 6 4 2       □          ♡ 9
◇ J 10 9                   ◇ 8 6 5 2
♣ J 7 2                    ♣ 10 9 3
              ♠ 10 5
              ♡ A Q 10 8 5 3
              ◇ A K 3
              ♣ Q 8
```

2.
```
              ♠ K Q 7 6
              ♡ K 6 4
              ◇ K J 9
              ♣ Q 6 4
♠ 8 2                      ♠ 9 3
♡ Q J 10 7 2    □          ♡ A 9 5 3
◇ A 6 5 3                  ◇ Q 10 7
♣ 5 3                      ♣ J 10 9 8
              ♠ A J 10 5 4
              ♡ 8
              ◇ 8 4 2
              ♣ A K 7 2
```

You have a complete count. Declarer had five spades, four clubs, one heart—and three diamonds. So you duck the second diamond and let him sweat it out.

Declarer's play was poor. True, he made it very easy for you to count his hand, but better technique would have given him a sure thing. After ruffing the second heart and drawing trumps, he should have played four rounds of clubs, ruffing the fourth. After ruffing the heart king, he could lead a diamond to the jack, endplaying East.

Problems

3. Dlr: West
   Vul: N-S

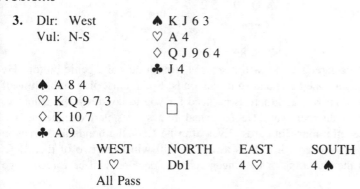

```
              ♠ K J 6 3
              ♡ A 4
              ◇ Q J 9 6 4
              ♣ J 4
♠ A 8 4
♡ K Q 9 7 3     □
◇ K 10 7
♣ A 9
```

WEST	NORTH	EAST	SOUTH
1 ♡	Dbl	4 ♡	4 ♠
All Pass			

Back to rubber bridge, Chicago scoring, or IMPs—try to set the contract. You, West, lead the king of hearts. Declarer wins the ace and leads a trump to his queen and your ace. You try to cash the heart queen, but declarer ruffs and draws two more trumps, partner discarding hearts. Next, declarer cashes the diamond ace, partner playing the two, and continues with the diamond three. How do you defend?

4. Dlr: South
   Vul: Both

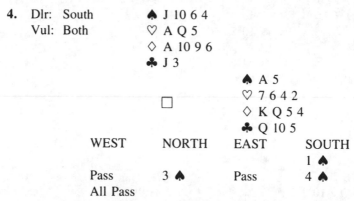

♠ J 10 6 4
♡ A Q 5
◇ A 10 9 6
♣ J 3

♠ A 5
♡ 7 6 4 2
◇ K Q 5 4
♣ Q 10 5

WEST	NORTH	EAST	SOUTH
			1 ♠
Pass	3 ♠	Pass	4 ♠
All Pass			

West, your partner, leads the ten of hearts to dummy's ace. When the spade jack is led, you take your ace and exit with a trump, partner following suit low to both tricks. Declarer cashes the queen and king of hearts, partner following with the nine and eight. Now the diamond jack is led and passed to your queen. How do you defend?

Solutions

3.

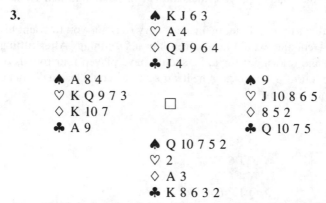

♠ K J 6 3
♡ A 4
◇ Q J 9 6 4
♣ J 4

♠ A 8 4
♡ K Q 9 7 3
◇ K 10 7
♣ A 9

♠ 9
♡ J 10 8 6 5
◇ 8 5 2
♣ Q 10 7 5

♠ Q 10 7 5 2
♡ 2
◇ A 3
♣ K 8 6 3 2

A count of declarer's tricks will keep you from hitting the panic button. He has four spades, one heart and four diamonds. So he must play clubs himself to make the contract, and there is no need for you to lay down the club ace.

Look at it another way: Declarer had five spades and one heart, and therefore seven minor-suit cards. Even after he leads diamonds five times in all and throws some of his clubs away, he still will have two of them left. If East has the club king or the queen and ten, declarer will be forced to go down.

4.

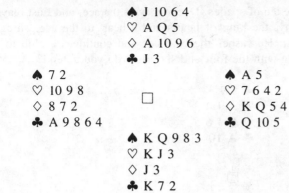

♠ J 10 6 4
♡ A Q 5
◇ A 10 9 6
♣ J 3

♠ 7 2   ♠ A 5
♡ 10 9 8   ♡ 7 6 4 2
◇ 8 7 2   □   ◇ K Q 5 4
♣ A 9 8 6 4   ♣ Q 10 5

♠ K Q 9 8 3
♡ K J 3
◇ J 3
♣ K 7 2

Return a diamond. Declarer has five spades and three hearts—therefore, five cards in clubs and diamonds combined. If he started with two diamonds and three clubs, a diamond return won't help him—it will only allow him to pitch a club he could have ruffed in dummy. He still will go down if West has the club ace.

Even if declarer has two clubs and three diamonds and avoids a second diamond loser, he can't make the contract unless he has the club ace. And if declarer started with

♠ K Q 9 8 x
♡ K J x
◇ J x x
♣ A x,

he has woefully misplayed the hand. After stripping out the majors, he could have exited with ace and another club, snaring the defenders in an endplay.

Problems

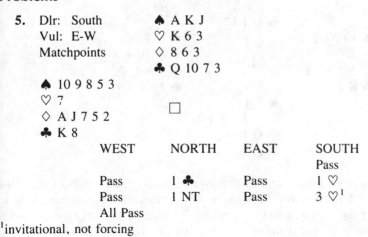

5. Dlr: South
Vul: E-W
Matchpoints

♠ A K J
♡ K 6 3
◇ 8 6 3
♣ Q 10 7 3

♠ 10 9 8 5 3
♡ 7
◇ A J 7 5 2   □
♣ K 8

WEST	NORTH	EAST	SOUTH
			Pass
Pass	1 ♣	Pass	1 ♡
Pass	1 NT	Pass	3 ♡[1]
All Pass			

[1] invitational, not forcing

You, West, lead the ten of spades. Declarer wins the ace, and East plays the seven. Declarer plays the king of hearts and a heart to the ace, shrugging when you show out. He cashes the club ace and continues a club to your king, East following with the four and six. How do you defend?

6. Dlr: South
   Vul: N-S

♠ J 9 3
♡ A J 4 3
◇ Q J 6 5
♣ A 10

♠ 6 5
♡ K Q 10 8
◇ K 7 2
♣ 5 4 3 2

□

WEST	NORTH	EAST	SOUTH
			1 ♠
Pass	2 NT	Pass	3 ♣
Pass	3 ♠	Pass	4 ♠
All Pass			

You, West, lead the king of hearts—three, two, six. What do you lead to trick two?

Solutions

5. Declarer will have a six-card heart suit for his jump, so you can place him with the heart ace and jack for 5 HCP. He already has shown the club ace—that's 9 HCP—so he cannot have the diamond king. Even if he has the queen of diamonds, he has a hand some players would open. Lead a low diamond.

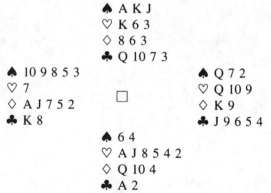

♠ A K J
♡ K 6 3
◇ 8 6 3
♣ Q 10 7 3

♠ 10 9 8 5 3
♡ 7
◇ A J 7 5 2
♣ K 8

□

♠ Q 7 2
♡ Q 10 9
◇ K 9
♣ J 9 6 5 4

♠ 6 4
♡ A J 8 5 4 2
◇ Q 10 4
♣ A 2

6. Declarer's bidding suggests at least nine black cards—probably his pattern is 5-2-2-4. He would have no reason to duck the opening lead with a singleton heart, and if he had three hearts, it would be too dangerous to duck. You should shift to a diamond. Even if declarer has the diamond ace, this play will cost you nothing. (Declarer would have finessed in hearts and discarded his little diamond anyhow.) However, if partner has the diamond

ace, you must cash your two diamond tricks right away before declarer can take a discard.

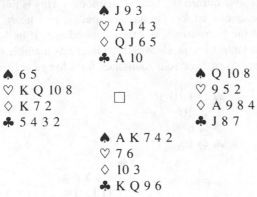

                    ♠ J 9 3
                    ♡ A J 4 3
                    ◇ Q J 6 5
                    ♣ A 10
  ♠ 6 5   ♠ Q 10 8
  ♡ K Q 10 8   ♡ 9 5 2
  ◇ K 7 2   □   ◇ A 9 8 4
  ♣ 5 4 3 2   ♣ J 8 7
                    ♠ A K 7 4 2
                    ♡ 7 6
                    ◇ 10 3
                    ♣ K Q 9 6

Problems

7. Dlr: South   ♠ Q J 10 5
    Vul: None   ♡ A 10
               ◇ A 6 5 4
               ♣ Q J 8

  ♠ 9 6 2
  ♡ Q 8 5 2
  ◇ K 3   □
  ♣ A 7 5 2

WEST	NORTH	EAST	SOUTH
			2 ♠
Pass	4 ♠	All Pass	

You, West, lead the two of hearts. Dummy's ace wins and partner discourages with the three. Declarer draws trumps with the queen, jack, and ace, East unhelpfully pitching three hearts. Now the four of clubs is led toward dummy. Plan your defense.

8. Dlr: South   ♠ A 8 6 4 3
    Vul: Both   ♡ A 5
               ◇ J 9 6 4
               ♣ 3 2

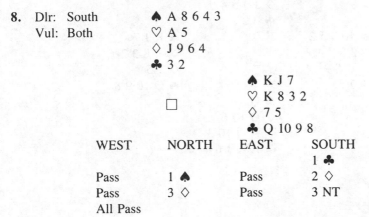

                              ♠ K J 7
                  □   ♡ K 8 3 2
                              ◇ 7 5
                              ♣ Q 10 9 8

WEST	NORTH	EAST	SOUTH
			1 ♣
Pass	1 ♠	Pass	2 ◇
Pass	3 ◇	Pass	3 NT
All Pass			

West, your partner, leads the four of hearts, ducked to your king. How do you continue?

281

Solutions

7. Win the club ace and shift to the king of diamonds. This is not a difficult play if you count declarer's tricks. He has six spades, two hearts (East has denied possession of the heart king), and the diamond ace. If he has another club, he can set up a tenth trick in clubs. (If declarer has a singleton club he has either a third heart to ruff, or four diamonds for a long-card trick in that suit). The full deal:

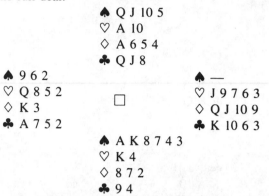

The deal is from the 1979 Bermuda Bowl final, United States vs. Italy. The contract was four spades at both tables and, remarkably, *both* Wests ducked the first club. The contract could no longer be beaten.

8. Partner's opening lead marks declarer with three hearts, probably with the queen. South's reverse, especially when followed by his 3 NT bid, promises greater length in his first suit—he is likely to have four diamonds and at least five clubs. (If his pattern were 2-3-4-4, he would have jumped to 2 NT at his second turn, or perhaps opened 1 NT.) Since all the evidence suggests that declarer is short in spades, you should try the spade king at trick two.

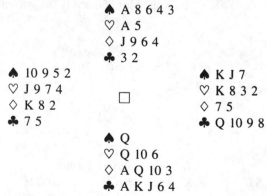

Problems

9. Dlr: North   ♠ A K 4 3
     Vul: Both   ♡ K J 10 4
              ◇ 10 4
              ♣ Q 10 4

♠ J 9 7 5
♡ A 5
◇ K 9 7 5 2   □
♣ A 3

WEST	NORTH	EAST	SOUTH
	1 ♡	Pass	1 NT
All Pass			

You, West, lead the five of diamonds—four, queen, ace. Declarer plunks down the heart queen and another. You win the second heart, partner following low-high. How do you continue?

10. Dlr: South   ♠ K Q 10 4
     Vul: N-S   ♡ K 10 4
             ◇ J 9 2
             ♣ K 6 4

♠ A J 7 2
♡ Q 5
◇ Q 8 3   □
♣ Q J 10 5

WEST	NORTH	EAST	SOUTH
			1 ♡
Pass	1 ♠	Pass	2 ◇
Pass	3 ♡	Pass	4 ♡
All Pass			

You, West, lead the queen of clubs, holding the first trick. The club ten also wins, but declarer ruffs the third club. At trick three, declarer leads the three of spades. How do you defend? (If you win the ace, East plays the nine.)

Solutions

9. Declarer has shown 6 HCP so far, and he must have the diamond jack since East played the queen at trick one. To beat this contract, you must give partner both missing club honors. True, declarer is unlikely to have the club king, which would give him 10 HCP. But if declarer holds even the club jack (and East has the queen of spades), the defense can do no better than take two spades, one diamond, one heart, and two clubs before they have to give declarer a seventh trick in either diamonds or clubs.

Furthermore, if declarer has the spade queen he has seven tricks unless you cash out. Cash the diamond king and then shift to ace and another club.

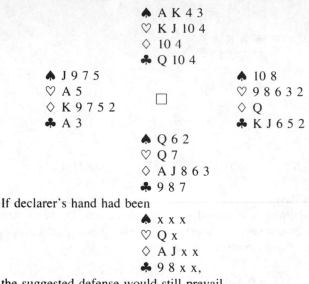

```
                  ♠ A K 4 3
                  ♡ K J 10 4
                  ◇ 10 4
                  ♣ Q 10 4
  ♠ J 9 7 5                        ♠ 10 8
  ♡ A 5            □              ♡ 9 8 6 3 2
  ◇ K 9 7 5 2                      ◇ Q
  ♣ A 3                            ♣ K J 6 5 2
                  ♠ Q 6 2
                  ♡ Q 7
                  ◇ A J 8 6 3
                  ♣ 9 8 7
```

If declarer's hand had been

```
                  ♠ x x x
                  ♡ Q x
                  ◇ A J x x
                  ♣ 9 8 x x,
```

the suggested defense would still prevail.

10. Win the spade ace. Declarer accepted a game invitation with at most 12 HCP, so he surely has good shape to compensate. When partner plays the spade nine, showing an even number, you know that declarer is 1-5-5-2 or 1-6-4-2. If he has six hearts, the outcome is out of your hands. However, if declarer is 5-5 in the reds, you can beat the hand for sure by leading a trump. This will give up any chance of scoring your heart queen, but declarer will have at most five heart tricks, two spades and two diamonds. The full deal:

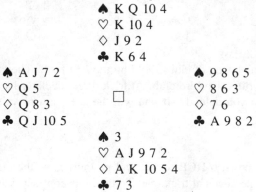

```
                  ♠ K Q 10 4
                  ♡ K 10 4
                  ◇ J 9 2
                  ♣ K 6 4
  ♠ A J 7 2                        ♠ 9 8 6 5
  ♡ Q 5            □              ♡ 8 6 3
  ◇ Q 8 3                          ◇ 7 6
  ♣ Q J 10 5                       ♣ A 9 8 2
                  ♠ 3
                  ♡ A J 9 7 2
                  ◇ A K 10 5 4
                  ♣ 7 3
```

If you lead anything but a heart, the contract might make.

Problems

11. Dlr: North   ♠ A Q 7 6
     Vul: None   ♡ Q 8
                 ◇ K 8 5 3
                 ♣ K 5 4

♠ J 3
♡ K J 5 2
◇ J 10 6   □
♣ Q J 10 7

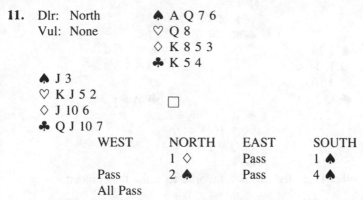

WEST	NORTH	EAST	SOUTH
	1 ◇	Pass	1 ♠
Pass	2 ♠	Pass	4 ♠
All Pass			

You, West, lead the queen of clubs, winning. Declarer ruffs the second club and draws two rounds of trumps with the ace and queen, East discarding a club. Dummy's last club is ruffed, and declarer plays the ace and ten of hearts to your king. How do you defend?

12. Dlr: South   ♠ A 10 6 4
     Vul: Both   ♡ Q J 9 5 3
                 ◇ 9 3
                 ♣ A 6

♠ 5
♡ K 8 4 2
◇ K 7   □
♣ K J 9 7 5 3

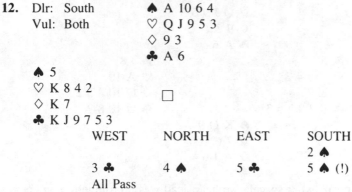

WEST	NORTH	EAST	SOUTH
			2 ♠
3 ♣	4 ♠	5 ♣	5 ♠ (!)
All Pass			

South's undisciplined five-spade bid is odd. You, West, try a surprise attack with the heart two. Your heart freezes when you see dummy. However, East wins the ace and returns the heart ten to your king, declarer following twice. What do you play to trick three?

Solutions

11. Declarer had six spades, one club and thirteen cards in all. If he began with a doubleton heart, as it appears, then he had four diamonds, and a ruff-and-discard will be of no use to him. You should exit with a heart.

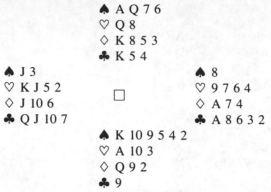

♠ A Q 7 6
♡ Q 8
◇ K 8 5 3
♣ K 5 4

♠ J 3　　　　　　　　　　　　♠ 8
♡ K J 5 2　　　　　　　　　　♡ 9 7 6 4
◇ J 10 6　　　　□　　　　　　◇ A 7 4
♣ Q J 10 7　　　　　　　　　　♣ A 8 6 3 2

♠ K 10 9 5 4 2
♡ A 10 3
◇ Q 9 2
♣ 9

On any other lead, declarer is a favorite to make the contract.

12. Declarer has six spade tricks, plus at most two aces in the minors. If you lead a third heart, allowing partner to ruff one of dummy's winners, declarer will take only two heart tricks, and the contract must come up a trick short. The full deal:

♠ A 10 6 4
♡ Q J 9 5 3
◇ 9 3
♣ A 6

♠ 5　　　　　　　　　　　　　♠ J 8
♡ K 8 4 2　　　　　　　　　　♡ A 10
◇ K 7　　　　　□　　　　　　◇ Q 10 8 5 2
♣ K J 9 7 5 3　　　　　　　　♣ Q 10 8 2

♠ K Q 9 7 3 2
♡ 7 6
◇ A J 6 4
♣ 4

As it happens, your speculative heart lead was no triumph. You could have made things easier by leading some other suit.

Problems

13. Dlr: West
Vul: Both

♠ K J 4
♡ 8 6 3
◇ K Q J 3
♣ Q 10 4

♠ Q 10 6 5 2
♡ A 10 4 2
◇ 8 7
♣ K 9

□

WEST	NORTH	EAST	SOUTH
Pass	1 ◇	Pass	2 NT[1]
Pass	3 NT	All Pass	

[1] 13-15 HCP, balanced

You, West, lead the five of spades. Dummy's jack wins, partner signaling with the nine. At trick two, the queen of clubs is led and passed to your king. How do you continue?

14. Dlr: West   ♠ K Q 10 8 3
    Vul: E-W   ♡ 7 5 3
                     ◇ K Q 4
                     ♣ 6 5

♠ A 6
♡ A Q 8 4 2   □
◇ J 10 9
♣ K 8 4

WEST	NORTH	EAST	SOUTH
1 ♡	1 ♠	Pass	2 NT
All Pass			

You, West, lead the four of hearts—five, nine, jack. A spade to dummy's king wins, and a spade is returned to declarer's jack and your ace. How do you continue?

Solutions

13. Take stock of declarer's high-card points. He has the spade ace and the ace and jack of clubs. (He would not lead the queen of clubs when his club holding was at best A-8-x-x.) What about the diamond ace? If declarer lacked that card, his first play might well have been a diamond. If he does have the diamond ace, that's 13 HCP, so his hearts can be no better than queen-high. Even in the unlikely event that declarer lacks the diamond ace, his hearts would have to be K-J-x or better.

It cannot cost for you to shift to a low heart. On the actual deal, it is necessary to beat the contract.

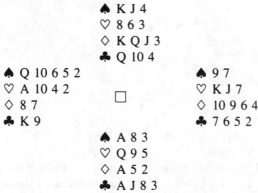

                 ♠ K J 4
                 ♡ 8 6 3
                 ◇ K Q J 3
                 ♣ Q 10 4

♠ Q 10 6 5 2   ♠ 9 7
♡ A 10 4 2   □   ♡ K J 7
◇ 8 7   ◇ 10 9 6 4
♣ K 9   ♣ 7 6 5 2

                 ♠ A 8 3
                 ♡ Q 9 5
                 ◇ A 5 2
                 ♣ A J 8 3

14. Lead the eight of clubs. Even if this goes into the jaws of the ace-queen, declarer still has only seven tricks—four spades, a heart, and two clubs— and he cannot make the hand unless he has the diamond ace. Note that if you return the diamond jack and find declarer with the ace, he has at least eight tricks.

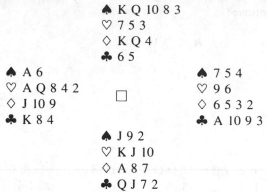

    ♠ K Q 10 8 3
    ♡ 7 5 3
    ◇ K Q 4
    ♣ 6 5

♠ A 6   ♠ 7 5 4
♡ A Q 8 4 2   ♡ 9 6
◇ J 10 9   ◇ 6 5 3 2
♣ K 8 4   ♣ A 10 9 3

    ♠ J 9 2
    ♡ K J 10
    ◇ A 8 7
    ♣ Q J 7 2

A club lead would lose only if declarer's hand were something like

    ♠ J 9 x
    ♡ K J 10
    ◇ x x x x
    ♣ A Q 10.

After winning the club queen, declarer would run spades, catching you in a strip squeeze. You would either have to bare the club king, throw a winning heart (making it safe for declarer to knock out the diamond ace), or pitch all your diamonds (letting declarer endplay you with a heart lead). However, for all this to happen, declarer must hold the club ten as well as the ace and queen.

Problems

15. Dlr: East   ♠ K J 7 5 3
    Vul: Both   ♡ Q 7
                       ◇ A Q 2
                       ♣ K 10 5

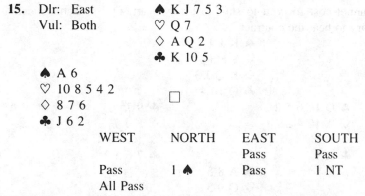

♠ A 6
♡ 10 8 5 4 2
◇ 8 7 6
♣ J 6 2

WEST	NORTH	EAST	SOUTH
		Pass	Pass
Pass	1 ♠	Pass	1 NT
All Pass			

You, West, lead the four of hearts. Declarer calls for dummy's queen, and partner's king is allowed to hold. East's heart jack wins the next trick, and declarer takes the heart ace on the third round. Declarer leads a diamond to the ace and plays the diamond queen. When East's jack falls, declarer overtakes with the ace and leads a low spade toward dummy. Hopefully, you have been doing some counting. Do you win or duck?

288

16. Dlr: South ♠ J
Vul: Both ♡ A 10 8
◇ J 10 6 4
♣ K J 7 6 3

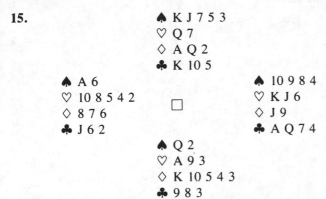

♠ K 10 9 7 3
♡ 7 5 2
◇ A 7
♣ A 10 4

WEST	NORTH	EAST	SOUTH
			1 ♠
Pass	2 ♣	Pass	2 ♡
Pass	2 NT	Pass	4 ♡
All Pass			

The defense gets off to a flying start when West leads the three of diamonds to your ace. You return a diamond to his king and ruff a third round of diamonds. Declarer has followed with the eight, queen, and two. What do you play next?

Solutions

15. ♠ K J 7 5 3
♡ Q 7
◇ A Q 2
♣ K 10 5

♠ A 6   ♠ 10 9 8 4
♡ 10 8 5 4 2   ♡ K J 6
◇ 8 7 6   ◇ J 9
♣ J 6 2   ♣ A Q 7 4

♠ Q 2
♡ A 9 3
◇ K 10 5 4 3
♣ 9 8 3

So far, declarer has shown 7 HCP. East has produced only 5 HCP, but it must be assumed that he has the club ace, for a total of 9.

Declarer must have one black queen, else East would have 13 HCP and would have opened the bidding. However, declarer cannot have both black queens—with 11 HCP, he would be too strong to respond 1 NT. Which black queen does declarer have? Clearly, the spade queen. He would not lead a spade, putting himself to a needless guess, if he could knock out the club ace for a certain seventh trick.

You should win the spade ace, cash your hearts, and lead a club, expecting to find East with the setting tricks.

16.

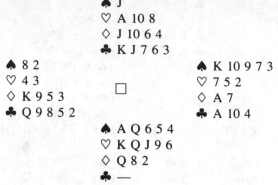

Shift to a trump. The club ace will not cash, since declarer showed no fewer than ten major-suit cards in the bidding and already has followed to three rounds of diamonds.

Count tricks. After a trump shift, declarer can take no more than five hearts, two spades (with a finesse of the queen if he has it), and two ruffs in dummy. He cannot score dummy's fourth diamond while you still have a trump, but if he draws your trumps he loses one of his ruffs. Either way, nine tricks are the limit.

A Problem-Solver's Game: Drawing Inferences

There is more to good bridge than just memorizing a set of rules or even paying heed to principles and tendencies. Bridge appeals because it is a game of problem-solving and logic.

Quiz 8 dealt with making assumptions on defense. As we saw, many assumptions amount to no more than hopeful speculation. An *inference*, however, is an assumption supported by the logical analysis of evidence.

If your opponents play logically and observe accepted practices and conventions, they'll reveal something about what they have and what their plans are. Useful inferences abound in the bidding and play. I can remember deals when I let a beatable contract slip through, and at the time I saw nothing to indicate the winning defense. Later, after some reflection, I realized I had missed a subtle but telling inference.

There are several sources of inferences. To start at trick one, analysis of the bidding may guide you to a killing opening lead. Suppose you hold as West:

♠ K 10
♥ A J 8 5 2
♦ J 4
♣ K Q 10 3

WEST	NORTH	EAST	SOUTH
1 ♥	Pass	1 ♠	Pass
2 ♣	Pass	Pass	2 ♦
All Pass			

Partner bid spades, but the spade king would be a poor lead when he must have a very weak hand. A better shot is to find him short in hearts—he failed to raise directly or even take a preference over your two-club rebid. Perhaps half the time, partner will hold a singleton heart, so ace of hearts and another is an attractive form of attack. The full deal might be:

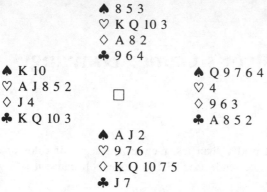

♠ 8 5 3
♥ K Q 10 3
♦ A 8 2
♣ 9 6 4

♠ K 10　　　　　　　　♠ Q 9 7 6 4
♥ A J 8 5 2　　　　　♥ 4
♦ J 4　　　　　　　　♦ 9 6 3
♣ K Q 10 3　　　　　♣ A 8 5 2

♠ A J 2
♥ 9 7 6
♦ K Q 10 7 5
♣ J 7

After heart ace, heart two, East can put you back in twice with clubs for another ruff and to kill dummy's fourth heart. Then declarer will have to maneuver an endplay to go down just one.

If you can assume partner is thinking clearly, some valid inferences may be available from *his* opening lead and subsequent defense.

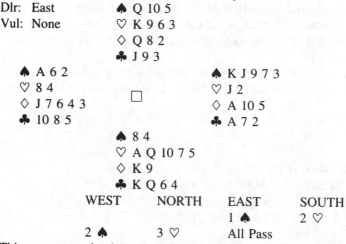

Dlr: East　　　♠ Q 10 5
Vul: None　　　♥ K 9 6 3
　　　　　　　♦ Q 8 2
　　　　　　　♣ J 9 3

♠ A 6 2　　　　　　　　♠ K J 9 7 3
♥ 8 4　　　　　　　　♥ J 2
♦ J 7 6 4 3　　　　　♦ A 10 5
♣ 10 8 5　　　　　　♣ A 7 2

♠ 8 4
♥ A Q 10 7 5
♦ K 9
♣ K Q 6 4

WEST	NORTH	EAST	SOUTH
		1 ♠	2 ♥
2 ♠	3 ♥	All Pass	

This was at matchpoints. West led the four of diamonds, and East took the ace. Reluctant to lead away from the spade king despite partner's raise, East returned a low club. This allowed declarer to make a valuable overtrick by drawing trumps and depositing a spade on the diamond queen.

Players are reluctant to lay down aces, even in a suit partner has bid, for fear of setting up an intermediate card for declarer. (Here, West doubtless reasoned that there always would be time to cash E-W's spade tricks, since East had opened the bidding and had to have some entries.) East therefore should have played partner for the spade ace and led a spade at trick two. If West had held three or four small spades, would not his opening lead have been a spade?

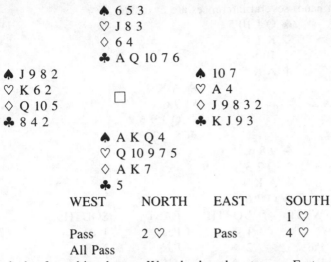

```
              ♠ 6 5 3
              ♡ J 8 3
              ◇ 6 4
              ♣ A Q 10 7 6
♠ J 9 8 2                        ♠ 10 7
♡ K 6 2          □              ♡ A 4
◇ Q 10 5                        ◇ J 9 8 3 2
♣ 8 4 2                         ♣ K J 9 3
              ♠ A K Q 4
              ♡ Q 10 9 7 5
              ◇ A K 7
              ♣ 5
```

WEST	NORTH	EAST	SOUTH
			1 ♡
Pass	2 ♡	Pass	4 ♡
All Pass			

For lack of anything better, West leads a low trump. East wins the ace and returns a trump. Now West should happily lead a third round. Should he not be afraid of dummy's club suit? No—unless East had the clubs all sewed up, he surely would have shifted to a diamond or spade.

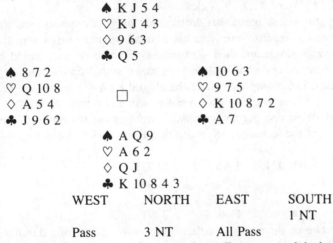

```
              ♠ K J 5 4
              ♡ K J 4 3
              ◇ 9 6 3
              ♣ Q 5
♠ 8 7 2                         ♠ 10 6 3
♡ Q 10 8         □              ♡ 9 7 5
◇ A 5 4                         ◇ K 10 8 7 2
♣ J 9 6 2                       ♣ A 7
              ♠ A Q 9
              ♡ A 6 2
              ◇ Q J
              ♣ K 10 8 4 3
```

WEST	NORTH	EAST	SOUTH
			1 NT
Pass	3 NT	All Pass	

West led the two of clubs—five, ace, three. East expected declarer to have either the club jack or king, since declarer might have put up dummy's queen if lacking both of those honors. East decided to shift to a diamond—but was it the right time for the honor-trapping lead of the *ten*?

East knew that declarer had five clubs. The lead of the ten might save a trick if declarer had three diamonds, but that meant he would have only two cards in one of the majors. West then would have had a four-card major suit, and he likely would have preferred to lead that suit instead of a club. So East rejected the tempting "surrounding" play and led a pedestrian diamond seven, playing declarer for 3-3-2-5 pattern. As you can see, the fancy lead of the ten would have caused a disaster this time.

On the next hand, several inferences are available.

```
                    ♠ Q J 10 5
                    ♥ K J 5
                    ◇ 10 8
                    ♣ A K 5 2
   ♠ 3 2                          ♠ A K 7
   ♥ A 10 8 4 2         □         ♥ 9 6
   ◇ 7 5 3                        ◇ Q J 9 6 2
   ♣ J 10 9                       ♣ 8 4 3
                    ♠ 9 8 6 4
                    ♥ Q 7 3
                    ◇ A K 4
                    ♣ Q 7 6
```

WEST	NORTH	EAST	SOUTH
	1 ♣	Pass	1 ♠
Pass	2 ♠	Pass	2 NT
Pass	4 ♠	All Pass	

West leads the jack of clubs. Declarer wins in dummy and leads the queen of spades to East's king. Back comes the nine of hearts. If West wins and returns a heart, the defense is through except for the spade ace. However, if West thinks about it, the right play of ducking is clear.

The bidding strongly suggests that declarer has only four spades (and East's defense would make no sense unless he had a small trump to ruff with). But if East's heart nine is singleton, then declarer has four hearts and would have responded one heart to one club, showing his major suits "up the line."

Finally, if East had a singleton heart, he should *cash the spade ace* before leading his heart, giving West no choice but to win and return the suit.

On that deal, West can get an *inferential* count of the distribution. Here's another example of the technique. Suppose that East hears this bidding:

WEST	NORTH	EAST	SOUTH
			1 NT
Pass	2 ♣	Pass	2 ♥
Pass	2 ♠	Pass	2 NT

West leads the two of diamonds. East's pattern is 4-3-2-4, while dummy hits with 5-2-3-3 shape. Right away, East can figure that declarer is 2-4-4-3.

Another illustration:

```
              ♠ A 7 4
              ♡ A J 6 3
              ◇ K J 6 2
              ♣ 7 2
♠ J 9 6 5                        ♠ K 3 2
♡ Q 10 4          □            ♡ 9 7 5 2
◇ 7 5                            ◇ A 10
♣ K 10 6 3                      ♣ J 9 5 4
              ♠ Q 10 8
              ♡ K 8
              ◇ Q 9 8 4 3
              ♣ A Q 8
```

WEST	NORTH	EAST	SOUTH
			1 ◇
Pass	1 ♡	Pass	1 NT
Pass	3 ◇	Pass	3 NT
All Pass			

West leads a spade, ducked to the king. Before leading to the next trick, East tries to figure out declarer's pattern. Declarer did not rebid one spade, nor did he raise hearts directly or show a preference when invited to. Therefore, he should have at most two hearts and three spades. (West's lead indicates that declarer has exactly three spades.) If declarer had been 4-4 in the minors, he probably would have opened one club—there is little point to opening in the higher ranking of two four-card minor suits when you plan to rebid 1 NT. So East is inclined to place declarer with a five-card diamond suit, and he can assume that declarer has the spade queen for his 3 NT bid.

Desperate measures are needed. The spade suit won't provide enough tricks to beat the contract, and a passive defense isn't a favorite, either—declarer's long suit should let him set up nine tricks eventually. So East shifts aggressively to the club jack—and this time he strikes gold.

Defenders must take careful note of unusual plays by declarer. If a capable declarer does something a bit out of the ordinary, you can bet he has something up his sleeve.

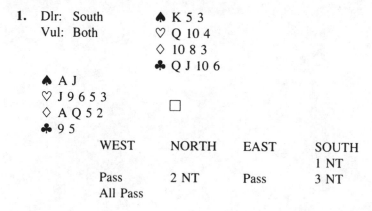

Dlr: South
Vul: E-W

♠ A Q 6
♡ A Q J 9 5
♢ 10 4
♣ J 10 2

♠ 8 7 2   ♠ K J 10 5
♡ 7 6 3   ♡ 10 8 4
♢ Q 9 8 3   ☐   ♢ K J 2
♣ K 7 4   ♣ 8 6 5

♠ 9 4 3
♡ K 2
♢ A 7 6 5
♣ A Q 9 3

WEST	NORTH	EAST	SOUTH
			1 ♣
Pass	1 ♡	Pass	1 NT
Pass	3 NT	All Pass	

Unwilling to break the diamond suit, West leads the spade eight. Declarer considers going up with the ace, but he fears that East has five spades. Finally, he concocts an alternative scheme—he plays dummy's queen. If East wins and returns a spade, declarer will win and take a club finesse—he knows that if West produces the club king and has a spade left to lead, the defenders will take only four tricks in all.

East should wonder why declarer didn't play *low* from dummy at trick one, keeping dummy's spade tenace intact and gaining some time. The most likely explanation—declarer is nervous about some other suit and wants to make it easy for the defenders to continue spades! So East finds the good switch to a diamond honor, and down declarer goes.

Many of our Quiz problems deal with drawing inferences from declarer's play. It is appropriate that this Quiz, which covers the various sources of inferences, is the longest one in this book—because bridge *is* a problem-solver's game.

Problems

1.   Dlr: South
     Vul: Both

♠ K 5 3
♡ Q 10 4
♢ 10 8 3
♣ Q J 10 6

♠ A J
♡ J 9 6 5 3
♢ A Q 5 2   ☐
♣ 9 5

WEST	NORTH	EAST	SOUTH
			1 NT
Pass	2 NT	Pass	3 NT
All Pass			

You, West, lead the five of hearts. Dummy's ten holds, East playing the eight. At trick two, declarer leads a spade to his queen, East contributing the ten. How do you defend?

2. Dlr: South   ♠ K 7 5
    Vul: Both   ♡ Q 8 5 2
                    ◇ A 4
                    ♣ K 7 5 2

    ♠ J 9 4 2
    ♡ 4
    ◇ Q J 8 3   ☐
    ♣ J 10 8 4

	WEST	NORTH	EAST	SOUTH
				1 ♡
	Pass	3 ♡	Pass	4 NT
	Pass	5 ◇	Pass	6 ♡
	All Pass			

You, West, lead the jack of clubs, which wins. At trick two, you shift to the queen of diamonds, expecting declarer to have a singleton club on the bidding. Declarer wins the ace, ruffs a club, cashes the king of diamonds, and ruffs a diamond. Next, declarer runs his remaining four trumps. Your last five cards are your original four spades and the jack of diamonds. What do you discard on declarer's last trump? (No doubt you would like to know what your partner discarded on the trumps. Well, I'm not telling, so you'll have to reason things out on your own. Anyway, your partner is notoriously un-reliable.)

Solutions

1. Declarer has shown the spade queen and the heart ace-king. He could have three heart tricks or four, but he is a big favorite to have both the ace and king of clubs. He must have at least one high club on the bidding, and if he had the club king, say, and no club ace, his first move would have been to set up his clubs. Declarer would not be attacking spades, where he has only the king and queen. (Partner's spade ten suggests that he has a sequence.)

Given that declarer has both high clubs, that's 16 HCP, so East must hold the diamond king. Shift to a low diamond, hoping for a full deal like this:

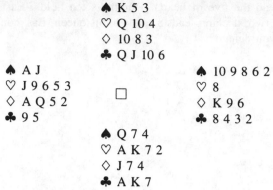

$\spadesuit$ K 5 3
$\heartsuit$ Q 10 4
$\diamondsuit$ 10 8 3
$\clubsuit$ Q J 10 6

$\spadesuit$ A J
$\heartsuit$ J 9 6 5 3
$\diamondsuit$ A Q 5 2
$\clubsuit$ 9 5

$\spadesuit$ 10 9 8 6 2
$\heartsuit$ 8
$\diamondsuit$ K 9 6
$\clubsuit$ 8 4 3 2

$\spadesuit$ Q 7 4
$\heartsuit$ A K 7 2
$\diamondsuit$ J 7 4
$\clubsuit$ A K 7

Declarer was trying to steal his ninth trick when he led a spade.

2. A simple problem. Declarer cannot have another diamond, else he would have ruffed it in dummy. You can safely let go the diamond jack and cling to your spades.

$\spadesuit$ K 7 5
$\heartsuit$ Q 8 5 2
$\diamondsuit$ A 4
$\clubsuit$ K 7 5 2

$\spadesuit$ J 9 4 2
$\heartsuit$ 4
$\diamondsuit$ Q J 8 3
$\clubsuit$ J 10 8 4

$\spadesuit$ 10 3
$\heartsuit$ 9 7 3
$\diamondsuit$ 10 9 7 2
$\clubsuit$ A Q 9 6

$\spadesuit$ A Q 8 6
$\heartsuit$ A K J 10 6
$\diamondsuit$ K 6 5
$\clubsuit$ 3

Declarer might have played on spades after drawing just two rounds of trumps, but that wouldn't have worked either as the cards lay. Note that a club continuation at trick two would have let declarer get home on a dummy reversal.

Problems

3. Dlr: South
Vul: N-S

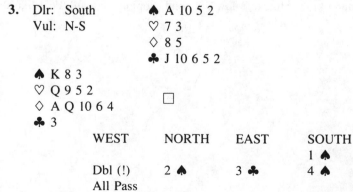

$\spadesuit$ A 10 5 2
$\heartsuit$ 7 3
$\diamondsuit$ 8 5
$\clubsuit$ J 10 6 5 2

$\spadesuit$ K 8 3
$\heartsuit$ Q 9 5 2
$\diamondsuit$ A Q 10 6 4
$\clubsuit$ 3

WEST	NORTH	EAST	SOUTH
			1 $\spadesuit$
Dbl (!)	2 $\spadesuit$	3 $\clubsuit$	4 $\spadesuit$
All Pass			

You, West, lead the three of clubs. East obliges with the ace, and declarer drops the queen. You ruff the club nine return, declarer playing the king. How do you continue?

4. Dlr: South
   Vul: E-W

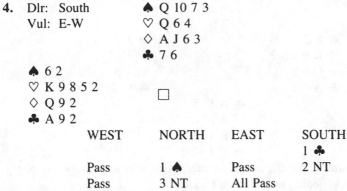

♠ Q 10 7 3
♡ Q 6 4
◇ A J 6 3
♣ 7 6

♠ 6 2
♡ K 9 8 5 2
◇ Q 9 2
♣ A 9 2

WEST	NORTH	EAST	SOUTH
			1 ♣
Pass	1 ♠	Pass	2 NT
Pass	3 NT	All Pass	

You, West, lead the five of hearts—six, ten, jack. Declarer plays off the ace-king of spades and continues with a spade to the queen; East follows high-low as you pitch a club. Now the diamond ace is cashed and a diamond is led to the seven, ten, and your queen. Do you get out passively with a diamond, risk a heart continuation, or break new ground in the club suit?

Solutions

3.

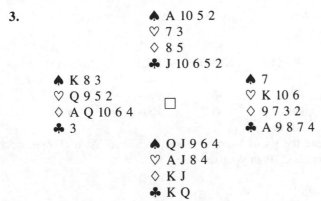

♠ A 10 5 2
♡ 7 3
◇ 8 5
♣ J 10 6 5 2

♠ K 8 3
♡ Q 9 5 2
◇ A Q 10 6 4
♣ 3

♠ 7
♡ K 10 6
◇ 9 7 3 2
♣ A 9 8 7 4

♠ Q J 9 6 4
♡ A J 8 4
◇ K J
♣ K Q

Having made a takeout double of one spade, you can be counted on for four cards in the other major. The key clue is that East did not compete in hearts, as he surely would have done with four of them. So declarer is likely to have four hearts in addition to his (probably five) spades.

You must cash the ace of diamonds. If you don't, declarer will throw his diamonds on dummy's clubs. Hearts, however, can wait—if declarer has a heart loser, he will be unable to avoid it.

4. Continue with a low heart. Declarer is marked with three spades. His method of attacking diamonds suggests he has four cards there—if he had only three diamonds, he has left a winner stranded in dummy! Declarer must

have at least four clubs—he would have opened one diamond otherwise. Therefore, he should have just two hearts, and a heart continuation is safe.

```
                    ♠ Q 10 7 3
                    ♡ Q 6 4
                    ◇ A J 6 3
                    ♣ 7 6
    ♠ 6 2                          ♠ J 9 8 4
    ♡ K 9 8 5 2          □        ♡ 10 7 3
    ◇ Q 9 2                        ◇ 7 5
    ♣ A 9 2                        ♣ Q 8 5 4
                    ♠ A K 5
                    ♡ A J
                    ◇ K 10 8 4
                    ♣ K J 10 3
```

If you punt with a diamond, declarer might win in dummy and play a club to his jack, setting up the ninth trick.

Problems

5. Dlr: South   ♠ K 9 3
Vul: Both   ♡ 5 4 3 2
              ◇ J
              ♣ A Q 10 8 3

♠ 7 2
♡ J 10 7 6
◇ A 10 8 3   □
♣ 9 7 2

WEST	NORTH	EAST	SOUTH
			1 ♠
Pass	2 ♣	Pass	2 ◇
Pass	2 ♠	Pass	3 ♠
All Pass			

You, West, lead the six of hearts—two, queen, ace. At trick two, declarer leads a low diamond. Plan your defense.

6. Dlr: South   ♠ 7 5
Vul: N-S   ♡ A J 5 4
              ◇ Q J 10 4
              ♣ Q 7 5

♠ K 10 6 2
♡ 7 6
◇ A 8 7   □
♣ K J 9 4

WEST	NORTH	EAST	SOUTH
			1 ♡
Dbl	Redbl	Pass	Pass
1 ♠	2 ♡	Pass	4 ♡
All Pass			

You, West, choose a trump lead. Declarer draws two rounds, partner following, and tables the diamond king. You win the second diamond, East playing high-low. How do you continue?

Solutions

5. For starters, grab the diamond ace—declarer could easily have the king and queen. Then shift to a trump. Declarer's diamond play indicates that he is interested in ruffing losers in dummy. If instead he wanted to make use of dummy's clubs, he would be trying to draw trumps himself.

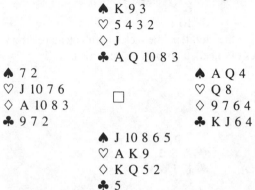

```
              ♠ K 9 3
              ♡ 5 4 3 2
              ◇ J
              ♣ A Q 10 8 3
 ♠ 7 2                        ♠ A Q 4
 ♡ J 10 7 6                   ♡ Q 8
 ◇ A 10 8 3        □          ◇ 9 7 6 4
 ♣ 9 7 2                      ♣ K J 6 4
              ♠ J 10 8 6 5
              ♡ A K 9
              ◇ K Q 5 2
              ♣ 5
```

On your trump switch, partner will clear three rounds, leaving declarer a trick short of his contract.

It is true that a very subtle declarer might lead a diamond, trying to induce you to lead trumps and resolve a guess in the trump suit for him. Luckily, there aren't many declarers around who are that tricky.

6. When North redoubled, East's first duty was to bail your side out to a playable spot if he could. When he failed to bid one spade, he patently denied four cards in spades, so you can place declarer with four. East echoed in diamonds, so declarer's pattern probably is 4-5-2-2.

You must realize that a club shift cannot lose even if declarer has the ace. Declarer always could throw his clubs on dummy's diamonds and lose at most two spade tricks, making the contract. However, two *spade* discards on the diamonds won't help declarer one bit—he'd just be throwing away cards that he just as easily could ruff in dummy. The full deal:

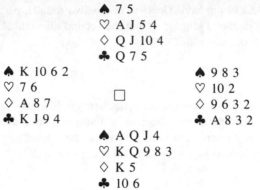

```
                    ♠ 7 5
                    ♡ A J 5 4
                    ◇ Q J 10 4
                    ♣ Q 7 5
♠ K 10 6 2                        ♠ 9 8 3
♡ 7 6                             ♡ 10 2
◇ A 8 7          □               ◇ 9 6 3 2
♣ K J 9 4                        ♣ A 8 3 2
                    ♠ A Q J 4
                    ♡ K Q 9 8 3
                    ◇ K 5
                    ♣ 10 6
```

With declarer holding the club ten, the jack of clubs lead (or the king of clubs followed by the jack) is needed to beat the contract.

Problems

7. Dlr: East   ♠ 8 5 3
     Vul: None   ♡ 7 5 2
               ◇ A 8 2
               ♣ K J 6 3

```
♠ K Q 9 2
♡ J 10 8
◇ K 3         □
♣ A 9 5 2
```

WEST	NORTH	EAST	SOUTH
		Pass	Pass
1 ♣	Pass	1 ♠	2 ◇
2 ♠	3 ◇	All Pass	

You, West, lead the king of spades and continue the suit. Declarer ruffs the third spade and plays a diamond to the ace and a diamond to the jack, queen, and king. You shift to the heart jack—two, four, king. Now comes the inevitable low club. Are you ready for this? Do you win or duck?

8. Dlr: South   ♠ A 8 3
     Vul: N-S   ♡ J 3 2
               ◇ K J 9 5 4
               ♣ J 5

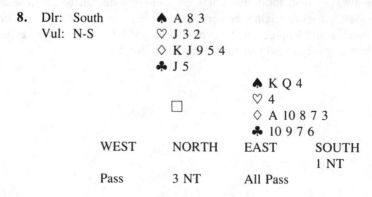

```
                    ♠ K Q 4
                    ♡ 4
          □         ◇ A 10 8 7 3
                    ♣ 10 9 7 6
```

WEST	NORTH	EAST	SOUTH
			1 NT
Pass	3 NT	All Pass	

West, your partner, leads the spade two, ducked to your queen. The spade king holds the next trick, and a third spade knocks out dummy's ace. A diamond is led from dummy. What do you play?

If you jump in with your ace, South and West play low. What would you return?

Solutions

7.

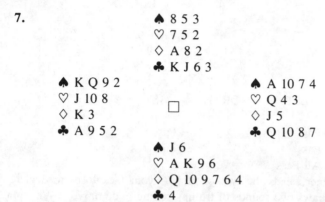

♠ 8 5 3
♡ 7 5 2
◇ A 8 2
♣ K J 6 3

♠ K Q 9 2
♡ J 10 8
◇ K 3
♣ A 9 5 2

♠ A 10 7 4
♡ Q 4 3
◇ J 5
♣ Q 10 8 7

♠ J 6
♡ A K 9 6
◇ Q 10 9 7 6 4
♣ 4

Win the club ace. An inferential count is available. Declarer has six diamonds and two spades. East would have responded one heart with four hearts and four spades, so declarer is marked with four hearts and a singleton club.

If you win the club ace, you will get a heart trick later for down one.

8. Partner led from a four-card spade suit, and you can infer he has a singleton diamond. (With a diamond void, he would have had a five-card heart or club suit to lead from.) Partner's pattern should be 4-4-1-4, and declarer's, therefore, is probably 3-5-2-3.

Rising with the diamond ace will not cost you a fast trick since the suit will be blocked. Upon winning, you should return a club. The only danger is that declarer has all the heart honors. If partner has a fast entry in hearts, declarer is always doomed—he cannot take nine tricks without leading a heart. However, if the full deal is:

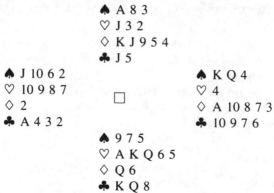

♠ A 8 3
♡ J 3 2
◇ K J 9 5 4
♣ J 5

♠ J 10 6 2
♡ 10 9 8 7
◇ 2
♣ A 4 3 2

♠ K Q 4
♡ 4
◇ A 10 8 7 3
♣ 10 9 7 6

♠ 9 7 5
♡ A K Q 6 5
◇ Q 6
♣ K Q 8

a heart return would be fatal.

Note that if you do not grab your diamond ace on the first lead, declarer can win and shift to clubs for nine tricks.

Problems

9. Dlr: South   ♠ Q 7 4
     Vul: N-S   ♡ Q 10 8 2
                 ◇ K 5 4 3
                 ♣ 8 3

                             ♠ J 9 3 2
                             ♡ 9
                 □   ◇ A 8 6 2
                             ♣ J 9 7 4

WEST	NORTH	EAST	SOUTH
			2 ♣
Pass	2 ◇	Pass	2 ♡
Pass	3 ♡	Pass	6 ♡
All Pass			

West, your partner, leads the two of clubs—your jack loses to declarer's king. Declarer draws two rounds of trumps ending in dummy, as West plays the four and seven. You shed a club. Now declarer calls a low diamond from dummy. What do you play?

If you duck, declarer wins the queen, returns to dummy with a trump (West throwing a middle spade), and leads another low diamond from dummy. What do you do this time?

10. Dlr: North   ♠ K Q J 5
     Vul: Both   ♡ 8 5 3
                 ◇ A K Q 2
                 ♣ J 3

♠ A 2
♡ Q 10 6 2
◇ 10 8 7 4 3   □
♣ K 2

WEST	NORTH	EAST	SOUTH
	1 ◇	Pass	2 ♣
Pass	2 ♠	Pass	3 ♣
Pass	4 ♣	Pass	5 ♣
All Pass			

You, West, lead the two of hearts—three, king, ace. Declarer leads the nine of diamonds to dummy, East playing the six, and leads the club jack—five, four, king. How do you defend?

Solutions

9. You can confidently duck the first diamond, since partner surely would have preferred a diamond lead from J-10-9-x to a club from Q-10-x-x.

You also can duck the second diamond because the slam is cold if declarer has both the queen and jack. Declarer would have six hearts, two clubs, a club ruff, and two diamonds, and he must have the spade ace since he wouldn't leap to slam with less than three aces. The full deal:

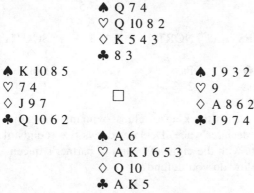

10. You can't be sure why declarer went to dummy for a trump play, but in any case it cannot be right to try cashing the queen of hearts. If declarer has a heart loser, he also must have three diamonds. If his hand were something like

♠ x x
♡ A x
◇ x x
♣ A Q x x x x x,

he would attempt to throw his heart away on the top diamonds before taking the trump finesse. You should lead a diamond, hoping partner can ruff.

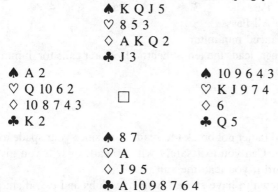

Obviously, declarer could have made the contract simply by playing ace and another club. His club play was correct considering the suit in isolation, but perhaps not within the context of the whole hand.

Problems

11. Dlr: South   ♠ 10 6 2
     Vul: Both   ♡ J 3
              ◇ Q J 8 3
              ♣ J 9 6 3

♠ Q 8 4
♡ 10 9 7 5 4 2
◇ 7 5
♣ A 4

WEST	NORTH	EAST	SOUTH
			1 ◇
2 ♣	Pass	Pass	Dbl
Pass	2 ◇	2 ♡	3 ◇
All Pass			

West, your partner, leads the king of clubs, winning. He shifts to the king of hearts, taken by declarer's ace. Declarer draws two rounds of trumps, all following, and exits with the eight of hearts to partner's queen. A low club goes to your ace. How do you defend?

12. Dlr: South   ♠ J 9 4
     Vul: N-S   ♡ Q J 9 4
              ◇ 7 6
              ♣ A K 8 4

♠ 5 3
♡ A 7 3 2
◇ J 8 5
♣ Q 10 9 3

WEST	NORTH	EAST	SOUTH
			1 ♠
Pass	2 ♣	Pass	2 NT[1]
Pass	3 ♠	Pass	4 ♠
All Pass			

[1]balanced minimum

West, your partner, leads the ten of hearts. Declarer calls for dummy's queen. Plan your defense.

Solutions

11. You would rather not break the spade suit, since your spade tricks aren't going anywhere. Can you exit safely with a heart, or will you give declarer a ruff-and-discard if you lead the suit?

Partner is known to have started with five clubs and two diamonds. If he had three good cards in each major, do you suppose he might have doubled one diamond for takeout instead of overcalling? It would have been a much more flexible action and, especially at IMPs or rubber bridge, less likely to lead to a disaster. Play the ten of hearts.

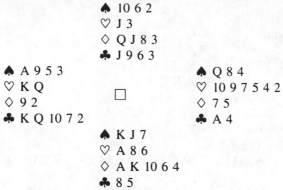

```
              ♠ 10 6 2
              ♡ J 3
              ◇ Q J 8 3
              ♣ J 9 6 3
♠ A 9 5 3                    ♠ Q 8 4
♡ K Q           □           ♡ 10 9 7 5 4 2
◇ 9 2                        ◇ 7 5
♣ K Q 10 7 2                 ♣ A 4
              ♠ K J 7
              ♡ A 8 6
              ◇ A K 10 6 4
              ♣ 8 5
```

If you lead a spade, it costs the setting trick. (This is based on a deal from *All 52 Cards*, an excellent book by Marshall Miles.)

12.   Declarer would not have rebid 2 NT if he had a four-card heart suit to show, so partner's heart ten cannot be a singleton. You should signal with the seven of hearts at trick one.

```
              ♠ J 9 4
              ♡ Q J 9 4
              ◇ 7 6
              ♣ A K 8 4
♠ A 8 2                     ♠ 5 3
♡ 10 5           □          ♡ A 7 3 2
◇ K 9 4 3 2                 ◇ J 8 5
♣ 7 6 5                     ♣ Q 10 9 3
              ♠ K Q 10 7 6
              ♡ K 8 6
              ◇ A Q 10
              ♣ J 2
```

When declarer leads trumps, partner will win the ace and play his second heart, obtaining a ruff. The diamond king will be the setting trick. Note that it is vital for you to duck the first heart, retaining your entry.

Problems

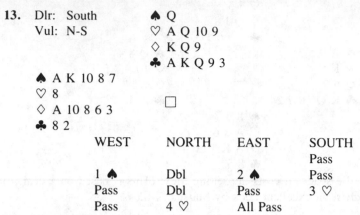

13. Dlr: South
Vul: N-S

♠ Q
♡ A Q 10 9
◇ K Q 9
♣ A K Q 9 3

♠ A K 10 8 7
♡ 8
◇ A 10 8 6 3
♣ 8 2

☐

WEST	NORTH	EAST	SOUTH
			Pass
1 ♠	Dbl	2 ♠	Pass
Pass	Dbl	Pass	3 ♡
Pass	4 ♡	All Pass	

You, West, lead the king of spades. East plays the two, declarer the four. How do you continue?

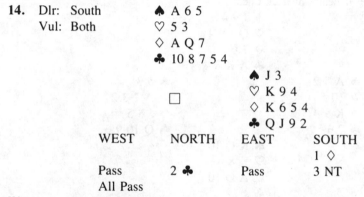

14. Dlr: South
Vul: Both

♠ A 6 5
♡ 5 3
◇ A Q 7
♣ 10 8 7 5 4

☐

♠ J 3
♡ K 9 4
◇ K 6 5 4
♣ Q J 9 2

WEST	NORTH	EAST	SOUTH
			1 ◇
Pass	2 ♣	Pass	3 NT
All Pass			

West, your partner, leads the two of hearts. Declarer captures your king with the ace and leads a low diamond. Partner plays the eight, dummy the queen, and your king wins. How do you continue?

Solutions

13. Clearly, you must play East for the heart king, and he also must obtain a diamond ruff. You could try ace of diamonds and another, playing him for a singleton, but if he has a doubleton diamond, you need to underlead your ace at this point. Which shall it be?

Doubletons are more common, to be sure, but there also is a slight inference. East is likely to have J-9-x-x-(x) of spades to justify a raise with so few high cards; but if his hand were

♠ J 9 x x
♡ K x x
◇ x
♣ x x x x x,

he might have jumped to *three* spades, preemptive, over North's double.

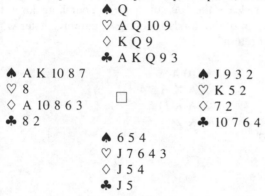

```
              ♠ Q
              ♡ A Q 10 9
              ◇ K Q 9
              ♣ A K Q 9 3
♠ A K 10 8 7                  ♠ J 9 3 2
♡ 8                           ♡ K 5 2
◇ A 10 8 6 3       □          ◇ 7 2
♣ 8 2                         ♣ 10 7 6 4
              ♠ 6 5 4
              ♡ J 7 6 4 3
              ◇ J 5 4
              ♣ J 5
```

14. Partner led from a four-card heart suit, marking declarer with four. Furthermore, partner can have no more than four spades, else his lead would have been a spade, so declarer has four cards there. Declarer opened one diamond, so he is likely to have at least four diamonds (and partner's play of the diamond eight substantiates this). So it looks like declarer has a singleton club. You should win the king of diamonds and shift to a *low* club.

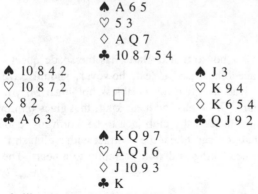

```
              ♠ A 6 5
              ♡ 5 3
              ◇ A Q 7
              ♣ 10 8 7 5 4
♠ 10 8 4 2                    ♠ J 3
♡ 10 8 7 2         □          ♡ K 9 4
◇ 8 2                         ◇ K 6 5 4
♣ A 6 3                       ♣ Q J 9 2
              ♠ K Q 9 7
              ♡ A Q J 6
              ◇ J 10 9 3
              ♣ K
```

If you don't like declarer's 3 NT bid, I'm with you. But that's no reason to let him steal a game.

Problems

15. Dlr: North
Vul: None

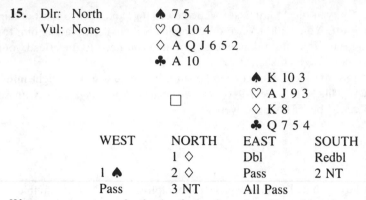

♠ 7 5
♡ Q 10 4
◇ A Q J 6 5 2
♣ A 10

♠ K 10 3
♡ A J 9 3
◇ K 8
♣ Q 7 5 4

WEST	NORTH	EAST	SOUTH
	1 ◇	Dbl	Redbl
1 ♠	2 ◇	Pass	2 NT
Pass	3 NT	All Pass	

West, your partner, leads the four of spades. Your king loses to the ace. Declarer leads the ten of diamonds, ducking in dummy. After winning your king, what do you return?

16. Dlr: North
Vul: N-S

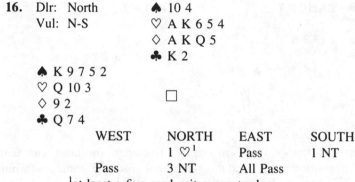

♠ 10 4
♡ A K 6 5 4
◇ A K Q 5
♣ K 2

♠ K 9 7 5 2
♡ Q 10 3
◇ 9 2
♣ Q 7 4

WEST	NORTH	EAST	SOUTH
	1 ♡[1]	Pass	1 NT
Pass	3 NT	All Pass	

[1] at least a five-card suit guaranteed

You, West, lead the five of spades—four, queen, ace. Declarer continues with ace, king, and another heart. Partner discards the eight of spades, and declarer's jack loses to your queen. How do you continue?

Solutions

15. You can bet your house that declarer has the spade queen—he would have held up his ace otherwise. (West, however, should have the spade jack—he shouldn't lead low from a worthless holding.) So you can count eight tricks for declarer. If he has the heart king, that gives him only 9 HCP, and he still must have at least the club jack to be worth his redouble.

All this means that you can't beat the contract with a club shift. You must play partner for the heart king and shift promptly to a heart. The full deal:

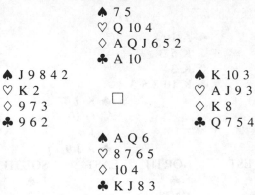

♠ 7 5
♡ Q 10 4
◇ A Q J 6 5 2
♣ A 10

♠ J 9 8 4 2
♡ K 2
◇ 9 7 3
♣ 9 6 2

♠ K 10 3
♡ A J 9 3
◇ K 8
♣ Q 7 5 4

♠ A Q 6
♡ 8 7 6 5
◇ 10 4
♣ K J 8 3

If you return anything but a low heart at trick three, declarer will make at least one overtrick.

16. You can cash the spade king and exit with a diamond, trying to endplay dummy, but this won't work if declarer has the diamond jack (or any four diamonds). The alternative is a club shift, but that is risky, too—it could give away the ninth trick if declarer has the club jack.

To shed some light on the problem, ask yourself this: Why did declarer respond 1 NT with three-card heart support, avoiding the normal raise? He must have a really terrible hand and was afraid that a raise would sound too encouraging. South already has shown 6 HCP. If your inference is valid, he can't have any more. Prefer the club shift.

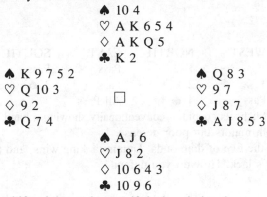

♠ 10 4
♡ A K 6 5 4
◇ A K Q 5
♣ K 2

♠ K 9 7 5 2
♡ Q 10 3
◇ 9 2
♣ Q 7 4

♠ Q 8 3
♡ 9 7
◇ J 8 7
♣ A J 8 5 3

♠ A J 6
♡ J 8 2
◇ 10 6 4 3
♣ 10 9 6

The club shift might work even if declarer's hand were

♠ A J x
♡ J x x
◇ x x x
♣ J 10 x x

If he misguessed and played the king from dummy, partner would win and return a club to your queen. Then you could cash your spade king, exit with a diamond, and score a diamond in the end.

Problems

17. Dlr: North   ♠ A 10 8
      Vul: Both   ♡ K 5 3
                     ◇ K 3
                     ♣ K 10 8 5 3

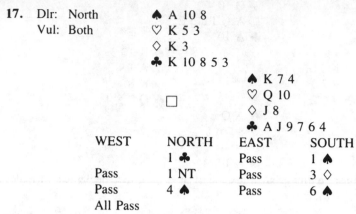

                     ♠ K 7 4
                     ♡ Q 10
                     ◇ J 8
                     ♣ A J 9 7 6 4

WEST	NORTH	EAST	SOUTH
	1 ♣	Pass	1 ♠
Pass	1 NT	Pass	3 ◇
Pass	4 ♠	Pass	6 ♠
All Pass			

West, your partner, leads the six of hearts, dummy's king holding. At trick two, declarer calls for the three of clubs. Do you play your ace? Why or why not?

18. Dlr: East   ♠ K J 10 7 4
      Vul: N-S   ♡ K Q 10 6 2
                     ◇ K
                     ♣ 9 2

♠ 9 2
♡ A 3
◇ Q 10 8 5 2   □
♣ A J 7 3

WEST	NORTH	EAST	SOUTH
		Pass	Pass
1 ◇	2 ◇ [1]	Pass	3 ♠
Pass	4 ♠	All Pass	

[1] A "Michaels cuebid," conventionally showing a hand with length in both majors but poor defense.

You, West, lead the five of diamonds. Dummy's king wins, and a low heart is led to declarer's jack. How do you defend?

Solutions

17.

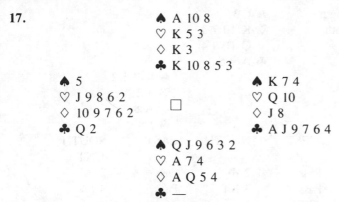

♠ A 10 8
♡ K 5 3
◇ K 3
♣ K 10 8 5 3

♠ 5
♡ J 9 8 6 2
◇ 10 9 7 6 2
♣ Q 2

♠ K 7 4
♡ Q 10
◇ J 8
♣ A J 9 7 6 4

♠ Q J 9 6 3 2
♡ A 7 4
◇ A Q 5 4
♣ —

Duck the first club. Two strong inferences are available. First, declarer simply leaped to slam without using Blackwood, so he must not be worried about first-round controls—he is likely to have two aces and a void. There is an outside chance that declarer's club control is a singleton, but in that case West also would have a singleton. With the very weak hand West seems to have, he surely would have led a singleton if he had one.

18. You must hope for two club tricks and a spade. However, there is no need to play East for a specific holding like the club king and the queen of trumps. If declarer had the ace of spades, he would have come to hand and taken a club discard on the diamond ace. Win the heart ace and lead a trump.

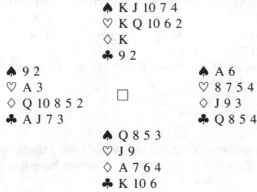

♠ K J 10 7 4
♡ K Q 10 6 2
◇ K
♣ 9 2

♠ 9 2
♡ A 3
◇ Q 10 8 5 2
♣ A J 7 3

♠ A 6
♡ 8 7 5 4
◇ J 9 3
♣ Q 8 5 4

♠ Q 8 5 3
♡ J 9
◇ A 7 6 4
♣ K 10 6

Problems

19. Dlr: South ♠ 6 3
      Vul: Both ♡ K 10 7 4
                  ♢ Q 10 9 4
                  ♣ A 9 5

                           ♠ K 9 5 2
                           ♡ 3 2
                □   ♢ A 8 5 3
                           ♣ J 8 2

WEST	NORTH	EAST	SOUTH
			1 NT
Pass	2 ♣	Pass	2 ♠
Pass	3 NT	Pass	4 ♡
All Pass			

West, your partner, leads the jack of diamonds. Plan your defense.

20. Dlr: East ♠ Q 9 4 3
      Vul: None ♡ 9 5 2
                  ♢ J 5
                  ♣ A 10 7 6

♠ 8 2
♡ K 10
♢ Q 10 7 6 4 2   □
♣ J 4 3

WEST	NORTH	EAST	SOUTH
		Pass	1 ♠
Pass	2 ♠	Pass	4 ♠
All Pass			

You, West, lead the six of diamonds. East wins the ace and cashes the ace of hearts. Plan your defense.

Solutions

19. Duck the first diamond, since partner cannot have a singleton. Declarer showed four cards in each major, so clearly he cannot have four diamonds.

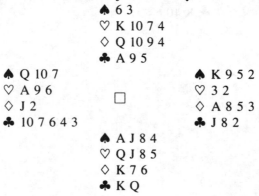

                ♠ 6 3
                ♡ K 10 7 4
                ♢ Q 10 9 4
                ♣ A 9 5

♠ Q 10 7   ♠ K 9 5 2
♡ A 9 6   ♡ 3 2
♢ J 2   □   ♢ A 8 5 3
♣ 10 7 6 4 3   ♣ J 8 2

                ♠ A J 8 4
                ♡ Q J 8 5
                ♢ K 7 6
                ♣ K Q

314

If you play the eight of diamonds at trick one, declarer can do no better than lead a trump. Partner will take the ace and continue with his other diamond—now you can give him a ruff.

20. If East's hearts were headed by only the ace, he would be tempted to *underlead* his holding to put declarer to a guess or keep communications intact. He would infer that declarer couldn't have a singleton king, since you definitely would have led a heart from Q-J-10-(x)-(x).

It is far more likely that East has both the ace and queen of hearts and is content to cash whatever tricks he can in the suit. In that case, you may have to dump your king of hearts under his ace to defeat the contract. The full deal is:

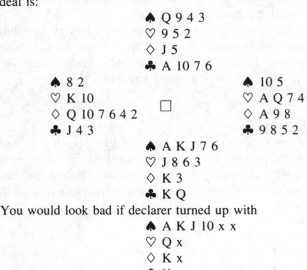

```
              ♠ Q 9 4 3
              ♡ 9 5 2
              ◇ J 5
              ♣ A 10 7 6
♠ 8 2                        ♠ 10 5
♡ K 10                       ♡ A Q 7 4
◇ Q 10 7 6 4 2    □          ◇ A 9 8
♣ J 4 3                      ♣ 9 8 5 2
              ♠ A K J 7 6
              ♡ J 8 6 3
              ◇ K 3
              ♣ K Q
```

You would look bad if declarer turned up with

```
              ♠ A K J 10 x x
              ♡ Q x
              ◇ K x
              ♣ K x x
```

However, that would leave East with

```
              ♠ x
              ♡ A J 9 x x x
              ◇ A x x
              ♣ Q x x,
```

and not many players would have passed throughout with that hand.

Quiz 22

Picking Up Partner

It's common knowledge that most partners need all the help they can get. Bridge is a partnership game, and like it or not, our results depend on what that person across the table does. Regardless of what sadistic impulses we may harbor, winning bridge means helping partner avoid mistakes.

Players often forget that a good partner will take note of every little thing that happens at the table—for instance, he will watch the spots like a hawk, looking for subtle inferences. In the simple situation below, East would have to consider his partner's problems to avoid a potentially costly play.

```
            A 7 6
   9 3        □        J 8 5 4 2
            K Q 10
```

West leads the nine of this suit, and dummy ducks. If East plays the jack and declarer wins the king, the position will be unclear to West—he may cherish the belief that he has found partner with the queen-jack and continue the suit in vain. If East wants to make sure that West loses interest in this suit, he should play the two.

Dlr: North   ♠ Q 7
Vul: None   ♡ K 6 3
           ◇ 9 7 5
           ♣ A K J 10 4

```
♠ K 3                        ♠ 8 5 2
♡ 9 8 5 4 2                  ♡ A Q
◇ 8 3          □             ◇ K Q J 6 4 2
♣ 9 8 6 3                    ♣ 7 5
            ♠ A J 10 9 6 4
            ♡ J 10 7
            ◇ A 10
            ♣ Q 2
```

WEST	NORTH	EAST	SOUTH
	1 ♣	1 ◇	1 ♠
Pass	2 ♣	Pass	3 ♠
Pass	4 ♠	All Pass	

West leads the diamond eight. East can see that there is little hope for the defense unless West has a trump trick and he can be encouraged to shift to hearts. So East unconventionally plays the diamond *king* at trick one. When West wins the spade king, he will place declarer with the diamond queen, and a heart shift will be much more attractive.

Perhaps West should reason out the heart switch in any case, but East is trying to preserve his partner's supply of mental energy for other hands down the road.

This deal, from one of Alfred Sheinwold's fine books, illustrates the same idea.

```
                    ♠ 10 5
                    ♡ 7 4 3
                    ◇ K J 8 3
                    ♣ K Q J 3
    ♠ A 9 8 6 4                 ♠ K Q
    ♡ 8 5 2                     ♡ J 10 9 6
    ◇ A 6 4          □          ◇ 7 5 2
    ♣ 7 5                       ♣ 9 8 6 2
                    ♠ J 7 3 2
                    ♡ A K Q
                    ◇ Q 10 9
                    ♣ A 10 4
```

West leads the six of spades against 3 NT, and East holds the first two tricks with the queen and king. Now the defense can take no more than West's two aces, and the contract is made.

As the cards lie, West could have beaten the game by overtaking the spade king and leading the nine. Declarer cannot get home without a diamond trick. When a diamond is led, West grabs the ace and cashes two more spades. However, as West protested, this defense would be spectacularly unsuccessful if declarer's hand were

```
        ♠ J 3 2
        ♡ A K Q 6
        ◇ Q 10 9
        ♣ A 10 4
```

Sheinwold points out that East was mainly at fault for putting partner to a guess. He should have played his spade honors out of order—the king first, then the queen. The message that he had only two cards in the suit would have been clear.

Declarer made another impossible game on the next deal. Which defender do you think was more to blame?

Dlr: South   ♠ Q 3
Vul: N-S   ♡ 10 7 4
           ◇ A 7
           ♣ A J 9 5 4 2

♠ A 9 7 6   ♠ 10 8 5 4
♡ A J 8   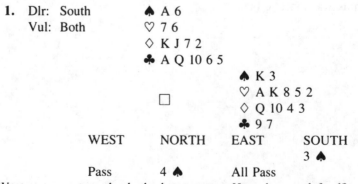   ♡ K 9 6 2
◇ J 9 8 2   ◇ 10 6
♣ Q 8   ♣ 7 6 3

           ♠ K J 2
           ♡ Q 5 3
           ◇ K Q 5 4 3
           ♣ K 10

WEST	NORTH	EAST	SOUTH
			1 ◇
Pass	2 ♣	Pass	2 NT
Pass	3 NT	All Pass	

West led the six of spades. Dummy's queen held, East playing the five. Declarer tried a club to the ten and queen. Now West found the killing shift to the heart eight, but East, on winning the king, switched back to spades. The defense could take no more than four tricks.

We hold East almost blameless. West just as easily could have held

           ♠ A J x x
           ♡ A 8 x
           ◇ J 9 x x
           ♣ Q x

(although with that hand he might have laid down the heart ace first). As East argued in the postmortem, if West wanted a spade return, it *would* be correct for him to lead a high heart to discourage a heart continuation—and the eight looked pretty high.

Perhaps West should have removed partner's losing option by *cashing the spade ace* before shifting to hearts.

Problems

1.   Dlr: South   ♠ A 6
    Vul: Both   ♡ 7 6
                ◇ K J 7 2
                ♣ A Q 10 6 5

                      ♠ K 3
                      ♡ A K 8 5 2
             ☐   ◇ Q 10 4 3
                      ♣ 9 7

WEST	NORTH	EAST	SOUTH
			3 ♠
Pass	4 ♠	All Pass	

West, your partner, leads the heart queen. How do you defend?

2. Dlr: North   ♠ 9 6
       Vul: Both   ♡ A K Q 7 5
                  ◊ Q 3
                  ♣ K Q 8 3

♠ 5 3 2
♡ 9 8 4 2
◊ K 8 6 5 2   □
♣ 2

WEST	NORTH	EAST	SOUTH
	1 ♡	Pass	1 ♠
Pass	2 ♣	Pass	3 ♠
Pass	4 ♠	All Pass	

You, West, lead your singleton club. Partner obligingly captures dummy's king with the ace and returns the four of clubs, which you ruff. Declarer has followed with the seven and ten. How do you continue?

Solutions

1. Overtake with the heart king, cash the heart ace, and lead a diamond. If you leave West on lead, he may shift to clubs or underlead the diamond ace. Remember, he cannot know that you are looking at a surprise trick in trumps.

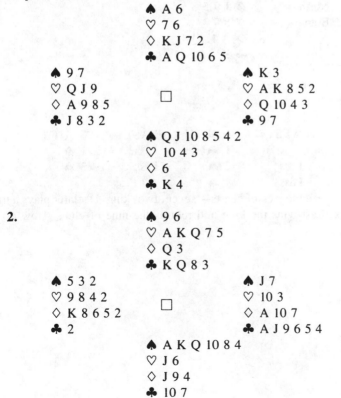

♠ A 6
♡ 7 6
◊ K J 7 2
♣ A Q 10 6 5

♠ 9 7   ♠ K 3
♡ Q J 9   ♡ A K 8 5 2
◊ A 9 8 5   □   ◊ Q 10 4 3
♣ J 8 3 2   ♣ 9 7

♠ Q J 10 8 5 4 2
♡ 10 4 3
◊ 6
♣ K 4

2.   ♠ 9 6
          ♡ A K Q 7 5
          ◊ Q 3
          ♣ K Q 8 3

♠ 5 3 2   ♠ J 7
♡ 9 8 4 2   ♡ 10 3
◊ K 8 6 5 2   □   ◊ A 10 7
♣ 2   ♣ A J 9 6 5 4

♠ A K Q 10 8 4
♡ J 6
◊ J 9 4
♣ 10 7

Lead the king of diamonds. Partner's club four is a suit–preference signal requesting a diamond return—presumably, he has the diamond ace. However, if you return a low diamond, you give him a problem. He might decide to play you for the queen of spades instead of the king of diamonds. (Indeed, on your defense, he *should*.) If he returns a third round of clubs, trying for a trump promotion, declarer will ruff high, draw trumps, and claim.

Problems

3. Dlr: East
Vul: N-S

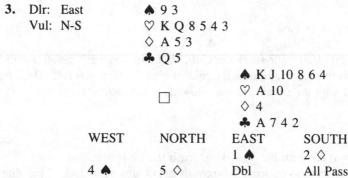

♠ 9 3
♡ K Q 8 5 4 3
◇ A 5 3
♣ Q 5

♠ K J 10 8 6 4
♡ A 10
◇ 4
♣ A 7 4 2

WEST	NORTH	EAST	SOUTH
		1 ♠	2 ◇
4 ♠	5 ◇	Dbl	All Pass

West, your partner, leads the two of hearts. Plan your defense.

4. Dlr: North
Vul: Both

♠ J 9 5 3
♡ 8 7
◇ A K Q
♣ K J 10 4

♠ 7
♡ J 10 9 6 3
◇ J 8 2
♣ A 8 6 2

WEST	NORTH	EAST	SOUTH
	1 ♣	Pass	1 ♠
Pass	2 ♠	Pass	3 ♠
Pass	4 ♠	All Pass	

You, West, lead the jack of hearts—seven, two, king. Declarer plays a trump to the jack. East wins the king and returns the nine of clubs. How do you defend?

Solutions

3.

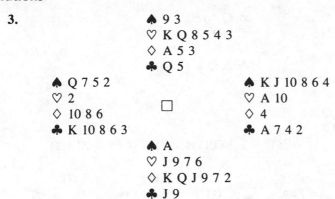

$\spadesuit$ 9 3
$\heartsuit$ K Q 8 5 4 3
$\diamondsuit$ A 5 3
$\clubsuit$ Q 5

$\spadesuit$ Q 7 5 2
$\heartsuit$ 2
$\diamondsuit$ 10 8 6
$\clubsuit$ K 10 8 6 3

$\spadesuit$ K J 10 8 6 4
$\heartsuit$ A 10
$\diamondsuit$ 4
$\clubsuit$ A 7 4 2

$\spadesuit$ A
$\heartsuit$ J 9 7 6
$\diamondsuit$ K Q J 9 7 2
$\clubsuit$ J 9

No disasters! Cash the club ace at trick two, then give partner his heart ruff. If you return the heart ten immediately, partner is a cinch to return a spade, your bid suit, after ruffing. (Note that a suit-preference mixup is likely because fate dealt you just one heart, and it happens to be a high one. Declarer could add to the confusion by following with the nine and jack on the two heart leads.)

4.   Declarer would take a finesse if he were missing only the spade king, so East must hold the ace also. If you trust your partner, you will duck the club, playing him for a doubleton. If partner had a singleton club, he would have cashed his spade ace before leading it, removing your option of ducking.

$\spadesuit$ J 9 5 3
$\heartsuit$ 8 7
$\diamondsuit$ A K Q
$\clubsuit$ K J 10 4

$\spadesuit$ 7
$\heartsuit$ J 10 9 6 3
$\diamondsuit$ J 8 2
$\clubsuit$ A 8 6 2

$\spadesuit$ A K 2
$\heartsuit$ Q 5 4 2
$\diamondsuit$ 10 9 6 5
$\clubsuit$ 9 5

$\spadesuit$ Q 10 8 6 4
$\heartsuit$ A K
$\diamondsuit$ 7 4 3
$\clubsuit$ Q 7 3

Problems

5. Dlr: South   ♠ Q 10 5
     Vul: N-S   ♡ Q J 7
                  ◇ J 6 2
                  ♣ A Q 4 3

♠ J 8 7 4 2
♡ K 6
◇ A Q 4 3   □
♣ 10 7

WEST	NORTH	EAST	SOUTH
			1 ◇
Pass	2 ♣	Pass	2 NT
Pass	3 NT	All Pass	

You, West, lead the four of spades—five, six, nine. Declarer continues with a club to the queen and the queen of hearts, passed to your king. How do you continue?

6. Dlr: South   ♠ K 9 5 3
     Vul: Both   ♡ 6
                  ◇ Q 6 3
                  ♣ K Q 10 6 4

♠ 10 6 2
♡ J 9 7 5 2
◇ K 10 7 5   □
♣ A

WEST	NORTH	EAST	SOUTH
			1 ♠
Pass	3 ♠	Pass	4 ♠
All Pass			

You, West, lead the ace of clubs—four, two, five. Interpreting partner's play as suit preference, you shift to the five of diamonds. Dummy plays low and East's jack wins. Next, partner lays down the diamond ace, to which declarer follows. What do you play to this trick?

Solutions

5. Continue spades, by all means—but take care to lead the *jack*. The full deal:

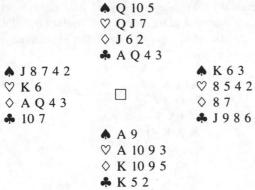

```
              ♠ Q 10 5
              ♡ Q J 7
              ◇ J 6 2
              ♣ A Q 4 3
♠ J 8 7 4 2                      ♠ K 6 3
♡ K 6                           ♡ 8 5 4 2
◇ A Q 4 3         □             ◇ 8 7
♣ 10 7                          ♣ J 9 8 6
              ♠ A 9
              ♡ A 10 9 3
              ◇ K 10 9 5
              ♣ K 5 2
```

If you led a second low spade, East is probably still sitting there, trying to
figure out your holding. Since you have J-x-x-x-x, he can defeat the contract
by playing low again. But if you had A-x-x-x-x and no ace of diamonds,
he'd never live it down if he ducked. Lead the jack, and he'll *know* it can't
gain to play the king.

6.

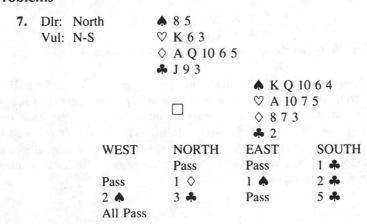

```
              ♠ K 9 5 3
              ♡ 6
              ◇ Q 6 3
              ♣ K Q 10 6 4
♠ 10 6 2                        ♠ J
♡ J 9 7 5 2                     ♡ K 10 8 4
◇ K 10 7 5        □             ◇ A J 8 4
♣ A                            ♣ 8 7 3 2
              ♠ A Q 8 7 4
              ♡ A Q 3
              ◇ 9 2
              ♣ J 9 5
```

Partner is unsure where the setting trick lies. Help him out by throwing the
king of diamonds under the ace, forcing a club return.

Problems

7. Dlr: North
Vul: N-S

```
♠ 8 5
♡ K 6 3
◇ A Q 10 6 5
♣ J 9 3
                    ♠ K Q 10 6 4
         □          ♡ A 10 7 5
                    ◇ 8 7 3
                    ♣ 2
```

WEST	NORTH	EAST	SOUTH
	Pass	Pass	1 ♣
Pass	1 ◇	1 ♠	2 ♣
2 ♠	3 ♣	Pass	5 ♣
All Pass			

323

West, your partner, leads the two of spades, and your queen loses to declarer's ace. Declarer leads a diamond to the queen and finesses the club nine, losing to partner's king. At trick four, partner leads the heart queen, and dummy plays low. How do you defend?

8. Dlr: South
Vul: E-W

♠ A 6 3
♡ Q 7 4
◇ J 5 3
♣ A K Q J

♠ K
♡ A J 10 5 2
◇ A Q 6
♣ 9 8 5 2

□

WEST	NORTH	EAST	SOUTH
			3 ♠
Pass	4 ♠	All Pass	

You, West, lead the heart ace, and declarer drops the king. Plan your defense.

Solutions

7. From West's point of view, a heart shift is needed if declarer has the diamond king and you have the A-x-x of hearts and a six-card spade suit. Since you know from partner's lead of the spade two that declarer has another spade, you *must* overtake the heart queen with the ace and cash the spade king.

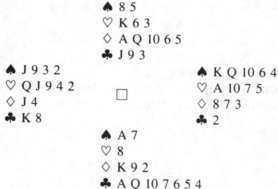

♠ 8 5
♡ K 6 3
◇ A Q 10 6 5
♣ J 9 3

♠ J 9 3 2   ♠ K Q 10 6 4
♡ Q J 9 4 2   ♡ A 10 7 5
◇ J 4   □   ◇ 8 7 3
♣ K 8   ♣ 2

♠ A 7
♡ 8
◇ K 9 2
♣ A Q 10 7 6 5 4

If you let West hold the queen of hearts, he is sure to lead the suit again.

8. Clearly, you must shift to diamonds, playing partner for the king. However, even if he has that card there are a couple of pitfalls. First, you mustn't lead low—if dummy ducked, partner might sagely play the nine from K-9-x-x. If you lead the ace, be sure to follow with the six. If you lead the queen the second time, partner might play you for ace-queen alone and overtake to give you a ruff! The most elegant sequence is to lead the queen, then the ace and another.

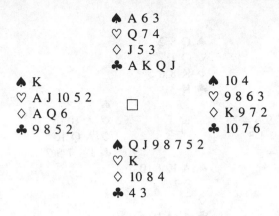

```
              ♠ A 6 3
              ♡ Q 7 4
              ◇ J 5 3
              ♣ A K Q J
  ♠ K                        ♠ 10 4
  ♡ A J 10 5 2    ☐         ♡ 9 8 6 3
  ◇ A Q 6                    ◇ K 9 7 2
  ♣ 9 8 5 2                  ♣ 10 7 6
              ♠ Q J 9 8 7 5 2
              ♡ K
              ◇ 10 8 4
              ♣ 4 3
```

Problems

9. Dlr: South
    Vul: Both

```
              ♠ Q 8 2
              ♡ Q J 3
              ◇ K 8 6 5 2
              ♣ K 3
                        ♠ 7 5 3
              ☐         ♡ A 10
                        ◇ A Q 10
                        ♣ J 8 7 5 2
```

WEST	NORTH	EAST	SOUTH
			1 ♠
Pass	2 ◇	Pass	2 ♠
Pass	3 ♠	Pass	4 ♠
All Pass			

West, your partner, leads the four of hearts. You capture dummy's queen, declarer following with the seven. How do you continue?

10. Dlr: South
    Vul: Both

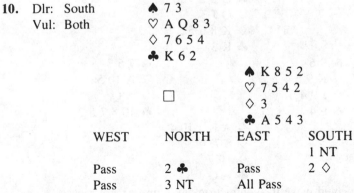

```
              ♠ 7 3
              ♡ A Q 8 3
              ◇ 7 6 5 4
              ♣ K 6 2
                        ♠ K 8 5 2
              ☐         ♡ 7 5 4 2
                        ◇ 3
                        ♣ A 5 4 3
```

WEST	NORTH	EAST	SOUTH
			1 NT
Pass	2 ♣	Pass	2 ◇
Pass	3 NT	All Pass	

West, your partner, leads the jack of diamonds, won by declarer's queen. A club is led to the eight, king, and your ace. How do you continue?

Solutions

9.

                        ♠ Q 8 2
                        ♡ Q J 3
                        ◇ K 8 6 5 2
                        ♣ K 3
      ♠ 9 6   ♠ 7 5 3
      ♡ K 9 6 4 2   □   ♡ A 10
      ◇ J 9 4 3   ◇ A Q 10
      ♣ 9 4   ♣ J 8 7 5 2
                        ♠ A K J 10 4
                        ♡ 8 7 5
                        ◇ 7
                        ♣ A Q 10 6

Cash the ace of diamonds and return a heart.

Suppose you return the heart ten at trick two instead. Declarer will falsecard with the eight, leaving partner in the dark as to who has the missing five. Looking at all four hands, the right defense is easy; but if declarer had

                        ♠ A K J x x
                        ♡ 8 7
                        ◇ x x
                        ♣ A Q 10 x

a diamond switch by West would be the winner.

You know from the opening lead that West has exactly five hearts to the king—he would not lead low from a worthless suit, nor would declarer be likely to rebid two spades with a four-card heart suit. A heart ruff is available. Furthermore, if declarer is void in diamonds (with, say, 6-3-0-4 pattern) the contract is probably unbeatable.

West might guess right even if you return a heart immediately. He might reason that you would be in no hurry to return a heart unless you had a doubleton. However, if the full deal were:

                        ♠ Q 8 2
                        ♡ Q J 3
                        ◇ K 8 6 5 2
                        ♣ K 3
      ♠ 9 6   ♠ 7 5 3
      ♡ K 9 6 4 2   □   ♡ A 10 5
      ◇ J 9 4 3   ◇ A Q
      ♣ 9 4   ♣ 10 8 7 5 2
                        ♠ A K J 10 4
                        ♡ 8 7
                        ◇ 10 7
                        ♣ A Q J 6

declarer could make the contract on any return except a heart.

10. The bidding marks partner with four spades, so a spade switch must be right. But start by leading the *king*, which can't lose anything and may gain. The full deal:

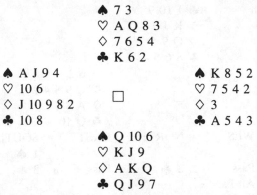

♠ 7 3
♡ A Q 8 3
◇ 7 6 5 4
♣ K 6 2

♠ A J 9 4
♡ 10 6
◇ J 10 9 8 2
♣ 10 8

♠ K 8 5 2
♡ 7 5 4 2
◇ 3
♣ A 5 4 3

♠ Q 10 6
♡ K J 9
◇ A K Q
♣ Q J 9 7

If you lead the two, declarer's ten loses to partner's jack. But will partner continue the suit? As it is, the defense has to cash out, but partner may see things differently—he doesn't know that declarer has 18 HCP, leaving you with no minor honors in clubs or hearts. From his vantage point, your spades could be four to the *queen*—in that case a spade continuation would give away a possibly vital trick. Partner may choose to exit passively with another diamond.

It's true that declarer could have something like

♠ A J x
♡ K J x
◇ K Q x
♣ Q J 9 x

and East does better in the short run to lead a low spade. However, declarer has nine tricks if he holds that hand. Unless West owns the spade ace, the contract is probably on ice.

Problems

11. Dlr: West
    Vul: Both

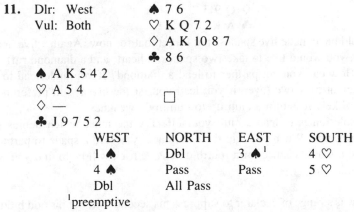

♠ 7 6
♡ K Q 7 2
◇ A K 10 8 7
♣ 8 6

♠ A K 5 4 2
♡ A 5 4
◇ —
♣ J 9 7 5 2

WEST	NORTH	EAST	SOUTH
1 ♠	Dbl	3 ♠[1]	4 ♡
4 ♠	Pass	Pass	5 ♡
Dbl	All Pass		

[1]preemptive

You, West, lead the spade ace—six, queen, eight. How do you proceed to earn the maximum penalty?

12. Dlr: South
Vul: Both

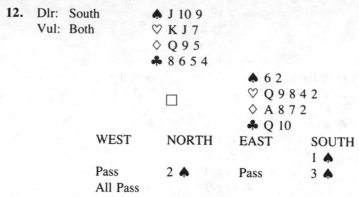

♠ J 10 9
♡ K J 7
◇ Q 9 5
♣ 8 6 5 4

♠ 6 2
♡ Q 9 8 4 2
◇ A 8 7 2
♣ Q 10

WEST	NORTH	EAST	SOUTH
			1 ♠
Pass	2 ♠	Pass	3 ♠
All Pass			

West, your partner, leads the ten of diamonds. Guessing well, you win the ace immediately and return a diamond, partner ruffing. Partner continues with the seven of clubs, and your queen loses to the ace. Declarer now plays ace and another spade, partner's king winning. West cashes the club king and continues with the club jack. What do you discard on this trick?

Solutions

11.

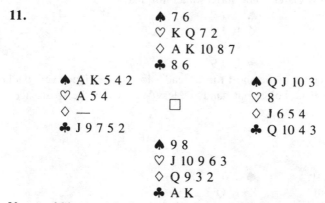

♠ 7 6
♡ K Q 7 2
◇ A K 10 8 7
♣ 8 6

♠ A K 5 4 2
♡ A 5 4
◇ —
♣ J 9 7 5 2

♠ Q J 10 3
♡ 8
◇ J 6 5 4
♣ Q 10 4 3

♠ 9 8
♡ J 10 9 6 3
◇ Q 9 3 2
♣ A K

You could have made five spades, but forget that for now. Against five hearts doubled, you would like to take two spades, a heart, and a diamond ruff, for +500. How can you get partner to lead a diamond? If you underlead to his spade jack at trick two (even if you lead your spade *five* as suit preference), he is too likely to return a club up to dummy's weakness.

The solution is to lead a club yourself. Try the nine, which denies any interest in clubs. When you win the trump ace, you lead a spade to partner's jack, and his only chance for a fourth defensive trick will be to find you with a diamond void.

12. It was strange of declarer to suppress his second suit, but his odd bidding may pay off if you aren't careful. Partner doesn't know that declarer started with ten cards in spades and diamonds. If declarer ruffs the third club and leads a heart, partner may think that it cannot cost to duck, giving declarer a chance to misguess for two down, −200. But *you* know that declarer can have one heart at most, so you must prevent partner from ducking by discarding the heart queen on the third round of clubs.

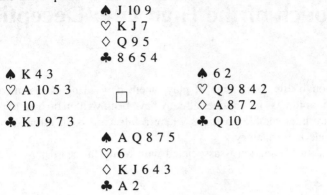

♠ J 10 9
♡ K J 7
◇ Q 9 5
♣ 8 6 5 4

♠ K 4 3
♡ A 10 5 3
◇ 10
♣ K J 9 7 3

♠ 6 2
♡ Q 9 8 4 2
◇ A 8 7 2
♣ Q 10

♠ A Q 8 7 5
♡ 6
◇ K J 6 4 3
♣ A 2

A Touch of the High Life: Deception

Although this is one area of play where new wrinkles are uncovered every so often, volumes and volumes already have been written on how to fool declarer. There are innumerable positions where a falsecard is desirable, and still others where one is mandatory.

The J-9 combination is associated with many falsecards:

$$\begin{array}{ccc} & 10\ 8\ 2 & \\ K\ 5\ 4\ 3 & \square & J\ 9 \\ & A\ Q\ 7\ 6 & \end{array}$$

Declarer leads the two from dummy. If East plays the nine, declarer's queen loses to the king. But the jack drops under the ace next, giving declarer three tricks. Note the effect if East plays his jack on the *first* round. Declarer's queen will lose to the king again, but on regaining the lead declarer will finesse dummy's eight, playing West for K-9-5-4-3.

$$\begin{array}{ccc} & K\ Q\ 10\ 8\ 4\ 2 & \\ A\ 7\ 3 & \square & J\ 9 \\ & 6\ 5 & \end{array}$$

Needing to set up this suit, declarer leads low to the king. Say East follows with the nine. Declarer sees that if West has A-J-7-3, two tricks must be lost in any case, so he comes back to hand and leads low to the queen. But if East drops his jack on the first lead, declarer surely will play to dummy's eight next.

$$\begin{array}{ccc} & 10\ 7\ 6\ 3 & \\ K & \square & A\ J\ 9 \\ & Q\ 8\ 5\ 4\ 2 & \end{array}$$

This suit is trumps, and declarer leads low from dummy. If East follows with the nine, declarer may duck, playing West for a singleton honor. But suppose East deviously puts up the jack! Declarer will surely cover with the queen, and the defense will take three tricks.

$$\begin{array}{ccc} & A\ 10\ 8\ 4 & \\ J\ 9\ 5\ 2 & \square & 3 \\ & K\ Q\ 7\ 6 & \end{array}$$

Declarer, who is known to have four cards in this suit, starts by leading low to his king. If West follows with the two, declarer has no choice but to continue with the queen from hand, and the third-round finesse against West will become marked. However, West can offer declarer a losing option by dropping his *nine* on the first round. If the nine is in fact a singleton, declarer must play to the ace next to set up a finessing position against East.

The J-9 situations are part of one big family of deceptive plays. Q-9 holdings belong to another branch.

                    10 8 2
A 5 4   □   Q 9
                    K J 7 6 3

Declarer leads low from dummy, and East must put the queen up.

On board 77 of the 1976 Bermuda Bowl final, the contract at one table was three spades and the trump suit was:

                    10 6 5 3
A   □   Q J 9
                    K 8 7 4 2

When dummy led a trump at one point, East, Benito Garozzo, deceptively played the *queen*. This beautiful move failed to gain a trick only because Hugh Ross, the U.S. declarer, had a good idea where the missing high cards were from the bidding. He ducked in hand, refuting Garozzo's gambit.

Even the 10-8 tandem may come in for a share of deception.

                    K J 7 6
2   □   A 10 8 3
                    Q 9 5 4

Declarer leads low to dummy's jack. If East wins the ace, declarer will cash the king next, catering to A-10-8-3 in East. So East should let the jack hold, offering his *eight*. Declarer will probably lead back to his queen, expecting West to have A-10-3-2.

                    K J 7 6
A 10 8   □   Q 5 4
                    9 3 2

If declarer leads low toward dummy, West might produce a third trick from thin air by following with the *ten*. Assuming that the jack loses to the queen and the defenders place the lead in dummy, declarer may proceed to run the seven, playing East for Q-8-5-4 or A-Q-8-5-4.

Following with a higher card than you need to is the idea behind other deceptive plays. On the next deal, East pulled off a beautiful swindle.

Dlr: South   ♠ 10 5 4
Vul: None   ♡ 10 7 5 3
                    ◇ Q J 10 6
                    ♣ A Q

♠ A J 6 2   ♠ K 9 7 3
♡ 9 6 2   ♡ K J 8
◇ 8 7   □   ◇ K 5 2
♣ 9 8 6 4   ♣ 10 7 2

                    ♠ Q 8
                    ♡ A Q 4
                    ◇ A 9 4 3
                    ♣ K J 5 3

WEST	NORTH	EAST	SOUTH
			1 NT
Pass	2 ♣	Pass	2 ◇
Pass	3 NT	All Pass	

This was the auction at both tables in a team-of-four match. At one table West led the normal spade, and the defenders took their book immediately. Declarer saw that the contract depended on the location of the diamond king, so he discarded hearts from his hand and dummy. Winning the heart shift, he cashed the ace and queen of clubs and took the diamond finesse for his contract.

At the other table West preferred to lead a passive nine of hearts. Dummy played low and East followed with the *jack*. Declarer eyed this card hopefully, won the queen of hearts, and followed with the ace. Sure enough, East dropped the *king*.

Declarer now thought he was home—he could finesse the seven of hearts for a fourth heart trick, and there were five top tricks available in the minors. But when East produced the eight of hearts, the defense took four spades for down one.

Winning a trick with a higher card than necessary sometimes can produce strange results.

```
              Q 10 9
  6 5 4         □         K J 3
              A 8 7 2
```

Declarer attacks this suit by leading low to the nine. If East wins the jack, declarer will lead the queen from dummy later, picking up the suit. Winning the king, however, would induce declarer to finesse the ten next in case West has J-x-x x.

On other occasions a defender may do best not to win a trick at all.

```
Dlr: North        ♠ J 5
Vul: Both         ♡ A J 6
                  ◇ A Q J 3 2
                  ♣ A J 5
♠ Q 10 8 2                      ♠ K 7 6 3
♡ Q 9 4 3          □            ♡ 10 7 5
◇ 8 7                           ◇ K 10 4
♣ Q 10 9                        ♣ K 7 2
                  ♠ A 9 4
                  ♡ K 8 2
                  ◇ 9 6 5
                  ♣ 8 6 4 3
```

WEST	NORTH	EAST	SOUTH
	1 ◇	Pass	1 NT
Pass	3 NT	All Pass	

West leads the two of spades to the jack, king, and ace. Declarer immediately finesses the queen of diamonds, and East should *duck*. (However, the effect is lost unless he makes up his mind in advance to play low *without pause*.) Now declarer doesn't know whether to repeat the diamond finesse for the ninth trick or switch to hearts and try the finesse in that suit—and with only one entry left to his hand, he can't do both.

Opportunities for deception on the opening lead are common. For example, suppose you are on lead against 3 NT with K-Q-J-10-4 of spades and no other face cards. You might steal a trick by leading the *queen*. A possible deal, at matchpoint duplicate:

```
Dlr: East        ♠ 7 6 3
Vul: N-S         ♡ K 4
Matchpoints      ◊ 5 3
                 ♣ A J 9 6 5 3
♠ K Q J 10 4              ♠ 8 5
♡ 8 7 2          ☐        ♡ 10 9 6 5 3
◊ 9 8 6                   ◊ A K 10 7
♣ 8 7                     ♣ K 4
                 ♠ A 9 2
                 ♡ A Q J
                 ◊ Q J 4 2
                 ♣ Q 10 2
```

WEST	NORTH	EAST	SOUTH
		Pass	1 NT
Pass	3 NT	All Pass	

If the opening lead is the king of spades, declarer will realize that holding up the ace once is free—even if the club finesse works, only ten tricks are available. But suppose West leads the spade *queen*. Now declarer may take a different view. If the queen is a true card, holding up twice cannot gain—if East, a passed hand, has both black kings, West must have a diamond honor for an entry. And when East plays low on the first spade, declarer may not even hold up once, sensing that East has forgotten to unblock with K-x.

Problems

Here is a departure from the usual format. In each problem, a full deal, a bidding sequence, and (except in Problem 1) an opening lead are shown. You must visualize the likely course of the play and spot a defender's chance for deception.

The problems would be too easy if we led you along and asked for your play at the critical point—and we're sure you wouldn't appreciate it if we made things too soft on you.

1. Dlr: South   ♠ K 7 3
      Vul: N-S   ♡ K J 3
                ◇ Q 6 4
                ♣ J 10 9 5

♠ J 9 6 2		♠ 8 4
♡ A 9 7 2	□	♡ 10 8 6 5
◇ A 10 8		◇ J 9 7 2
♣ A 4		♣ 8 7 6

                ♠ A Q 10 5
                ♡ Q 4
                ◇ K 5 3
                ♣ K Q 3 2

WEST	NORTH	EAST	SOUTH
			1 NT
Pass	3 NT	All Pass	

The contract went down one. What was West's opening lead?

2. Dlr: West   ♠ 10 7 5 2
      Vul: Both   ♡ K 7 5 2
                ◇ K Q
                ♣ Q 5 4

♠ Q 9		♠ J 6
♡ J 9 6 4	□	♡ A Q 10 8
◇ 8 7 3		◇ 9 5 2
♣ 10 9 7 6		♣ A K J 3

                ♠ A K 8 4 3
                ♡ 3
                ◇ A J 10 6 4
                ♣ 8 2

WEST	NORTH	EAST	SOUTH
Pass	Pass	1 NT	2 ♠
Pass	3 ♠	Pass	4 ♠
All Pass			

Opening lead: six of clubs.

3. Dlr: South
Vul: None

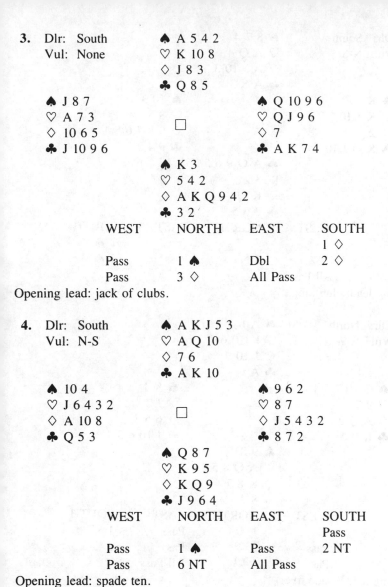

♠ A 5 4 2
♡ K 10 8
◇ J 8 3
♣ Q 8 5

♠ J 8 7
♡ A 7 3
◇ 10 6 5
♣ J 10 9 6

♠ Q 10 9 6
♡ Q J 9 6
◇ 7
♣ A K 7 4

♠ K 3
♡ 5 4 2
◇ A K Q 9 4 2
♣ 3 2

WEST	NORTH	EAST	SOUTH
			1 ◇
Pass	1 ♠	Dbl	2 ◇
Pass	3 ◇	All Pass	

Opening lead: jack of clubs.

4. Dlr: South
Vul: N-S

♠ A K J 5 3
♡ A Q 10
◇ 7 6
♣ A K 10

♠ 10 4
♡ J 6 4 3 2
◇ A 10 8
♣ Q 5 3

♠ 9 6 2
♡ 8 7
◇ J 5 4 3 2
♣ 8 7 2

♠ Q 8 7
♡ K 9 5
◇ K Q 9
♣ J 9 6 4

WEST	NORTH	EAST	SOUTH
			Pass
Pass	1 ♠	Pass	2 NT
Pass	6 NT	All Pass	

Opening lead: spade ten.

5. Dlr: South
Vul: N-S

		♠ 8 7 4
		♡ A Q 4
		◇ A J 10 3
		♣ A 8 3

♠ K J		♠ 10 3
♡ K J 10 9 7 6		♡ 8 5
◇ 2	□	◇ 9 8 7 6 5 4
♣ K Q J 10		♣ 9 4 2

	♠ A Q 9 6 5 2
	♡ 3 2
	◇ K Q
	♣ 7 6 5

WEST	NORTH	EAST	SOUTH
			1 ♠
2 ♡	3 NT	Pass	4 ♠
All Pass			

Opening lead: club king.

6. Dlr: North
Vul: E-W

		♠ A 6 3 2
		♡ K 10 6 4
		◇ J 10 9
		♣ A Q

♠ Q 10 7 5 4		♠ K J
♡ 9 7		♡ J 2
◇ A Q 2	□	◇ 6 5 3
♣ K 9 7		♣ J 10 6 5 4 2

	♠ 9 8
	♡ A Q 8 5 3
	◇ K 8 7 4
	♣ 8 3

WEST	NORTH	EAST	SOUTH
	1 ◇	Pass	1 ♡
Pass	2 ♡	Pass	3 ◇
Pass	4 ♡	All Pass	

Opening lead: spade five.

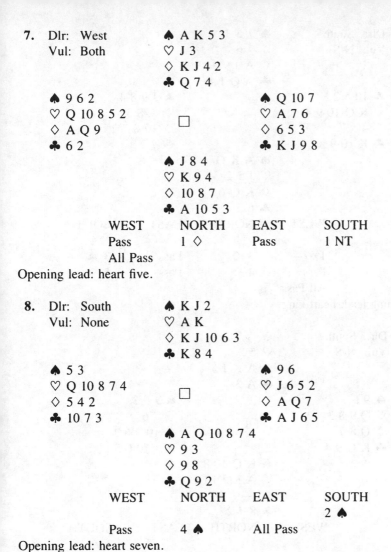

7. Dlr: West   ♠ A K 5 3
     Vul: Both   ♡ J 3
                ◇ K J 4 2
                ♣ Q 7 4

♠ 9 6 2   ♠ Q 10 7
♡ Q 10 8 5 2   ♡ A 7 6
◇ A Q 9   ◇ 6 5 3
♣ 6 2   ♣ K J 9 8

                ♠ J 8 4
                ♡ K 9 4
                ◇ 10 8 7
                ♣ A 10 5 3

WEST	NORTH	EAST	SOUTH
Pass	1 ◇	Pass	1 NT
All Pass			

Opening lead: heart five.

8. Dlr: South   ♠ K J 2
     Vul: None   ♡ A K
                ◇ K J 10 6 3
                ♣ K 8 4

♠ 5 3   ♠ 9 6
♡ Q 10 8 7 4   ♡ J 6 5 2
◇ 5 4 2   ◇ A Q 7
♣ 10 7 3   ♣ A J 6 5

                ♠ A Q 10 8 7 4
                ♡ 9 3
                ◇ 9 8
                ♣ Q 9 2

WEST	NORTH	EAST	SOUTH
			2 ♠
Pass	4 ♠	All Pass	

Opening lead: heart seven.

9. Dlr: South
Vul: N-S

```
              ♠ 7 6 3
              ♡ 7 6
              ◇ A J 9 3
              ♣ A Q J 4
♠ 10 5 2                    ♠ J 9 8 4
♡ K Q 10 9 4               ♡ A 8 3
◇ 4           □            ◇ 10 8 7 2
♣ K 10 9 8                 ♣ 7 2
              ♠ A K Q
              ♡ J 5 2
              ◇ K Q 6 5
              ♣ 6 5 3
```

WEST	NORTH	EAST	SOUTH
			1 ◇
1 ♡	3 ◇	Pass	3 ♠
Pass	4 ◇	Pass	5 ◇
All Pass			

Opening lead: heart king.

10. Dlr: South
Vul: N-S

```
              ♠ A 7 2
              ♡ 5 2
              ◇ A K J 5 4 3
              ♣ A 3
♠ 9 6                      ♠ J 5 3
♡ Q 9 8 3                  ♡ 7 6
◇ Q 8 7       □            ◇ 10 9 6 2
♣ K Q 9 4                  ♣ J 10 6 5
              ♠ K Q 10 8 4
              ♡ A K J 10 4
              ◇ —
              ♣ 8 7 2
```

WEST	NORTH	EAST	SOUTH
			1 ♠
Pass	2 ◇	Pass	2 ♡
Pass	3 ♠	Pass	4 ♡
Pass	5 ♣	Pass	6 ♠
Pass	7 ♠	All Pass	

Opening lead: club king.

11. Dlr: South
Vul: N-S

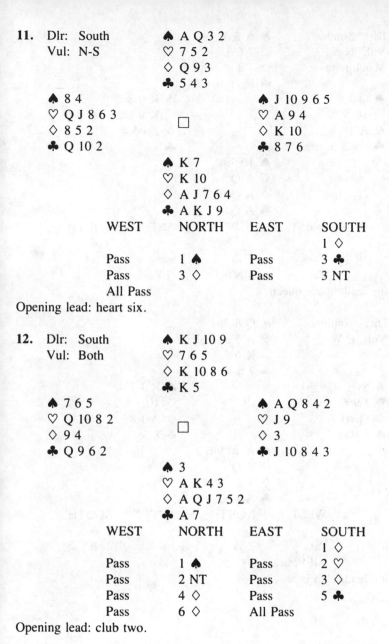

♠ A Q 3 2
♥ 7 5 2
♦ Q 9 3
♣ 5 4 3

♠ 8 4
♥ Q J 8 6 3
♦ 8 5 2
♣ Q 10 2

♠ J 10 9 6 5
♥ A 9 4
♦ K 10
♣ 8 7 6

♠ K 7
♥ K 10
♦ A J 7 6 4
♣ A K J 9

WEST	NORTH	EAST	SOUTH
			1 ♦
Pass	1 ♠	Pass	3 ♣
Pass	3 ♦	Pass	3 NT
All Pass			

Opening lead: heart six.

12. Dlr: South
Vul: Both

♠ K J 10 9
♥ 7 6 5
♦ K 10 8 6
♣ K 5

♠ 7 6 5
♥ Q 10 8 2
♦ 9 4
♣ Q 9 6 2

♠ A Q 8 4 2
♥ J 9
♦ 3
♣ J 10 8 4 3

♠ 3
♥ A K 4 3
♦ A Q J 7 5 2
♣ A 7

WEST	NORTH	EAST	SOUTH
			1 ♦
Pass	1 ♠	Pass	2 ♥
Pass	2 NT	Pass	3 ♦
Pass	4 ♦	Pass	5 ♣
Pass	6 ♦	All Pass	

Opening lead: club two.

13. Dlr: South
Vul: N-S
Matchpoints

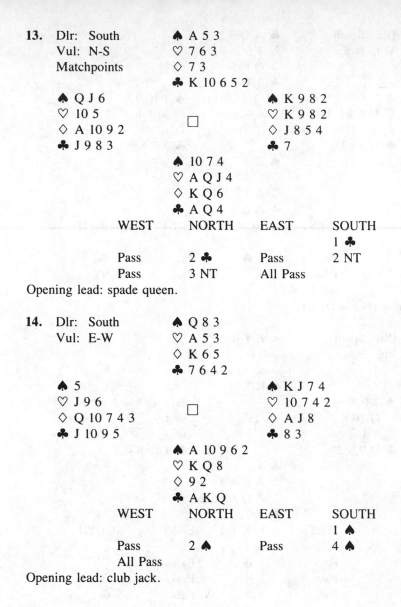

         ♠ A 5 3
         ♡ 7 6 3
         ◇ 7 3
         ♣ K 10 6 5 2

♠ Q J 6   ♠ K 9 8 2
♡ 10 5   ♡ K 9 8 2
◇ A 10 9 2   ◇ J 8 5 4
♣ J 9 8 3   ♣ 7

         ♠ 10 7 4
         ♡ A Q J 4
         ◇ K Q 6
         ♣ A Q 4

WEST	NORTH	EAST	SOUTH
			1 ♣
Pass	2 ♣	Pass	2 NT
Pass	3 NT	All Pass	

Opening lead: spade queen.

14. Dlr: South
Vul: E-W

         ♠ Q 8 3
         ♡ A 5 3
         ◇ K 6 5
         ♣ 7 6 4 2

♠ 5   ♠ K J 7 4
♡ J 9 6   ♡ 10 7 4 2
◇ Q 10 7 4 3   ◇ A J 8
♣ J 10 9 5   ♣ 8 3

         ♠ A 10 9 6 2
         ♡ K Q 8
         ◇ 9 2
         ♣ A K Q

WEST	NORTH	EAST	SOUTH
			1 ♠
Pass	2 ♠	Pass	4 ♠
All Pass			

Opening lead: club jack.

15. Dlr: South
Vul: None

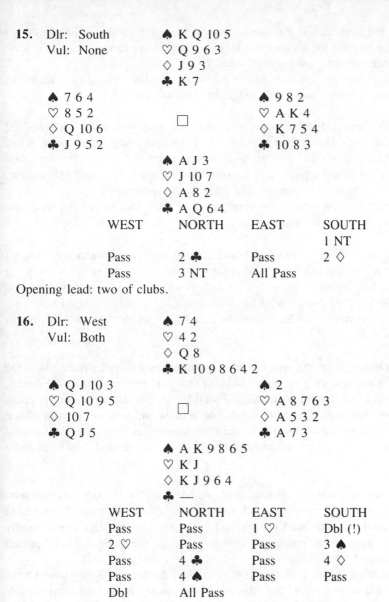

♠ K Q 10 5
♡ Q 9 6 3
◇ J 9 3
♣ K 7

♠ 7 6 4
♡ 8 5 2
◇ Q 10 6
♣ J 9 5 2

♠ 9 8 2
♡ A K 4
◇ K 7 5 4
♣ 10 8 3

♠ A J 3
♡ J 10 7
◇ A 8 2
♣ A Q 6 4

WEST	NORTH	EAST	SOUTH
			1 NT
Pass	2 ♣	Pass	2 ◇
Pass	3 NT	All Pass	

Opening lead: two of clubs.

16. Dlr: West
Vul: Both

♠ 7 4
♡ 4 2
◇ Q 8
♣ K 10 9 8 6 4 2

♠ Q J 10 3
♡ Q 10 9 5
◇ 10 7
♣ Q J 5

♠ 2
♡ A 8 7 6 3
◇ A 5 3 2
♣ A 7 3

♠ A K 9 8 6 5
♡ K J
◇ K J 9 6 4
♣ —

WEST	NORTH	EAST	SOUTH
Pass	Pass	1 ♡	Dbl (!)
2 ♡	Pass	Pass	3 ♠
Pass	4 ♣	Pass	4 ◇
Pass	4 ♠	Pass	Pass
Dbl	All Pass		

Opening lead: heart five.

The contract was set *two* tricks. How?

Solutions

1. West, with 13 HCP, knew his partner would play no part in the defense, so he led the *seven* of hearts. Declarer won and knocked out the club ace. West continued with the heart two, masquerading as a man with a five-card heart suit and no further entry. Now declarer thought he couldn't afford to set up the ninth trick in diamonds, lest the defenders get three hearts and two aces, so he tried for his contract by cashing the three top spades. As it was, this established the *setting* trick—for West!

If West had led a normal fourth-best heart, declarer would have made the contract, judging it safe to dislodge the diamond ace.

2. Declarer ruffed the third club, went to dummy with a diamond, and led the spade ten, playing East for Q-9-6 or J-9-6 and trying to induce an error. But when East covered with the jack and declarer won the king, West realized that the Q-9 were equals, and he smoothly dropped the *queen*. Of course, declarer went back to dummy and finessed the spade eight.

Declarer might have gone wrong even if West had played the nine, but the play of the queen was virtually sure to work.

3. After ruffing the third club and drawing trumps, declarer went after a heart trick by leading low to the eight (the correct percentage play, winning if West had the nine plus either the jack or queen). East saw that if he won with the nine, declarer would have no option but to lead straight to the king on the next round. So East won the jack, allowing declarer to lead low to the ten next.

4. Declarer won the opening lead in dummy and played a diamond to the king. West, knowing from the bidding that declarer must have the queen, too, was ready for this—he ducked with the proper degree of indifference. Declarer could have taken the club finesse now and won all thirteen tricks, but he had no reason to believe the club queen was right and the diamond ace was wrong. He returned to dummy, led another diamond, and went down three!

5. Declarer won the opening lead and tried for fast pitches on diamonds. West ruffed the second diamond with the *king* of spades, cashed two clubs, and exited with the heart jack, won by dummy's queen. Declarer naturally placed East with the rest of the trumps, so he led the spade eight and passed it. Unlucky!

Had West ruffed with the jack of spades, declarer probably would have picked off the now-bare king, playing the opponent who had bid for that card.

6. South ducked the first spade and won the second. He drew trumps in two rounds and finessed the diamond jack. West won with the *ace* of diamonds and returned the nine of clubs. Declarer thought he had an overtrick in the bag by winning the club ace and picking up the diamonds to discard the club queen. But when he took another diamond finesse, West perversely produced the queen and cashed the club king for down one!

7. At one table in a team event, declarer won the third heart and led a diamond to the nine and jack. Judging that both diamond honors were on his left, he tried a low spade from dummy. East won the queen but could do no better than exit with a spade. Declarer won the jack and led a second diamond, making the contract.

In the replay, the contract was the same, and again declarer held up the heart king until the third round. However, when he led the seven of diamonds toward dummy, West played the *queen*. The king won. Declarer naturally continued with a diamond to the eight and was irritated to see it lose to the nine. West cashed his hearts and shifted to a club, setting up a seventh trick for the defense.

8. Declarer won the heart, drew trumps, and passed the nine of diamonds to East's queen. East saw that a club switch was mandatory, but to give himself an extra chance he led the *jack*. Declarer ducked this, winning dummy's king. When East won the diamond ace, he continued with a low club. Understandably, declarer misguessed, playing low again, and the defense prevailed.

9. East overtook the heart king at trick one, as though with a doubleton, and returned the three. West won and played a third heart. Taken in, declarer ruffed in dummy with the jack. Later, to his chagrin, he found that he had to lose a trump trick for down one.

10. South won the club ace and tried to combine his chances. He played the top diamonds, discarding his clubs. Had everyone followed low, declarer planned to ruff a third diamond. If the queen dropped, thirteen tricks would be there; if not, declarer planned to fall back on a heart play.

The diamond chance was fated to come in—at least until West dropped the diamond queen on the *second* round of the suit (following a well-known falsecarding principle by playing a card he soon would be known to hold.) Declarer eyed this suspiciously, but he finally changed his plan. He drew two rounds of trumps with the ace and king and continued with the ace, king, and jack of hearts, ruffing. East overruffed, and West had to get the heart queen later, for two down.

11. There are deceptive possibilities for *both* defenders. After winning the heart king, declarer may test the water by cashing the ace-king of clubs. If the queen happens to drop from West, declarer can finesse the club nine, taking nine tricks without the diamond suit. Since West would hate to see declarer play diamonds, he can cooperate by following with the queen on the second club!

As for East—if declarer immediately goes to dummy and leads a low diamond, East definitely should put up the king. As it happens, declarer has nine tricks now. But if he gets greedy and finesses the diamond nine, trying to make five or six, he'll be sorry.

12. After winning the first trick in hand and drawing trumps, declarer is likely to lead a spade to the nine. East knows from the bidding that declarer has a singleton spade. If East wins the spade queen, declarer later will lead the king for a ruffing finesse (by far his best play), obtaining two discards for heart losers.

Note the effect if East wins the first spade with the *ace*. Declarer may try to ruff out "West's" spade queen for the second discard or play for a non-existent major-suit squeeze against West.

13. Suppose declarer wins the third spade and correctly leads a diamond to the king. West might duck this, leaving declarer to ponder whether he should play diamonds or hearts for the ninth trick. But let us say that West wins the diamond ace and exits with the ten to declarer's queen. Declarer has a chance for an overtrick, but he needs two entries to dummy for two heart finesses. He cashes the club ace, all following low, but when the club queen is played next, West can drop the *jack*. Now declarer thinks he can afford to overtake with the king, saving the ten as a second entry. When East shows out, even nine tricks are suddenly beyond reach.

14. Lacking entries to dummy, declarer probably will attack trumps by leading low to the queen. If East wins, declarer will go to the heart ace and finesse for the spade jack later. But suppose East *ducks*. Declarer surely will lead low to the ace next.

Ducking completely also might work if declarer's first play is low to the *eight*.

15. The opening lead marks declarer with four clubs. The defense has a chance only if declarer has three diamonds and West holds the diamond queen. Even so, it won't help if East shifts to a low diamond. Declarer ducks this to the queen and can always guess right if West continues the suit.

Instead, East should try leading the *king* of diamonds (the less pause for thought, the better). Now declarer will fear that East holds K-Q-10-x and West has the remaining high heart for an entry. If declarer ducks, and ducks again when East continues with a low diamond, he is beaten.

16. The famous deal is from the 1963 Bermuda Bowl. Benito Garozzo was East. Winning the heart ace, Garozzo shifted to a trump, won by declarer! South now led a diamond to the queen, and Garozzo ducked smoothly! He ducked again when the diamond eight was continued. Reasonably enough, declarer judged to pass the eight, hoping it would drive out the ace from West, and Garozzo had created a second diamond trick from thin air.

Quiz 24

Don't Be Endplayed!

The side that gets to play last to a trick enjoys an obvious advantage. In particular, if one side has to break open a brand-new suit, it'll wind up costing them a trick a substantial part of the time. Therefore, a useful technique in play is to exit purposely, forcing the opponents to help you by leading.

Declarers use this technique so often that the defense constantly must be alert. There may be signs that declarer is planning a throw-in (also called an endplay, an elimination or a strip), and there also are ways the defenders may be able to thwart declarer's plans.

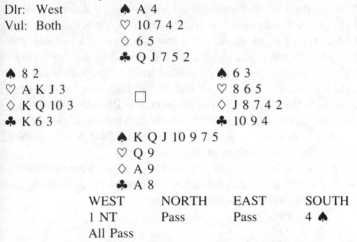

Dlr: West
Vul: Both

♠ A 4
♡ 10 7 4 2
◇ 6 5
♣ Q J 7 5 2

♠ 8 2
♡ A K J 3
◇ K Q 10 3
♣ K 6 3

♠ 6 3
♡ 8 6 5
◇ J 8 7 4 2
♣ 10 9 4

♠ K Q J 10 9 7 5
♡ Q 9
◇ A 9
♣ A 8

WEST	NORTH	EAST	SOUTH
1 NT	Pass	Pass	4 ♠
All Pass			

South's blast into game was indelicate—a slower approach might have reached the laydown 3 NT. Against the four-spade contract, West cashed two top hearts and shifted to the king of diamonds. Declarer won and ran off seven rounds of trumps. East threw one card in each red suit and all three clubs, while West came down to the guarded king of clubs and the queen of diamonds. Declarer then led his diamond, endplaying West.

West knew from the discards that declarer had the ace and a small club, so he should have tried to avoid the throw-in by pitching his high diamond, hoping East had the jack.

On many hands, a defender will lack the luxury of picking his discards in comfort. This deal is from the 1980 World Team Olympiad final.

Dlr: East   ♠ J
Vul: None   ♡ K J 10 8 2
                  ◇ K 6 5
                  ♣ J 8 4 3

♠ Q 9 8 5 4   ♠ 10 7 6 3
♡ A 7   ♡ 6 5
◇ A 10 7 4   □   ◇ Q 8 2
♣ Q 6   ♣ A 10 7 2

                  ♠ A K 2
                  ♡ Q 9 4 3
                  ◇ J 9 3
                  ♣ K 9 5

WEST	NORTH	EAST	SOUTH
		Pass	1 ♣
1 ♠	Dbl	3 ♠	Pass
Pass	Dbl	Pass	4 ♡
All Pass			

Mike Passell, West for the United States, led a spade, won by dummy's jack. Declarer, Henri Szwarc of France, led trumps. Passell took his ace and got out with a trump. Declarer won in hand and led a low diamond. Passell saw the danger and dashed up with the ace, exiting with a diamond to dummy's king. Now declarer came to hand with a trump, cashed his spades, ruffed his last diamond, and led a club to the king. If West had played low here, another club lead would have entangled the defenders in an endplay. But Passell came through again by unblocking his queen, and there was nothing declarer could do but lose two more tricks. The United States won ten IMPs when their South, Bobby Wolff, got home with the same contract at the other table.

That was a solo performance by Passell, but avoiding endplays are more often a matter of partnership cooperation. Edgar Kaplan and Norman Kay collaborated beautifully on this hand from the 1966 Reisinger Teams.

Dlr: South   ♠ Q 10 6 3
Vul: Both   ♡ A 7 6 3
                  ◇ K 7
                  ♣ 8 7 5

♠ K J   ♠ 4
♡ Q J 5   ♡ K 10 8 2
◇ A Q J 4 3   □   ◇ 10 9 8 2
♣ Q 10 4   ♣ 9 6 3 2

                  ♠ A 9 8 7 5 2
                  ♡ 9 4
                  ◇ 6 5
                  ♣ A K J

WEST	NORTH	EAST	SOUTH
			1 ♠
1 NT	Dbl	Pass	Pass
2 ◇	2 ♠	Pass	4 ♠
All Pass			

346

Kaplan, West, led the heart queen. Declarer ducked this, and Kay grabbed the chance to overtake with the king. Declarer won the club shift and immediately led a diamond to the jack and king. Kay subsequently found himself on lead with the diamond ten, and another club lead saved Kaplan from the impending club endplay. The defense ended with one trick in each suit.

Incidentally, Kaplan knew it was safe to duck the first diamond lead—declarer could not hold a singleton. Kay almost certainly had only one spade, and with a five-card diamond suit, he would have removed 1 NT doubled to two diamonds.

Avoiding endplays requires lots of foresight. On this deal from a matchpoint event, West had to be careful about his choice of leads.

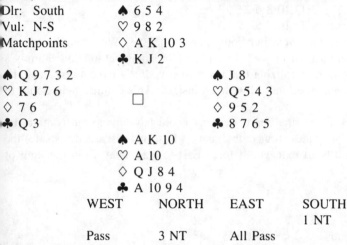

Dlr: South
Vul: N-S
Matchpoints

♠ 6 5 4
♡ 9 8 2
◇ A K 10 3
♣ K J 2

♠ Q 9 7 3 2
♡ K J 7 6
◇ 7 6
♣ Q 3

♠ J 8
♡ Q 5 4 3
◇ 9 5 2
♣ 8 7 6 5

♠ A K 10
♡ A 10
◇ Q J 8 4
♣ A 10 9 4

WEST	NORTH	EAST	SOUTH
			1 NT
Pass	3 NT	All Pass	

West led the three of spades to the jack and king. Declarer cashed four diamonds, as West discarded two spades, and then misguessed in clubs, losing a finesse to West's queen. West could count declarer for 3-2-4-4 pattern, and he felt obliged to switch to hearts—declarer, who had shown 14 HCP, might well have just Q-x of hearts. So a low heart lead went to queen and ace. Declarer then cashed two more clubs. forcing West down to the heart king and the Q-9 of spades. A heart exit endplayed West for a valuable second overtrick.

West could have saved himself by leading the heart king, a no-cost play.

We've seen that the defenders routinely duck winners to preserve their communication or deceive declarer. However, the technique may leave declarer holding an exit card for a throw-in. This deal, which was reported in *The Bridge World*, is from the 1967 European Championship.

Dlr: South   ♠ A J 7 6 4
Vul: None   ♡ K 10
                 ◇ A 3
                 ♣ A K J 3

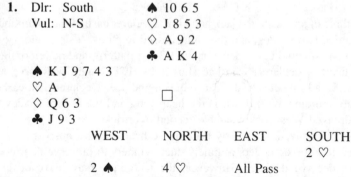

♠ Q 9 8 5   ♠ 10 3 2
♡ 9 8 6   ♡ A Q 5 4 2
◇ J 9 4   ◇ K 7 5
♣ 8 4 2   ♣ 9 6

                 ♠ K
                 ♡ J 7 3
                 ◇ Q 10 8 6 2
                 ♣ Q 10 7 5

The bidding was not given, but South played in 3 NT. West found the nine-of-hearts lead, and East must have been tempted for a moment to allow dummy's ten to hold. Fortunately, realizing that his partner couldn't have a fast entry, he played off the queen, ace, and a low heart instead. This defense held South to his eight top tricks.

Had East ducked the first heart, declarer could have made the contract by cashing the king of spades, four clubs, and (if East had discarded a spade) the spade ace. Then a heart exit would force East to lead away from the king of diamonds.

Problems

1. Dlr: South   ♠ 10 6 5
     Vul: N-S   ♡ J 8 5 3
                 ◇ A 9 2
                 ♣ A K 4

♠ K J 9 7 4 3
♡ A
◇ Q 6 3
♣ J 9 3

WEST	NORTH	EAST	SOUTH
			2 ♡
2 ♠	4 ♡	All Pass	

You, West, lead the seven of spades. To your relief, East wins the ace and returns a spade, declarer's queen falling to your king. What do you play to trick three?

2. Dlr: South
Vul: E-W

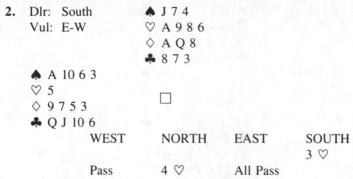

♠ J 7 4
♡ A 9 8 6
◇ A Q 8
♣ 8 7 3

♠ A 10 6 3
♡ 5
◇ 9 7 5 3
♣ Q J 10 6

WEST	NORTH	EAST	SOUTH
			3 ♡
Pass	4 ♡	All Pass	

You, West, lead the queen of clubs. Partner wins the ace and returns the two, declarer's king winning. At trick three, declarer leads a low spade. Do you go up with your ace? Why or why not? If you win, what do you lead next?

Solutions

1. With a balanced hand in dummy, there is no reason not cash the heart ace. If you don't, you may be endplayed with it. The full deal:

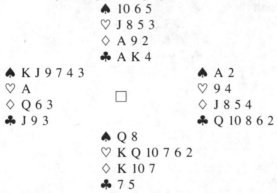

♠ 10 6 5
♡ J 8 5 3
◇ A 9 2
♣ A K 4

♠ K J 9 7 4 3
♡ A
◇ Q 6 3
♣ J 9 3

♠ A 2
♡ 9 4
◇ J 8 5 4
♣ Q 10 8 6 2

♠ Q 8
♡ K Q 10 7 6 2
◇ K 10 7
♣ 7 5

If you continue with the spade jack at trick three, declarer ruffs, plays ace, king, and another club, ruffing, and leads a heart. Now you must lead a diamond, giving declarer a chance to pick up the suit, or concede a fatal ruff-and-discard.

2. Declarer would be reluctant to open with a preempt with two black kings outside his long suit. His spade play before drawing trumps suggests that he wants to eliminate the suit in preparation for an endplay. Since declarer may well have a singleton spade, fly with the spade ace and shift to the nine of diamonds.

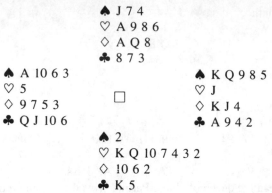

```
                      ♠ J 7 4
                      ♡ A 9 8 6
                      ◇ A Q 8
                      ♣ 8 7 3
        ♠ A 10 6 3                    ♠ K Q 9 8 5
        ♡ 5                           ♡ J
        ◇ 9 7 5 3          □          ◇ K J 4
        ♣ Q J 10 6                    ♣ A 9 4 2
                      ♠ 2
                      ♡ K Q 10 7 4 3 2
                      ◇ !0 6 2
                      ♣ K 5
```

Your side could have made four spades, but that's no reason to let the enemy
make four hearts. If you do not defend as indicated, declarer will strip out
the black suits and lead a diamond to the eight, endplaying East.

Problems

3. Dlr: North   ♠ 5
    Vul: N-S   ♡ K 7 5 2
                     ◇ A K 8 5
                     ♣ J 9 6 3

    ♠ Q 10 8 4 3
    ♡ Q J 10 4
    ◇ 7 6   □
    ♣ K 5

WEST	NORTH	EAST	SOUTH
	Pass	Pass	1 ◇
Pass	1 ♡	Pass	2 ◇
Pass	4 ◇	Pass	5 ◇
All Pass			

You, West, lead the queen of hearts, which holds. Declarer ruffs the second
heart, plays a diamond to the king, and comes back to the club ace. He cashes
the spade ace-king (dummy discards a club), ruffs a spade, ruffs a heart, goes
to the diamond ace (East showing out), and ruffs another heart.

Ten tricks have been played. What are your last three cards?

4. Dlr: East   ♠ K 6 4
     Vul: None   ♡ 6 5
                ◇ J 10 5 4
                ♣ Q J 4 2

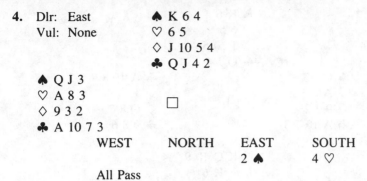

♠ Q J 3
♡ A 8 3
◇ 9 3 2
♣ A 10 7 3

WEST	NORTH	EAST	SOUTH
		2 ♠	4 ♡

All Pass

You, West, lead the spade queen and continue the suit. Declarer ruffs the second spade and leads the king of hearts to your ace, partner dropping the jack. How do you continue?

Solutions

3. Your last three cards should be two spades and the *five* of clubs. East is marked with the club queen, else declarer would have had a finesse to take, and declarer's innocent-looking play of the club ace should arouse your suspicions. Such a play early in the hand is a sure sign that declarer needs a throw-in and wants to make his preparations before the need for you to unblock becomes obvious.

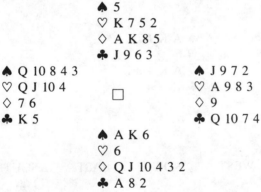

         ♠ 5
         ♡ K 7 5 2
         ◇ A K 8 5
         ♣ J 9 6 3

♠ Q 10 8 4 3   ♠ J 9 7 2
♡ Q J 10 4   ♡ A 9 8 3
◇ 7 6   ◇ 9
♣ K 5   ♣ Q 10 7 4

         ♠ A K 6
         ♡ 6
         ◇ Q J 10 4 3 2
         ♣ A 8 2

You can see what happens if you hang on to the club king. After declarer finishes stripping the hand, a second club endplays you.

4.

                    ♠ K 6 4
                    ♡ 6 5
                    ◇ J 10 5 4
                    ♣ Q J 4 2

    ♠ Q J 3   ♠ A 10 8 7 5 2
    ♡ A 8 3   □   ♡ J
    ◇ 9 3 2   ◇ Q 8 7
    ♣ A 10 7 3   ♣ 9 8 6

                    ♠ 9
                    ♡ K Q 10 9 7 4 2
                    ◇ A K 6
                    ♣ K 5

Return the eight of hearts. If you carelessly get out with a spade, you have wasted a vital exit card and will be ripe for an endplay. After ruffing and drawing trumps, declarer will lead the club king. You can duck and win the second club, but with only minor-suit cards left, you must concede the rest one way or another.

It's different if you put declarer back in his hand with a trump at trick four. Now you can get out safely with a spade after winning the second club. Unable to reach dummy, declarer must lose to the diamond queen in the end.

Problems

5. Dlr: North
       Vul: None

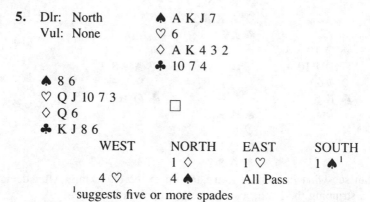

                    ♠ A K J 7
                    ♡ 6
                    ◇ A K 4 3 2
                    ♣ 10 7 4

    ♠ 8 6
    ♡ Q J 10 7 3   □
    ◇ Q 6
    ♣ K J 8 6

          WEST   NORTH   EAST   SOUTH
                    1 ◇   1 ♡   1 ♠[1]
          4 ♡   4 ♠   All Pass

[1]suggests five or more spades

You, West, lead the queen of hearts. Partner overtakes with the king and shifts to the two of clubs. Declarer plays the three, and your jack wins. How do you continue?

6. Dlr: South   ♠ A 8
    Vul: None   ♡ A K Q J
                         ♢ Q 2
                         ♣ K Q 5 4 3

♠ Q J 10 7 2
♡ 4 3
♢ A J 10 9 8 6   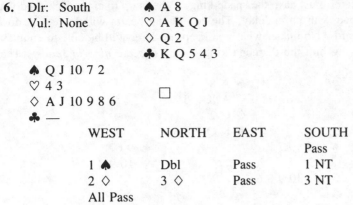
♣ —

WEST	NORTH	EAST	SOUTH
			Pass
1 ♠	Dbl	Pass	1 NT
2 ♢	3 ♢	Pass	3 NT
All Pass			

The occasion is the 1967 Bermuda Bowl. You are playing for Italy, and as the auction indicates, you like to bid. Against 3 NT you lead the diamond jack. Dummy's queen wins, partner playing the seven. At trick two declarer plays a club to his jack. Plan your defense.

Solutions

5. Your play can matter only if declarer has three clubs to the ace and three small diamonds. Think it over before returning the club six. If partner has to put up the queen, that will leave you holding your side's club winner. You'll be vulnerable to an endplay.

On a low-club return, declarer wins the ace, draws trumps, ruffs the losing heart, cashes the top diamonds, and exits with a club to you. You must give a ruff-and-discard, and declarer's diamond loser disappears. To avoid this ignominy, lead the club *king* at three.

     Partner did well not to try a deceptive lead of the club *queen*, which would have led to a certain endplay.

6. Partner appears to have ducked the club ace! If he has another diamond, you will have a few well-chosen words for him after the session. But for now, consider whether the contract can still be beaten.

Declarer must have the spade king, so he is up to eight tricks and you are threatened with an endplay. The run of the hearts will force you down to seven cards. No matter what you keep, declarer will be able to endplay you into giving him the diamond king—*if he has the nine of spades.* The full deal:

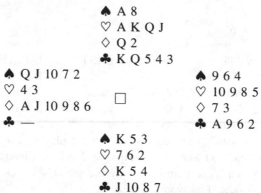

```
                    ♠ A 8
                    ♡ A K Q J
                    ◇ Q 2
                    ♣ K Q 5 4 3
   ♠ Q J 10 7 2                    ♠ 9 6 4
   ♡ 4 3                           ♡ 10 9 8 5
   ◇ A J 10 9 8 6                  ◇ 7 3
   ♣ —                            ♣ A 9 6 2
                    ♠ K 5 3
                    ♡ 7 6 2
                    ◇ K 5 4
                    ♣ J 10 8 7
```

In 1967, Giorgio Belladonna at once began to discard his spades from the top. By the time declarer finished the hearts, Giorgio had only the seven and two left. Now no endplay was possible, and declarer had to concede down one.

Italy won a swing on the deal when their N-S pair reached the same contract at the other table and West led the spade queen.

Problems

7. Dlr: West   ♠ 9 8 3
   Vul: Both   ♡ Q 10 7 6
                     ◇ K Q 9
                     ♣ A Q 2

```
   ♠ A 7 2
   ♡ K 5 3
   ◇ A 10 4
   ♣ K J 10 5
```

WEST	NORTH	EAST	SOUTH
1 ♣	Pass	Pass	1 ♡
Pass	3 ♡	Pass	4 ♡
All Pass			

You, West, lead the jack of clubs—queen, nine, three. Declarer plays a heart to the ace and another heart. You win, as East throws the four of spades, and you continue with the king of clubs. Declarer wins, draws your last trump (East discarding a low diamond), and leads the king of diamonds. You win and try the club ten, but declarer ruffs. He cashes the diamond jack and queen, East following. Then comes the nine of spades—ten, queen. How do you defend?

354

8. Dlr: North   ♠ K 10 5 3
Vul: None   ♡ J 8 6 3
              ◇ A K 5
              ♣ 10 3

                     ♠ 9 8 2
                     ♡ A Q 10 9
                     ◇ 7
                     ♣ K Q 6 5 4

WEST	NORTH	EAST	SOUTH
	Pass	1 ♣	Dbl
Pass	2 ♣	Pass	2 ♠
Pass	4 ♠	All Pass	

Now it's the 1970 Bermuda Bowl. You lately became a free agent, so you now are playing for Norway. West, your partner, leads the seven of hearts. Plan your defense.

Solutions

     7. Declarer is known to have 3-5-3-2 shape, and he must have the spade king as well as the queen for his four-heart bid. Assuming partner has the jack, the six becomes a crucial card. To make sure of beating the contract, you must let the spade queen hold. The full deal:

               ♠ 9 8 3
               ♡ Q 10 7 6
               ◇ K Q 9
               ♣ A Q 2

♠ A 7 2   ♠ J 10 5 4
♡ K 5 3   ♡ 4
◇ A 10 4   ◇ 8 7 6 2
♣ K J 10 5   ♣ 9 8 7 4

               ♠ K Q 6
               ♡ A J 9 8 2
               ◇ J 5 3
               ♣ 6 3

If you win, you must return a spade. Declarer then will make the contract by playing low from dummy—he knows East has the spade jack, since that card would have given you enough to open 1 NT.

8. Partner's lead is a heavy favorite to be a singleton. To avoid later complications, win the heart ace and return the *queen*.

```
               ♠ K 10 5 3
               ♡ J 8 6 3
               ◇ A K 5
               ♣ 10 3
♠ 7 6                          ♠ 9 8 2
♡ 7                            ♡ A Q 10 9
◇ Q 9 6 4 3 2        □         ◇ 7
♣ J 9 7 2                      ♣ K Q 6 5 4
               ♠ A Q J 4
               ♡ K 5 4 2
               ◇ J 10 8
               ♣ A 8
```

In 1970, East for Norway won the heart ace and returned the nine. Declarer, Bobby Wolff, ducked, and West ruffed. Wolff won the club shift, drew trumps, and finessed in diamonds. After eliminating that suit, he exited with a club. Whichever defender won was endplayed. Note that the return of the heart queen, letting West ruff out the king, would have left declarer with no chance.

In the other room, the contract was four hearts, down, so the United States gained a big swing.

Problems

9. Dlr: South
Vul: N-S

```
               ♠ 10 6 5 3
               ♡ Q 6
               ◇ A K 2
               ♣ J 5 4 2
♠ K Q 7 2
♡ K 9 5 3
◇ 7 6                □
♣ Q 9 7
```

WEST	NORTH	EAST	SOUTH
			1 ◇
Pass	1 ♠	Pass	2 ◇
Pass	3 ◇	Pass	5 ◇
All Pass			

You, West, lead the king of spades—three, nine, four. How do you continue?

10. Dlr: East   ♠ 8 5 3
  Vul: None   ♡ 7 5 2
      ◊ Q 3
      ♣ K Q 10 9 2

              ♠ K J
      ☐   ♡ Q 10 8 3
              ◊ K J 10 9
              ♣ A 4 3

WEST	NORTH	EAST	SOUTH
		1 ◊	1 NT
Pass	2 NT	Pass	3 NT
All Pass			

As usual, West leads his own suit instead of yours—he starts with the six of spades. Declarer allows your king to win. How do you continue?

Solutions

9. Shift to a trump, not to stop ruffs but to avoid helping declarer strip you out of your exit cards in spades. The dummy is lean, and you have hearts and clubs under control, so there is no hurry to cash any more spade tricks. The full deal:

                ♠ 10 6 5 3
                ♡ Q 6
                ◊ A K 2
                ♣ J 5 4 2
    ♠ K Q 7 2   ♠ A J 9 8
    ♡ K 9 5 3   ☐   ♡ J 10 8 4
    ◊ 7 6   ◊ 8 3
    ♣ Q 9 7   ♣ 10 8 6
                ♠ 4
                ♡ A 7 2
                ◊ Q J 10 9 5 4
                ♣ A K 3

If you continue spades, the play will go: ruff by declarer, diamond to the ace, spade ruff, diamond to the king, spade ruff, club ace, club king, club. Now you have to lead away from the king of hearts. However, declarer cannot succeed if you refuse to play a second spade.

Partner could have bailed you out, of course, by overtaking at trick one to return a heart.

10. Declarer accepted an invitation to game, so assuming West has the queen of spades, declarer must have the missing 17 HCP. Suppose you return the jack of spades at trick two. Declarer wins and leads a club to the nine. You must hold off, of course, and declarer continues with a heart to the jack, the ace and king of hearts, and more clubs. When you finally take your ace of clubs, you can cash the queen of hearts, but then you must lead away from the king of diamonds, giving dummy the lead to finish the clubs. Declarer will make an overtrick.

The only chance to beat the contract is to lead the jack of diamonds *now*, before dummy's clubs are set up.

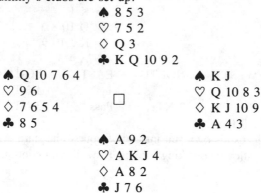

```
              ♠ 8 5 3
              ♡ 7 5 2
              ◇ Q 3
              ♣ K Q 10 9 2
♠ Q 10 7 6 4                    ♠ K J
♡ 9 6                           ♡ Q 10 8 3
◇ 7 6 5 4          □            ◇ K J 10 9
♣ 8 5                           ♣ A 4 3
              ♠ A 9 2
              ♡ A K J 4
              ◇ A 8 2
              ♣ J 7 6
```

Problems

11. Dlr: South   ♠ A 10 6 3
      Vul: None   ♡ Q 7
                     ◇ A Q 4
                     ♣ 7 5 4 2

```
                              ♠ K 8
                              ♡ 8 6 4 3
              □               ◇ K J 9 6 5
                              ♣ 9 3
```

WEST	NORTH	EAST	SOUTH
			1 ♠
Pass	3 ♠	Pass	4 ♠

West, your partner, leads the two of hearts. Dummy's queen wins, and declarer drops the jack. Declarer calls for a low club—three, jack, queen. Partner cashes the club ace, dropping declarer's king, and continues with the club ten. What do you discard?

12. Dlr: South   ♠ Q 10 4
      Vul: N-S   ♡ A J 2
                     ◇ Q 10 4
                     ♣ K 5 4 2

```
♠ K 5 3
♡ 8
◇ J 9 7 5 2          □
♣ Q J 10 7
```

WEST	NORTH	EAST	SOUTH
			1 ♡
Pass	2 ♣	Pass	2 ♡
Pass	3 ♡	Pass	4 ♡
All Pass			

You, West, lead the queen of clubs, winning the first trick. Declarer ruffs your club continuation and plays the heart king and a heart to the ace, East following with the ten and two. Next, the spade ten is led—six, two, king. How do you continue?

Solutions

11. You had better "discard" the spade king! The early play suggests that declarer has 5-3-3-2 pattern with the A-K-J of hearts. Suppose you throw a high diamond on the club ten. Declarer will ruff, cash hearts (throwing a diamond) and play ace and another spade. You win and must lead into dummy's diamond tenace. The full deal:

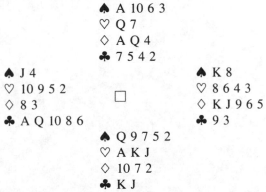

♠ A 10 6 3
♡ Q 7
◇ A Q 4
♣ 7 5 4 2

♠ J 4
♡ 10 9 5 2
◇ 8 3
♣ A Q 10 8 6

♠ K 8
♡ 8 6 4 3
◇ K J 9 6 5
♣ 9 3

♠ Q 9 7 5 2
♡ A K J
◇ 10 7 2
♣ K J

To avoid being endplayed, you must ruff in with the trump king on the third club and exit with a trump or heart. Declarer can get rid of one diamond as you ruff, but he still has a diamond to lose.

Partner could have made it much easier on you by switching to diamonds. (If West held a singleton spade, with declarer having 6-3-2-2 pattern, a diamond shift would be necessary to beat the contract.)

12. You have two tricks in, and partner seems to have the trump queen. He may have an ace as well, in which case you can relax. But if partner's other honor is the diamond king, you must be careful—again, you mustn't help declarer establish an endplay. Return a passive spade, preserving partner's exit cards.

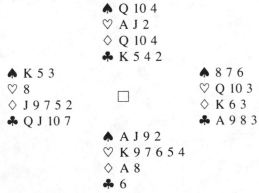

♠ Q 10 4
♡ A J 2
◇ Q 10 4
♣ K 5 4 2

♠ K 5 3
♡ 8
◇ J 9 7 5 2
♣ Q J 10 7

♠ 8 7 6
♡ Q 10 3
◇ K 6 3
♣ A 9 8 3

♠ A J 9 2
♡ K 9 7 6 5 4
◇ A 8
♣ 6

If you mistakenly play a third club, declarer ruffs, goes to the spade queen, ruffs the last club and cashes spades. If partner does not ruff in, he is thrown in with a trump lead to play away from the diamond king.

On a spade exit by you, declarer can win the queen, ruff a club, and play two more spades, discarding dummy's last club. Partner need only discard a diamond to defeat the contract.

At Your Club: Defense at Duplicate Bridge

At matchpoint duplicate (tournament) bridge, your scores are compared with those of other pairs who hold your cards on an identical deal. The distribution of the cards, the dealer, and the vulnerability are the same every time the deal is played—only the players change. Your *matchpoint* score, which determines whether you win the event, is based on how many of your competitors you beat (by any margin). Very small differences in the scores can swing a lot of matchpoints, and this can profoundly affect your strategy.

Dlr: South
Vul: N-S
Matchpoints

```
              ♠ 10 7 4
              ♡ J 5
              ◇ 6 5 4
              ♣ A Q J 9 4
                           ♠ 8 6 5 3
                           ♡ A 7
        □                  ◇ Q 10 9 2
                           ♣ 7 3 2
```

WEST	NORTH	EAST	SOUTH
			1 ♡
Pass	1 NT	Pass	3 ♡
Pass	4 ♡	All Pass	

West, your partner, leads the king of spades. Declarer wins the ace and plays a trump to the jack and your ace. What do you return?

There would be no choice at rubber bridge or IMPs—you return the diamond ten, since partner must hold the ace if you are to have any chance of setting the contract. But at matchpoints, your goal is not to set the contract but to beat the many other pairs who will defend four hearts with your cards. (On this deal, the contract is "normal"—four hearts will be reached at almost every table— so the matchpoints will be won in the *play*. This won't always be the case.)

On the bidding, the diamond ace probably resides in declarer's hand, so at matchpoints you should return a spade and cash what tricks you can—at least one spade should cash since West might have bid at the vulnerability with K-Q-J-x-x. If you return a diamond and find declarer with a hand like

```
              ♠ A x
              ♡ K Q 10 9 x x
              ◇ A x
              ♣ K x x,
```
your matchpoint score will be poor.

```
Dlr:  South          ♠ 8 6 3
Vul:  Both           ♡ K 6 3
Matchpoints          ◇ A 10 9 5 4
                     ♣ 8 7
                              ♠ K 10 4
                              ♡ J 10 9 8
              □               ◇ K Q 2
                              ♣ 9 6 3
```

South opens 1 NT (16-18 HCP), and all pass. West, your partner, leads the five of spades—three, king, ace. Declarer runs the eight of diamonds to your queen, and you return a spade to declarer's queen, West playing the two. Now the jack of diamonds is passed to your king.

At any other form of scoring, you would return a club, since partner must have something in clubs to beat the contract. At matchpoints, though, there is a fair case for a spade return, allowing partner to take his tricks. Declarer will make no more than two this way, whereas he might make three if you return a club. (He could have the heart ace and club ace-king, or the club ace or ace-jack and heart ace-queen.)

This hand appeared in a best-selling bridge book, and a spade return was suggested. In fact, a spade return gains in three situations, while a club also gains in three: when declarer has the club king, club king-jack, or the heart queen and club ace-queen-jack.

Even a *heart* return could be best. If declarer's holding is heart ace and club ace-queen, he might judge from your failure to return a club that you have the club king and take the club finesse. At any rate, you can see how the matchpoint conditions can give extra headaches to both sides.

Opening leads at matchpoints also demand a different approach. There is a stronger tendency toward safety. Aggressive leads that offer only nebulous hope of beating the contract have less to gain and more to lose at matchpoints. Once again, beating the contract may be a secondary consideration.

```
WEST          NORTH        EAST         SOUTH
                           1 NT         Pass
3 NT          All Pass
As South you hold
```

```
              ♠ K Q 10
              ♡ A 7 5 4 2
              ◇ K 3 2
              ♣ 8 7
```

Lead the king of spades, making sure of a couple of tricks. The chance of establishing hearts is too uncertain to lead that suit.

WEST	NORTH	EAST	SOUTH
		1 ♠	Pass
2 ♠	Pass	3 ♡	Pass
4 ♡	All Pass		

As South you hold

♠ 5
♡ K 6 3
♢ K Q 10 4
♣ K 10 7 5 2

Try the king of diamonds. Leading the singleton spade would gain a bushel of points when it works, but that's irrelevant at pairs. What matters is that it rates to lose *a trick* more often than it gains one.

WEST	NORTH	EAST	SOUTH
		1 ♡	Pass
3 ♣	Pass	3 ♡	Pass
4 ♣	Pass	4 NT	Pass
5 ♡	Pass	6 NT	All Pass

As South you hold

♠ A 10 6 4
♡ 9 7 3
♢ Q J 10
♣ 8 7 3

Cash the ace of spades—there is a good chance the opponents have thirteen tricks as soon as they gain the lead. You might score a lot of matchpoints by holding them to six. You would lead the queen of diamonds against an auction like 1 NT-4 NT-6 NT, and even on this auction you might lead a diamond at IMPs or rubber bridge.

At rubber bridge, your goal is scoring as many points as possible. At pairs, some scores are as much as you want or need. You must evaluate the contract and decide what your target should be.

Dlr: West   ♠ 7 6
Vul: N-S   ♡ K Q 7 6
Matchpoints   ◇ A 9 6 2
           ♣ K 8 7

♠ A J 9 5 4   ♠ Q 10 8 3 2
♡ 2   ♡ A 8 5 4 3
◇ K J 8 3   □   ◇ 10 7 5
♣ A 3 2   ♣ —

           ♠ K
           ♡ J 10 9
           ◇ Q 4
           ♣ Q J 10 9 6 5 4

WEST	NORTH	EAST	SOUTH
1 ♠	Dbl	4 ♠	5 ♣
Dbl	All Pass		

Thinking E-W are trying to steal, South unsoundly tries five clubs. West leads to the heart ace and receives a ruff. At rubber bridge, he might underlead the ace of spades now, hoping for another ruff and a tasty + 800. At pairs it is right to *cash* the ace of spades. Few Souths will bid five clubs vulnerable against not, and + 500 will beat all the E-W pairs who score + 480 in four spades.

Dlr: East   ♠ J 8 4 2
Vul: Both   ♡ J 9 4 2
Matchpoints   ◇ A K 4
           ♣ 9 8

♠ K 7   ♠ 9 5
♡ Q 10 8   ♡ A 5 3
◇ Q 10 9 8 3   □   ◇ J 6 5 2
♣ A J 3   ♣ K 5 4 2

           ♠ A Q 10 6 3
           ♡ K 7 6
           ◇ 7
           ♣ Q 10 7 6

WEST	NORTH	EAST	SOUTH
		Pass	Pass
1 ◇	Pass	1 NT	All Pass

South leads the six of spades. Dummy's king wins, North signaling with the eight. A diamond goes to North's king, and the spade jack is played.

South's decision never to bid looks very doubtful. Declarer probably has the heart ace and club king; nevertheless, N-S can make three spades, and many N-S pairs will get into the bidding one way or another.

South can beat 1 NT one trick by leaving partner on lead to switch to a heart, and that would be the right defense at IMPs. But + 100 will be worth few matchpoints if everybody else is + 140. Instead, South must go all out for down two (at the risk of letting the contract make) by overtaking the spade and shifting to a low heart.

Declarer probably will try dummy's ten, winning the ace when North's jack covers. But when North wins the diamond ace, he can lead another spade, and now another low heart from South makes declarer guess.

Problems

1. Dlr: South   ♠ K Q 4 2
     Vul: Both   ♡ A 9 6
                ◊ K 6
                ♣ K 8 6 2

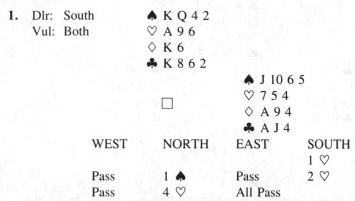

                     ♠ J 10 6 5
                     ♡ 7 5 4
                     ◊ A 9 4
                     ♣ A J 4

WEST	NORTH	EAST	SOUTH
			1 ♡
Pass	1 ♠	Pass	2 ♡
Pass	4 ♡	All Pass	

West, your partner, leads the jack of diamonds. Dummy's king covers. How do you defend?

2. Dlr: South   ♠ 8 6 3
     Vul: N-S   ♡ A Q 10 6 4
                ◊ K 4 3
                ♣ 5 4

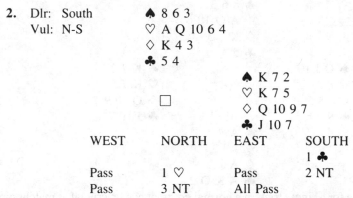

                     ♠ K 7 2
                     ♡ K 7 5
                     ◊ Q 10 9 7
                     ♣ J 10 7

WEST	NORTH	EAST	SOUTH
			1 ♣
Pass	1 ♡	Pass	2 NT
Pass	3 NT	All Pass	

West, your partner, leads the queen of spades. Plan your defense.

Solutions

1. Win the diamond ace and cash the club ace. Declarer is likely to have six heart tricks, three spades, and a diamond. If he has either a third diamond to ruff or the club queen, you can never do better than hold the hand to five anyway. The full deal is:

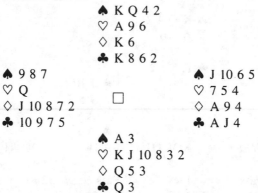

```
                    ♠ K Q 4 2
                    ♡ A 9 6
                    ◇ K 6
                    ♣ K 8 6 2
    ♠ 9 8 7                         ♠ J 10 6 5
    ♡ Q                             ♡ 7 5 4
    ◇ J 10 8 7 2      □             ◇ A 9 4
    ♣ 10 9 7 5                      ♣ A J 4
                    ♠ A 3
                    ♡ K J 10 8 3 2
                    ◇ Q 5 3
                    ♣ Q 3
```

If you exit passively at trick two, declarer will squeeze you in the black suits to make two overtricks. This will give you a matchpoint zero.

2.

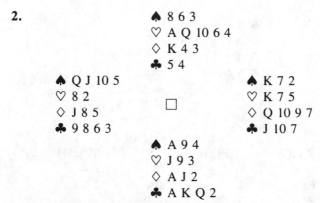

```
                    ♠ 8 6 3
                    ♡ A Q 10 6 4
                    ◇ K 4 3
                    ♣ 5 4
    ♠ Q J 10 5                      ♠ K 7 2
    ♡ 8 2                           ♡ K 7 5
    ◇ J 8 5          □              ◇ Q 10 9 7
    ♣ 9 8 6 3                       ♣ J 10 7
                    ♠ A 9 4
                    ♡ J 9 3
                    ◇ A J 2
                    ♣ A K Q 2
```

The battle for a single trick in a normal contract can be crucial at matchpoints. West should have at least Q-J-9-x of spades, so East can afford to overtake the first trick, trying to look like a man with K-x. Declarer might win the second round of spades anyway, since he stands a good chance for twelve tricks if the heart finesse works; but there is nothing wrong with giving him a nudge in the wrong direction.

Along the same lines, a defender might decline to overtake with K-x if he *wants* declarer to hold up an ace twice.

Problems

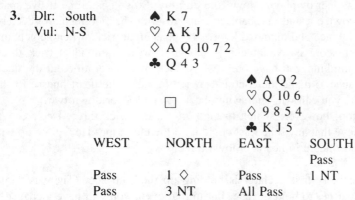

3. Dlr: South
Vul: N-S

♠ K 7
♥ A K J
♦ A Q 10 7 2
♣ Q 4 3

□

♠ A Q 2
♥ Q 10 6
♦ 9 8 5 4
♣ K J 5

WEST	NORTH	EAST	SOUTH
			Pass
Pass	1 ◇	Pass	1 NT
Pass	3 NT	All Pass	

West, your partner, leads the four of spades. Dummy's king loses to your ace, declarer playing the six. When you cash the spade queen, declarer plays the eight and West the three. How do you continue?

4. Dlr: South
Vul: None

♠ A 3
♥ 8 3
♦ A J 10 7 6 2
♣ 7 5 4

□

♠ 10 8 4
♥ K Q 6
♦ Q 9 8 4
♣ K J 9

WEST	NORTH	EAST	SOUTH
			1 NT
Pass	3 NT	All Pass	

West, your partner, leads the two of clubs. Your king holds the first trick, and your jack of clubs wins at trick two. How do you continue?

Solutions

3.

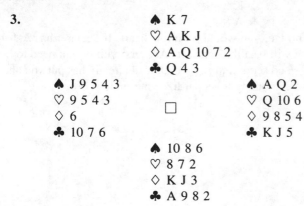

♠ K 7
♥ A K J
♦ A Q 10 7 2
♣ Q 4 3

♠ J 9 5 4 3
♥ 9 5 4 3
♦ 6
♣ 10 7 6

□

♠ A Q 2
♥ Q 10 6
♦ 9 8 5 4
♣ K J 5

♠ 10 8 6
♥ 8 7 2
♦ K J 3
♣ A 9 8 2

Partner must have the spade jack—if declarer had J-x-x, he could have made sure of a stopper by playing low from dummy. So you can run off five spade tricks for down one and a probable average result. (The bidding marks declarer with the club ace and diamond king, so he has eight tricks when he gets in.)

A better score is available if you switch to a diamond at trick three. Declarer, thinking you have only two spades, will be gratified at the unexpected chance to make the contract. When he takes the heart finesse for his ninth trick, you can win and switch back to spades for down two.

For a top, however, switch to the *club jack* at trick three. Declarer will never believe that any sane East could hold the club king. He will go up with the ace and finesse in hearts—down three!

4. It is likely that declarer is holding up the club ace. (There is barely room for partner to hold the ace, but in that event you will have a chance to cash out later.)

Partner seems to have gotten off to a good opening lead. His club two shows four cards there; he can have no more than one diamond, and he would have preferred to lead a heart or spade with five cards in either suit. So his pattern is 4-4-1-4. At many tables, West will lead a major suit, which may give declarer an extra spade trick or time to set up hearts.

Since there is nothing to gain by continuing clubs, switch to the king of hearts, setting up a fourth defensive trick while you still have a probable diamond entry. The full deal:

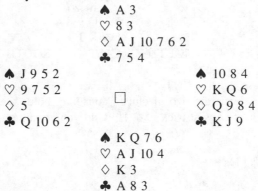

```
              ♠ A 3
              ♡ 8 3
              ◇ A J 10 7 6 2
              ♣ 7 5 4
♠ J 9 5 2                      ♠ 10 8 4
♡ 9 7 5 2          □          ♡ K Q 6
◇ 5                           ◇ Q 9 8 4
♣ Q 10 6 2                    ♣ K J 9
              ♠ K Q 7 6
              ♡ A J 10 4
              ◇ K 3
              ♣ A 8 3
```

At IMPs or rubber bridge, you would try a *low* heart. If declarer has A-J-9-x and misguesses, you will beat the contract. At pairs, you do not need to beat the contract to get a good score. Partner's club lead already has put you ahead of the other pairs, so do nothing to jeopardize your good score.

Problems

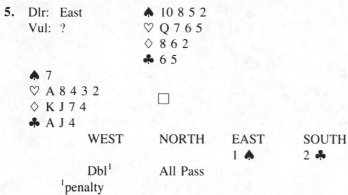

5. Dlr: East
    Vul: ?

           ♠ 10 8 5 2
           ♡ Q 7 6 5
           ◇ 8 6 2
           ♣ 6 5

♠ 7
♡ A 8 4 3 2
◇ K J 7 4   ☐
♣ A J 4

WEST	NORTH	EAST	SOUTH
		1 ♠	2 ♣
Dbl[1]	All Pass		

[1]penalty

You, West, lead the seven of spades. East wins the ace and returns the jack. Declarer's king covers and you ruff. You lead a diamond to partner's ace, and he cashes the queen of spades as you discard the eight of hearts. A diamond return goes to your jack, and South's queen falls under your diamond king. The contract is down one already. What do you lead next (a) if neither side is vulnerable? (b) if you are vulnerable and they are not?

6. Dlr: South
    Vul: None

      ♠ A 8 2
      ♡ A 7 3
      ◇ J 9 4 2
      ♣ A J 7

                 ♠ Q 4
        ☐   ♡ Q J
                 ◇ A 10 8 5
                 ♣ 9 8 5 4 2

WEST	NORTH	EAST	SOUTH
			1 ♠
Pass	2 NT	Pass	3 ♡
Pass	3 ♠	Pass	4 ♠
All Pass			

West, your partner, leads the three of diamonds, and declarer's king drops under your ace. How do you continue?

369

Solutions

5.

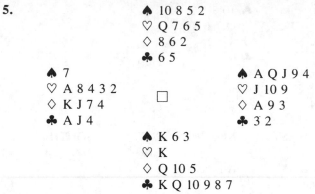

<pre>
              ♠ 10 8 5 2
              ♡ Q 7 6 5
              ◇ 8 6 2
              ♣ 6 5
♠ 7   ♠ A Q J 9 4
♡ A 8 4 3 2   □   ♡ J 10 9
◇ K J 7 4   ◇ A 9 3
♣ A J 4   ♣ 3 2
              ♠ K 6 3
              ♡ K
              ◇ Q 10 5
              ♣ K Q 10 9 8 7
</pre>

At equal vulnerability, cash your heart ace, ensuring three down. That is all you need to get a good matchpoint score.

It's a different story if you are vulnerable against not. The problem is that there is a game available your way, and most E-W's will bid it. Your decision to double two clubs for penalties will not appeal to many of the other Wests. There will be some two-heart bids and a few negative doubles, and E-W eventually will arrive in 3 NT or four hearts. +500 will do you no good if the other pairs are +620 or +630, so you must try for +800 by underleading the heart ace. You hope partner can win the king and play a fourth spade, promoting a third trump trick for you.

The same principle applies whenever the opponents take a good sacrifice against you. You may be booked for a poor matchpoint score unless you beat them more than the value of your game.

6. Return a diamond. Ordinarily this would be a mistake because declarer would have a chance to gain a trick with a loser-on-loser play. Here, though, you can tell that the hearts, clubs and trumps all lie well for declarer (although he doesn't know it). If you leave him to play wide open, he probably can take the rest of the tricks.

<pre>
              ♠ A 8 2
              ♡ A 7 3
              ◇ J 9 4 2
              ♣ A J 7
♠ 10 7 6   ♠ Q 4
♡ 9 8 6 5   □   ♡ Q J
◇ Q 7 6 3   ◇ A 10 8 5
♣ Q 10   ♣ 9 8 5 4 2
              ♠ K J 9 5 3
              ♡ K 10 4 2
              ◇ K
              ♣ K 6 3
</pre>

Declarer is likely to look with favor on your diamond return. He will discard a heart, planning to discard another heart eventually on the jack of diamonds.

However, holding him to just one overtrick in this normal contract should be a very good result for you because twelve tricks can be made.

If you return, say, the queen of hearts, declarer takes the heart ace and king, plays the ace and king of trumps, cashes the ten of hearts, and ruffs his heart loser with dummy's last trump as West follows helplessly. A diamond ruff lets declarer draw trumps, and the winning club finesse lets him claim the balance.

Problems

7. Dlr: East
   Vul: None

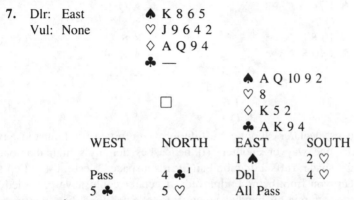

♠ K 8 6 5
♥ J 9 6 4 2
♦ A Q 9 4
♣ —

♠ A Q 10 9 2
♥ 8
♦ K 5 2
♣ A K 9 4

WEST	NORTH	EAST	SOUTH
		1 ♠	2 ♥
Pass	4 ♣[1]	Dbl	4 ♥
5 ♣	5 ♥	All Pass	

[1]strong heart raise, short in clubs

West, your partner, leads the jack of clubs. Declarer ruffs in dummy, playing a small club from his hand. He draws trumps with the king and ace, West's queen dropping on the second round. The jack of diamonds is led and passed to your king. What do you return?

8. Dlr: West
   Vul: Both

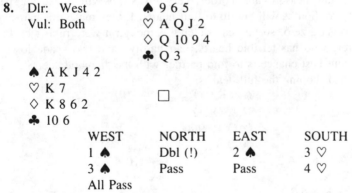

♠ 9 6 5
♥ A Q J 2
♦ Q 10 9 4
♣ Q 3

♠ A K J 4 2
♥ K 7
♦ K 8 6 2
♣ 10 6

WEST	NORTH	EAST	SOUTH
1 ♠	Dbl (!)	2 ♠	3 ♥
3 ♠	Pass	Pass	4 ♥
All Pass			

You, West, lead the ace of spades, felling the queen from declarer. How do you continue?

7. Should you cash the spade ace to hold declarer to his contract? Try counting his tricks. He has five hearts in hand, three ruffs in dummy and at most three diamonds. That's only eleven tricks in all, so the spade ace can't go away. Get out with a high club and await developments.

                  ♠ K 8 6 5
                  ♡ J 9 6 4 2
                  ◊ A Q 9 4
                  ♣ —
    ♠ J 7   ♠ A Q 10 9 2
    ♡ Q 7   ♡ 8
    ◊ 10 8 7 3   □   ◊ K 5 2
    ♣ J 10 8 7 3   ♣ A K 9 4
                  ♠ 4 3
                  ♡ A K 10 5 3
                  ◊ J 6
                  ♣ Q 6 5 2

As it happens, declarer cannot get off dummy comfortably and must lose two more tricks one way or another. (If he cashes dummy's high diamonds, discarding a spade, ruffs a diamond and leads a spade, West must put up the jack to keep you from being endplayed.) Declarer could have prevailed by saving a top trump in his hand as an entry to take a second diamond finesse.

Note West's brave five-club bid, which would have been unthinkable at any other form of scoring. Even though West didn't lead a spade, which would make it easy to set five hearts, it would be a shame if you failed to make the most of his bidding enterprise.

8. Desperate measures are in order. Very few Norths will double one spade, and still fewer Souths will bid up to four hearts. If they make this game, you are sure to get a zero, so you can defend as though it were rubber bridge.

Declarer, who has terrible hearts, can hardly have two spade losers as well, so your best chance is to find partner with the diamond ace. Shift to a low diamond, hoping the full deal is:

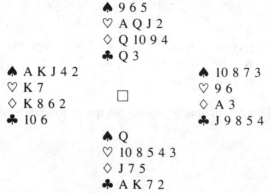

                  ♠ 9 6 5
                  ♡ A Q J 2
                  ◊ Q 10 9 4
                  ♣ Q 3
    ♠ A K J 4 2   ♠ 10 8 7 3
    ♡ K 7   ♡ 9 6
    ◊ K 8 6 2   □   ◊ A 3
    ♣ 10 6   ♣ J 9 8 5 4
                  ♠ Q
                  ♡ 10 8 5 4 3
                  ◊ J 7 5
                  ♣ A K 7 2

True, a diamond switch might concede an overtrick if declarer had

♠ Q
♡ 10 8 x x x
◇ A x
♣ K x x x x.

But in that case you weren't getting many matchpoints anyway.

Problems

9. Dlr: South
Vul: None

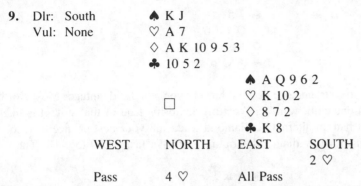

♠ K J
♡ A 7
◇ A K 10 9 5 3
♣ 10 5 2

♠ A Q 9 6 2
♡ K 10 2
◇ 8 7 2
♣ K 8

WEST	NORTH	EAST	SOUTH
			2 ♡
Pass	4 ♡	All Pass	

West, your partner, leads the four of clubs. After capturing your king with the ace, declarer plays a trump to the ace and a trump back. Do you take this trick? If you take it, partner and declarer play low. What do you return?

10. Dlr: North
Vul: N-S

♠ A K J 9
♡ A J 3
◇ Q 9
♣ K J 9 3

♠ 10 8 6 4 2
♡ K 9 5
◇ A 6 2
♣ 8 7

WEST	NORTH	EAST	SOUTH
	1 ♠ (!)	Pass	1 NT
Pass	3 NT	All Pass	

West, your partner, leads the two of clubs. Declarer puts in dummy's nine, winning, and continues with a club to his ace. Next, the heart ten is run to your king, West following with the eight. What do you return?

Solutions

9. You rise with the heart king because there will be a ruff to take if partner has the club queen. However, before returning a club, *cash the spade ace.* Oddly, this cannot cost. If partner has the club queen, he can't both give you a ruff and lead a spade through, so you will get just three more tricks no matter how you proceed. But if declarer has the club queen, cashing the spade ace will save a trick.

373

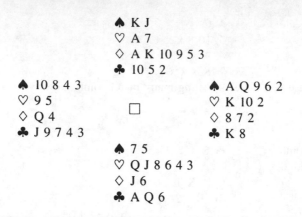

```
        ♠ K J
        ♡ A 7
        ◇ A K 10 9 5 3
        ♣ 10 5 2
♠ 10 8 4 3              ♠ A Q 9 6 2
♡ 9 5                  ♡ K 10 2
◇ Q 4          □       ◇ 8 7 2
♣ J 9 7 4 3            ♣ K 8
        ♠ 7 5
        ♡ Q J 8 6 4 3
        ◇ J 6
        ♣ A Q 6
```

10. North's strange opening bid has put you at a disadvantage. Most Norths will open one club, warning West off the losing lead of that suit. It is likely that West had an alternative diamond lead, and your best chance to recover is to shift to a low diamond, hoping you have fast tricks to cash. The full deal:

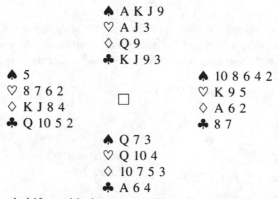

```
        ♠ A K J 9
        ♡ A J 3
        ◇ Q 9
        ♣ K J 9 3
♠ 5                    ♠ 10 8 6 4 2
♡ 8 7 6 2              ♡ K 9 5
◇ K J 8 4      □       ◇ A 6 2
♣ Q 10 5 2            ♣ 8 7
        ♠ Q 7 3
        ♡ Q 10 4
        ◇ 10 7 5 3
        ♣ A 6 4
```

A diamond shift could give away still another trick if declarer had the king of diamonds instead of the queen of spades, but that's a risk you must take. The bidding and the opening lead have booked you for a bad score unless you can make something good happen.

11. Dlr: West   ♠ K 9 5 3
      Vul: Both   ♡ 8
                  ◊ A Q 10 6
                  ♣ K 10 5 4

♠ 7 2
♡ A K J 7 6 5 2   □
◊ K J 2
♣ 2

WEST	NORTH	EAST	SOUTH
1 ♡	Dbl	2 ♡	4 ♠
5 ♡	Pass	Pass	5 ♠
Pass	Pass	Dbl	All Pass

You, West, lead the two of clubs. When dummy plays low, partner puts up the ace and returns the club seven for you to ruff. Declarer has followed with the three and nine. What do you play next?

12. Dlr: North   ♠ 9 5
      Vul: None   ♡ A Q 10 9 6 4
                  ◊ A 8
                  ♣ K J 3

♠ A 10 8 6 3
♡ J 5
◊ Q 9 5   □
♣ A 10 6

WEST	NORTH	EAST	SOUTH
	1 ♡	Pass	2 ◊
Pass	2 ♡	Pass	2 NT
Pass	3 NT	All Pass	

You, West, lead the six of spades—five, jack, king. Declarer goes to the heart queen and leads a club, covering partner's eight with the queen. How do you defend?

Solutions

11.

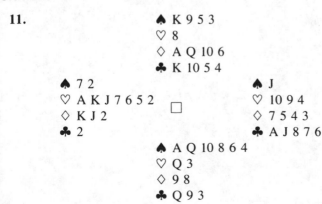

             ♠ K 9 5 3
             ♡ 8
             ◊ A Q 10 6
             ♣ K 10 5 4

♠ 7 2   ♠ J
♡ A K J 7 6 5 2   □   ♡ 10 9 4
◊ K J 2   ◊ 7 5 4 3
♣ 2   ♣ A J 8 7 6

             ♠ A Q 10 8 6 4
             ♡ Q 3
             ◊ 9 8
             ♣ Q 9 3

Your side already has had the best of the deal. South made a doubtful decision to bid five spades, and East made good decisions to double five spades and put up the club ace. You should settle for down one by cashing a heart.

You could, of course, go for the throat by underleading in hearts. If partner had the queen, another club ruff would produce +500. However, +200 should be worth most of the matchpoints anyway, while −850 will be a sure zero.

12.

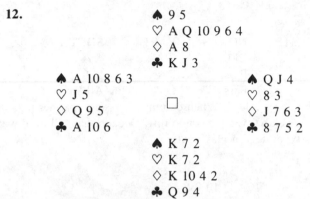

```
                  ♠ 9 5
                  ♡ A Q 10 9 6 4
                  ◇ A 8
                  ♣ K J 3
  ♠ A 10 8 6 3                    ♠ Q J 4
  ♡ J 5                           ♡ 8 3
  ◇ Q 9 5           □             ◇ J 7 6 3
  ♣ A 10 6                        ♣ 8 7 5 2
                  ♠ K 7 2
                  ♡ K 7 2
                  ◇ K 10 4 2
                  ♣ Q 9 4
```

The correct play at matchpoints is the spade ace. Partner will unblock the queen, and you can cash out.

You might as well assume declarer has a hand that will allow to you score well matchpointwise. Declarer appears to hold K-x-x of hearts, and many pairs will play in four hearts. If declarer has the alternative hand for his bidding:

```
              ♠ K Q x
              ♡ K x x
              ◇ J x x x
              ♣ Q 9 x
```

he will make 4 NT whatever you do. You will score poorly, since four hearts will make only four. However, on the actual deal you can't afford to defend passively. It will be a disaster if declarer takes ten tricks in notrump here, because the marked lead of the spade queen will hold four hearts to four.

The Dreaded Final Exam

Prepare for a real workout!

The subjects here are the same as in Quizzes 1 to 25—everything from second-hand play to counting distribution by inference—but the problems are even more challenging. I have tried to avoid obscure "textbook" techniques, such as underruffing to avoid being endplayed in trumps—you might play for ten years without encountering one of these situations. Instead, I've included hands that I believe have a touch of practical value. Nevertheless, this is a tough batch of problems. Only an expert can expect to get most of them right—or even "sort of right."

Problems

1. Dlr: South:
Vul: N-S

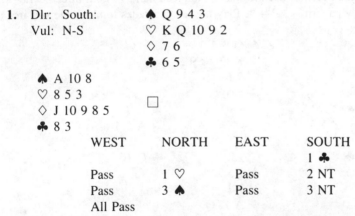

♠ Q 9 4 3
♡ K Q 10 9 2
◇ 7 6
♣ 6 5

♠ A 10 8
♡ 8 5 3
◇ J 10 9 8 5
♣ 8 3

WEST	NORTH	EAST	SOUTH
			1 ♣
Pass	1 ♡	Pass	2 NT
Pass	3 ♠	Pass	3 NT
All Pass			

You, West, lead the jack of diamonds—six, four, queen. Declarer leads the heart jack and overtakes with dummy's queen, East ducking. A club to the jack wins, East playing the two. A second heart is won by East's ace, and he returns the two of diamonds to declarer's king. Now declarer tables the two of spades. Which spade do you play, and why?

2. Dlr: South: ♠ J 10 8 7
   Vul: N-S   ♡ 8 7
                   ◇ A K Q 6 5
                   ♣ 10 6

                        ♠ Q 9 5 4
             □   ♡ A 10 6
                      ◇ 8 7 3
                      ♣ 8 7 2

WEST	NORTH	EAST	SOUTH
			1 NT
Pass	2 ♣	Pass	2 ♠
Pass	4 ♠	All Pass	

West, your partner, leads the heart four, and declarer drops the queen under your ace. You choose to shift to the club seven. Declarer plays low, and partner wins the queen and cashes the ace. A third club is won by declarer's jack. He leads the two of diamonds to the queen and calls for the jack of spades. Do you cover?

Solutions

1. On the bidding, declarer has a balanced hand without three hearts—his most likely pattern is 3-2-4-4. Play the ten of spades to block the suit in case he has J-x-x.

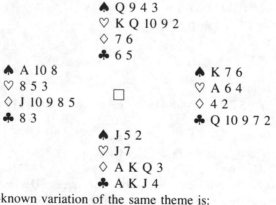

               ♠ Q 9 4 3
               ♡ K Q 10 9 2
               ◇ 7 6
               ♣ 6 5

♠ A 10 8   ♠ K 7 6
♡ 8 5 3   □   ♡ A 6 4
◇ J 10 9 8 5   ◇ 4 2
♣ 8 3   ♣ Q 10 9 7 2

               ♠ J 5 2
               ♡ J 7
               ◇ A K Q 3
               ♣ A K J 4

A better-known variation of the same theme is:

               K 10 4
J 5 3   □   9 8 7 6
               A Q 2

Needing a second dummy entry, declarer leads the two, planning to insert the ten. But West puts up his jack, and declarer's guns are spiked.

2.

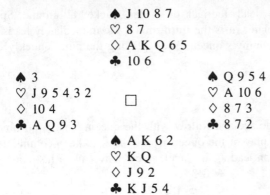

You should cover. Declarer has to have both the ace and king of spades. If you play low, declarer will pass the jack. He will have no option but to continue with the ten next, and the position will be disclosed. If you cover the jack, declarer wins the king; however, he must decide whether to lay down the ace or ten next.

Problems

3. Dlr: South
Vul: E-W

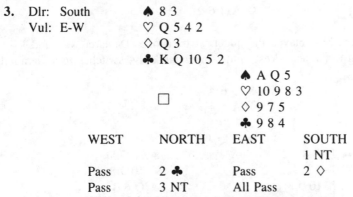

WEST	NORTH	EAST	SOUTH
			1 NT
Pass	2 ♣	Pass	2 ◊
Pass	3 NT	All Pass	

West, your partner, leads the four of spades. Plan your defense.

4. Dlr: North
Vul: N-S

♠ Q 6 4
♡ A 5 4
◊ 7
♣ A Q J 10 7 4

□ ♠ A K 5
♡ 10 9 8
◊ Q 6 3
♣ K 8 3 2

WEST	NORTH	EAST	SOUTH
	1 ♣	Pass	1 ♡
Pass	2 ♣	Pass	2 ◊
Pass	2 ♡	Pass	3 ◊
Pass	4 ♡	All Pass	

West, your partner, leads the jack of spades, ducked all around. Spades are continued, and declarer ruffs the third round. He immediately leads the club five and finesses dummy's queen, West playing the nine. Quickly! How do you defend?

Solutions

3. Play the spade ace and follow with the queen. This is no time for the learned third-hand play of the queen from A-Q-x to keep communication—you will never be on lead again, while West may have a fast entry.

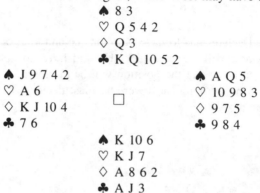

```
                    ♠ 8 3
                    ♡ Q 5 4 2
                    ◇ Q 3
                    ♣ K Q 10 5 2
    ♠ J 9 7 4 2                      ♠ A Q 5
    ♡ A 6                            ♡ 10 9 8 3
    ◇ K J 10 4          ☐           ◇ 9 7 5
    ♣ 7 6                            ♣ 9 8 4
                    ♠ K 10 6
                    ♡ K J 7
                    ◇ A 8 6 2
                    ♣ A J 3
```

In practice, East played the queen at trick one. Declarer won and led the heart king to the ace. West, quite understandably, switched to a diamond.

4.

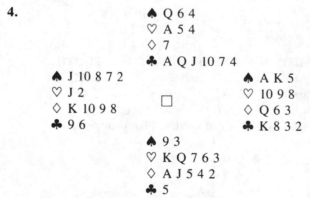

```
                    ♠ Q 6 4
                    ♡ A 5 4
                    ◇ 7
                    ♣ A Q J 10 7 4
    ♠ J 10 8 7 2                     ♠ A K 5
    ♡ J 2                            ♡ 10 9 8
    ◇ K 10 9 8         ☐            ◇ Q 6 3
    ♣ 9 6                            ♣ K 8 3 2
                    ♠ 9 3
                    ♡ K Q 7 6 3
                    ◇ A J 5 4 2
                    ♣ 5
```

At the table, East grabbed the club king. After that, there was no way to keep declarer from taking the rest.

Terence Reese wrote that, especially when declarer's trump holding is tenuous, a defender must avoid relinquishing his control of declarer's best side suit. (This deal, in fact, is based on one noted by Reese.) If East had smoothly allowed dummy's club queen to hold, declarer probably would have continued with the club ace and another, expecting to ruff out the king from West. And even if East betrayed his club holding with a reluctant duck, declarer might well go down.

Problems

5. Dlr: East
    Vul: None

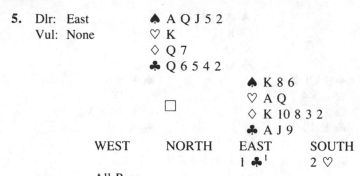

♠ A Q J 5 2
♡ K
◇ Q 7
♣ Q 6 5 4 2

♠ K 8 6
♡ A Q
◇ K 10 8 3 2
♣ A J 9

WEST	NORTH	EAST	SOUTH
		1 ♣[1]	2 ♡
All Pass			

[1]artificial, strong

West, your partner, leads the three of clubs. Dummy plays low, and your jack wins. You cash the ace and queen of trumps and get out with the club nine, ruffed by declarer. Next, declarer leads the three of spades to the four and queen. How do you defend?

6. Dlr: South
    Vul: N-S

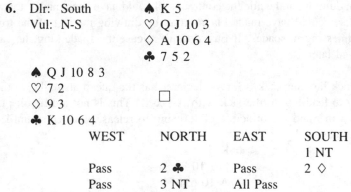

♠ K 5
♡ Q J 10 3
◇ A 10 6 4
♣ 7 5 2

♠ Q J 10 8 3
♡ 7 2
◇ 9 3
♣ K 10 6 4

WEST	NORTH	EAST	SOUTH
			1 NT
Pass	2 ♣	Pass	2 ◇
Pass	3 NT	All Pass	

You, West, lead the queen of spades—five, two, six. Dummy's king wins the next spade, and declarer calls for the two of clubs. East plays the nine and declarer the jack. Right now! Do you win or duck?

Solutions

5.

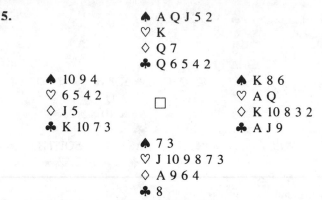

```
            ♠ A Q J 5 2
            ♡ K
            ◇ Q 7
            ♣ Q 6 5 4 2
♠ 10 9 4              ♠ K 8 6
♡ 6 5 4 2            ♡ A Q
◇ J 5        □        ◇ K 10 8 3 2
♣ K 10 7 3           ♣ A J 9
            ♠ 7 3
            ♡ J 10 9 8 7 3
            ◇ A 9 6 4
            ♣ 8
```

The deal is from the 1976 Bermuda Bowl final, United States vs. Italy. In one room, poor defense let the Italians get home with a spade partial on the N-S cards. The U.S. South at the other table could have gotten most of this back by making two hearts. At the crucial point, when declarer took a spade finesse, Arturo Franco, East, won and *returned a spade*. This cut declarer off from dummy, and while the contract still could have been made, it wasn't.

Declarer could have made his contract by drawing the rest of the trumps before finessing in spades. If East doesn't release the spade king, he can be endplayed later.

6. Duck the club jack. (Surely declarer has the queen also—he would be unlikely to lead low to the jack with A-J-x-x.) This is not a difficult play if you keep in mind the principle of refusing to release your entry until your suit is established.

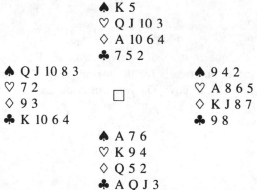

```
            ♠ K 5
            ♡ Q J 10 3
            ◇ A 10 6 4
            ♣ 7 5 2
♠ Q J 10 8 3         ♠ 9 4 2
♡ 7 2               ♡ A 8 6 5
◇ 9 3        □        ◇ K J 8 7
♣ K 10 6 4          ♣ 9 8
            ♠ A 7 6
            ♡ K 9 4
            ◇ Q 5 2
            ♣ A Q J 3
```

When the club jack holds, declarer is likely to shift to hearts. Partner wins the ace and returns his last spade. To land his contract now, declarer must guess which minor-suit finesse to take.

Note that if you win the first club, declarer will have no problem making the contract.

Problems

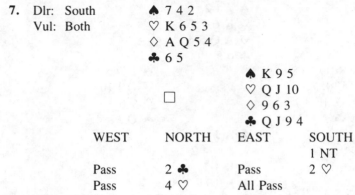

7. Dlr: South
Vul: Both

♠ 7 4 2
♥ K 6 5 3
♦ A Q 5 4
♣ 6 5

♠ K 9 5
♥ Q J 10
♦ 9 6 3
♣ Q J 9 4

WEST	NORTH	EAST	SOUTH
			1 NT
Pass	2 ♣	Pass	2 ♥
Pass	4 ♥	All Pass	

West, your partner, leads the six of spades—two, king, ace. Declarer draws two rounds of trumps with the ace and king, West following. Next come the king and jack of diamonds and a diamond to the queen (West following).

Declarer continues with the diamond ace. Do you ruff? If so, what do you return? If not, what do you discard?

8. Dlr: North
Vul: Both

♠ J 3
♥ A K J 3
♦ A K 6
♣ 10 8 6 3

♠ A K 2
♥ 7 5
♦ J 9 5 3 2
♣ A 5 2

WEST	NORTH	EAST	SOUTH
	1 NT	Pass	4 ♠
All Pass			

You, West, lead the seven of hearts. Declarer wins the queen in hand and continues with the king and ace of hearts, pitching the club queen. After ruffing, how do you continue?

Solutions

7.

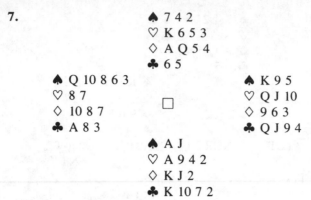

```
            ♠ 7 4 2
            ♡ K 6 5 3
            ◇ A Q 5 4
            ♣ 6 5
♠ Q 10 8 6 3              ♠ K 9 5
♡ 8 7          ☐         ♡ Q J 10
◇ 10 8 7                 ◇ 9 6 3
♣ A 8 3                  ♣ Q J 9 4
            ♠ A J
            ♡ A 9 4 2
            ◇ K J 2
            ♣ K 10 7 2
```

Ruffing the diamond ace is clearly wrong—you can't stop declarer from taking one pitch, and you would prefer to get in and use your queen of hearts to draw two of declarer's trumps.

Take care with your discard, however. Look ahead to what happens if you pitch a spade and find declarer with 2-4-3-4 pattern. After throwing his spade loser on the fourth diamond, he plays a club to the queen, king, and ace. After ruffing West's spade return, he puts you in with a trump and scores the club ten in the end for the tenth trick.

You can beat the contract if you save both your remaining spades—you'll have a winner to cash when you win your trump trick. (This is based on a deal reported by Hugh Kelsey.)

8. Switch to a diamond. If declarer's pattern is 6-2-4-1, as it seems, you can give partner a diamond ruff after winning the first trump.

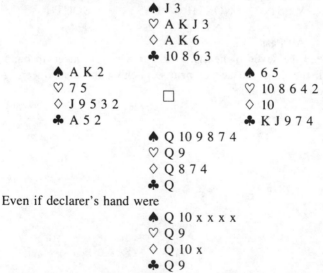

```
            ♠ J 3
            ♡ A K J 3
            ◇ A K 6
            ♣ 10 8 6 3
♠ A K 2                   ♠ 6 5
♡ 7 5          ☐         ♡ 10 8 6 4 2
◇ J 9 5 3 2              ◇ 10
♣ A 5 2                  ♣ K J 9 7 4
            ♠ Q 10 9 8 7 4
            ♡ Q 9
            ◇ Q 8 7 4
            ♣ Q
```

Even if declarer's hand were

```
            ♠ Q 10 x x x x
            ♡ Q 9
            ◇ Q 10 x
            ♣ Q 9
```

the suggested defense would succeed. Declarer could win the diamond ace and throw his other club on the last heart as you ruffed with a high trump. But you could play a second diamond and still give partner a third-round ruff.

384

Problems

9. Dlr: South ♠ 9 8 7 5
Vul: Both ♡ K Q 10 4 3
◇ Q
♣ J 7 2

                                ♠ 10 6 2
                                ♡ J 8 6 2
             □   ◇ K J 9 6
                                ♣ 10 4

WEST	NORTH	EAST	SOUTH
			1 ♣
Pass	1 ♡	Pass	2 ◇
Pass	3 ♣	Pass	3 NT
All Pass			

West, your partner, leads the king of spades, won by declarer's ace. Declarer tries the ace, king, and queen of hearts, but West discards a diamond on the third round. Next come the ace-king of clubs and a club surrendered to West's queen. What do you discard on this trick?

10. Dlr: West ♠ A K Q 10 7
Vul: None ♡ J 10 5
◇ Q 5 2
♣ 10 8

♠ J 8 5
♡ 8 6
◇ A 10 8 6 4 3   □
♣ 9 6

WEST	NORTH	EAST	SOUTH
Pass	1 ♠	Pass	2 ♡
Pass	2 ♠	Pass	3 NT
Pass	4 ♡	All Pass	

You, West, lead the nine of clubs. East wins the king and returns the jack of diamonds, on which declarer plays the seven. How do you defend?

Solutions

9.

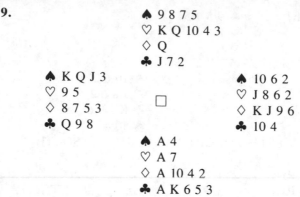

♠ 9 8 7 5
♡ K Q 10 4 3
◇ Q
♣ J 7 2

♠ K Q J 3
♡ 9 5
◇ 8 7 5 3
♣ Q 9 8

♠ 10 6 2
♡ J 8 6 2
◇ K J 9 6
♣ 10 4

♠ A 4
♡ A 7
◇ A 10 4 2
♣ A K 6 5 3

Gene Prosnitz, playing in the 1985 Spring North American Championships in Montreal, knew that the contract could be set. But how could he get partner to underlead in spades instead of playing a diamond? Prosnitz came up with a beautiful discard—the diamond king. West got the message and led his low spade to the ten. Prosnitz cashed the heart jack, and the spade return sank a contract that had looked impregnable.

Declarer could have made 3 NT by conceding a club before cashing the hearts, but his play would have been a winner if the heart jack fell while spades were 5-2.

10. Win the diamond ace and return a club. Partner will win the ace and play a third club. You ruff with the six, forcing an honor from dummy and establishing a trick for partner's Q-9-7.

♠ A K Q 10 7
♡ J 10 5
◇ Q 5 2
♣ 10 8

♠ J 8 5
♡ 8 6
◇ A 10 8 6 4 3
♣ 9 6

♠ 4 3 2
♡ Q 9 7
◇ J 9
♣ A K 4 3 2

♠ 9 6
♡ A K 4 3 2
◇ K 7
♣ Q J 7 5

The deal arose in the 1979 Vanderbilt Teams and was analyzed in *The Bridge World* magazine. In practice, both Easts played three rounds of clubs immediately, overlooking the necessity of taking side-suit winners before trying for an uppercut. (From East's point of view, the contract is unlikely to be set unless West has the diamond ace or a trump honor.) Declarer overruffed West's trump six, cashed the ace and king of trumps, and followed with four rounds of spades, throwing his diamonds. Making four.

In his writeup of the deal, Edgar Kaplan also pointed out that, on the jack-of-diamonds return at trick two, West should know to win and switch back to clubs instead of trying to give partner a diamond ruff. If East had a singleton diamond, Kaplan noted, he should *cash the club ace* before returning his diamond.

Problems

11. Dlr: South ♠ K 7 3
    Vul: N-S   ♡ J 6 5
                ◊ 7 6
                ♣ K J 10 8 2

			♠ A 10 8 6
			♡ 8 7
	□		◊ 9 5 4 2
			♣ A Q 3

WEST	NORTH	EAST	SOUTH
			1 ♡
Pass	2 ♡	Pass	4 ♡
All Pass			

West, your partner, leads the queen of diamonds. Declarer wins the king and cashes the ace and king of hearts, West's queen falling doubleton. Then comes the club nine—four, two. How do you defend?

12. Dlr: South ♠ K 5 3
    Vul: N-S   ♡ 10 6
                ◊ K J 10 4
                ♣ K 10 6 2

♠ Q 10 7 2			
♡ K J 8 5 3			
◊ A 8 5 3		□	
♣ —			

WEST	NORTH	EAST	SOUTH
			1 ♣
Dbl	1 ◊	1 ♡	1 ♠
2 ♡	3 ♣	Pass	4 ♣
Pass	5 ♣	All Pass	

You, West, lead the five of hearts—six, ace, nine. Partner returns the heart two, and declarer's queen falls to your king. How do you continue?

Solutions

11. Return the spade *ten*, hoping declarer has specifically Q-9-x. Presumably, declarer will let your lead run to dummy's king. When you win the next club, a low spade will force him to guess.

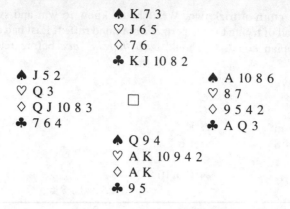

♠ K 7 3
♡ J 6 5
◇ 7 6
♣ K J 10 8 2

♠ J 5 2
♡ Q 3
◇ Q J 10 8 3
♣ 7 6 4

♠ A 10 8 6
♡ 8 7
◇ 9 5 4 2
♣ A Q 3

♠ Q 9 4
♡ A K 10 9 4 2
◇ A K
♣ 9 5

12. Lead a *low* diamond. Declarer has two spade tricks and at most seven clubs, for a maximum of nine in all. Even if he wins the singleton queen of diamonds, he must concede a spade trick to you in the end. (If he has a diamond, he can have no more than six clubs, so no squeeze is possible.)

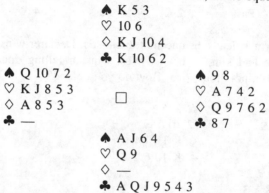

♠ K 5 3
♡ 10 6
◇ K J 10 4
♣ K 10 6 2

♠ Q 10 7 2
♡ K J 8 5 3
◇ A 8 5 3
♣ —

♠ 9 8
♡ A 7 4 2
◇ Q 9 7 6 2
♣ 8 7

♠ A J 6 4
♡ Q 9
◇ —
♣ A Q J 9 5 4 3

If you try to cash the diamond ace, you deserve your fate. Declarer's void should come as no surprise on this bidding. He ruffs, draws trumps, and cashes the ace and king of spades. When the queen doesn't fall, he takes a ruffing finesse against East's diamond queen, setting up a second spade discard.

Problems

13.   Dlr: South   ♠ K 9 3
        Vul: None   ♡ J 9 4 2
                      ♢ 6 5
                      ♣ K 10 7 3

                               ♠ 8 5
                   □   ♡ K 7 3
                               ♢ 9 2
                               ♣ A J 9 6 4 2

WEST	NORTH	EAST	SOUTH
			1 ♡
2 ♢	2 ♡	3 ♣	4 ♡
All Pass			

West, your partner, leads the queen of clubs. Declarer plays the three from dummy. How do you defend?

14.   Dlr: East   ♠ 6 3
        Vul: None   ♡ K 10 4
                      ♢ Q 6 5
                      ♣ A K J 5 4

♠ 4
♡ Q 9 7 6 2
♢ K 10 7 2   □
♣ 9 7 2

WEST	NORTH	EAST	SOUTH
		Pass	Pass
Pass	1 ♣	1 ♠	2 NT
Pass	3 NT	All Pass	

You, West, lead the six of hearts, willing to risk partner's wrath if a spade lead is better. Declarer plays dummy's king, partner wins the ace, and declarer follows with the five. East returns the heart three, South playing the eight. How do you defend?

Solutions

13.   South has advertised a good hand, so West's overcall must have been fairly light. He surely has at most one heart. If his club queen is singleton, he might have bid differently—with seven diamonds, he might have preferred to preempt at this vulnerability; with five spades, he could have tried an initial Michaels cuebid or introduced the spade suit over four hearts.

     Assuming that West's clubs are Q-x, why did he prefer a club lead to a diamond? His diamonds can't be headed by the ace-king, probably not by king-queen-jack. It's more like he has a tenace holding that he preferred not to lead away from, like king-jack or ace-queen. In that case, it must be right for you to overtake with the club ace and shift to a diamond.

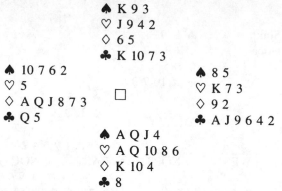

♠ K 9 3
♡ J 9 4 2
◇ 6 5
♣ K 10 7 3

♠ 10 7 6 2
♡ 5
◇ A Q J 8 7 3
♣ Q 5

♠ 8 5
♡ K 7 3
◇ 9 2
♣ A J 9 6 4 2

♠ A Q J 4
♡ A Q 10 8 6
◇ K 10 4
♣ 8

Three rounds of diamonds allow you to overruff dummy for the setting trick.

14. Declarer must have the jack of hearts left, since East would have led that card at trick two. The question is, why did declarer decline the normal play of the heart four from dummy at trick one? There is only one good answer: He is desperate to gain the lead. Win the heart queen and shift to the two of diamonds.

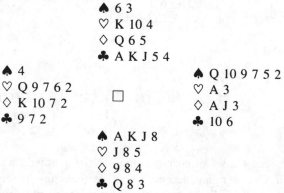

♠ 6 3
♡ K 10 4
◇ Q 6 5
♣ A K J 5 4

♠ 4
♡ Q 9 7 6 2
◇ K 10 7 2
♣ 9 7 2

♠ Q 10 9 7 5 2
♡ A 3
◇ A J 3
♣ 10 6

♠ A K J 8
♡ J 8 5
◇ 9 8 4
♣ Q 8 3

As it happens, declarer could (and perhaps should) have made his game by ducking the opening lead. With East on lead, the defense can take only three diamond tricks.

Problems

15. Dlr: South
Vul: None

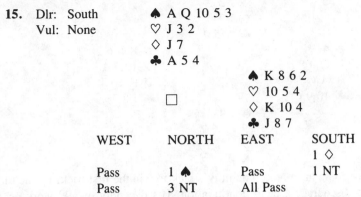

♠ A Q 10 5 3
♡ J 3 2
◇ J 7
♣ A 5 4

♠ K 8 6 2
♡ 10 5 4
◇ K 10 4
♣ J 8 7

WEST	NORTH	EAST	SOUTH
			1 ◇
Pass	1 ♠	Pass	1 NT
Pass	3 NT	All Pass	

West, your partner, leads the heart six. Dummy plays low, and declarer wins your ten with the ace. Declarer passes the spade nine, which you duck. The spade jack comes next; partner discards the two of clubs, and dummy plays low. How do you defend?

16. Dlr: East
Vul: N-S

♠ 6 5
♡ J 10 7 4
◇ K 6 5 4 3
♣ K 3

♠ A Q 7 2
♡ 9 5
◇ A J 10 9
♣ A 6 5

WEST	NORTH	EAST	SOUTH
		3 ♣	Dbl
Redbl	3 ◇	Pass	3 ♡
4 ♣	4 ♡	All Pass	

You, West, lead the ace of clubs—three, eight, nine. How do you continue?

Solutions

15. Declarer is certain to have good hearts. (If his holding were A-x-x, why did he not try dummy's jack at trick one or, failing that, hold up his ace?)

Partner's club discard offers no encouragement there, so diamonds is the only suit left to try. Lead the ten in case you have to unblock. The full deal:

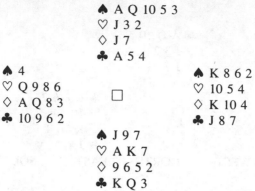

<pre>
                    ♠ A Q 10 5 3
                    ♡ J 3 2
                    ◇ J 7
                    ♣ A 5 4
   ♠ 4   ♠ K 8 6 2
   ♡ Q 9 8 6   ♡ 10 5 4
   ◇ A Q 8 3   □   ◇ K 10 4
   ♣ 10 9 6 2   ♣ J 8 7
                    ♠ J 9 7
                    ♡ A K 7
                    ◇ 9 6 5 2
                    ♣ K Q 3
</pre>

Declarer could have put up dummy's jack to win the first trick, but he didn't want to discourage a heart continuation. His deception would work against most defenders.

16.

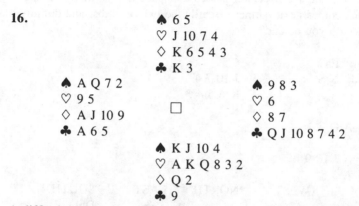

<pre>
                    ♠ 6 5
                    ♡ J 10 7 4
                    ◇ K 6 5 4 3
                    ♣ K 3
   ♠ A Q 7 2   ♠ 9 8 3
   ♡ 9 5   ♡ 6
   ◇ A J 10 9   □   ◇ 8 7
   ♣ A 6 5   ♣ Q J 10 8 7 4 2
                    ♠ K J 10 4
                    ♡ A K Q 8 3 2
                    ◇ Q 2
                    ♣ 9
</pre>

A difficult hand—the winner is a club continuation, which deprives declarer of a chance to pull off the feared Morton's Fork Coup. On the bidding, declarer must have a club singleton, and he is likely to have four spades as well as six hearts, otherwise he'd have overcalled three hearts directly instead of stopping off to make a takeout double. (Declarer could, of course, have 3-6-3-1 pattern, but then East, with his singleton diamond, might not have signaled with a middle club spot.)

Suppose you exit with a trump. Declarer pulls two rounds and leads the two of diamonds—and you are about to be impaled on one of the tines of Morton's Fork.* If you duck, dummy's king wins. Declarer then discards the diamond queen on the club king and concedes two spades. If you take the diamond ace, declarer gets *three* discards for spades—one each on the diamond king, the fifth diamond (which he can establish), and the club king.

---

*The name originates from an episode in English history. Cardinal Morton was charged with keeping full the coffers of King Henry VII. He obtained money from the affluent businessmen and nobles around London, using the following approach: If they lived well, they must have plenty of money to contribute to the king; if they lived frugally, they must have money saved of which the monarch could avail himself. No matter what their lifestyle, they were fair game for the Cardinal.

However, the timing for this delicate sequence of plays is destroyed if you continue clubs at trick two. Declarer must take a discard prematurely, and you can hold him to nine tricks whatever his choice.

Problems

17. Dlr: West
    Vul: Both

♠ 10 8 7 3
♡ Q 10 5
◇ Q 10 4 3
♣ K 7

♠ Q 2
♡ K
◇ A 7 5
♣ J 9 8 6 5 3 2

□

WEST	NORTH	EAST	SOUTH
Pass	Pass	3 ♡	3 ♠
Pass	4 ♠	All Pass	

You, West, win the first trick with the king of hearts, East signaling with the nine. You shift to a club. Declarer wins the king, playing the queen from his hand, and plays a spade. Partner's king pops up and declarer's ace wins. Declarer cashes the club ace, East following, and leads the trump jack. What do you play to the next trick?

18. Dlr: South
    Vul: E-W

♠ 10 9
♡ A J 10 6 5
◇ K Q 4 3
♣ 9 8

♠ J 7 6 4 2
♡ 9
◇ A J 8 2
♣ K 10 3

□

WEST	NORTH	EAST	SOUTH
			1 ♣
Pass	1 ♡	Pass	3 ♣
Pass	3 ◇	Pass	3 ♡
Pass	4 ♣	Pass	4 ♠
Dbl	Pass	Pass	6 ♣
All pass			

West, your partner, leads a low spade, won by declarer's queen. Declarer cashes the spade ace, ruffs a spade (partner's king falling), and plays a club to the queen, winning. Next comes the club ace, partner throwing a diamond, and a club to your king, partner throwing a heart. What is your next play?

Solutions

17. A very tricky problem. *Your play to the next trick depends on what declarer leads.* You should have thrown your spade queen under the ace!

Declarer's 6-2-3-2 pattern is clear from the bidding and play. He surely has the diamond king for his three-level overcall. (And East wouldn't preempt with the heart ace and *two* side kings.) However, East must hold the diamond jack (and nine) for the defense to have a chance.

Strangely, if you cling to your sure trump trick, it costs *two* tricks. When you take your spade queen, you face a choice of evils—you can either break the diamonds, giving declarer three winners and a discard for his heart loser, or you can lead a club, conceding a ruff-and-discard. Declarer can ruff in dummy, pitching a diamond, and establish dummy's fourth diamond.

If you dump the spade queen under the ace, declarer has no way to prevail.

18.

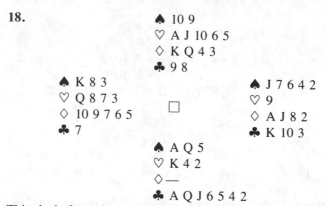

This deal, from the 1968 Vanderbilt, saw a classic defense by Alvin Roth. Winning the club king, Roth returned the *eight* of diamonds, judging that declarer had a diamond void from his leap to slam (no Blackwood) and his failure to try for a diamond pitch on the hearts.

The idea was to make declarer think that West had the diamond ace. Then declarer might be apt to misguess hearts in the end. Sure enough, South, Ira Rubin, ruffed the diamond and ran his trumps. With three cards left, dummy and declarer had three hearts. Rubin cashed the heart king and led a heart,

West following low. Now if West's remaining card were the diamond ace, as seemed indicated, the heart queen would drop from East under the ace. But Roth's reputation for subtle defense betrayed him—giving East due credit for a good play, Rubin finessed the heart jack and made the slam.

Problems

19. Dlr: East
     Vul: N-S

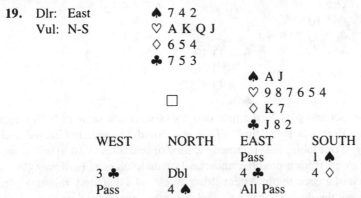

WEST	NORTH	EAST	SOUTH
		Pass	1 ♠
3 ♣	Dbl	4 ♣	4 ◊
Pass	4 ♠	All Pass	

West, your partner, leads the two of hearts. Dummy wins and leads a spade. You take your ace. What do you return?

20. Dlr: South   ♠ 5
     Vul: Both   ♡ J 6 5
     Matchpoints   ◊ A K 4 3
                    ♣ A K Q 3 2
     ♠ K J 9 4
     ♡ A K Q 8 3   □
     ◊ 10 5
     ♣ 9 6

WEST	NORTH	EAST	SOUTH
			2 ♠
Pass	2 NT	Pass	3 ♠
Pass	4 ♠	Pass	Pass
Dbl	All Pass		

You, West, lead the heart ace. (At the sight of dummy, you are thankful you didn't overcall three hearts.) You continue with the heart king, ruffed. Declarer shrugs, goes to dummy with a diamond, and leads a spade to the two, ten, and your jack. Down one is assured. Do you see any chance for down two, and all the matchpoints?

19.

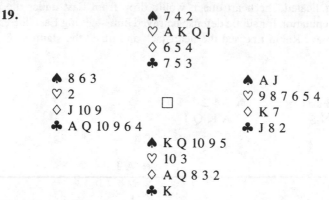

♠ 7 4 2
♡ A K Q J
◇ 6 5 4
♣ 7 5 3

♠ 8 6 3
♡ 2
◇ J 10 9
♣ A Q 10 9 6 4

♠ A J
♡ 9 8 7 6 5 4
◇ K 7
♣ J 8 2

♠ K Q 10 9 5
♡ 10 3
◇ A Q 8 3 2
♣ K

The contract and play to the first two tricks were the same at both tables in the 1977 Bermuda Bowl final. (This was board 83, near the end of a close match.) At one table, East returned the nine of hearts for West to ruff, warning partner away from a possible underlead of the club ace. However, this was too much of a good thing. After ruffing, West led a diamond, thinking partner might have the diamond ace and declarer either a club void or K-x. Declarer won, drew trumps, and threw his club king on a high heart. (He had taken care to unblock in trumps and so could reach dummy with the spade seven.) A diamond was lost, making four.

In the replay, East, Bob Hamman, thoughtfully returned the heart six at trick three. "This noncommittal card neither invited North to lead a diamond nor encouraged any such adventure as underleading the club ace," says the official book of the championship. "Bobby Wolff took the hint and made the essential play of cashing the club ace. Since declarer couldn't help losing a diamond trick, he went down a trick."

Perhaps the first West should have cashed the club ace no matter what, but Hamman's careful signal certainly made things easier on *his* partner.

20.

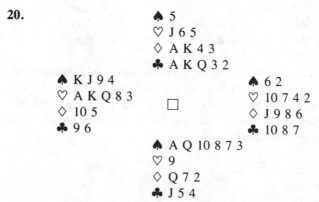

♠ 5
♡ J 6 5
◇ A K 4 3
♣ A K Q 3 2

♠ K J 9 4
♡ A K Q 8 3
◇ 10 5
♣ 9 6

♠ 6 2
♡ 10 7 4 2
◇ J 9 8 6
♣ 10 8 7

♠ A Q 10 8 7 3
♡ 9
◇ Q 7 2
♣ J 5 4

A little subterfuge is needed to achieve five defensive tricks. Declarer has heard your double. After ruffing your heart continuation, he probably will lay down the spade ace and start cashing minor-suit winners. He'll plan to concede two tricks to your king and nine of trumps, but he keeps control for down only one.

To deflect declarer, drop your spade nine when he lays down the ace. Now he may think you doubled in the hope of two heart tricks and two spades. If spades are 3-3, he can play a third round of the suit and claim. However, you win the spade king and force out declarer's last trump with another heart lead. Your last trump and last heart are good for two down.

Problems

21. Dlr: East
Vul: E-W

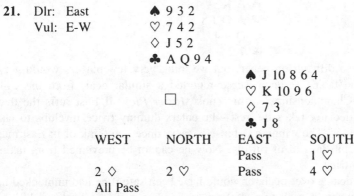

♠ 9 3 2
♡ 7 4 2
◇ J 5 2
♣ A Q 9 4

♠ J 10 8 6 4
♡ K 10 9 6
◇ 7 3
♣ J 8

WEST	NORTH	EAST	SOUTH
		Pass	1 ♡
2 ◇	2 ♡	Pass	4 ♡
All Pass			

West, your partner, leads the ace and king of diamonds. You encourage, and declarer follows with the four and nine. At trick three, partner leads the diamond eight. Plan your defense.

22. Dlr: South
Vul: Both

♠ K J 5 4
♡ A Q 6
◇ J 5
♣ Q 10 7 4

♠ A 10 8 6
♡ 9 7 4 2
◇ 8 4 3
♣ A 2

WEST	NORTH	EAST	SOUTH
			1 ◇
Pass	1 ♠	Pass	1 NT
Pass	3 NT	All Pass	

West, your partner, leads the three of clubs. Low from dummy. Plan your defense.

21.

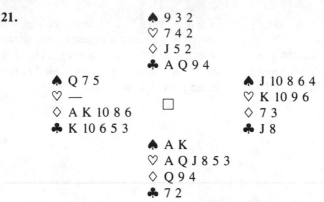

♠ 9 3 2
♡ 7 4 2
◇ J 5 2
♣ A Q 9 4

♠ Q 7 5
♡ —
◇ A K 10 8 6
♣ K 10 6 5 3

♠ J 10 8 6 4
♡ K 10 9 6
◇ 7 3
♣ J 8

♠ A K
♡ A Q J 8 5 3
◇ Q 9 4
♣ 7 2

This isn't so difficult on paper, but we think very few players would get it right at the table. Terence Reese reported a similar deal, from the 1948 European Championships, in his book *Master Play*. If East ruffs the third diamond, declarer takes the rest—he enters dummy twice in clubs to take trump finesses. The winning defense is easy, once you think of it: East must discard a club instead of ruffing. Now he cannot be prevented from taking two trump tricks.

On the deal above, declarer would have been safe if he had unblocked his diamond queen at trick two. If East declined to ruff, the lead would have been in dummy for a heart finesse.

22.   You win the club ace, but the outlook is gloomy. A club return looks fruitless, and so does a diamond when declarer bid the suit. Your best chance is in spades, where declarer may be weak. The full deal could be:

♠ K J 5 4
♡ A Q 6
◇ J 5
♣ Q 10 7 4

♠ Q 3 2
♡ 10 8 3
◇ K 9 6
♣ J 9 6 3

♠ A 10 8 6
♡ 9 7 4 2
◇ 8 4 3
♣ A 2

♠ 9 7
♡ K J 5
◇ A Q 10 7 2
♣ K 8 5

Even if this is the layout, you must be careful. The only card to beat the contract is the spade *ten*. Partner withholds the queen, of course, and declarer wins. (It does him no good to duck.) When West wins the diamond king, his return of the spade queen blots out declarer's nine, and you take three spade tricks, and five in all. (The deal is based on a position first studied, we believe, by Terence Reese.)

Problems

23. Dlr: South
Vul: Both

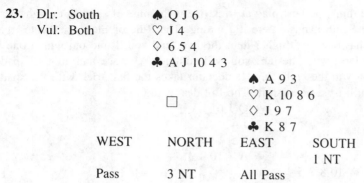

♠ Q J 6
♡ J 4
◇ 6 5 4
♣ A J 10 4 3

♠ A 9 3
♡ K 10 8 6
◇ J 9 7
♣ K 8 7

WEST	NORTH	EAST	SOUTH
			1 NT
Pass	3 NT	All Pass	

West, your partner, leads the five of spades, and dummy plays low. How do you defend?

24. Dlr: North
Vul: Both

♠ Q 7 5
♡ K J 6 3
◇ A 10 3
♣ 9 3 2

♠ 10 6
♡ Q 10 4
◇ 9 6 4 2
♣ A K Q 4

WEST	NORTH	EAST	SOUTH
	Pass	Pass	1 NT
Pass	2 ♣	Pass	2 ♠
Pass	3 NT	Pass	4 ♡
All Pass			

West, your partner, leads the five of clubs. Plan your defense.

Solutions

23. We think the best play at trick one is the nine of spades, though there are some South hands where it's wrong. The Rule of Eleven indicates that declarer has one card higher than the five, and you'll find out which one it is. If declarer wins the ten, you will continue with ace and another spade when you win the club king. If declarer takes the first trick with the spade king, you'll try a heart shift. The full deal could be:

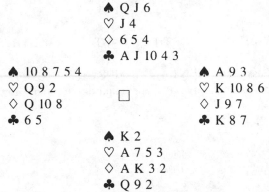

```
                    ♠ Q J 6
                    ♡ J 4
                    ♢ 6 5 4
                    ♣ A J 10 4 3
 ♠ 10 8 7 5 4                    ♠ A 9 3
 ♡ Q 9 2                         ♡ K 10 8 6
 ♢ Q 10 8        □               ♢ J 9 7
 ♣ 6 5                           ♣ K 8 7
                    ♠ K 2
                    ♡ A 7 5 3
                    ♢ A K 3 2
                    ♣ Q 9 2
```

Declarer could have forced a guess on you by playing the spade queen.

If declarer's hand is:

```
                    ♠ K 2
                    ♡ Q 7 5 3
                    ♢ A K Q 3
                    ♣ Q 9 2
```

it looks as though East needs to take the spade ace at trick one and shift to a heart. However, declarer could still make the contract. He unblocks the spade king, wins the third heart, cashes two spades and four diamonds, and tosses East in with the fourth heart to lead away from the king of clubs.

Nor can declarer's hand be:

```
                    ♠ K 4 2
                    ♡ Q 7 3
                    ♢ A K Q 3
                    ♣ Q 9 2
```

since West would have led a heart from A-9-x-x rather than a spade from 10-x-x-x. However, declarer could have:

```
                    ♠ K 2
                    ♡ Q 7 3
                    ♢ A K Q 3
                    ♣ Q 9 5 2
```

or

```
                    ♠ K 4 2
                    ♡ A 7 5 3
                    ♢ A K Q 3
                    ♣ 9 2
```

and the alternative defense would be right. If you played declarer for one of those hands, you may consider that you answered correctly.

A more familiar example of a defensive *discovery play* is seen here:

♠ A 9 6
♡ 9 6 3
◇ 8 6
♣ K J 10 5 4

♠ 8 3 2   ♠ K 5
♡ 10 8 7 5 2   ♡ K J 4
◇ A Q 4   ◇ J 10 9 5 3
♣ 8 7   ♣ 9 3 2

♠ Q J 10 7 4
♡ A Q
◇ K 7 2
♣ A Q 6

At matchpoints, South plays in four spades and West leads the heart five. Declarer is known to have the ace, so East should play the jack. When South is able to produce the queen, East knows to shift to a diamond later.

24.

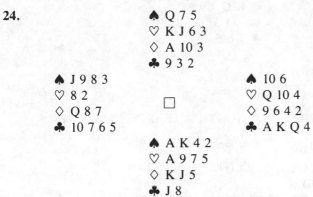

♠ Q 7 5
♡ K J 6 3
◇ A 10 3
♣ 9 3 2

♠ J 9 8 3   ♠ 10 6
♡ 8 2   ♡ Q 10 4
◇ Q 8 7   ◇ 9 6 4 2
♣ 10 7 6 5   ♣ A K Q 4

♠ A K 4 2
♡ A 9 7 5
◇ K J 5
♣ J 8

Concealment is an advanced defensive technique. Here you must win the club *ace*, cash the *queen*, and continue with the four. If you play normally in clubs—queen, then king, and ace—and later you show up with the heart queen, declarer will know that West has the queen of diamonds since you didn't open the bidding. Conceal your club holding from him and he may get the diamonds wrong.

Problem

25.　Dlr: South　　♠ A Q 4 2
　　　Vul: N-S　　　♡ A 7
　　　　　　　　　　◇ J 5
　　　　　　　　　　♣ Q 7 6 3 2

♠ J 8
♡ Q J 10 9 4
◇ K 10 6 3　　　□
♣ J 9

WEST	NORTH	EAST	SOUTH
			1 ♣
Pass	1 ♠	Pass	1 NT
Pass	3 NT	All Pass	

You, West, lead the queen of hearts—seven, six, king. At trick two, declarer lays down the club ace. Plan your defense.

The Last Chance

Dlr: North　　♠ 4
Vul: Both　　　♡ K Q J 9 8 7
　　　　　　　　◇ A J 3
　　　　　　　　♣ 7 6 5

♠ J 2
♡ A 6 3
◇ Q 6 5 2　　　□
♣ 10 9 8 4

WEST	NORTH	EAST	SOUTH
	1 ♡	1 ♠	Dbl[1]
Pass	2 ♡	Pass	2 NT
Pass	3 NT	All Pass	

[1]penalty

You, West, lead the jack of spades, winning the first trick. How do you continue?

Solution

25. Drop the club jack under the ace. This can't cost anything, and it should gain if the full deal is:

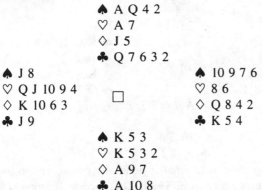

```
                ♠ A Q 4 2
                ♡ A 7
                ◇ J 5
                ♣ Q 7 6 3 2
♠ J 8                          ♠ 10 9 7 6
♡ Q J 10 9 4        □          ♡ 8 6
◇ K 10 6 3                     ◇ Q 8 4 2
♣ J 9                          ♣ K 5 4
                ♠ K 5 3
                ♡ K 5 3 2
                ◇ A 9 7
                ♣ A 10 8
```

Unless declarer is very suspicious, he will go to dummy and lead a club to the eight, a necessary play if East has K-9-5-4. Now you can shift to a diamond and set the contract.

Without your falsecard, declarer will merely continue with the eight of clubs toward dummy. When your jack appears, declarer will score an easy overtrick.

The Last Chance Solution

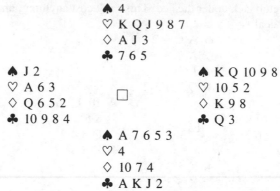

```
                    ♠ 4
                    ♡ K Q J 9 8 7
                    ◇ A J 3
                    ♣ 7 6 5
    ♠ J 2                         ♠ K Q 10 9 8
    ♡ A 6 3             □         ♡ 10 5 2
    ◇ Q 6 5 2                     ◇ K 9 8
    ♣ 10 9 8 4                    ♣ Q 3
                    ♠ A 7 6 5 3
                    ♡ 4
                    ◇ 10 7 4
                    ♣ A K J 2
```

It is fitting that we close with what is generally considered to be one of the finest defensive plays ever made. The deal is recorded, among other places, in Louis Watson's *Play of the Hand at Bridge*. The great Oswald Jacoby held the West cards in a 1932 tournament, and Watson was his partner.

South ducked the first trick, correctly judging that West had a doubleton spade. Jacoby now found the devastating shift to the *queen of diamonds*, and declarer was finished. No other card will beat the contract.

No one, as far as I know, has commented on Watson's contribution to the defense. Most players would have overtaken the spade jack at trick one. If declarer had ducked, Watson could have achieved the same coup as Jacoby by shifting to a low diamond from his side. Do you suppose Louis analyzed the situation correctly but chose to let Jacoby have a chance for immortality?